BUSINESS ETHICS

BUSINESS ETHICS

Foundation for Corporate Social Responsibility and Governance

P. KAMATCHI
Director
SVT Lauren Institute of International
Management Studies, Bangalore

TECHSAR™
NEW DELHI

Published and Printed by
Techsar Pvt. Ltd.
4435–36/7, Ansari Road, Daryaganj
New Delhi-110002 (India)
E-mail: tech_info@techsarworld.com
Website: www.techsarworld.com

ISBN 978-93-84588-13-7

Reprint 2025

Preface

Ethics is beyond business, whereas there should be perfection between business and ethics. Ethics is for sustainability in a long run both for the personal and business life. Corporates are morally and socially responsible to customer in particular and society in general. Indian inherited values are fading away due to cultural changes in the society. Hence, inculcating ethics and ethical values are expected among younger generations and managers. Stress, work pressure, competitions, lifestyle, lack of work-life balance and so on are the major hurdles in practising ethics. The study of business ethics is gaining importance among the management students to realise values and practise of ethics.

All over the globe many universities introduced ethics as a subject. Code of ethics has been formulated by American Marketing Association and enforced on corporatist seriously.

Quality, continuous improvement, sustainability, transparency, etc., are some of the core expectations in the business for long survival and economic growth. Hence, the study of ethics will help managers and business organisation to develop conceptual skill to identify the core issues both ethical and non-ethical and arrive at on appropriate suggestions. It also formulates alternative course of action, evaluate ethical performance and understand the meaning and importance of corporate social responsibility.

"Good governance leads to Good business" is wide accepted mantra among business houses. Corporatist with good governance is practising strongly by improving their business and profits worldwide. This brings a sea change in standard of living modifying the way of life and thinking and wide open to consumers need. Ethics and good governance stand as strong tool for economic growth and also for the international business. The study of ethics mends oneself with personal ethics which extends to organisational ethics and expand in making quality services and products. It also setup the correct and alternative decision process and creates a balance between work and life among managers and employees.

This book is focussed more on research study by the author covering the various aspects on business ethics, perception and practice, corporate social responsibility and their performances and wide coverage of marketing ethics.

The main tool for learning is the corporate opinion or perception and suggestion of their business practices. Author also incorporated various ideas and tools for implementation of ethics with the help of qualitative and quantities analysis and interpretation.

The book is divided into five major topics and with two research topics which are the strength of quality information.

The structure of book is with, Chapter 1 covering various factors, basics of ethics corporate social responsibility, issue management, crisis management, and arguments for and against on business ethics.

Chaper 2 ethics is more of personal phenomena and each individual is unique by oneself. Our ethos is focussed on individual happiness which leads to practice of individual ethics, which also important for the organisation towards success. This chapter is masterpiece which gives the basic idea about individual perception and attitude, values, morality, virtue, old ethics and new ethics based on Bhagavad Gita.

Chapter 3 is covering with wide range of management and functional areas like ethics in management, human resource, marketing, finance, technology and profession.

Chapter 4 touches on corporate social responsibility features, principles, issues and also models on corporate governance in India.

Chapter 5 includes the role of corporate culture in business, concept, functions, impact, cross-cultural ethics and so on.

Chapter 6 research contribution of the author, covering the perception and practices of ethics in marketing segment. It also covers valuable primary data and various quotes and opinions towards ethics in marketing and business activities.

Chatper 7 lays the foundation of ethics and ethical stamina for corporatist for setting up of Model Ethical House.

Value addition in the book is the various live and practical examples in form of exhibit in each and every chapter.

Hope the book will bring a change in the mind, thoughts and action in adopting ethics both by individuals and corporations and interesting educative study input to the students.

P. Kamatchi

Contents

Preface v

1. **Business Ethics** **3**
   - Introduction 3
   - Ethics, Business Ethics and Corporate Ethics 5
   - Scope of Business Ethics 6
   - Types of Ethics 10
   - Factors Influencing Business Ethics 15
   - Moral Standards 16
   - A Detailed Note on Moral Theory 17
   - Additional Factors Influencing Business Ethics 25
   - Basics of Business Ethics 27
   - Why Ethics? Argument for Business Ethics 28
   - Research Outcome on Ethics in Business 31
   - Corporate Social Responsibility 34
   - Issues in General Business Ethics 37
   - Crisis Management 41
   - Responses to Crisis Situations or Crisis Management 43
   - Types of Crises 44
   - Brief Note of Case Studies on Ethical Issues 45
   - Neil Armstrong to Sue Barber 48

2. **Personal Ethics** **57**
   - Understanding Personal Ethics 57
   - Value of Self 59
   - Evaluatory Changes in Personal Ethics 65
   - Contemporary Ethical Theories Related to Personal Ethics 68
   - Promote Happiness 73
   - Karma Yoga 78
   - Understanding Karma Yoga 79
   - Classic Yogas 79
   - Proactive 83
   - Understanding Proactive 83
   - Proactive Steps for Personal Ethics 84

Commentary on Plato 99
Ethics of Virtue vs Ethics of Principle 100

3. Ethics in Management 107
Introduction 107
Ethics in Human Resource Management 112
Human-centric Model 128
Approaches 134
Processes 135
Roadblocks 136
Getting Results 137

4. Marketing Ethics 149
Marketing of Product and Ethical Issues in Product 152
Pricing and Ethical Issues in Pricing 164
Advertising and Ethical Issues in Advertising 167
Sales and Distribution : Ethics and Ethical Issues 178
American Marketing Association's Code of Ethics 182
Ethical Aspects of Financial Management 184
Ethics in Financial Management 185
Technology Ethics 193

5. Corporate Social Responsibility 219
Introduction 219
Corporate Social Responsibility 222
Cases on CSR in Brief 229
Corporate Governance 258
Models of Corporate Governance in India 261
Ethical Issues on Good Corporation 277

6. Role of Corporate Culture in Business 281
Introduction 281
Culture 282
Corporate Culture 282
Research View on Corporate Culture and Ethical Values 283
Corporate Culture vs Organisational Culture 285
Corporate Culture and Change 286
Core Components of Corporate Culture 287
Corporate Culture with the Logistics Management 289
Culture and Ethical Behaviour 291

	Functions of Corporate Culture	294
	Research Study on Change in the Corporate/Organisational Culture	296
	Change in the Organisational Culture	297
	Element of Corporate Culture	309
	Cross-culture and its Issues in Ethics	317
	Overview on Different Cases Related Culture	319
	Organisational Culture	320
	Organizational Culture and Managerial Ethical Behaviours	322
7.	**Perception and Practices of Marketing in Business Ethics**	**327**
	Code of Ethics	334
	Corporate Opinion and Practices Towards Stakeholders	346
	Model for Corporate Ethical House	352
Index		**353**

"Ethics is a study of what constitutes good and bad human conduct, including related activities and values."

—Barry (1979)

1

Chapter

Business Ethics

INTRODUCTION

India is blessed with value based system of life since ages. Indians are originally known for "Dharma and Karma", theory in their daily practices. Consciousness, god fearing and traditional practices still exist in the hearts of the individuals. Values are looked at as the foundation of ethics. If these values are distorted it will be reflected in the unethical actions. In the modern and advanced technology era, it is observed the unethical activities are multiplying day by day. Many individuals are very ethical or spiritual in private life, but in business they unethical. Individuals are to build "ethical stamina" both in private and business life. The society and its various groups of individuals are watching continuously the ethical or unethical practices of the businesses and corporates. For continuous sustainability and benefit in the long run ethical foundation in the organization is necessary.

Right from 1980 the West started focussing on ethics and made it compulsory by passing various regulations, code of ethics and legislations on good governance, etc. It is realised, the unethical practices will work only for the short-run but ethical practices are to be implanted gradually only through high level continuous practices of ethical values in the organisation.

Several factors influence the level of ethical behaviour in an organisation. An individual's knowledge level regarding an issue can help to determine ethical behaviour. A decision maker with a greater amount of knowledge on a subject or situation may take steps to avoid unethical problems, whereas a less informed person may unknowingly take action which may lead to an ethical conflict. One's moral values and value-oriented attitude clearly influences his or her business behaviour. Most people join organisation to accomplish personal goals. The types of personal goals an individual aspires to and the manner in which these goals are pursued have significant impact on individual's behaviour in the organisation.

The value oriented and ethical business practices enable the management to lead a much better life and a much more superior business life. This may bring a great fulfilment in the corporate world and it will turn to "socially responsible management". Such management will help ordinary people to produce extraordinary results, will lead to increase in productivity, quality of work life and higher returns.

A corporate with good corporate ethics will recognise the diverse interests of its stakeholders namely, shareholders, employees, suppliers, customers, government and society at large. There is a demand for good corporate governance in the wake of economic liberalization, deregulation and business policies and legislation. There is also increasing focus and demand for corporate ethics and ethical practices in the business all the over the world. The situation on policies, culture exchanges, economic status, quality of life of the people and so on, compute the business world to imbibe ethical practices in the organizations, management and also daily businesses.

Business ethics Business ethics is the study of business situations activities and the decisions where issues of right and wrong are addressed. Business ethics is the study of business action with special reference to its moral adequacy. Again it is a study of existing corporate policies that have an impact on human and environmental well-being. The actual business policies and behaviour constitute business morality, which is expressed as a given set of convictions and activities, both inside and outside of any business organisation. Business ethics is concerned with the application of moral standards through the conduct of individuals involved in organizations through which the society is benefited through goods and services.

Business ethics is also a type of applied ethics which is concerned with clarifying the obligations and dilemmas of managers and other decision makers in business. Business ethics is a comprehensive study of corporate policies and not the study of isolated issues on events or topics. Business activities are expected to note the internal and external factors of organization. It is a type of applied ethics which is concerned with classifying the obligations and dilemmas of managers and other decision-makers of business. The concept of business ethics has been highlighted, when the concept of social responsibility was raised among business people and corporates as a response to the fast changing social and economic values of society.

Corporate ethics In general there is not much difference between business ethics and corporate ethics. However, it need to be differentiated as both of them function differently. Corporate ethics touches both society and business. It is directly related to its contribution to the societal well- being. Corporate ethics is described as a systematic study of moral matters pertaining to the functional areas of business and industry. It is also a comprehensive study of corporate policies. Corporate ethics is setting up of moral standards appropriate for corporate actions, it also includes issues such as frauds and bribes. The ethically responsible company is one which has developed a culture of caring for people and the environment. A culture is an ethical practice which flows downward from the top managers and the leaders to the lower level management. It should also consider the interest of customers, shareholders, employees, suppliers, traders, locality and the wider community.

ETHICS, BUSINESS ETHICS AND CORPORATE ETHICS

Ethics

Ethics is operationally defined as "a study of rightness or wrongness, good or bad, which determines human and moral values."

According to Barrey (1979) "Ethics is a study of what constitutes good and bad human conduct, including related activities and values."

"Ethics is concerned not only with distinguishing right from wrong and good from bad but also with commitment to do what is right or what is good. The concept of ethics is inextricably linked to that of value, that is, enduring belief that influences the choices we make from among available means and ends." —Kenneth Kernaghan.

"Ethics is the inquiry concerned with the justification for persons in actions. Such justification is the search for a coherent set of rules or norms which guide our actions when they cause conflict with others." —R. Edward Feeman

"Ethics is relating to morals; treating of moral questions; morally correct; honorable. It is also the study of morals and moral choices. It focuses on standards, rules and codes of conduct that govern the behaviour of individuals and groups."

— Concise Oxford Dictionary

Business Ethics

"Business ethics is the process of evaluating decisions, either pre or post with respect to the moral standards of the society's culture." —David J. Fitzsche

"Business ethics is the policies and methods for rightness and wrongness, desirable or undesirable based on practices of reliability, honesty, transparency, equality, continuous improvement, responsibility and sincerity." —Kamatchi, P

"Business ethics is a systematic study of moral (ethical) matters pertaining to business, industry or related activities or practices and beliefs. It can also refer to the actual standards, values or practices or beliefs. In other words it is simply referred to the systematic handling of values in business and industry." —John Donaldson

"Business ethics is application of general ethical rules to business behaviour."

—Keith Davis

"Business ethics attempts to apply general moral principles to business activities in order to resolve or at least to clarify, the moral issues which typically arise in business."

—Elizabeth Vallance

Corporate Ethics

Corporate ethics and ethical practices are to act according to the environmental factors which are mainly based on social environment, legal environment and ethical environment. Hence, corporate ethics is laid on moral theories, moral values and judgements and ethical standards.

According to Sachin (1999) "Business or corporate ethics can also be referred to as an act within business for non-business reasons. It should concern itself with designing and developing an organisation for managing who like all human beings, display the normal range of ethical instincts and see that these instincts are not compromised at work."

Again, Shivaraman (1997) puts it as, "The ethically responsible company is one which has developed a culture of caring for people and the environment."

It is expected that the established corporations will always be ethical. The elements of corporate business ethics which may also influence factors are shown below:

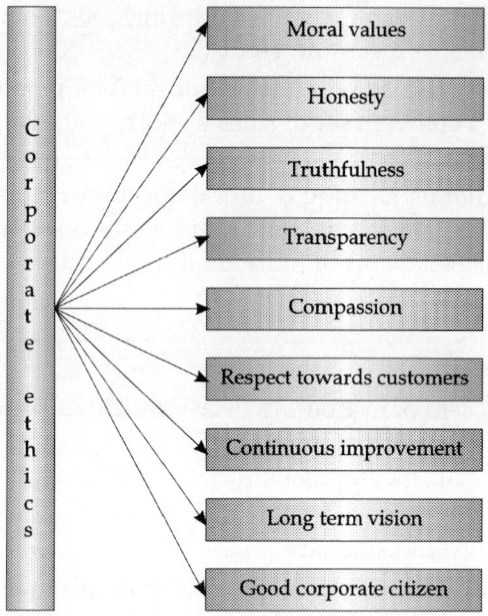

Fig. 1.1 Factors influencing corporate ethics

Extract Banerjee R.B (2001)

Business is beyond profit and it should be based on ethical and moral values. The corporates are not expected to lie. They are expected to adopt the principles of reliability and truthfulness in their business activities. They should focus on respect towards customers, and long-term vision to make themselves as good corporate citizen.

SCOPE OF BUSINESS ETHICS

Ethics is beyond business. Businesses are supposed to contribute the man's happiness and meet his material needs. The business houses have become a dominant form of modern business organisations. Every business needs society's approval in order to function with better understanding between the self and society. The business units are social institutions. As Keith Davis (1973) put it as, business and society interact with each other and are mutually dependent on both internal and external factors. Internal factors are shareholders, employees, suppliers, financial institutions and the external factors like government, law and social interest groups. Business is directly connected to the both sides, namely, society and consumer. Hence, business ethics should extend to all corners of the business activities and society. There is no limited scope. Again the corporate are to act according to the environmental factors of social, legal and ethical environment, like given in below diagram:

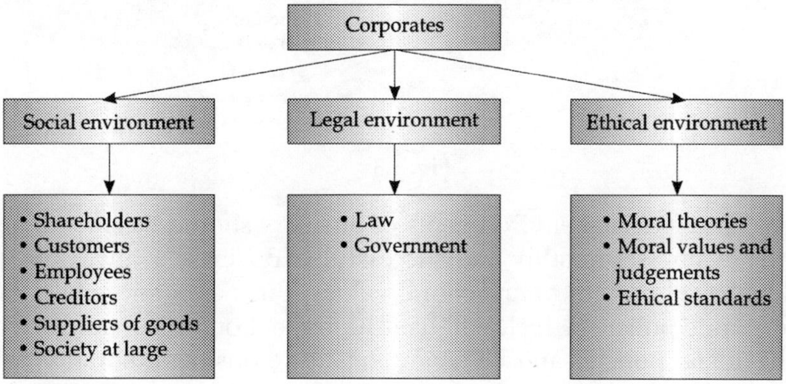

Fig. 1.2 Corporate environment

Framework for Scope of Business Ethics

As ethics should spread and be practised in all activities of business, there is no set of standards or boundaries for business ethics. However, the following framework has to be outlined before the business activity starts as a part of its scope:

1. **Criminal behaviour and legal framework:** Every business needs a code of ethics pertaining to criminal behaviour and legal issues. The employee in a business needs to be trained sufficiently regarding legalities of the business and the consequences of their actions would have upon them and the business.
2. **Human values and personal behaviour:** Every business needs an ethical framework or policy for human values and behaviour. Employees should be given training to interact with people, customers, suppliers and competitors. They need to behave with people at different levels and any inappropriate behaviour will have adverse consequences.
3. **Corporate and business ethics:** Though the study refers to business ethics, this strictly pertains to the corporate ethics, ethical policies for business and actions that are going to be under check. They need to be in compliance with legal framework and standards.

However, for the purpose of study the scope of business ethics can be studied on the basis of business environment of the individual organization and the same is understood as stakeholders which is divided into two as given under.

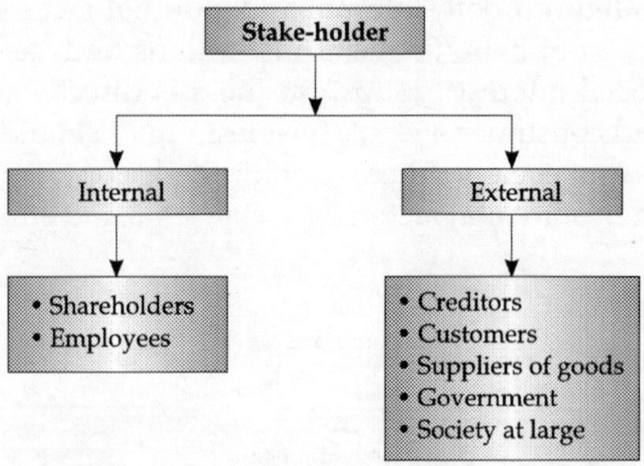

Fig. 1.3

Both internal and external environments of business should be smooth and clean in order to run the business smoothly and successfully. Business is always beyond profit and it should be based on ethical and moral values. Business ethics mainly focuses on the existing corporate policies which will have an impact on human and environmental well-being. The actual policies and behavior constitute business morality, which is expressed as a given set of convictions and activities, both inside and outside the business houses. There is a general belief in India that ethics is inherited in the society. But this is gradually fading away. It may be for the reasons like change in mindset, westernisation, crime, bad politics, concept corruption, misappropriation and malpractices. Today the business and corporates are also becoming a part of these unwarranted activities. Hence, the scope of ethics is to be extended to each and every activity of the business both to the functional areas and non-functional areas.

Functional Areas of Business Ethics

1. **Towards Shareholders:** The responsibility any business is to make the enterprise is stability and enterprising. It would then be capable of providing those who commit their investments/capital to it with a fair and adequate reward for risk taken.The following are ethical acts of business towards shareholders:
    - Investments into profitable scheme
    - Timely payment of dividends
    - Providing requisite information
    - Informing the progress of the business
    - Ensure capital appreciation
    - Protect minority shareholder's interest
    - Not to window-dress balance sheets
    - Protect interests during mergers, amalgamations and takeovers.
2. **Towards Employees:** The basic responsibilities of business houses is to make profit and wealth through the knowledgeable, skilled and strong manpower

or employees. It is the bounded duty of business to extend its ethical acts in the organization for employees by:

- Providing with a fair salary and wages
- Providing job security
- Providing good working conditions
- Providing opportunity for training and career development
- Opportunity in participating management activities
- Providing education and welfare facilities
- Providing strong HR department for caring and compassion

3. **Towards Creditors:** Creditors are banking and lending institutions and they stand as a supportive tool for continuous financial flow for the business. The business organisation should practise ethic through:
   - Determining proper terms and conditions of loans
   - Proper utilisation of debt capital
   - Regular payment of interest and advances
   - Providing requisite information
4. **Towards Customers:** Customer satisfaction is the ultimate aim of any business. Advanced marketing management aims at customers' delight. Customers are treated as kings in the business world. Many of the present corporate businesses are building marketing strategies to stabilise customer relationship and create "relationship-marketing". But many a times customers are duped through fake advertisements and products. Hence, the business houses should be honest towards customers and extend the ethical activities by,
   - Determining fair prices
   - Making available goods and services whenever they are needed
   - Providing quality goods
   - Satisfying customers through proper solutions to their problems
   - Avoid discriminating pricing
   - Avoid duping customers through wrong and fake advertisement
   - Playing fair and just in marketing activities through 4 Ps, namely, product, place, price and physical condition.
5. **Towards Suppliers of Goods:** Debtors are integral part of business activities. Businesses depend upon their goods and goods depend upon its suppliers. Hence, the businesses should act ethically by,
   - Paying fair prices in reasonable time and by purchasing on reasonable terms and conditions
   - Information about the change in demands and preferences
   - Promotion of healthy competition

6. **Towards Government:** Businesses cannot function independently without the support of the government. Government's main aim is to develop and promote economy and its development. This is possible only through industry and business growth. Business in turn should be honest and just in giving back all possible contribution and dues to the government. The following are the core areas to be extended in the ethical practices:
   - Timely payment of taxes and dues.
   - Keeping away from politics of business.
   - Following legal provisions.
   - Co-operation with the government during times of crisis.
   - Acting as partner in the progress of the country.
7. **Towards Societal Level:** Society and business are interwoven hence, they cannot function separately. For the success of the business best practices of human activities in all standard sectors and areas, communities are important. The following are the extended areas for business ethics:
   - Care and concern for economically weaker sections of the people.
   - Discriminating among different classes of people and customers should be avoided.
   - Concern and protection of clean environment.
   - Contributing to the better quality of life.

TYPES OF ETHICS

Ethics essentially is something which deals with human beings. As we all know human beings are rather complex, based on emotions, conscience and mental status. Thus, it is very hard to classify ethics into different categories. However, this can be based on conduct, customs or character. The meaning and practice of ethics differ from person to person, family to family, country to country and business to business. A lot of people talk about right or wrong, the acceptable and unacceptable principles and protocol, all these pertain to ethics. Ethics can also be based on moral philosophy. Doing something "moral" can also be vaguely said that it is the same as doing something "good". It is difficult to really classify "good" as different types of good, but there is only good or bad. Similarly, there are only ethical practices. But for the sake of understanding one can classify ethics into different types. Hence, it can be broadly classified into two major types.

The above types of ethics are based on research study and each of them is discussed briefly.

Individual Ethics

1. **Transactional ethics:** In transactional ethics, there are two parties involved with a common interest. Common interest may or may not be the same. But

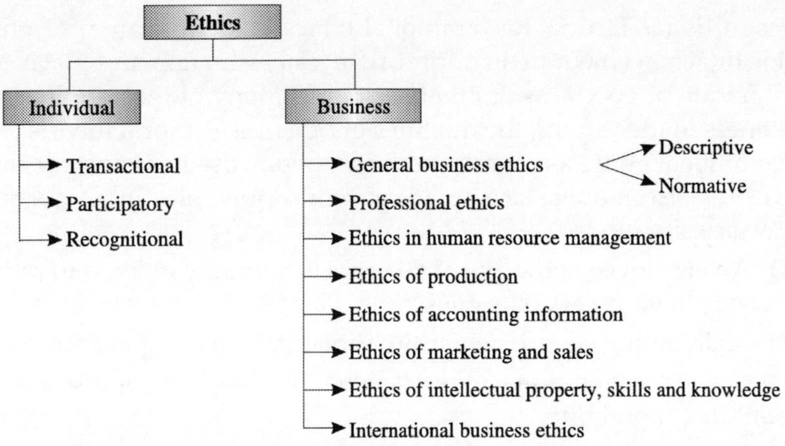

Fig. 1.4

two of them have a "symbiotic relationship". Therefore they depend on each other. Morality is involved in this relation. In order to let each party's transactions run smoothly, all parties have to accept the principle of equality and allow every party to act and enjoy the same amount of freedom, i.e., one should not try to take the upper hand on the others as this would break the symbiosis. It is based on two basic moral principles, namely:

- Principle of honesty – Here one should act in good faith fairly and equitably not betraying the confidence.
- Principle of reciprocity – Here one should avoid free riding on somebody else's efforts.

Hence, "equality, "honesty" and "reciprocity" in combination is known as transactional ethics.

2. **Participatory ethics:** This type of ethics appears both at the individual and business level. Here the common interest is the main criteria. The parties join the alliance voluntarily, committing themselves to a self-imposed and non-enforceable obligation. This entails a specific type of social relation.

   Participatory ethics is about the shape of solidarity in an age of individualisation. In simple understanding, when an individual or a company participates for a common cause, which is helpful to all parties and also the society or general public, is known as participatory ethics. The participation should be voluntary. In common projects on behalf of general welfare, an individual or business corporation demonstrate its citizenship through:

   (1) Voluntary services of individuals by joining the hands with forces armed during emergency and crisis.

   (2) Business or corporate joins the government in raising the fund or contributing financial help towards establishment of community health centres, public washrooms and so on.

3. **Recognitional Ethics:** Recognitional ethics is identification of one's quality, value or achievement in an appropriate time, situation and place. Many times recognition of goodness of others is scarce. Many of the people may not have openness in identifying the qualities of others. The moral theories support the recognitional ethics as moral standards, to practise in almost all areas of business. It is also emphasized to adopt moral principles in an appropriate and necessary situations.
   (1) An employee at the age of 60 years is normally obliged to retire and give way to younger colleagues.
   (2) Maintaining silence, when situation demands to speak the truth.

In simple terms the recognitional ethics is when one has to recognise a party for performance/results as a moral duty.

Business Ethics

Business ethics is basically principles of applied ethics, which analyse various ethics rules and ethical or moral problems that may take place in commercial environment.

Business ethics can be of two kinds: descriptive and normative.

- Descriptive discipline is applied in the academic world.
- Normative discipline is basically implemented as a corporate device and it is also utilized in the form of career specialization.

However, for the sake of studying, the different forms of business ethics can be categorized into the following and each stands as a separate topic in the business world.

General business ethics: Ethics applicable in almost all business fields and tackling various issues raised thereby are known as general business ethics. This type of ethics is practised by administrative and higher level of managerial field. Managing or tackling the various issues is known general business ethics. The issues are:

- Corporate Social Responsibility (CSR)
- Fiduciary responsibility (employee welfare)
- Corporate governance
- Individual espionage
- Hostile takeover (takeover)
- Corporate manslaughter
- Political contributions

Professional Business Ethics

Any business fair and just with appropriate co-ordination of work-forces and dealing with the various issues successfully is professional business ethics. The following are the issues related to professional ethics:

- Ethics of human resource management (HRM)
- Ethics in accounting information.

- Ethics in production.
- Ethics in marketing and salesmanship.
- Ethics of intellectual property, skill and knowledge.
- International business ethics.

Some of the research studies classify the ethics into five major branches, based on the moral philosophy. Moral philosophy addresses morality as good and bad, noble and ignoble, right and wrong, justice and virtue.

The five branches may be referred to the types as:

1. **Meta ethics** refers to moral propositions and how the truth and values (if any) may be determined.
2. **Normative ethics** refers to the practical means of determining a normal course of action.
3. **Applied ethics** refers to the ways and means of moral outcomes which may be achieved in specific situations.
4. **Moral psychology** refers to how moral capacity or moral agency develops and identifies its nature.
5. **Descriptive ethics** refers to moral values people actually abide by, within each of these branches are many different schools of thoughts. There is still further sub-fields of study. The branches of ethics have been explained under theories of ethics.

Characteristics of Business Ethics

Before discussing the characteristic features of business ethics, the term ethics should be analysed on the basis people, history, religion, nation and races.

So according to the Greeks, ethics means "a code of conduct, the manners or customs and the characterisation of the person's morals. It would also mean in a positive way of accepting responsibilities."

Whereas in India any act based on "dharma" is ethics. Right action, good practices, honesty, caring, compassion, respect, good habits, respect to elders, parenting and so on are some of the acts of dharma. However, the quality characteristics of ethics are based on good ethics and good ethics should follow the following characteristics.

- Right – which is morally correct
- Equitable – which is just and equal
- Good – which brings the highest good for all concerned
- Proper – which is appropriate and acceptable
- Fair – which is honest and due
- Just – which is perceived and practised

Added to the above, ethics is also based on moral standards. Moral standards depend upon the value system. The value system of people depends upon their background and childhood experience. Ethical decision taken both by the individual or by the corporates should be filled with obligations.

Taking into count, of the above said nature of ethics the following can be said as the various characteristics of business ethics.

1. **Ethics differs from individual to individual:** Every individual organisation has its own perception or opinion on ethics. Ethical decisions differ from one individual to another. Each individual's views may be based on one's own value system and the same may be unique or otherwise. Whereas ethical decisions do not have unique solutions. The question of ethics arises when each organisation views in terms of one's own frame of reference.
2. **Ethics and ethical decisions affect the situations:** Many times ethics are situational. When the situation demands a person may act ethically or otherwise he may simply follow rules and regulations or law. Many times an unethical act is considered a pebble thrown into a pond of water, which produces endless ripples in the pond, until the water of the entire pond gets disturbed by it. Likewise, simple unethical act of an individual may tempt or influence others to follow the same and spread negativity in the organisation or in a particular situation.
3. **Ethical compromise:** In life there are always two extremes. One extreme involves practices which lead to maximum profit or personal interests. In the other extreme there is social responsibility or personal responsibility. There may be a few cases when profit and responsibility go hand in hand. But in all other cases, there needs to be a trade-off or a compromise. This compromise can be either classified into ethical or unethical practices.
4. **Consequential ethical practices:** Consequences of ethical practices are not always clear. These are always ambiguous. One cannot expect that one's ethical practice will definitely bring positive results. Similiarly, when one follows unethical practices, it is not neccessary that there will be negative results.

   But one can assertively say that somehow, somewhere and sometimes ethical practices will lead to positive results and unethical practices will lead to negative results.

   Thus, one just has to follow ethics and not expect any result. Only then ethics will do its magic somehow, somewhere, at sometime!
5. **Ethics is one's own responsibility:** Everybody makes decisions, i.e., either one makes a decision for oneself, someone else or for organisation. For all these decisions one makes only the person who makes the decisions is responsible for it. Thus, each person is individually responsible for the ethical or unethical decision he or she takes. Taking ethical or unethical decision depends upon the individual and unique value system, along with his moral standards. Whether this decision is ethical or unethical will depend on his conscience. Thus, ethics is one's own responsibility.

6. **Ethical actions are voluntary human actions:** In the previous section it is mentioned that ethics is one's own responsibility. Not only is a person responsible for his decisions but is also liable to them. One cannot give excuses to the circumstances where such that he / she would not take an ethical decision. Whatever the situation is, if any ethical decision is not taken, that person is liable for his action. Hence, all the actions either ethical or unethical are results of voluntary human actions and not of situations beyond control.
7. **Ethics is based on moral standards:** Moral standards are code of conduct like (1) maximise use of society and people, (2) Respecting the moral rights, (3) Distribution of profits or benefits justly and (4) Care for self, enterprise or organisation and society. Based on these moral standards, ethics is trying to seek factual information like concerning the policies and behavior of the organisation. Later it will be trying to arrive at the moral judgement which include rightness or wrongness of the policy, institution or behavior.
8. **Ethics is beyond Law:** An individual or business cannot violate the law in the society. The laws and regulations established by the government sets the minimum standards for ethical behaviour. Laws represent the values of a society that have the formal authority of threat and punishment,. This makes everybody to follow the law compulsorily. It checks the external activities whereas ethics is beyond law, which studies internal qualities.
9. **Ethics is oxymoron:** Ethics is always contradictory to explain its concept clearly. The perception and practice of ethics both by an individual and business differ. The differences may be due to economic, political, or societal environment. This difference can be based on the standard set by two types of ethics, namely, old ethics and new ethics. Like old ethics is refered as, if a person is ethical he is to "hold responsibility", whereas in the new ethics the word "responsibility" changes to "rights".

FACTORS INFLUENCING BUSINESS ETHICS

As already said, business is beyond profit and it should be based on ethical and moral values. The business and business houses are not expected to lie. They are expected to adopt the principles of reliability and truthfulness in their business activities. It is also expected that the business houses should possess the parentalistic attitude towards shareholders and respect the customers' feelings. Social commitment and corporate citizenship are the core values of any business.

Factors influencing business ethics are based on:

- Moral values
- Honesty
- Truthfulness

- Compassion
- Respect towards customers
- Continuous improvements
- Long term vision
- Good corporate citizen

The moral values and moral standards and factors influencing the business ethics can be understood deeply only through ethical theories.

"Look at the problem from the position of another partly affected by the decision and try to determine what response the other person would expect as the most virtuous", is coined sayings in the set golden rules. —Golden rules

Theories of Ethics

There are two major theories and subdivided theories under each category. The diagram depicts the same.

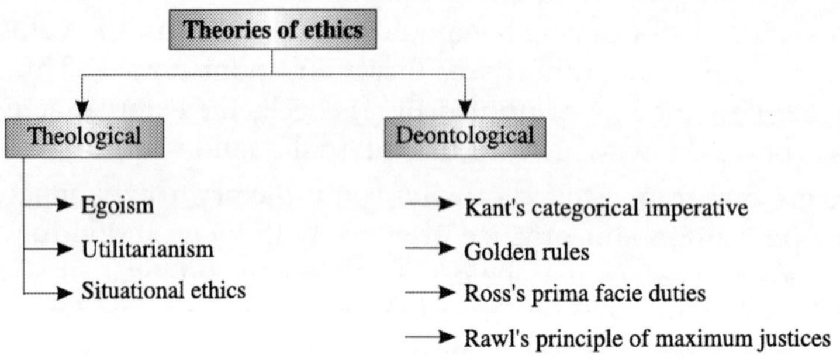

Fig. 1.5

The details of the above theories are extracted and explained under moral theories.

MORAL STANDARDS

Moral standards are expected to be followed by the business which may be divided in four categories.

- Maximising social utility (utilitarianism)
- Respecting moral rights
- Distributing benefits and burden
- Exercising caring

Whatever the **moral theories explain** the business houses should follow the standard theories for best ethical practice he business ethics differs on the basis of law of the land, nature of the business, support of the government policies, type of society, standard of life, stakeholders and so on.

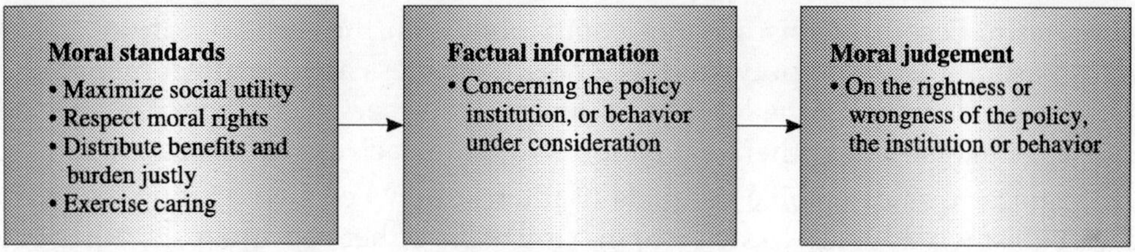

Fig. 1.6

Source Velasquez- (1998) p.129 quoted by Shivaramu (2000) p 78

A DETAILED NOTE ON MORAL THEORY

Moral theories help in understanding both individual ethical philosophy and organizational ethics. It is a means of ethical understanding to tackle any situation in the organization. It is also a tool for solving various ethical issues. A brief note of each moral theory explained below.

Teleogical Theories

There is an ethical school of thought that argues that the moral rightness of an action can be determined by looking at its consequences. If the consequences are good, the action is good. If the consequences are bad, the action is wrong. Teleologists determine what is right by examining the ratio of good to bad that action produces. In general, the right action is the one that has produced or is intended to produce the greatest ratio of good to bad results. Three schools of thought have developed from the teleological viewpoint –egoism, utilitarianism, and situational ethics.

(a) Egoism Egoism suggests that an act is ethical when it promotes the individual's best long-term interests. In other words, if an action produces or is intended to produce the greatest ratio of good to bad for that individual, then the individual must choose that course of action. Egoists will make sacrifices in the short run for the purpose of long-term gain. Furthermore, egoism can be compatible with characteristics such as honesty, generosity, and self-sacrifice.

Advantages: From a marketing perspective, marketing policies and decisions are judged to be good if they promote the long-term interests of the organization. All marketing professionals must take responsibility for evaluating their own actions. Although most organizations have codes, these codes serve only as guidelines, encouraging certain kinds of activities and discouraging others. In this respect, egoism provides an answer: an action is good if it is in the long-term best interest of the individual, the organization, or both. Egoism requires that all action be judged solely on the basis of the "best" long-term interests.

Disadvantages: There are several problems associated with ethical egoism. First, egoism ignores blatant wrongs. When long-term self-interests are the measure, egoism takes no stand against actions that are blatantly wrong, if the results of those actions are best in the long-term. Second, egoism is not compatible with the basic nature of business. Business is part of a larger society, and as a result, business actions affect many. Egoists operate without considering the long-term interests of others. Yet others are affected by the decisions of egoists, and others have inputs into the decisions of egoists.

Third, egoism cannot resolve conflicts of interest between two or more egoists. Because each egoist would want to strive to maximize his or her self-interests, other egoists involved in the decision would have to make sacrifices. Although egoism does allow for self-sacrifice, egoists often find it difficult to engage in sacrificial behaviors when their goal is to maximize self-interests. In other words, when groups make decisions, everyone cannot maximize his gain. Any alternative selected will not be in the best long-term interests of all concerned.

Finally, egoists do not see things from others' points of view. When the best long-term interests are the evaluation criteria, the judgments of egoists are influenced only by those self-interests. Any guidance, suggestions, recommendations, or decisions will be self-serving.

(b) Utilitarianism Utilitarianism is an ethical philosophy that emphasizes the best interests of all concerned. As a philosophy, utilitarianism recommends that an act that is undertaken produces the greatest ratio of good to bad for everyone. There are two types of utilitarian ethics act utilitarianism and rule utilitarianism.

Act utilitarianism: Act utilitarianism is a philosophy that maintains that the right course of action is the one that produces the greatest ratio of good to bad for all concerned. The consequences for everyone resulting from alternative courses of action must be considered.

Rule utilitarianism: Rule utilitarianism asks decision makers to consider the worth of a rule under which an action is undertaken. If keeping a rule produces more good than breaking it, we should keep the rule.

Advantages: Using utilitarian standards, a course of action is considered good if it provides more good than any other alternative. Rules, policies, and standards are not accepted blindly. They are to be tested against the criterion of the best interests of everyone. Furthermore, utilitarianism provides a way of resolving conflicts of self-interest. Individuals in organizations make decisions and evaluate their actions. This is not the case with the egoist orientation.

Utilitarianism also recognizes the importance of others in marketing decision making. Customers, society, owners, and employees must all be considered under the philosophy of choosing the course of action that provides the greatest ratio of good to bad for everyone. Finally, utilitarianism provides latitude for marketing decision marking. Decisions can be made that fit the circumstances at the time of decision. No specific action is always judged to be good.

Disadvantages: Utilitarianism, as an ethical philosophy, also suffers from several drawbacks. First, utilitarianism ignores actions that appear to be wrong in and of themselves.

Both act and rule utilitarianism focus on ends rather than means. So the end justifies the means. If this is the case, the next time a fly lands on your nose, let your friend smash it with a rock.

Under utilitarianism, it is difficult to formulate satisfactory rules. For example, suppose you were about to declare bankruptcy. Suppose also that you know that the rule "Never use privileged information for personal gain" is codified by your organization. You encounter a situation in which you have access to privileged information that will result in your receiving a large sum of money and help you avoid bankruptcy. You might reason that the harm done to others by using the information much less than the good that will come from using the information. So you use the information. You have just changed the rule to read, "Never use privileged information for personal gain…except in case of bankruptcy."

(c) Situational Ethics Situational ethics contends that the ethical action is the one that produces the greatest amount of Christian love of all the alternatives possible. Situational ethics arose because of the contention that other ethical theories were inappropriate. Specifically, ethical philosophies that are legalistic, that sought absolute laws that must always be obeyed, are overly directive. Furthermore, ethical philosophies that are existentially based, that espouse conditions of no guidelines, are nondirective. They provide no guidelines for actions. Situational ethics is proposed to fall somewhere in between these two extremes.

Advantages: According to situational ethics, rules and principles are valid only if they serve in a specific situation. Therefore, ethical decision makers must be fully acquainted with all the circumstances in a particular decision-making situation. The situational philosophy humanizes business marketing decision making. The philosophy emphasizes the importance of people and their welfare in marketing decision making. Furthermore, situational ethics rejects legalism. Legalism dictates decisions and, in a strict sense, allows for no deviation-no thought. Legalists would argue that the law represents all that we need in the way of guidelines for ethical decision making. This, of course, is not true. Conformity to the law is necessary, but not sufficient, to be ethical.

Disadvantages: Situational ethics suffers from several weaknesses. First, it is not a definite decision procedure. The same motives may procure two completely different results. Let's look at the pharmaceutical industry. One marketing decision maker who wants to provide for the welfare of society might argue that introducing a drug with possible harmful side effects will maximize the amount of love for everyone concerned. A second marketing decision maker, who wants to provide for the welfare of society, might argue that the drug should not be introduced because the side effects are such that the welfare of society will not be served. The same motives produce different decisions.

Second, situational ethics really endorses the existential philosophy. Situational ethics denies general rules (e.g., telling the truth is always good.) Such rules are legalistic. Therefore, there is latitude in decisions about telling the truth. There must be certain situations in which telling the truth is not good. So individuals are left to decide for themselves under what circumstances telling the truth is good.

Finally, although situational ethics espouses Christian love in its definition, it is not a Christian ethics. Although situational ethicists use the concept of agape love in their reasoning—unselfish love epitomized by Christ's sacrifice on the cross. Agape love is considered valid only if it serves love in every situation. In other words, such pronouncements as the Ten Commandments are reduced to the 10 suggestions by situational ethicists. They are viewed as cautious generalizations, not the absolutes espoused by Christianity, because the situational ethicist may encounter situations in which he or she, as a decision maker, will justify sidestepping the absolute.

Deontological Theories

Deontological ethicists argue that more than the consequences of an action must be considered in making ethical decisions. Several deontological theories are presented below.

(a) Kant's Categorical Imperative Immanuel Kant believed that nothing was good in itself except a "good will." A good will was understood by Kant to mean the human ability to act according to the concept of law or principles. Personality characteristics such as sensitivity, talent, and so on are good and desirable only to the extent that the human will makes good use of them. Kant believed that good will took precedence over all else.

The concept of a good will is rooted in duty, and only when an individual acts from a sense of duty does the action have any moral worth. The critical issue in following Kant's logic lies in what constitutes duty. For example, what motivates a retailer not to overcharge a customer? Does that retailer act from a perspective of serving the customer or from the perspective of avoiding legal problems if caught? According to Kant, if the action was not willed from the retailer's sense of moral duty to be honest and fair, then the action has no moral worth.

Advantages: From a marketing decisions-making perspective, Kant's philosophy has some merit. For one think, some actions (e.g., lying) are always judged to be wrong. Therefore, Kant's approach to ethics has the advantage of eliminating some uncertainty from decision making by automatically eliminating some alternatives. Second, Kant's philosophy implies a moral obligation to act from a respect for rights and recognition of responsibilities. In other words, we act ethically when we act according to our duties, that is, according to the law. The law acknowledges certain rights and responsibilities, something that marketers must consider in making ethical decisions.

Disadvantages: Kant's ethics are not without problem. First, like other ethical theories, no clear way of resolving conflict is provided. Duties come in conflict-maximizing shareholder profits versus charging reasonable prices to the consumer. How is the conflict between these two duties resolved? One might argue that serving customers' needs is in the long-term best interests of the stockholder. Although, philosophically, this is true, will serving customers needs result in shareholder profits in the future? No one can be sure.

(b) Golden Rule The golden rule commands us to treat others as we would like others to treat us. In other words, if you want to be treated fairly, you should treat others fairly. The hallmark of the gold rule is impartiality. That is, we should not make exceptions for ourselves. We should not do to others what we would not want them to do to us.

Advantages: The golden rule offers the advantage of personalizing marketing decisions. It is difficult to think of a better directive for dealing with others than treating them as we would like to be treated. The golden rule asks marketing decision makers to put themselves in other people's shoes, to empathize with their concerns.

Disadvantages: Unfortunately, the golden rule does not recognize that inequalities may exist between the parties to a marketing decision. Parties in an exchange are rarely equal. Those who argue this go on to say that because of these inequalities, parties in the exchange may not be in a position to return the behaviour. But that is not what is advocated by the golden rule. The golden rule does not imply a "scratch my back and I'll scratch yours" philosophy. Rather, it is a directive that asks individuals to treat others fairly, as they would like to be treated if the circumstances were turned around.

A second argument against the golden rule is that we cannot really know how others feel. Although this is true in a rigorous sense, it is my contention that this argument is also flawed. It is not necessary to know, precisely, how others feel. We do not know how to accurately predict the reactions of others to certain circumstances. There is always uncertainty. If we desired to act under conditions of complete certainty, we would never act because conditions of complete certaintly never exist.

(c) Ross's Prima Facie Duties William David Ross held the belief that there are duties or obligations that bind us morally. Marketing decision makers using this ethical philosophy must evaluate alternatives with respect to duties involved and determine the duty that is most obligatory. The term, prima facie, means "on the surface" or "at first sight." For Ross, prima facie duties are those that ordinarily impose a moral obligation but under certain circumstances, may not apply. We recognize a prima facie duty at first sight as being obligatory when all other things are equal and there are no conflicting duties. According to Ross, there are six categories of prima facie duties:

1. **Duties of fidelity** are those that rest on prior acts of our own. Such duties include the duty not to lie, the duty to remain faithful to contracts, and the duty to keep promise.
2. **Duties of gratitude** are those that rest on acts of other people toward the individual. Individuals are bound by obligations that originated from relationships that we have with others.
3. **Duties of justice** are those that rest on the possibility of distributing pleasure or happiness in a way not in accord with the merits of those concerned. Is justice being served when the president's son or daughter, the worst salesperson in the organization, receives the highest raise?
4. **Duties of beneficence** are those that rely on the fact that there are people in the world whose situation we can improve. It is this duty that appears to be one of the driving forces behind the socially responsible actions of marketing organizations.

5. **Duties of self-improvement** are those that rest on the fact that we can improve ourselves. In other words, individuals should strive to use their talents to their fullest potential.
6. **Duties of no injury** are those that do not harm others. Ross interprets the importance of not harming others as more important than the duties of beneficence.

Advantages: The Rose prima facie duties are set up in a way that leads individuals to think about those duties and to set aside those duties only when other duties have priority. The six sets of duties have clear implications for how marketing professionals should operate as they make marketing decisions. Furthermore, Ross' approach combines the utilitarian perspective of consequences with moral duties. One of the difficulties of utilitarian thinking is that it has the means by which results are achieved.

Disadvantages: The obvious disadvantage of Ross' prima facie duties lies in the question. How do we know what prima facie duties we have to begin with? Although Ross claims that these duties are self-evident; others have argued that we cannot be certain that our duties as individuals include such things as obligation to tell the truth. In order words, there are individuals who are proponents of lying if circumstances dictate such behaviour. A second disadvantage concerns the relative weight and merit of the six duties proposed. In the face of conflicting duties, how is a marketing professional to decide which duty is more important?

(d) Rawls' Principle of Maximum Justice John Rawls (1971) published **A Theory of Justice** in which he tried to combine the merits of deontological and teleogical theories. Rawls' theory attempts to establish principles of justice. His principles rest on the notion of the "original position," a hypothetical situation in which all people are ignorant of their talents and socioeconomic status. Rawls claims that in this position, people are mutually self-interested, rational, and similar in their needs. He then proposes to ask these people what principle of justice should be followed and surmises that they would choose two such principles—the liberty principle or the difference principle.

Liberty principle: People in the original position would expect all those participating in some practice to have an equal right to the greatest amount of liberty that is compatible with a similar liberty for all.

Difference principle: People in the original position would allow for inequalities only as they serve each individual's advantage and that those inequalities arise under conditions of equal opportunity.

Advantages: Rawls'principles carry with them respect for others. Rawls argues that it is never right to exploit even one individual for the benefit of others. Furthermore, Rawls' philosophy outlines areas of broad social responsibility for business organizations through the implementation of the liberty and difference principles. Finally, Rawls' principles require marketing decision makers to consider the preferences of individuals and groups who cannot act for themselves. For a marketing professional, the entire area of consumer-related problems fits in here. Consumers have relatively little input into marketing professionals' decisions, beginning with the conception of a product idea through to the introduction of that product to the marketplace. Because consumers are the ones who will ultimately purchase the product, however, their viewpoints should be considered.

Disadvantages: The primary disadvantage of Rawls' theory is that it is based on several questionable assumptions. One is that Rawls assumes that individuals will act rationally if they are in the original position. He further assumes that people all have similar needs, interests, and capabilities in this original position. Also, the theory conceals from those in the original position any knowledge of their interests, talents, plans and conceptions of what is good. Finally, Rawls assumes that differences will be tolerated as long as those who are worst off see some benefit resulting from decisions.

(e) Principle of Proportionality Thomas Garrett's principle of proportionality has three elements: (a) what we intend, (b) how we carry out that intention, and (c) what happens. Garrett's approach brings together intentions, means, and ends. According to Garrett's philosophy, an individual is responsible for whatever he or she wills as a means or an end. So if both the means and the needs are good in and of themselves, then the individual may ethically risk foreseen but unwilled side effects if and only if there exists a proportionate reason for doing so.

According to Garrett, it is unethical to will anything bad on oneself or others. For example, a marketing manager who attempts to destroy the image of a competitive product wills something bad on that competitor and is acting unethically. Furthermore, it is unethical to risk or permit something harmful to oneself or others without a proportionate reason. Risk involves probabilities concerning means and ends. There is no absolute way that any one means will lead to a particular end. Permit means that an individual may allow something to happen but not will it to happen. A proportionate reason exists when the intended good result of an action is greater than the negative consequences associated with that action.

Advantages: Garrett's principle of proportionality provides a synthesis of most ethical theories. Consequences, goodness of the will, and duties are all taken into account by the proportionality principle through the employment of the concepts of intention, means, and ends. Furthermore, the principle of proportionality provides marketing professionals with flexibility while at the same time not approving of unethical behaviour. This principle does not rely exclusively on consequences to judge the ethical nature of an action. Intentions and actions are also judged as ethical or unethical in this principle. So the end justifies the means only if the individual decision maker does not will something bad to happen to others.

Disadvantages: A key disadvantage of the principle is that it is vague on the subject of what constitutes bad outcomes. Furthermore, the factors surrounding proportionality are vague. Garrett uses the terms necessary and useful in his explanations of proportionality.

But what is necessary and what is useful? Because deciding what is necessary and useful is a matter of subjective judgment, the decisions concerning what constitutes proportionality are also somewhat subjective (Source: Laurence B. Chonko (1995))

Summary of possible questions of an individual towards ethical decision making

Consideration	*Typical questions you might ask yourself*	*Theory*
(1) One's own interests	Is this really in my, or my organization's best long-term interests? Would it be acceptable and expected for me to think only of the consequences to myself in this situation?	Egoism.
(2) Social consequences	If I consider all the possible consequences of my actions, for everyone who is affected, will we be better or worse off overall? How likely are these consequences and how significant are they?	Utilitarianism
(3) Duties to others	Who do I have obligations to in this situation? What would happen if everybody acted in the same way as me? Am I treating people only to get what I want for myself (or my organization) or am I thinking also of what they might want too?	Ethics of duty
(4) Entitlements of	Whose rights do I need to consider here? Am I respecting fundamental human rights and people's need for dignity?	Ethics of rights of others
(5) Fairness	Am I treating everyone fairly here? Have processes been set up to allow everyone an equal chance? Are there major disparities between the 'winners' and 'losers' that could be avoided?	Theories of justice
(6) Moral character	Am I acting with integrity here? What would a decent, honest person do in the same situation?	Virtue ethics
(7) Care for others	How do (or would) the other affected parties feel in this situation? Can I avoid doing harm to others? Which solution is most likely to preserve healthy and harmonious relationships among those involved?	Feminist ethics and relationships
(8) Process of resolving conflicts	What norms can we work out together to provide a mutually acceptable solution to this problem? How can we achieve a peaceful settlement of this conflict that avoids'railroading' by the most powerful player?	Discourse ethics
(9) Moral impulse and emotions	Am I just simply going along with the usual practice here, or slavishly following the organization's code, without questioning whether it really feels right? How can I get closer to those likely to be affected by my decision? What do my emotions or gut feelings tell me once I'm out of the office?	Postmodern ethics

Source Andrew Crane and Dirk Matten (2007)

ADDITIONAL FACTORS INFLUENCING BUSINESS ETHICS

(a) **Leadership:** Ethical business activities can be influenced through the ethics of a leader. The character of a leader is the main quality which is expected to be very sound in business. A leader may be an authority, decision maker, the best teacher and a model in the organisation who designs, moulds and maintains stewardship of the organisation. A leader who may be a chief executive or CEO or proprietor of the organisation must be ethical to create, influence, plan and implement the ethical activities of the business. It is said "as is the ethical leader of the organisation so will be business with ethics." Hence, ethical leadership is necessary for the success of a business.

(b) **Strategy and Performance:** Strategies are long-term plans which are expected to be based on moral values. Corporate strategy, business strategy and functional strategy are different types of strategies where the ethical activities are to be strongly followed. Corporate mission, code of conduct and code of ethics are other formulated ethical standards in the organisation and on each of which, the ethical standards are strongly considered.

(c) **Ethical performance in Business:** It is expected that all the corporate or business units are influenced with ethical activities with are related to:
- Top management attitude
- Corporate culture and broad ethical standards
- Organisation changes related to employees
- Building up of ethical standard like:
    1. Code of ethics
    2. Ethics committee
    3. Ethics training programmes
    4. Ethics audits

Ethical Business Performance

Ethical business performance is understood as corporate social performance. Configuration of principle of social responsibility, processes of social responsiveness (willingness to help) and policies, programmes and observable outcome related to societal relationship by the firm. Social performance of a business be based on the principles of corporate social responsibility. There are three levels of principles where business houses or corporates social responsiveness is developed. The first level is the perspective of business as an economic institution, referred to as legitimacy (legal aspects) The public level is the organisational level of an enterprise, referred to as public responsibility (societal aspect) and the third is that of individual in an organisation where the principle is managerial discretion (administrative or managerial aspect).

An ethical corporate or business performance is explained with the following model:

Principle of corporate social responsibility

↓

- Institutional principle → Legitimacy
- Organisational principle → Public responsibility
- Individual principle → Managerial discretion

Principle of corporate responsibility

↓

- Environment assessment
- Stakeholder management
- Issue management

Outcome of corporate behaviour

↓

- Social impacts
- Social programmer
- Social policies.

Fig. 1.7

Ethical performance of a business should raise to the social performance. The social performance is combination of economic, legal, ethical and political performance.

Corporate houses with ethical business performance cannot ignore the law, government policies and society. These three areas also have greater influencing factors on the ethical business performance. But it is said that the business should perform more than the expectation of the law, for its ethical business activities.

Corporate Culture

Culture is ideas, attitude and other meaningful symbols to shape human behaviour in the society. Business houses which are referred to as corporates are to build these organizations with strong culture as the foundation for the best ethical business practices. Corporate culture is understood as the values, ideas, high principles based on legal and ethical theories. Perceptions, social responsibility, moral values and co-ordination between perception and practices in the organisation.

The corporates are to act in an ethically responsible way and develop a culture of caring for people and the environment. Culture flows downward from the top managers and leaders. Corporable culture mainly comprises two environments, i.e., internal and other being external. Internal is caring for employees, maintaining good and healthy work atmosphere, quality training to create organizational or work culture and meeting of the various requirements of the organisation. External refers to caring for stakeholders apart from shareholders and employees. The external environment consists of mainly customers, debtors, suppliers of goods, creditors and society. Many of the corporates include the people or society or general public as a part of their duty, to care and concern.

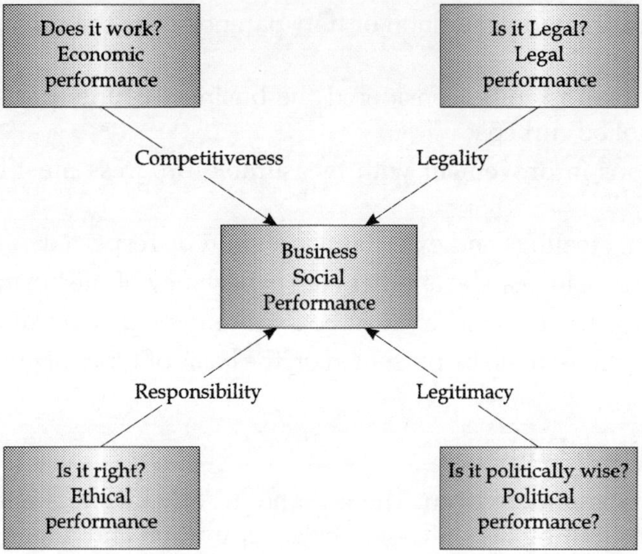

Fig. 1.8 Corporate culture

Environment protection is one of the major activities of the corporates. It is the moral and ethical responsibility of the corporate to clean up the environment where one's own business is functioning.

To sum up, the ethical activities of a business are influenced by individuals, moral theories, culture and values, humanity, traditional habits, morality, social responsibility, corporate social performance, corporate strategy, business strategy, functional strategy, code of ethics, leadership, management style, society, government and environments.

BASICS OF BUSINESS ETHICS

Basics or foundations are fundamental factors or qualities of any activities. Basics of business ethics are the various qualities or fundamental values followed by the business organisations. It is expected a good business is always to uphold the values of good ethics.

Good ethics and good business are synonyms from the moral, legal and human, point of view. Business ethics is science of conduct. Business houses are to be considered social institutions with ethical principles and rules of conduct that reflect their dignity, authority and social responsibility. Business houses must strive hard in their business and other business related activities to maintain a friendly environment.

Keeping the above views the following are qualified as basics of business ethics:

- Moral values are to be the foundations for the success of a business
- Honesty must be the best policy of the business.
- Reliability and truthfulness should always be the core point of the business.

- Transparency and promotion of transparency is be the core value of the business.
- Competitors are to be considered the business counterparts and their voice should not be curbed .
- Continuous improvement with measurable progress must be the mantra of business.
- Customers' feelings and expectations should be respected.
- Long-term vision can be another core expectancy of the business.
- Good corporate citizenship must be a continuous practice of business.
- Cultural values are to be presented on the basis of types of government, people and nation.

Argument on Business Ethics

Society and business are interwoven. There cannot be any business without the activity of a man who is contributing his skill, knowledge, education and might for the growth of business and its development. Business should have ethical foundation for its substanibility and long-term existence. It is expected every business should be based on moral values and human values.

Another view of argument for ethics are ethics drived from personal values and across the world there are many different cultures with different values as their base. Cultural values have a strong influence in the way business is conducted. As the economy expands and to become truly global it is inevitable that contradictory ethical stances will come into conflict.

For many years many of the government different countries have attempted to use trade to impact the culture of the countries. There are many examples in respect of unethical practices in the world today.

WHY ETHICS ? ARGUMENT FOR BUSINESS ETHICS

- Man absorbs impressions, attitudes behavioural patterns just as much as he can absorb which lead to teaching demonstrations and intellectual reasoning. Thus, ethics can be absorbed subjectively and objectively. This can be made to stand on rationality and universality with a systematic training.
- Ethics is a positive attitude of mind and character, just as much as it is a set of skills and knowledge.
- Ethics are gradually fading away especially in the countries like India where strong belief on ethics prevailed and the society was built whereas the new or modern ethics is gradually diversifying the regional ethics which is turning towards negativity and self-oriented activities. There need to inculcate practices of positiveness, continuous and upliftment attitude among traders, younger generation and society to build strong ethical foundation.

- The business houses or corporates should act as moral agents.
- Business ethics paves sense of obligation towards society to solve the problems created by the business.
- Organisational culture leads to moral behaviour of the company which leads to long-term success and profit.
- Ethical standards and practices lead to sound ethics for a good business.
- It is proved though studies and researches that the unethical practices and behaviour is be successful only in short run.
- Ethical business practices will be covering the areas of almost all dimensions of the business activities like stakeholders, environment, law and order and government policies.
- The global economy has shifted the power to impact the world in a lasting way from government to multinational companies. Developing countries are eager to form partnerships with these giants and are willing to conform to new requirements in order to do so. There is a refusual to deal with countries or businesses who engage in unethical practices. This can have a real effect on introducing common ethical standards for business across the world.
- Small businesses wanting to operate, do not have the same ability to force themselves with good business ethics; they do however have the ability to investigate how the goods they are purchasing from foreign sources are made. By choosing not to deal with companies who engage in questionable practices. Every business owner can establish higher standards.
- Marketeers in their business activities should possess ethical values to achieve market leadership by ensuring customer satisfaction through products and services of international standards.
- The unethical practices like misleading products and advertisements, false promises deceptions and unfair activities will have no way for long and continuous existence in the markets.
- The relationship marketing between customers and business can be strong only through ethical practices.
- Moving towards environmentally friendly products and operating practices. Over the past decades consumers prefer products that are environmentally friendly.
- As the world markets open up and individual cultures and business practices become more visible, consumers are again in a position to judge their brand choice, supporting companies who enforce high ethical standards.

Arguments Against Business Ethics

Few authors, businessmen and few people of philosophy believe that business being an economic entity should have only economic value and responsibility of the business is to earn profit.

Milton Friedman (1962) in his book **Capitalism and Freedom** believes as:

"There is one and only one responsibility of business to use its resources and engage in activities designed to increase its profits so long as it stays within the rules of the game which is to say, engages in open and free competition, without deception or fraud. Few friends could undermine the very traditions of our free society as the acceptance by corporate officials of a social responsibility other than to make as much as money for their stake holders as possible. This is fundamentally subversive doctrine".

From the above we can find that business ethics may be formed as a part of corporate culture and ultimately the customer would be called upon to bear the cost of the ethical practices of the organisation.

However, his views and general views of various people against business ethics are unacceptable and impracticable to the present marketing and business scenario.

To sum up, while it appears there is genuine opportunity to improve the standards of business ethics across the globe it should not be forgotten that the unethical practices are not restricted to any particular country or culture.

Global economy operates regardless of the ethical environment, and there is at least as much opportunity for promoting unethical practices as there is the chance for the better. It is the individual consumer, business people and share holder who have the powers insist on change.

Business culture followed by corporate culture, social responsibility, moralities, values, human-centric organisation, customer caring, code of conduct based on ethics, business strategy with strong business value honesty, transparency and truthfulness and so on so forth are various focusing areas for ethical foundation. In the business ethics, business and society go hand in hand. Diversion towards these areas will lead to collapsing of profits or sustainability of the business in the long run.

Ethics as a Tool

The following discussion will bring clear picture of the importance of ethics.

1. **Ethics corresponds to basic human needs:** On a deeper level we believe that most people want, and even need to be ethical not only in their private lives, but also in their business affairs. What is more important is most people want to be part of an organisation which they can respect and be publicly proud of, most top management would like to respond to this need of their employees, and they themselves feel an equal need to be genuinely proud of the company they are directing. These basic ethical needs are probably one of the most convincing reasons for ethical concern as the part of organisation.
2. **Ethical Value Create Credibility with the Public:** A company perceived to be ethically and socially concerned will be honoured and respected even by those who have no intimate knowledge of its actual working. TATA, Birla, Infosys and so on are the best examples. There will be an instinctive prejudice

in favour of its products, since people believe the company gives value for money. These are the companies, where the people eagerly invest their money when the opportunity arises.

3. **Ethical values give management credibility with employees:** Ethics and values of any company when perceived by employees as genuine, create common goals, values and language. The management has credibility with its employees precisely because it has sound corporate policies, employees management, etc. Strong basic law may not create any value or credibility among employees but only perceived moral philosophy, values or practices and social responsibility or responsiveness can create. Added to this employees will feel full secure and proud to work in ethical organizational climate.
4. **Ethical values help better decision making:** In recent past it has proved that the corporate business houses practising business ethics are attracting best decision making in the organisation. Decision on stakeholders policy towards internal and external business environments, strategy for marketing, human resource, finance and so on are decided on the basis of ethical foundation. Ethical decision making also renders a great helping hand in profit maximisation and best business policy or preparation of code of ethics.

RESEARCH OUTCOME ON ETHICS IN BUSINESS

During the period 2000 to 2003 a research study was undertaken on corporate business ethics, social resistibility, social performance, ethics and ethical issues in marketing. There was a overwhelming response by the corporates in discussing about the CSR CSP and ethical aspects. Basically, all human-beings are interested in practising ethics. But it may be situations, business opportunities, ups and downs make any business to slip from being ethical to unethical. There are certain extracts of the study and its findings, dialogues and discussions with the corporate given as the exhibits in the text. This makes the students, corporates or anybody to realise the practiability of business ethics. The various components like, moral values, honesty, truthfulness, transparency, continuous improvements, compassion towards employees, reliability, customer care, corporate citizenship and social responsibility are used to measure the perception and practice of business ethics.

Exhibit

Corporates Overall Perceptions and Practices on Business Ethics

The high value for business ethics by the multinational companies (93.9%) were followed by the public limited companies (92.9%). Whereas at the same time the MNCs are not keen on their business contribution to societal welfare and well-being.

The public limited companies show more interest towards the society. With regard to the business long-term vision, the public limited companies are more conscious than the multinational companies, who show less interest on this long-term vision. Again when the comparison is made between these two, it shows slight variation. The public limited companies desire to be a good corporate citizen, whereas multinational companies show less response towards corporate citizenship. They feel that they are tenants in this country and they must be very careful (IBM) and there must be continuous improvement process through teamwork (MICO).

- With regard to telling lies in business which is considered as common sense in some business places, the public sector companies disagree with this. As one of them said *"Honesty is fundamental, housekeeping boy, corporate ethics are beyond law and we are true almost"* (Karnataka Antibiotics and Pharmaceuticals Ltd.), *"I need not to tell lies and I need not tell everything to the customers"* (National Textile Corporation). The attitude of the private limited companies with regard to suppressing the voice of the competitors, good corporate citizenship is very high as compared to public sector companies. Regarding customers, one of the public sector expresses that *"Customers are Kings"*, (Mysore Sales International Ltd.) but collectively they show very little interest as regard to the respect towards customer feelings. Again the public sector companies are on a very low attitude level with respect to good corporate citizenship.
- The general attitudes towards business ethics by the different corporate sectors are very encouraging. The attitude on moral values, transparency, achieving continuous improvement, reliability and truthfulness and respect towards customers are very high in case of multinational companies and public limited companies.
- With regard to the business and the practice of moral and ethical values the public limited companies emerge very strong, as one of the corporates expressed that *"Our company is running in an ethical manner and it is integrated with 80 corporates (Wipro) and they have fear on expressing ethics, too much of ethics is to be avoided"* (TTK), *"our concept of business is family based"* (Bata India), *"In export business one must be ethical and we do follow that since ours is 100% export oriented organisation"* (Chestline), *"Ethics is our business and we are very much in right ways, no short cuts, we have open policy with nine branches"* (Aravind Mills), *"Ours is one of the TATA Group of Companies and ours is 100% transparent"* (Rallies India). Public sector companies are practising ethics to the minimum extent. They show again variation in trying to be a good corporate citizen. Public companies are among high to a good corporate citizen whereas public sectors are practising to a lower extent.
- Between multinational companies and private limited companies there is a variation with regard to the practice. Multinational companies are showing more transparency and they feel that, being transparent is good for a healthy business. Supporting this, one of the corporates said that *"we believe in being*

transparent and promote transparency, where we consider it as healthy sign of the business" (L.G), *"We are 100% transparent"* (Philips India). Whereas the private limited companies show very less interest in being transparent in their business.

- The private sector companies show high performance with regard to suppressing the voice of the competitors in the business, as compared to multinational companies. Further, in case of practice on long-term vision, private limited companies show high performance than multinational companies.
- Public sector and private limited companies show the same performance with regard to encouraging of healthy competition and not feeling sorry for other people, while they face problems. Further, the performance of the public sector and multinational companies in respect of continuous improvement in the business process is more or less the same.
- The attitude on telling lies in the business appears to favourable but the practice shows a lot of ambiguity especially by multinational companies. *"Ethics should be established for the long run, being honest and straight can solve many problems"* (Li and Fung) and another corporate lightly put it as *"Ethics is a matter of conscience."*
- There is a lot of variation by multinational companies both in attitude and practice with regard to the business contribution towards the welfare and well-being of society. Both public limited companies and private limited companies under private sector, individually differ in attitude and practice with respect to continuous improvement with measurable progress in the business. The public sector companies differ in this respect as one of companies feel *"We are going down as our research and development decision is not sound"*. (I.T.I) and also with respect to *"Long term vision and good corporate citizenship"*. Again the public sector shows the variation between the attitude and practice however, there is no difference between attitude and practice in respect of business reliability and trust, and respect towards customers feelings by all the corporate sectors.
- Many times attitude and practice differ. Different corporates put it as, *"It is difficult to be ethical in business, personally one may be ethical and to practice the same it is very difficult in the organisation, in the business world due to the competition, many are not ethical, even if he thinks to be ethical, the organisation may not allow and vice versa"* (Chestline), *"Even to be unethical, it is highly expensive (like tenders)"* (Indian Telephones Industries), *"Ethics is not beyond profit, every small businessman wants to make profit rather than being unethical, every individual goes for basic needs like food, shelter, education, meeting marriage expenditure and he will be in that sphere, there is no question of ethics, thus the same is applicable to the corporates and everybody is making lots of money by cheating the customers"* (NTC), *"Public sectors are more ethical and private sectors do not bother for ethics; people buy oil from us and fill in the other cylinders and sell it, it is very difficult to practice ethics in India,*

because everybody should get profit for the money invested" (Indian Oil Corporation), *"Private sectors are not practicing ethics"* (Hindustan Petroleum Corporation), *"Ethics depend upon the product and no quick money"* (Mysore Sales International Ltd.), *"Where is the question on ethics when we are running the company for the sake of the employees survival, though we are running on loss"* (Subadra Textiles), *"Ethics is partially agreeable and partially disagreeable"* (Shahi Exports), *"Ethics is a subject but being too ethical is not practical"* (TTK). Again one of the corporates put it as *"Ethics is an agency without teeth"* (Toyota) and another says that *"Corporates should be focused on the survival of the fittest logically ethics may be true and transparent and practically it is very difficult"* (Sangli Textile).

CORPORATE SOCIAL RESPONSIBILITY

Corporate social responsibility is an obligation of the organisation to act in a way that serves both its own interests and the interests of its many external communities. The corporates are to act ethically and develop a culture of caring for people and the environment.

Since business and society are interwoven there is an expectation from society as to what the appropriate business behaviour and outcome should be. Businesses today no longer exist only to maximise profits. They exist and operate for a number of reasons, one of which should be the welfare of the society in which they operate and grow (The topic CSR will be dealt in detail in the chapter 4)

Corporate ethics – The general concept of ethics was explained in previous topics. There are however three streams which oppose ethics in business. They are (1) Competitive free markets (2) Loyal agents (3) Obey the Law

1. **Competitive free markets:** This assumes that the pursuit of profits will ensure socially beneficial activities. However, this argument has several assumptions such as:
- Most individual markets are not perfectly competitive and they can make profits without being efficient.
- Rising profits may injure society by allowing pollution, deceptive advertisement, fraud, bribery prize fixing, etc.
- Companies produce what the buyers want, but many people are not buyers. Management should pursue profit.
2. **Loyal agent:** This assumes that managers and employees do whatever the employers want them to do:
    - Managers are expected to be loyal to the organisation. Is it an act of ethics?
    - Managers are duty-bound to serve the employees.
3. **Obey the Law:** In this context, obeying the law, is the act of ethics. However law and ethics do not always coincide. Sometimes the moral standards become law, for example in US, "The Foreign Corruption Practices Act".

Many MNC's which operate in more than one country face ethical dilemmas. The reason for this is the different countries have different standards and norms and the firms should act accordingly.

Corporates are more than economic institutions. They have a responsibility to help society to solve pressing social problems.

Corporates are not Merely Profit Making Bodies, but They are Responsible Entities

The following are the core areas of services, wherein the corporates can focus to meet various needs of general public:

(1) Health services:
  (i) Conducting health programmes
  (ii) Donation to the hospitals.

(2) Educational services
  (i) Promotion of education
  (ii) Starting up scientific research.
  (iii) Enchancing technical education.

(3) Community development:
  (i) Programmes for rural development
  (ii) Welfare of women and children
  (iii) Community services.

(4) Environmental protection:
  (i) Promotion of afforestation
  (ii) Consvervation of nature
  (iii) Study of ecology and safeguarding the environment.

(5) Promotion of culture:
  (i) Protection of heritage and arts
  (ii) Religion and values
  (iii) Promotion of arts and culture.

(6) General:
  (i) Road safety
  (ii) Sports and their promotion
  (iii) Any other core area related to society.

Issues Management

Society gives legitimacy and power to business. As business organizations have an impact on a variety of stakeholders (and not just equity shareholders) including government, customers, competitors, suppliers and employees, they are expected to operate in the interests of society. There are certain activities which are not expected from companies or prohibited by any economic, legal or ethical concerns. The problem with ethics is not that there is lack of knowledge about it or the acceptance of principles of behaviour underlying such knowledge. But ethics is to make the human behaviour naturally to practise as well as a part of making business decisions individually and collectively. Ethical decision making is a great challenge for the best and sound management. There are five conclusions concerning the complexity of managerial ethics. These are:

1. **Most ethical decisions have extended consequences:** The results of managerial decisions and actions do not stop with the first-level consequences. Rating level these results extends throughout the society and that extension constitutes the essence of the ethical argument. Bribes, pollution, unsafe products etc., are some of the issues which are directly related both to the management and society.
2. **Most ethical decisions have multiple alternatives:** It is commonly thought that ethical issues in management are primarily divided into two like a 'yes' and a 'no' choice as other alternative.

   For example (a) Should a manager pay a bribe or not (b) Should a company manufacture unsafe products or not ? (c) Should a factory pollute the air or not and so on. Whereas some of the situations create ethical issues like payment of bribery of import clearance.There are number of examples for ethical decision making.
3. **Most ethical decisions have mixed outcomes:** In management when there is imbalances in making ethical decisions may help in getting other things done. For example (a) pay an indirect bribe, but maintain the sales volume of imported goods through prompt delivery; (b) cause some air or water pollution but avoid the costs of installing and operating pollution control equipment; (c) design a slightly unsafe product but reduce the material and labour cost of manufacture. Here social benefits and costs as well as financial revenues and expenses are associated with almost all of the alternatives in ethical choices.
4. **Most of the ethical decisions have uncertain consequences:** It is commonly thought that ethical issues in management are free of risk or doubt, with a known outcome for each alternative, e.g., (a) pay the bribe, and receive the imported goods promptly; (b) invest in pollution control equipment, and emission will be reduced (c) produce an absolutely safe product at an additional cost. In this there is no clarity that what kind consequences will follow most ethical choices.
5. **Most ethical decisions have personal implications:** It is commonly thought that ethical issues in management are largely impersonal, divorced from the lives and careers of the managers, Individual benefits and costs, as well as financial and social benefits and costs are associated with most of the alternatives in ethical decisions.

The ethical decision making should be based on the following dimensions:

(1) Utilitarian dimension of ethical decision making: This is focussed on goal oriented factors. Like (a) Social goals.(b) Economic goals (c) Business goals. The above will be based on policy or goal making and maximisation of profit.

(2) Deontological dimension of ethical decision making: This consists of two types like (**i**) Right oriented which refers to legal right and moral right. (**ii**) Duty oriented; connected with contractual duties. (a) Obey laws (b) Moral duties. This dimension is based on the action or policy to fulfill our duties.

(3) Economic (distributive) justice: It is open to market returns and externalities: It is applicable to the action or policy most fairly alternative the benefits and burden among share holders.

ISSUES IN GENERAL BUSINESS ETHICS

General business ethics differ from organisation to organisation, corporate culture, environment, nature, type, climate quantative and qualitative of work, philosophy and so on are the basis for practising ethics and ethical decision making in the management. However, some study on business ethics brings out the various issues, which are as fallows:

- **Business ethics:** Many time it is based on philosophy of business. Here the aim of the business is to determine the fundamental purposes of the company. If a company's main purpose is to maximise the returns to its shareholders, then it should be seen as unethical for a company to consider the interests and rights of anyone else.
- **Corporate social responsibility:** It is an umbrella term under which the ethical rights and duties existing between companies and society is debated. Though business and society is interwoven and it is the moral responsibility of the corporate or businesses towards society and societal welfare, but this is not very seriously taken by many of the business houses since they want to maximise their profit, pay tax and increase the wealth.
- **Issues regarding the moral right and duties between a company and its shareholders:** Stakeholder concept in the management is not given full weightage by many of the small and medium companies as they give importance to the shareholders. Shareholders are mere investors. Only with the investment, the success of business is not measured. It is the stakeholders like employees, suppliers, customers, creditors, government along with the share holders are responsible for the total success of the business. There is a fiduciary relationship, i.e., relationship on trust or dependent on public confidence on stakeholders concept and not fully on share-holder concept.
- **Ethical issue:** It is concerning the relations between the companies creating unfriendly environment and spying the various business secrets.

- **Leadership issue:** Most of the ethical decision making is based on the leadership quality of the manager, corporate governance, corporate culture, corporate values, practices of the corporate. Corporate social performances are all the various dimensions with different issues in the organisation. This can be solved only with leadership quality a permanent issue in the organisations.
- **Political contribution:** Many business organisations are based on political environment. There is a lot of interlinked situations where both government and the corporate management interact. Both are independent as well dependent. Many times there will a contradictory viewpoints in respect of ethics and ethical decision making by the organisation.
- **Missusing of corporate ethics:** Many times the corporates perception and practising on ethics differ.

They do not follow what they think and say. Based on the market situation and business environment they change their policies. Altering the policies and programmes based on environment and organisational climate may not be an ethical activity, and this may result in conflicting issues in the organisations.

Understanding issues in management

Issues may be related to individual responsibility or moral responsibility. Moral responsibility is connected to the ethical dilemma in the organisation. For the sake of study the ethical issues, its management can be classified into:

1. Individual ethical issues.
2. Business ethical issues in general.
3. Ethical issues in functional areas of management like marketing, HR, finance, technology, etc.
4. Ethical issues related to internal and external environment.

1. **Individual ethics:** Practising of ethics differs from one person to another. What is ethical to one person may be unethical to another. Many times ethics is decided on the basis one's consciousness and values. An individual is expected to follow certain principles to be ethical, principles of purpose, perspective, patience, persistence and pride, being honest, punctual, fairness, integrated and so on when a person follows most of them may be termed non-issue persons in the management.
2. **Business ethical issues:**
   (i) Bribe: Taking bribes is unethical as this will result in loss of trust, uncertain transaction will lose its sustainability and it affects long-term investments.

   Giving bribes is unethical as in this process bribe-takers will be encouraged and all evil consequences will appear.

   (ii) Lack of moral values: These are considered the foundations for the success of the business.

(iii) Honesty: Telling lies in business is considered plain commonsense. But it is not always true and practised in the organisation, being honest to the customer, employees and to the society are important for the long-term existence of the business.

(iv) Transparency: Another important issue where the business will not reveal any other facts which are supposed to be revealed to its own shareholders. Transparency in all aspects of business, will help the business to grow healthy.

(v) Suppressing voice of the competitors: Many corporates try to suppress the competitiors through marketing or product, not letting the competitiors talk when they are supposed to talk. This is an unethical act. Here the small entrepreneurs are always discouraged by the big business houses.

(vi) Respect towards customer: Many countries follow, the "sellers market" rather than "buyers market". Many times customers' taste, interest, expectations, capacity and their knowledge are not considered by the corporates and customers are forced to accept the existing product in the market.

(vii) Long-term vision: The corporates should work upon the long-term vision. Their strategies, policies and programmes should be based on the vision. Many time corporates may be focusing on short-term vision rather than long-term vision.

(viii) Good corporate citizen: Corporates are expected, morally, and ethically very strong in framing the managerial decisions. Honesty towards internal and external environment leads to success in the organisation.

3. Ethical issues in functional areas of management:

1. **Marketing issues:** There are many issues in marketing areas since it involveds customers and general public. The issues are:
   (i) Mandatory to various laws not only related to customers but every activity of the marketing.
   (ii) Every activity should be based on ethical foundation.
   (iii) Unfair behaviour in the marketing.
   (iv) Deception in marketing of the products.
   (v) Influencing the customers to purchase their products through direct or indirect methods of marketing (like advertisement, direct selling, etc.)
   (vi) Fixing up of unfair prices
   (vii) Lack of customer care and after-sales services.
2. **Human resources issue:**
   (i) Bad human relationship and ineffective organizational structure.
   (ii) Poor working conditions.

(iii) Lack of opportunity for self-growth and career development.
(iv) Disparities in wages
(v) Unethical behaviour of HR manager.

3. **Financial Issues:**
(i) Improper determination of terms and conditions of loans.
(ii) Improper utilization of debt capital.
(iii) Irregular payment of interest and advances.
(iv) Lack of information to the shareholders and public.
(v) Poor assessment of investment opportunities.
(vi) Poor risk management.

4. **Ethical issues related to internal and external environment:** Internal environment may be related to and employees and shareholders.

(i) Issues related to shareholders are:
(i) Lack of transparency
(ii) Lack of investments into profitable shares
(iii) Untimely payment of dividends.
(iv) Lack of information towards progress of the business.

(ii) Issues related to employees:
(i) Not providing with a fair salary and wages.
(ii) Bad working conditions.
(iii) Unsatisfactory security needs
(iv) Poor recruitment policy
(v) Poor work culture
(vi) Stress, strain and pressure in the work spot.

External Environment

Most of the time related it is related to supplier of goods, environmental issues, government and society.

Issues towards supplier of goods:

(1) Lack of fair prices at the reasonable times.
(2) Unhealthy competition.
(3) Lack of information regarding changes in demand and preferences.
(4) Unfair prices in reasonable times.

Environmental Issues

(1) Actions that directly affect the livelihood and quality of human life.
(2) Actions that will affect the livelihood and quality of life of the future generation (e.g., unborn child)

(3) Actions that affect animals, plants ecology, etc.
(4) Improper installation of machinery for pollution control.
(5) Lack of environment awareness programme.
(6) Lack of safety devices.

Issues related to government:

(1) Untimely payment of taxes and duties.
(2) Indulging with bribing activities with the officials.
(3) Entering into politics and mixing with the business.
(4) Escaping from the legal aspect through political influence.
(5) Non-cooperation with the government during times of crisis and emergency.

Societal Issues

(1) Lack of social responsibility.
(2) Keeping away totally from societal problems.
(3) Depromotion of culture through western culture, with reference to carelessness towards, heritage, religion and values. Lack of promotion of art and culture.

CRISIS MANAGEMENT

Crises management refers to managing or methods to overcome a danger in the organisation. It may be a great difficulty or turning point in the organisation during various situations which may destruct or construct the opportunities to be a best or worst management. Many a times this sort of situation arise due the external environment.

Crisis can be of several types: Some cause surprise to management. While others are part of the usual risks of business operations.

According to Pearson and Clair, "an organisational crisis is a low-probability, and high impact event that threatens the organisation". There are different types of crisis where the corporates are expected to tackle them through their best managerial efficiency. Some of them are listed below:

(1) Product tampering
(2) Accident
(3) Copyright infringement
(4) Environmental spill
(5) Computer tampering
(6) Product/service boycott
(7) Natural disaster that disrupts a major product or service
(8) Natural disaster that destroys organisational information base.

(9) Bribery
(10) Terrorist attack
(11) Plant explosion
(12) Sexual harassment
(13) Product recall
(14) Natural disaster that destroys corporate headquarters and eliminates key stakeholders.

Crisis situations are the threat to the organisation. There are different reserach studies have been undertaken to tackle these situations. Different perspectives are thrown to analysis the crisis like:

(1) Psychological
(2) Socio-political
(3) Technological structure.

The above said perspectives are analysed though '4C's towards organisational crisis refered as, causes, consequences, caution and coping.

Crisis cannot always be fully expected, anticipated or predictable. Hence, it can be planned as it may or may not occur. And all that this can be managed when it arises. The management can with proper handling, defuse them, with the business related problems, such as the bankruptcy of a supplier, strike, hostile takeovers and cash shortage, and they may be known as crisis.

There are certain crises over which companies have no control like; (which occur naturally)

- Product hazards
- Natural disasters (floods, droughts or earthquakes)
- Civil unrest (riots, civil wars, strikes, etc)
- Hostile lobbies,
- Ownership battles,
- Technology problems.

There are some risks which uncontrollably arise due to certain situation. This may arise with lack of internal monitoring system in an organisation. Some of them are:

(i) Frauds: The reason for growing frauds are:
- Rapid business growth
- Leaner structures may create lack of operational knowledge.
- Modern technology and information capabilities.

(ii) IT Risks: Control services: This gets access to what within internal IT networks.
- Assurance services: Providing advice on the Internet services.
- Operational services: analysis of exposure to risk in workers day-to-day IT operations.

- E-commerce: Security tightening
- External security: Hacking, Internet fraud, pornography and damaging the image of the company.

(iii) Legal risks: A variety of threats ranging from criminal action, regulatory action, civil action by third parties, complaints or bad publicity. All these require timely and accurate legal risks advice.

(iv) Financial risks: It is another crisis that companies try to cover a variety of balance sheet risks, mostly foreign currency exchange fluctuations through derivatives. Insurance now covers the following:

- Future rent increases on commercial property.
- The residual value of assets and bridge short- term cash flow problems.
- Weather risk policies.

RESPONSES TO CRISIS SITUATIONS OR CRISIS MANAGEMENT

Organisational performance depends on proper planning and programming. This happens when certain successful activities become standardised into programmes for coping with certain situation.

Some of the suggestions to beat the crisis in the management:

(1) Avoid excuses: Emphasise prescriptions, which put stress on rationality, reliability, planning, agreement stability, hierarchical control and efficiency.

(2) Reject implicit assumptions, these are challenged and altered.

(3) Replace top manager: This is necessary to overcome the crisis. Such replacement should be total and not be limited to just one or two.

(4) Experiment with portfolios: Invest in new market products and technology.

Further the above aspects can be elaborated to include factors as intelligence failure, organisational learning crisis management and crisis marketing, which may all be studied deeply as a subject.

According to Marconi (1997)

The following are the various points or actions for crisis prevention:

- Be the first to comment.
- Show concern.
- Pledge co-operation
- Take responsibility
- Tell everyone about the action taken.
- Discuss with the larger context.
- Apologise, if wrong.
- Designate a single spokesperson.

- Raise company visibility.
- Advertise positively.
- Support causes.
- Talk to the public.
- Personalise the stay.
- Put it in the larger context.
- Redefine the company's positioning.
- Express sympathy.
- Recall the product.
- Give reward for information.
- Serve public notice.
- Crisis team setup.
- Arrest people for false reporting.
- No arrogance or doubt about bottlers.

TYPES OF CRISES

Pearson and Clair (1998) define an organisational crisis as followings:

An organisational crisis is a low-probability, high-impact event that threatens the viability of an organisation and is characterized by ambiguity of cause, effect, and means of resolution, as well as by a belief that decisions must be made swiftly.

They have listed the different types of crises as given below:

- Extortion
- Bribery
- Hostile takeover
- Information sabotage
- Product tampering
- Workplace bombing
- Vehicular fatality
- Terrorist attack
- Copyright infringement
- Plant explosion
- Environment spill
- Sexual harassment
- Computer tampering
- Escape of hazardous materials
- Security breach

- Executive kidnapping
- Personnel assault
- Product/service boycott
- Assault of customers
- Work-related homicide
- Product recall
- Malicious rumour
- Counterfeiting
- Natural disaster that disrupts a major product or service
- Natural disaster that destroys corporate headquarters
- Natural disaster that destroys organizational information base.
- Natural disaster that eliminates key stakeholders

Source Pearson and Clair [1998],. and S. Shivaraman (2000)

A brief note on different cases in respect of ethics and ethical issues on bribes, religious culture, and ethical decision making is followed.

BRIEF NOTE OF CASE STUDIES ON ETHICAL ISSUES

Bribes

(i) US Defence Contracts: A US Commerce Department report suggests that there is a lot of bribery in international defence contracts. Nearly half of the complaints received by the Department, are concerned with international defence procurement. Other industries involved include commercial aviation, communications, infrastructure and construction projects. Allegations of foreign bribery were made in 55 contracts valued at US $ 37 billion between May 1998 and April 1999. In the previous five years, bribery influenced 294 commercial contracts worth US $ 145 billion. US companies lost 77 contracts worth US $ 24 billion. They were at a disadvantage in international competition due to the US Foreign Corrupt Practices Act of 1977, which forbids US businesses from paying bribes.

In December 1997, the Organisation for Economic Cooperation and Development (OECD) drew up a legally binding treaty making corruption a criminal offence for companies operating in OECD countries to bribe foreign officials. Any illicit payment made to elected or appointed officials or to legislative, administrative or judicial posts fall swith in the treaty's scope, as also any bribe given to employees of public agencies or companies. Punishment is decided by each signatory's criminal courts.

Stofwever, Transparency International, a Berlin-based non-profit agency, is campaigning against graft and corruption worldwide. It published a corruption perception index that lists countries according to corruption perception, where specific allegations of bribes are made. Incidentally, one may recall that International Telephone & Telegraph (ITT), a US company had given bribes to overthrow the Allende regime in Chile in the 1970s.

(ii) The Bofors Guns Case in India The Bofors guns case is a long-running story. It led to the toppling of the government of Rajiv Gandhi in the 1980s when controversy raged over whether the administration had received kickbacks to buy weapons which did not meet the country's needs.

In 1990, India barred any further dealings with Bofors—even to buy spare parts or ammunition. The army was forced to cannibalize some of the weapons for spare parts to keep the rest in working order. However, during the fighting in Kashmir in 1999, reference was made to the Bofors battalion and its efforts. The cabinet approved to lift the ban at the end of June 1999.

(iii) IBM's Tangle in Argentina Allegations regarding IBM began in 1995. This was with reference to its local branch, which in 1993, paid US $ 37 million in kickbacks and bribes to obtain a US $ 250 million contract to supply the state-run Banco de la Nacion with a computer network to link up its 525 branches. A federal investigation was initiated, and only in April 1998 did it pick up speed as a result of the testimony of Gernaro Contartese, a former director of the Banco de la Nacion, who stated that he had profited by US $ 1.5 million (deposited in a Swiss bank).

Introducing Ethical Principles in Business

Two cases involving Philip Morris and Pepsi Co are discussed below to illustrate ethical principles in business.

(i) Phillip Morris's Troubles By 1995, 125 lawsuits were pending against Philip Morris. These related to health damages alleged to have been caused by the company's tobacco products. In addition, there were attacks on the company's beer segment claiming that alcoholic beverages imposed social costs including deaths attributable to drunken driving. The company was also accused of 'dirty money' made on the cigarette business.

- In 1954, the *Reader's Digest* published an article that linked smoking to cancer.
- In 1964, the Surgeon General of the US released its report linking smoking to cancer.
- In 1966, Congress required health warnings to be placed on all cigarette packages. This was further reinforced by amendments in 1969 and in 1985 to indicate the relation between cigarette smoking and other diseases.
- In 1994, the Federal Drug Administration (FDA) alleged that 4,00,000 Americans died of cases related to smoking each year.

Philip Morris argued that these studies were conclusive.

(ii) Pepsi's Burma Connection Pepsi Co announced on 23 April 1996 that it had decided to sell its 40 per cent stake in a bottling plant in Myanmar as a result of criticisms that, by remaining in Myanmar, the company was helping the repressive military regime which ruled the country.

Pepsi Co was one of several American companies which had responded to an invitation by the State Law and Order Restoration Council (SLORC) which came to power in Myanmar in September 1988. Other American companies were Levi Strauss, Amoco, Unocal, and Texaco. PepsiCo entered into a joint venture sought to set up a bottling plant with a 10-year licence to bottle and distribute PepsiCo-owned products in Myanmar, and did well.

However, there was criticism in the US questioning the ethics of doing business in Myanmar. A network of students on 100 campuses started boycotting PepsiCo products. Meanwhile, shareholders also submitted a resolution urging PepsiCo to leave Myanmar. In 1992, Levi Strauss withdrew from Myanmar; in 1994, Reebok and Liz Claiborne withdrew, and finally PepsiCo divasted in 1996.

Source S. Shivaram (2000)

Ethical Issues on Some of the Religious Culture

The recent use of a picture of Lord Ganesha on a beer bottle, the other controversial uses religious Indian motifs have been put to are:

(1) Putting Lord Ganesha and Godess Lakshmi on chapterles upper where the man keeps his heels and stamps.

(2) Pictures of gods have been painted on jeans; goddesses have been used on bikinis.

(3) Name of Wine Shops as Tirumala, Lord Venkateshwara, Krishna Rama, etc. (People question why not wicked ones like Ravana, Kamsa, Duryodhaya, etc.)

(4) In a recent issue of fashion magazine, a model was reporting a bracelet with a lotus and a picture of Godess Lakshmi. Probably she had no clue that it was a religious figure. While Hindus find it disrespectful.

(5) Lord Ganesha is treated like a funny comedian God. He has been shown in various forms on different occasions with different heads of politicians and funny people. Sometime back, Seshan's face (election commissioner) was shown as Lord Ganesha with a large belly during election period. So also Chief Minister like Dharma Singh, Lallu Prasad was shown like Ganesha with distorted funny faces.

(6) Ganesha's body is made in disintegrated into pieces in various modules as symbols in many of the logos of the company. The next god in turn who got into problem is Ling (Lord Iswara). Long back, one magazine showed women's breast in the form of Linga to bring up sex to the top and Bhakti at the lower.

(7) For the west, Ganesha would be an interesting figure – an elephant face, a human body and a big belly. Added to that he is sitting on a mouse with such large body. And to someone who knows nothing about Indian culture, it is only a beautiful picture.

A story was also written about Lord Shiva who were deer skin as *dhoti* and snakes as belt and also as an ornament. Vishnu from his place Vaikunta wanted to meet Lord Shiva. He came on Garuda (a high flying bird) to Kailasa the place of Lord Shiva. Both Garuda and snakes are bitter enemies. As soon as Lord Vishnu landed at Kailasa, the snake got frightened seeing Garuda. Snake vanished and the deer skin slipped from Shiva. Shiva stood naked and blushed seeing Vishnu. Such stories make our children to lose devotion on Gods.

A line may be drawn to eliminate such things or to reduce it to the minimum. Although a designer's psyche is to mix and match cultures, one would not dare to use religious symbols, but they should do some research beforehand. It is the responsibility of Indian designers to ensure religious Indian motifs are not misused. Lines have to be drawn by Indian themselves. While Indian designs are big abroad, India still is not. 'There need to create awareness about Indian culture'. There need a fashion council that can tell people about India. It may be an difficult task. India has such a diverse culture, before you know it something controversial will pop up again.

Source C.S.V. Murthy (2010)

Ethical Issues – Gambling

Gambling on the horses is like wise, a "game" that means the real wages made by venture capitalists of all kinds. Horse breeders trust their money to the quality of their bloodstock in every race without even needing to place a bet; investors judge that the skill of the manufacturer they back be of a chance and so trust their money to their own good judgement.

In and around the world gambling had become so common in every field on the election, sports match winning teams, films, beauty competitions, seat securing, love making challenges. Gambling can thus train and exercise in mind in taking real-life risks. But as its ancient symbolism shows, it is also a ritual honouring the dual influences of chance and skill in our world. To put one's trust in fortune alone is the mistake of gambling addict and mercury, the god of calculation, duly gets its revenge when the bean counters move in on the bankrupt. But both chance and skill are active in our lives all the time, we ignore either at our peril.

The sober citizen who has an annual flutter at the races should perhaps be seen as imitating the dice playing romans.

NEIL ARMSTRONG TO SUE BARBER

Apollo moon mission Astronant Neil Armstrong has threatened to sue a barber shop owner who collected Armstrong's hair after a turn and sold it for $3000 at Ohio. Armstrong, the first man to walk on the moon used to go to Marx's barber shop in Lebanon, Ohio about once a month for a cut. That stopped when he learned that owner Marx Sizemore had collected his hair from clippings from the floor and sold them in may 2004 to a collector at Connecticut John Reznikosf, who figures in the Guinness Book of World Records for having the largest collection of hair from celebrities like Abraham Lincon, Marilyn Monroe, Albert Einstein and Napoleon Bonaparte! Sizemore said "I did not deny it or anything. I told him I did it". He also said that Armstrong asked him to try to retrieve the hair, but the buyer did not want to give it back. "I called Neil back and told him that." Sizemore said. "Then I got this letter from his lawyer". The letter contents that the sale violated an Ohio law designed to protect the rights of famous people. It threatens legal action if Sizemore does not return the hair or contribute his project to charity. This is splitting Lunar hairs.

Armstrong can escape such hair-raising expencences in future by opting for a barber's shop in East instead of Ohio. Barbers in East, do not collect hair clippings but sweep them away to a pit and make wigs mixing differently hairs.

Neil Armstrong's hair may get distributed in different heads in a colourful way.

Ethical Issues – Environment Protection

(i) McDonald's McDonald's cooperated with Environmental Defence Fund (EDF), one of the leading environmental research and lobbying groups in the US, to solve its packaging problem by replacing polystyrene clamshells with quilted-paper wrappers.

The major innovation introduced by McDonald's in 1948 was to put food in paper bags. But environmental groups in 1988 started campaigning against the enormous amounts of rubbish McDonald's was producing, in particular its polystyrene clamshells. The company had selected the polystyrene packaging, which was a light-weight plastic foam with good insulating properties and at the time seemed ideal for packaging fast food. However, it was discovered that it took centuries to rot and young people started against the package.

- In 1989, McDonald's launched a test in ten restaurants to collect and recycle the polystyrene. The company found that it was technically feasible to collect the clamshells and turn them into pellets. However, many customers were carrying the packages out of restaurants and throwing them away. The company found that it was difficult to collect these for recycling and concluded that this was not the solution.
- In order to reduce the damaging publicity, McDonald's approached environmentalists for help and in August 1990, it signed an agreement with the EDF. This alliance had risks for both parties; EDF could be seen as ally of the company, and in case the company rejected EDF's advice, it could incur damaging publicity. However, an agreement allowed the company to meet its own expenses and publish its report independently if required.
- In October 1990, EDF advised the company to reduce the amount of packaging material used, rather than recycle it. McDonald's announced the replacement of the clamshell with a quilted-paper wrap made from a layer of tissue sandwiched between a sheet of polyethylene and a sheet of paper.
- The polystyrene industry immediately compared the environmental impact of the clamshell with the cardboard container made from virgin paper and found that the clamshell in fact was better leading to criticism of both EDF and

McDonald's EDF realized that McDonald's was genuinely concerned about the environmental damage to its business, and this led to a flourishing partnership between the two. The joint working party found that a third of all the waste was from packaging and a third was from food scraps. McDonald's is now trying to reduce the amount of packaging it uses and is also using plastics which are easier to recycle.

The partnership led to a reduction in protest letters, as also to some financial saving due to the use of the cheaper quilted wrap instead of the clamshell package. The example was followed by other fast food chains.

(ii) Dow Chemicals Activists alleged that Dow Chemicals had repeatedly spilled toxic dust intended for Dow's incinerator. As pressure increased from activists, Dow Chemicals announced that it was cooperating with state regulators. In 1996, Dow and the Natural Resources Defence Council (an environmental policy group based in New York) agreed to work together to improve the environment. Though both were initially sceptical, Dow managers discovered that it was profitable introduced new chemical catalysts and make other innovations in the manufacture of resins, combined with modifications in the processing equipment, and eliminate thereby, a nasty by-product, formaldehyde-laced tars. This involved a one-time investment of US $330,000 resulting in annual savings of US $3.3million to the waste-treatment plant.

The Natural Resources Defence Council worked with Dow and local environmentalists. Environmentalists selected 26 toxic chemicals with the objective of reducting toxics by 35 per cent. All the managers at Dow's 40 plants were asked to present their pollution prevention projects directly to the environmentalists. The project was known as the 'Michigan Source Reduction Initiative'.

The project was completed on 30 April 1999. Dow was able to cut the production of a list of toxic chemicals selected by the environmentalists by 37 per cent and reduce the release of chemicals in the air or water by 43 per cent (Feder, 1999). Both the company and the environmentalists realized that their cooperation would benefit by looking for and carrying out profitable ways to cut waste.

Several other types of alliances with activists are elaborated below.

Types of Alliances

Hartman and Stafford (1997) have identified six types of green alliances:

Since the accident, tankers navigating the Gulf of Alaska are escorted by tugboats and monitored far more closely. Disaster teams stand by ready to help in case of trouble. By the year 2015, all new tankers will be required to have double hulls.

(1) Mobil: On 12 January 1998, it was found that although Mobil's 57 offshore wells were in full production, the oil was not reaching the shore. The operation manger immediately ordered to shut down the supply. By that time, however, a 24-inch underwater pipeline from Mobil's production platform, 3.5 miles offshore, had already broken. There was 26 miles of oil spill. The oil drifted westwards and avoided Cameroonian waters. The bulk of the oil remained offshore and owing to warm winds and the light nature of Nigerian crude, the oil spill evaporated fairly rapidly. Thus, the damage caused by the spill was minimal and the shoreline was also spared a serious environmental disaster.

Although the Niger delta is the fifth-largest source of America's imported fuel, the people of the country have remained poor. More than 60 per cent of the revenue for Mobil's joint venture goes to the government.

Oil in the area was discovered by the Royal Dutch shell company in 1956, and exploited by Mobil, Chevron, Shell, Texaco and others. However, after the spill, Mobil started to get thousands of claims from the Akwa Ibom delta state, the resentment against the company having grown.

The damage caused by the oil spill amounted to US $600,000, but the cost to the company was about US $40 million (US $10 million for the clean-up and US $30 million for settling claims).

(2) Toxic Sludge: Boliden Ltd On 25 April 1998, the reservoir owned by Boliden Ltd, which produces mainly zinc, burst, and its toxic sludge flooded rivers and farms in southern Spain. The Spanish government started clean-up operations immediately releasing the first US $30 million on 25 May 1998. The estimated cost amounted to about US $120 million. Company executives said they would pay for the mopping up of some 3 million tonnes of sludge which spilled on to the riverbeds and banks, and would also reimburse farmers for their losses.

Whether the dike around the toxic reservoir burst because of human error, or because of movement inside the earth is currently being examined. The company argued that the dike was in good order but that it had broken because of the earth shifting under its foundations. Critics argued that the faults in the reservoir's structure had been detected over the past several years, but that these had been ignored by both government inspectors and the mine itself.

Boliden, the Canadian mining company spun off by Sweden's Trelleborg, announced in August 1998 that pre-tax losses for the quarter amounted US $52.1 million. This was blamed on falling metal prices and costs associated with a tailings dam rupture in Spain in 1998. Legal proceedings are underway to determine the responsibility and liability for the damages caused by the sludge. Operations at Boliden's Spanish mine were resumed at the end of 1998.

(3) Comeco Corporation: On 20 May 1998, a Kyrgyz truck driver hauling 20 tonnes of cyanide misjudged a turn and rolled his rig into a river six metres below. The cyanide was being taken to the Kumtor mountain top gold mine run by the uranium-mining giant, Comeco Corporation of Canada. The driver broke his arm and leg in the accident, but the river did not suffer much irrevocable damage.

Mistakes

- The miners negotiated directly with the President' team and isolated themselves by the lake from the local community. No local relationships were established.

- The Bishkek Evening News reported that the accident was 'worse than Hiroshima'. This led to panic; and a willingness to exploit the mine's readiness to pay compensation.

Source S. Shivaram (2000)

Case Study

Gurgaon Foods – Ethical decision making

Gurgaon Foods had a proposal for an international collaboration with Maxim Foods, USA, for exporting beef to the USA. The Managing Director Maxwell Jones was not sure if it would be sensible to start a beef factory in the area where the Hindu fundamentalists had a powerful hold. He gave the project to Rita Sharma, Govind Menon and Rusi Satarawallah for review. Rita was a devout Hindu and believed that the cow was sacred. She refused to be a party to the project. Govind had no such beliefs but was aware that the Directive Principles of the Indian Constitution mentioned that cow slaughter should be banned. Rusi was a total non-believer. He told Rita that it was well known that Aryans used to eat beef and that Hindu scriptures nowhere proscribed beef-eating. He also told Govind that the Directive Principles were not the law and cow slaughter was neither illegal nor unethical. He felt that even if such a law was moved, the company should bribe the legislator to see that the bill is not passed.

Maxwell was aware of the views of the three officers and hoped that Rusi would be able to convince the others. He was however surprised when they unanimously recommended that the project should not be taken up, even though they had found the project otherwise feasible and capable of yielding much better results than the company's financial cut-off norms. Maxwell asked Rita and Govind how they had managed to convince Rusi. He was intrigued to discover that they had been converted by Rusi and now agreed with him, except that they wished to draw, the line against bribing the legislators.

Govind said that Rusi's facts and arguments had been logical and rational, and had made him review his own ethical approach. The company had in fact got the project cleared by the government on the assurance that only old cows would be slaughtered. 'Old cows are dying anyway on the wayside – neglected, starved and diseased,' he said. But their meeting with Sakhlani, General Manager Procurement, made him and Rusi reconsider the matter, each for his own reasons. Sakhlani said that the argument of old cattle was a façade and the beef would meet international standards only if young cows were used. He saw no problem in assuring the company of a supply of young healthy cows as they were willing to offer much higher prices than normal. Govind was worried that this would result in loss of nutrition to the rural population, especially children, as milk production would come down.

Rita resisted this sudden and abrupt change in Govind; she believed that this was not necessarily bad as milk was too expensive a source of nutrition for the poor children, and milk products were being exported by the National Dairy Development Board and anyway not available in abundance. Rusi could foresee in this contentious issue a major public relations problem all along the 'cow routes' and a threat to the company's credibility and survival. He was not concerned with the social consequences but switched sides for pragmatic reasons. He again swung them all to his stand that the project should not be supported. Rita and Govind found this pragmatic approach irresistible and their earlier ethical foundations of little consequence in taking the decision.

(This case is fictional but the issues are real and have been developed on the basis of newspaper and television reports of several multinationals working in India. The most explosive of them involved the Kentucky Fried Chicken outlet at Bangalore and the most recent interview on television was with the chief executive of McDonald, USA.)

Ethics is easy to express and difficult to practice."

—Anonomous

2

Chapter

Personal Ethics

Ethics is a personal phenomenon. Business ethics cannot be adopted to the personal ethics, where each individual is unique by himself. General personal ethics forms the foundation of individual morality. The conscience, interpretation of what is good and bad, right and wrong are the consequences of personal ethics.

Personal ethics varies from person to person, depending on their own cultures, values, moral behaviour, beliefs, religious, practices, family, society, personal experiences, individual intuition, mindset and so on. Each of them is weighed differently by different persons based on the situations and places. Hence, one cannot clearly and assertively define this subject. There are different theories of ethics to determine, which may be referred to as moral theories.

In India it is generally accepted through our epics and Bhagavad Gita and the practice of ethics is the daily affair by the individual. But on analysis with the recent trends the inherited quality of ethics is fading away. The society needs ethical acts and ethical people for happiness and peace. 0

UNDERSTANDING PERSONAL ETHICS

Personal ethics is the moral foundation on which people build their lives. They assist in decision making and participating in actions that meet individual moral standards. Ethics represents the core value system used for every-day problem solving. They create a framework for determining "right" versus "wrong". Ethical life is based on a wide variety of factors. They are not absolutes rules. For many people, to define personal ethics is difficult. They simply consider their "inner-voice" as the ethical guidance which they need. After all, individual **intuition** plays an important role in what one finds ethical. Then what is "intuition"?

Capacity to use and understand the creative inner language is **intuition**. Our intuition is key to our personal creativity. It helps us to keep going in moments of uncertainty. It connects us to our inner compass. In life there are many situations for which no one gives you a recipe. It is our own intuition and the decision of an individual at that moment which saves him from an accident or protects from him negative influence. It is that inner voice that whispers to an individual in moments to help to decide.

With the intuition nobody will enter into a process of analyzing, doubting, intellectualizing or questioning. It helps to overcome the situations of uncertainty and chaos. Intuition cannot be **explained** but is **experienced**. It is cannot also be **expressed** but is **felt**.

If a person reacts to chaos with the automatic pilot of his habits and customs, complaints, anger, resistance, lack of acceptance, correction, it should be different etc., then the intuition does not work for the following reasons:

- Too much of involvement
- Considering self as saviour
- Trying to fix it and it gets worse
- Lack of clarity
- Choosing the sides, and losing equanimity
- Too much of noise and movement inside mind and heart.

With the above reasons the voice of intuition cannot be heard or felt.

Intuition is the capacity to use and understand the creative inner language. Eric Rolf describes it thus: "Life talks to each person in such a simple way that we can all understand it : it talks to us directly or through metaphors. Personal intuition, one that we each have, is the instrument to interpret it with."

To make it more clear, which is a great tool of personal ethics, more explanation is expected. This can be simplified with some more situations like: When we manage to be present, "Here and now", we are people with great potential, a lot of strength. All our energy and our strength are here. Out intuition and creativity align with our purpose and generosity, and what we do has an impact, it renews, and it generates trust and hope.

In order to be 'present', we develop the habit of stopping, reflecting and silencing. In the silence we get back strength. We let ideas take hold and we learn to trust in our intuition. Then we act from the heart of our being. The following are the outcomes of intuition:

(1) Regaining the inner strength which benefits both mind and body.

(2) Individual responses are based on love and trust.

(3) Avoidance of negative action like, selfishness, fears, voices which are not fruitful and bitterness.

(4) Offers true guidance, intelligence, spirituality and maturity.

(5) It inspires geniuses, and creativity.

It is said, the true power is within us. "It is not a question of filling oneself from the outside in, but of recovering that energy, that inner strength, inner voice, aligning consciousness with decision, word and action."

Hence, intuition is considered one of the fundamental and essential components of personal ethics. Naturally, with individual thoughts, intuition, mind and action, the personal ethics differs from person to person.

When defining personal ethics there are several aspects along with intuition, which vary from person to person. The different aspects influencing personal ethics and behaviour of the individuals generally fall into following:

- Value of self
- Value of others
- Value of society

VALUE OF SELF

Value of self is weighed as how a person presents himself, which may be the indicator of personal ethics. This refers to trustworthiness, honesty, reliability and consistency.

In other words, "you can see the physical manifestation of your personal ethics in decisions and behaviours that impact your relationships with others, your role in society and your personal identity". Though this framework is not necessarily comprehensive, it provides a basic platform on which to evaluate the role of ethics in everyday life.

Value of Others

Ethics relates considerably to how one person treats other persons in terms of respect, concern for their well-being and recognition of their autonomy. It strongly impacts the depth and longevity of relationships.

Value of Society

It is another aspect that how one interacts with society as a whole also speaks to their ethical standards. This includes compliance with the law, conforming to generally accepted social norms and contributing to the community.

Components of Personal Ethics

Personal ethics is based on the persons, society, area, nation, nature, climatic conditions, education, sex, religion, family and so on. Personal ethics can be concluded on one's own experiences. Howeve, there may be moral grounds to measure the ethics and the same may be considered as its components. Some of them are discussed in brief below.

(1) Perception: Perception represents how we interpret what we "see". No doubt you have attended some sporting event, watched a movie, or listened to the some lecture with your friends. Did you and your friends completely agree on what you saw and heard, or were there differences in what you perceived. Perception is based on information and we all selectively process information. As the risk of over-simplification, that means we choose to accept or reject information on the basis of how we see the world. For example, scientific advances, which are perceived by many to hold the promise of making the world better, are held back by the perceptions of others who are concerned about the dangers science can wield or command. Another example is that, the economic growth is constrained by growing environmental concerns. Many perceive that economic growth is outpaced by the growth of social problems. The question here is, "what happens when perceptions differ?" Obviously, the question is not easily answered. But there may be arguments and interpretations of that information which are based on their perceptions and on the values that hold. As each and every information discussed may be a direction, and direction of those thoughts influenced by individual perception, which is very important. When one discusses questions such as these, one will discover that disagreement or conflict arises because of one's perceptions and one's values often differ from those of others.

Perception has many implications in organizational situations in the sense that biased assessments of ourselves and others can occur in many ways. For example, perception distortions may occur during the hiring process and factors like stereotyping, halo effect or selective perception can affect the appraisal. There are several areas of performance appraisal where perceptual distortions occur. First, a work group is likely to blame other groups or departments for their own failure. For example, the marketing department may blame production department for poor sales or it may blame administration for low hiring and training budgets. Secondly, a superior may evaluate many subordinates at the same time and it is likely that first two or three subordinates in the beginning will be rated higher than the following subordinates due to possible fatigue and boredom. Also, if the first two evaluations happen to be excellent then the following subordinates will be judged by comparison thus creating a bias in the mind of the evaluator. Thirdly, research has indicated that in evaluating performance, both effort and ability are taken into consideration, but more weight is given to effort. Thus a poor performance would be seen as "not trying hard enough", rather than lack in ability. Finally, if the superior has a particularly favourable impression of a subordinate, the minor instances of poor performance may be ignored. Halo effect and stereotyping may also influence evaluation.

Our perception is also attributable to the knowledge of certain causes that may facilitate a certain type of behaviour. Knowing the cause of a behaviour contributes to the accuracy of our own perception about such a behaviour. For example, if a supervisor believes that poor productivity is attributed to the poor performance of subordinates, he will have a different behaviour towards them than if he believes the causes of poor performance to be beyond their control. Accordingly, we must ascertain whether the behaviour of other people is due to some of their inherent characteristics or whether such behaviour is in response to certain situational characteristics. This would affect our perception about other people.

(2) Compromise: Compromise may be referred to as a way of "quick fix" to resolve conflicts. We always struggle with compromise as expressed by familiar concept of good/evil, active/passive, positive/negative, light/dark, virtue/vice, male/female and so as these polar opposites are intentions, but they can complement and balance each other. Sometimes compromise may be good, if long-term considerations are evaluated. But when used as an easy "quick fix", there are danagers. There is a price to be paid for compromising one's values. Sometimes that price may be inconsequential as it relates to ethics and values. Sometimes the price of ethical compromise may seem very small, and we rationalize questionable behaviour on this basis. Generally, compromise at any level makes it easier to compare in future. Eventually, we might begin to rationalize to the point where we cannot distinguish between what we considred right and wrong.

Compromise is to bring amicable solutions without being unfair. Compromise is to give up the issues and values either partially or fully. Certain situations require series of compromises to drive the destiny to the desired point. This may be an arrangement with the client or with the workforce. Human situations cannot always have a definite package. Series of discussions may be needed to win over the people. Certain flexible postures have to be maintained, whereby both the parties may lose. This may be followed by three steps like (i) persuasion; when it fails, the next course is (ii) negotiation; when this also fails, the last would be (iii) litigation.

Compromise cannot be appreciated always since it is not healthy in all situations. During inevitable situations, one has to compromise without undue rigidity. It is always a great question, that how to make compromise without losing conviction. Whereas in losing situations, perhaps everybody has to make some compromise for the larger good. To an individual there may be four situations:

I win – you win
I win – you lose
I lose –you win
I lose – you lose.

The best and the most positive situation for compromise is "I win – you win". This sort of compromise will formulate a strong **personal ethics.**

Best saying is "Lose battles to win War".

(3) Values: Values are evident in all our behaviour. Our values represent the standards we use to guide our action. Each of us operates from a value system that is likely to be different from the value systems of others with whom we are associated. Furthermore, our values may change overtime, individually, or collectively as you will see shortly. Values change complicate the process by which we seek agreement with others and often are at the roots of ethical conflict. For each individual, values shape reality. Because each individual's values are unique, and perceptions of right or wrong are unique. Many of us however operate under the assumption that others will see things in the same ways we do. Sometimes this occurs whereas sometimes it does not occur. Where the assumption of similar values is false, we cannot tend to level those with different values as unethical. Because, there is no set of "ethical absolutes" to which every individual subscribe. Individuals differ. Although it is important to recognize that individuals differ, the mere recognition of differences is an over-simplification and does not provide a satisfactory guide for ethical decision making. Perhaps the best we can hope for this that each individual establishes a set of criteria that guide his or her actions and it does not change very often.

Each of us has our own unique set of values the way we see the world and react to the situations. We face continuing difficulty. Whereas our lives are such that we must live, work, and co-operate with others to survive as individuals; as organizations and as a society. Although we all want to be free to pursue our own viewpoints and feelings, left to our own freedom we would be in a constant state of conflict.

(4) Moral standards: Moral standards are norms imposed by an individual to practise or not practise of an act. Moral standards are based on influencing factors like family, religious places, organizations, institutions or even media. As the individual develops with his education, experiences, exposure and intellectual developments the moral standards set by a person may change with situations. Hence,

- Moral standards are associated with special emotions and a special vocabulary.
- Moral standards deal with matters that we think can seriously injure or benefit human beings.
- Moral standards are neither established nor changed by the decisions of particular authoritative bodies.
- Moral standards to be preferred to other values including self-interest.
- Moral standards are based on impartial consideration.

So, moral standards are standards that deal with matters that we think are of serious consequences and are based on good reasons and not on authority.

(5) Culture: Culture refers to complex values of ideas, attitudes and other meaningful symbols to shape human behaviour in the society. It may also be defined as the patterned way of thinking, feeling, and reacting that exist in a particular group. Culture allows an individual to "fill in the blanks", or behave automatically without having to specify everything in detail. When cultural values are violated, there tends to be emotional reactions and in extreme cases, complete disregard or even banishment of those who have committed the violations. Culture differs from person to person, family to family, place to place, religion to religion, society to society, organization to organization and nation to nation. Culture is based on values and behaviour both primarily and secondarily. Parenting and socialization represents the primary influence.

For example, for the first few years of life Japanese children are strapped to the bodies of their mothers, who encourage them to look at their faces, thus developing a relationship of dependency. These children also sleep with their parents until the age of 6 or 7, which strengthens this sense of dependency. Such parenting practices are consistent with the emphasis on harmony. This sort of practice also takes place in India and some of the eastern countries. By contrast, American children are strongly encouraged to explore the world as early in life as possible. So, the culture of two different persons from both Japan or eastern countries and America differ. Through this difference we can draw the conclusion as two styles of culture. The first style is **group-oriented style** as in the case of Japan, and second being the **individualistic style**, as in the case of the United States.

Religion is another primary influence of culture. Many citizens in several developing countries believe in astrology, and some of the business individuals will not undertake a course of action until it is approved by an astrologer. Whereas some religions oppose this kind a superstition. Family plays a vital role in culture. Organization culture also represents a potent secondary influence.

(6) Morale, Morality and Moral Character: Morale refers to confidence, and determination of an individual or a group of persons. A moralist may be a person who practises and teaches morality. He is also a follower of a natural system of ethics. Morality is the degree of conformity to moral principles. It is the right of moral conduct. It is a science and particular system or moral behaviour or character. Moral character is the quality of a person or group of persons who behave according to moral principles. There are generally accepted moral qualities which build an individual's character. Honesty, truthfulness, sincerity, timely-action, generosity, transparency, act of selflessness, co-operation, integrity, inner energy, strong will power and compassion are some of the qualities of moral character.

Morals stand as guiding principles and values, internal qualities and make to act and response to the situation at the right time and right place. We make moral decisions based on the practices without much debate and thought as these are well accepted principles and values. This is believed very deeply by many persons in the different parts of the world, especially in the east. Moral values are inherited from the parents, family system, teachers, religion, friends and well-wishers and experience. These provide the context or framework for our moral actions.

(7) Beliefs and family system: Beliefs are criteria of thoughts. They are the ways an individual expects people to think about the given concepts. Beliefs are different from norms, and do not find any action. Whereas the family system makes individual to act without raising question on belief.

Family systems in China, Japan, India, Arabian countries are entirely different from western countries. Here, there is a lot of cultural belief and system differences. Many of the systems are based on norms which may be natural or created. Long practices in the family system may be compulsory to practise, irrespective of acceptance to the present situations. There are lot of barriers between Hindu family and Mohamadean family system or any other family system.

To sum up, in respect of giving an insight on personal ethics, it raises a lot of variation in finalising the exact concept of personal ethics. However, some of the well accepted ideas/components/tools like perception, compromise, values, moral standards, morality, belief, family system culture and so on help in determining the meaning of personal ethics.

But there is a conflict on personal ethics, which may be clarified in the following explanation.

False Notion on Personal Ethics

While every person inevitably must decide for himself or herself how to regard his moral obligations. It is likely that personal conscience will embrace a wider range of values and beliefs that core universal ethical norms. When these "extra" values supplement ethical norms with personal moral convictions that are compatible with the dictates of normative ethics, there is no conflict between universal ethics and personal ethics. Unfortunately, some people are "moral imperialists" who seek to impose their personal moral judgments on others as if they were universal ethical norms. A bigger, (sometimes related) problem is that some people adopt personal codes of conduct that are inconsistent with universal ethical norms. Clearly, not all choices and value systems, however dearly held, are equally "ethical". If they were, there would be no legitimate basis for distinguishing between Hitler and Gandhi.

A person who believes that certain races are inferior to others and therefore it is "right" to oppress or persecute those races has adopted a personal value system that is inherently "unethical" according to the universal and consensus values associated with normative ethics. Similarly, an individual who has decided that lying is proper if it is necessary to achieve an important personal goal cannot assert personal ethics as a shield against impropriety.

Simply put, all individuals are morally autonomous beings with the power and right to choose their values, but it does not follow that all choices and all value systems have an equal claim to be called ethical. However, there are various norms and theories to determine ethics based on long practices, customs and universal acceptance.

Factors Influencing Personal Ethics

Though the ethics are inherited quality of an individual, there are certain factors which influence ethics to change or mould personally. These factors may be as external factors influencing personal ethics. Personal ethics act as the foundation for the moral compass; the internal guide that tells what's right and wrong. They drive one's actions and, to a certain extent, one's emotions, on a daily basis. But where do they come from? And why do people who appear similar sometimes have completely different sets of personal ethics?

So, you may not realize that the ethical principles you've built your life on are not an established set of rules handed to you at birth. They grow and develop with you over time and many things influence how they're crafted. These are discussed as direct speach to understand clearly. These are discussed below.

1. Family Influences Personal Ethics

While your parents can't dictate your morality, they are typically the first to voice and demonstrate ethical boundaries for you. Most parents consider it one of their critical jobs to instill a strong sense of right and wrong in their children. When parents tell their children that stealing is wrong, they are building a foundation for their child's personal ethics. Parents have a strong impact. How parents behave has a strong impact as well. Children absorb the actions of their family, which contributes heavily to their sense of morality.

2. Religious Beliefs Impact Personal Ethics

Religious beliefs have a unique impact on personal ethics. In general, religion allows people to accept an established set of moral rules. By following these spiritual laws, people feel they are behaving ethically. Religion often promises rewards as motivation for following the "rules". Interestingly, religion can inspire all kinds of acts, including violence. Some devout followers can come to embrace an ethical code that allows for incredible cruelty to be done in the name of a greater spiritual being, e.g., practising terriorism in the name of god.

3. Culture Affects Ethical Norms

Culture can dictate the ethical norms that people are used to and come to expect. The culture you live in may impact your ethical code more than you even realize, simply because it surrounds you. The customs and traditions of the society you inhabit become ingrained in your psyche, and the ethics of the group are generally accepted. Racism, gender discrimination and other forms of prejudice can become an accepted part of a person's ethical standards when surrounded by people who do it and allow it.

4. Personal Experiences

The events that happen in your life can also impact your ethics. Emotion and personal understanding may cause a powerful shift in beliefs. For example, many people claim to be against the death penalty. However, if a loved one is murdered, they may find themselves feeling differently when looking into the eyes of the person responsible.

5. Internal Reflection

Personal ethics are also developed by our feelings. When we do something that is against our moral code, we feel bad, guilty or ashamed. Likewise, when we do something that fits into our ethical idea of "right" we feel good, proud or happy. This causes a sort of immediate feedback for creating our moral standards and making ethical decisions.

The concept of personal ethics is incredibly complicated. It develops from a variety of factors and deserves in-depth exploration.

EVALUATORY CHANGES IN PERSONAL ETHICS

In recent past we see a tremendous changes in individual's underlying personal philosophies. When you begin your career, you can expect to encounter value conflicts. Such conflict can be very stressful and have serious effects on your life and your productivity. Differences in viewpoints will skew how people see the world.

There has been debate surrounding ethics and the human conditions. Ancient philosophers such as Aristotle, Plato and Socrates questioned the nature of ethics, asking if the concept was an innate human characteristic (existing at birth) or one created by the brain as a result of its environment. They also dealt deep into the core of the issue and asked, "Is it human nature to be ethical?" or are ethical choices the result of deliberate thoughtful consideration? Must one study "how" to be ethical or is it an unconscious routine? Are moral laws objective and defined by rational reason? Or are they based on personal, subjective feelings? Furthermore, the great philosophers asked, **"Must one be**

conscious of the ethical decision in order for it to be considered truly ethical?" Such questions still trigger debate. Many of the world's greatest minds concluded that the human condition is good and its overriding nature is to create happiness in strong bonds with others. These philosophical questions are an excellent way to begin questioning and evaluating your own sense of ethics and beliefs of human nature.

What ethics have been given by a ancient philosophies, moral theories, spirituality, different religions and so on have been tremendously changed with meaning with different dimensions based on the situation. This can be shown by differentiating two types of ethics, namely, old ethics and new ethics. The old ethics are age-old practices which are well accepted right from ancient days. Whereas new ethics started catching its identity right from 20th century. The society has gradually started accepting and adopting it. The following table shows the difference between old ethics and new ethics.

	Old Ethics favours		*New Ethics favours*
Difference between the old ethics and the new ethics.	Work	⟶	Leisure
	Savings	⟶	Debt
	Responsibility	⟶	Rights
	Competition	⟶	Protection
	Sex roles	⟶	Unisexism.
	Sacrifice	⟶	Self interest
	Equality/inequality	⟶	Equality
	Wealth accumulation	⟶	Wealth redistribution
	Absolutism	⟶	Situationalism
	Risk assumption	⟶	Risk aversion
	Efficiency / productivity	⟶	Quality of life
	Thrift / investment	⟶	Consumerism

Source: Lawrence B. Chonko, "Ethical Decision Making in Marketing" (1995).

When we discuss the above table, each item reflects values in its own way. Modern society with advancement of technology, research and development, modern education system, awareness among the rights and equality change in culture and practices in society, brought the new ethics into picture, which are also well accepted. Individuals strated replacing his hard work into leisure adopting the new technology. The banking system made people to invest in other assets by granting loans and he replaced the savings into debts which is more beneficial to him. Proponents of the old and new ethics accept the value of equality. But they disagree as to how equality should be viewed. The old ethics suggest that one person's advantage, gained through superior performance, does not create disadvantage for another person. Inequality is viewed as results oriented, not opportunity oriented. Performance and result are rewarded. Those who perform gain rewards. The new ethics, however, see such inequality as dehumanizing. Inequality is negatively viewed. An individual was commonly used to take responsibility irrespective of anything or any situation on moral grounds. Whereas in the new ethics the responsibility replaces into right. Every person started to be assertive in demanding the individual's right. More than competition which of old ethics, the individual status job, interest, wealth, identity, protections are the main focus to any person in the society. The new ethics are purely focusing on self-interest rather than sacrificing, which is old ethics. The word sacrifice has become an unwanted or a funny word to the younger generations. Sacrifice will take place only to protect self-interest, as the present society is gradually going away with the value of compassion or caring for others. The new ethics encourage action based on situations rather than absolution. Individuals are disinterested in risk taking, as every possible thing should be easy to understand in the new ethics, rather than risk assuming unlike in the old ethics. Work life balance and quality of life are present mantra for the new generation. Thrift and investment are considered old ethics and consumerism to be new ethics.

The present situation is where the east is looking west and west is trying to adopt east. According to Father Griffiths of England, who has been living a profound, sacred, and simple life in India since 1955, in reconstructing his orientation towards work and life which may form a part of personal ethics, says "India has been much more like a relevation to me, and I find living in this simplicity more enjoyable than I do living in the west with all its complications". The elaborate system of material conveniences built up in the west is not necessary for the real enjoyment of life. "The young Indians are looking to west, with that came all the cultural values of the west. But in our Ashram we are invaded by young people from the west, who are looking for what the east can give them" – Sadhguru.

Hence, there are various value systems in India which direct a lot towards personal ethics. The Gita, *Buddisam*, *Manusmurthi*, etc., give a lot of practical principles to practises ethics by the individuals. In the west many research studies have been undertaken to identify, define and practise individual ethics. A few of them are:

Perception on personal ethics of the research studies towards organisations

(1) According to Kenneth Blanchard, in his article, "Ethics in American Business," advocates **five principles** of ethical power for individuals as:

- **(i) Perspective:** A person believes that he is ethically sound and that he is guided by his conscience. A company's mission clearly stated and guided by values, hopes and behaviour is vital for its ethical stance.
- **(ii) Purpose:** An organization keeps to its purpose when work and life remain in perspective of employees, managers and employees need to take time to pause and reflect and evaluate where they are going and determine how they are going to get there.
- **(iii) Patience:** Patience is needed to an individual and to an employee in the organization. It is to believe that holding to their ethical values will lead them to success in the long run. This involves maintaining a balance between obtaining results and caring how they achieve those results.

(iv) **Persistence:** A person's behaviour must be consistent with his intentions. It involves having a commitment to live by ethical principles that does not falter over time.

(v) **Pride:** A person feels pride when he feels good about himself. There is a realization of self-esteem. When employees have patience and persistence and ethical principles they value, pride will be the result. This feeling gives way to ethical behaviour.

(2) According to Louise in his article on "Work Ethics Stress", he has given four principles of work ethics for an individual as:

(i) **Honesty:** It is the reputable, truthful and sincere attribute that is free of fraud or deception. "It is the most important ethics for me because it transforms ideal into reality, while of great value to communication and relationship."

(ii) **Punctuality:** It is arriving on time for work. It also demonstrates respect for co-workers and others who may be affected by its influence.

(iii) **Fairness:** It is being just and compassionate in communication and action. It is a trait that should be unbiased, without prejudice and demonstrating impartiality. "I believe that those who demonstrate fairness are more likely to receive the same."

(iv) **Integrity:** It is the soundness and consistency of actions that demonstrate ethics. It is my integrity and ensures that I adhere to the code of conduct that makes me an exemplary employee and role model.

CONTEMPORARY ETHICAL THEORIES RELATED TO PERSONAL ETHICS

Contemporary ethical theories are based on age-old ethical theories and practices. There are three major theories of contemporary ethics like; virture ethics, feminist ethics and discourse ethics. A brief discussion of the same follows:

(i) Virtue Ethics [Virtue of Humility]

Virtue refers to moral excellence, or goodness. Virtue of humility refers to a person when he is humble in expressing or acting with moral excellence or goodness. Virtue ethics is considered to be an alternative to moral principle. The act of virtue ethics refers to honesty, courage, temperance, integrity, compassion, and self control.

There are a lot of differences found in virtue ethics which looks at moral issues from a very different perspective than action based ethics. And it does not follow that the conclusions of virtue ethics will differ radically from the conclusions of an action based ethics.

It is said that the virtues are to be understood, as disposition which will not only sustain practices and enable us to achieve the good to practice, but will also sustain us in the relevant kind of quest for the good, by enabling us to overcome the harms, dangers temptations and situations which we encounter, and which will furnish us with increasing self-knowledge and increasing knowledge of the good. The word virtue is always accompanied with moral virtue. Moral virtue is an acquired disposition that is valued as part of the character of a morally good human being and that is exhibited in the person's habitual behaviour. There are different theories of virtue based on moral life which is to develop those general dispositions called moral virtues. And to exercise and exhibit them in the many situations that human life sets before us.

Theories of moral virtues based on habits and practices are:

(i) Aristotle: habits that enable a person to live according to reason.

(ii) Aquinas: habits that enable a person to live reasonably in this world, and be united.

(iii) Maclntyre: disposition that enables a person to achieve the good at which human "practices" aim.

(iv) Pincoff: dispositions that we use when choosing between person or potential future selves.

From the above theories it is understood that the moral virtues useful either "for everyone in general or for the possessor or of the quality."

Pincoff's theory of virtue seems more adequate than a theory, like Maclntyre's, which confines virtue to traits connected to practices. For the virtues, seem to be dispositions that enable us to deal with well with all of the emergencies of human life and not merely emergencies of practices. Both Aristotle and Aquinas, felt that in articulating the moral virtues, they were articulating those habits that enable a person to live a human life well and not merely to do well in social practices. There are four classical virtues both Aristotle and Aquinas agree as; courage, temperance, justice and prudence. Added to this, faith, hope and charity are also virtue ethics.

In India, dealing with the weak person or enjoying the materialistic benefit is not encouraged as the value of human being. Whereas quite often, we may hit the weak person instead of wrong person, because the wrong man is a strong person. It is the "wrong" which requires to be set right. Again it is practised that weak person may actually be strong enough individually, with due merit of his own personal values; but he is weak in the midst of powerful adversaries that operate around him. With the egoistic tempers, we more often lose sight of kindness. In such situations – *sama* – counselling, *dama* – rewarding, *bedha* – discriminating and *danda* – punishing are to be followed by orders, that should follow one after another. But many times the order or sequence is disturbed. If *danda* – punishing comes first and the last *sama* – counselling comes last may hit the morale of the people. This will lead to the situation where instead of making the "weak people" stronger, it may make the "strong people" weak.

In virtue ethics, "good actions come from good persons".

Virtue humility or ethics may be defined as, "virtue ethics contends that morally correct actions are those undertaken by actors with virtuous characters. Therefore, the formation of a virtuous character is the first step towards morally correct behaviours.

Hence, virtues are a set of acquired traits of character that enable a person to lead a good life. Virtue can be classified into two:

(i) Intellectual virtues – in this "wisdom" is the most prominent one.

(ii) Moral virtue – which comprises a long list of possible characteristics such as honesty, courage, friendship, mercy, loyalty, modesty, patience, etc.

All the above virtues are manifested in actions that are a habitual pattern of behaviour of virtuous person rather than just occurring once. As these traits are not ours by birth, we acquire them by learning, and most notably in business, by being in relationships with others.

(ii) Feminist Ethics

Feminist ethics are ethics where the individuals are deeply embedded in a network of interpersonal relations. Consequently, responsibility for members of this network and maintenance of connectedness, rather than allegiance to abstract moral principles. This is the predominant concern of feminist ethics. Male approach would focus on fair results, feminist perspectives stress social processes and particularly aim at the achievement of harmony, empathy and integration with regard to ethical issues. In respect of business and society there are differences between male and female approaches. The male approach is refered to ethics of rights, whereas the female ethics is referred to ethics of caring and relationships. The following Table shows the distinction between male and female ethics:

Contrasting gender–based view on ethics

Values	*Ethics of rights (male approach)*	*Ethics of care and relationship (female ethics)*
View of humans	Autonomous, separate, Interdependent independent, bearer of a function in the group.	Interdependent actors within a social web.
Moral goal	Fairness and impartiality, maintenance of rules.	Avoid maintenance of relationships.
Moral problem	Conflict of rights between individuals.	Conflict of responsibilities in network relationships.
Values	Rights, duties, fairness, due process, equal protection.	Harmony, empathy, community, caring, responsiveness integration.
Focus	Results	Processes.
Driving social force	Competition winning	Co-operation, compromise

Source: Andrew Crane, Disk Matten "Business Ethics" (2010)

Hence, feminist ethics is an approach that priorities empathy, harmonious and healthy social relationships and care for one another.

(iii) Discourse Ethics

It is to solve ethical conflicts by providing a process of norm generation through rational reflection on the real-life experience of all relevant participants. Discourse ethics may be based on philosophy and fundamentalists from different religions. The philosophical underpinning of the theorical approach may be referred to discourse ethics. Whereas the norms ultimately cannot be justified by rational arguments, but that they have, to be generated and applied to solve ethical conflict on a day-to-day basis. Many time discourse ethics, is more a recipe for practical conflict solution than an ethical theory. In simple terms, the only condition for it to work is the assumption that all human beings share the experience, and that the norms of peaceful resolution of conflict is the best way to organize social interaction. Nevertheless discourse ethics has been the underlying concept for the settlement of numerous disputes about environmental impacts of corporate decisions. In which various stakeholders with completely divergent value systems had to come to a common decision on certain controversial projects.

Exhibit

Ethical Issues at the Macro Level

(1) Tobacco is the Killer Unkilled: India is among the top consumers of tobacco in one form or the other. Its people spend Rs. 500 crore annually on tobacco. The Supreme Court directed the Government to ban smoking in all public places and public transport vehicles throughout the country because of its ill effects on health. Lot of advertisements have been put on TV and newspapers to educate people not to consume tobacco. In spite of all this, the Government seems to be less effective in its drive against smoking. WHO has estimated that 4.9 million people annually die in the world from smoking related diseases of which two-thirds are in the developing countries and tobacco may take 10 million lives every year by 2020. Over 150 million children in the world die of tobacco induced diseases, one-third of which under five years are due to acute respiratory infections and tobacco smoke. In India over eight lakh people are killed annually by tobacco related diseases and several lakh more are disabled. 20 million children in India are getting addicted to smoking every year; 50,000 children are becoming smokers every day as compared to 3000 in the US. Children are tempted to smoke by advertisements. Government has recently banned to films and serials show smoking scenes. There are 125 crore smokers worldwide over 40% being from developed countries. This figure is going to increase to 160 crore by 2020. There are 208 million tobacco users, of which 150 million smokers in India.

(2) Expensive Phones: People are getting mad enough to fling their expensive phones in anger. Hollywood star Russell Crowe was caught in the act, but pleading guilty and many enraged citizens who often throw their phones when angry. Crowe who was arrested and charged by the police for second degree assault, allegedly throw a phone at an employee of the hotel where he was staying and hit the man on the face. This may be the frustration-buster of the moment. Many admit that it is almost instinctive. More often than not, the phone is often irretrievably damaged.

(3) Security Concern: Former Indian Prime Minister Manmohan Singh voicing concern over the security of Pakistan's nuclear assets said that there had been reckless proliferation and there was a danger of extermists seizing power and taking control of the weapons. There is no doubt that Al Qaida network has a 'significant base' in Pakistan and there always a risk of Islamic militants seizing power. Thousand of schools (*madrasa*) as were set up to preach Jehad based on hatred of other religions.

(4) Computer Usage: City's corporators in India fail to evolve. Many missed computer training classes, but still they want computers to be purchased for them. Are corporations being pentium wise and paper foolish ? Some of the corporators do not know how to switch on a computer and do not want to click start either. Yet they were given computers and funds for furniture too. Some of the corporators would not have stuided even up to SSLC; some might not have even completed the course. Corporators must take thus seriously and acquire the skill. Only very few ministers have E-mail ID; bureaucrats are more computer savy; *netas* donot want to log on.

Case Study 1

(1) Overlook on Personal Ethics

Raghunath is running a small shop in a small town who is content with earning his frugal living. He is religious in appearance and compassionate towards others. One afternoon, when it was raining, a poor vendor of herbs named Satyadas came to his shop suffering from a high temperature. Raghunath provides him food and shelter next day he leaves for another destination leaving behind a pouch containing six gold coins and a ring studded with gems. Raghunath waits for him for several months to return and then on the persuasion of his wife Jamuna, he sells the contents of the pouch one by one, sets up a bigger shop, and builds a comfortable house for himself. He starts life with dignity in society. But one fine day, suddenly Satyadas makes his appearance. Raghunath is shocked. He is not as hospitable as before. On the contrary, he thinks as if a devil has turned up and wishes to leave quickly. As Satyadas is about to leave, conscientious Raghunath asks: "did you leave behind something here when you visited last time?" Satyadas says: "I don't know. God knows everything".

Questions:

1. In your opinion, Raghunath was with deep sense of guilt and remorse? If so, how and why?

2. Do you find the three imaginary characters are created for three conflicting aspects of a single mind? Morality, guilt and greed. Discuss these three characters based on your thinking.
3. Why could Raghunath not have the moral courage to practise transparency and tell Satyadas: "On your previous visit you left behind some gold coins and a ring. I waited for a long time for you to return. Only then I sold them to invest in my business and in building a his house. I want to repay you. Let us work out a repayment schedule. Comment.

(2) Recovery Police Style

Mr. X was then working in Delhi in the central police force on deputation. During a holiday in his home-town, a classmate of Mr. X invited him over to his place for tea. A deputy commissioner of police (DCP), a common friend. Mr. Y was the other invitee. Since it was raining, they had an extended tea session. When the rain stopped, Mr. X and Y both took leave of the host to return home.

Y requested X to drop him home as he had sent his vehicle away. X had parked his old car on the road. As he opened the door, he noticed that some burglar had broken into the car and had stolen the tape-recorder fitted in it. The rains had given the thief a good cover. X was aghast. Addressing the DCP, X said, "Look, both of us are senior police officers. Is it not ironical that X should be a victim of a theft, and that too in your jurisdiction, when both of us were socialising?"

The DCP, who was visibly embarrassed, muttered, "I am sorry about this theft. Please lodge a complaint. We will do our best to recover what was stolen". X said, "My friend, your are as much aware as a I am that there is no chance of recovering my stereo system. Why do you want me to lodge a complaint and add this to the long list of undetected cases in your town? Even if you do succeed, do you think I will come all the way from Delhi to depose in the court, spending more money on my travel than what the lost stereo costs?" X started the car, telling the DCP to forget the incident.

What is your opinion towards the status of police officers?

PROMOTE HAPPINESS

Happiness is internal joy/values experienced and expressed externally. Happiness and sadness are said to be the states of mind. As Hindu Upanishad says, "Mind itself is responsible for its bondage as well as liberation. Happiness never comes from the objects, events, personalities or even from the knowledge. The real happiness is in the subject, who is considered one's real self; our happiness is not on self start. But many times it depends on others. So our happiness and joyfulness is momentary and is dependent and it won't last longer. In other words an individual uses other person as a source of his happiness. The source may be family, friends, relatives, environment or any object. When he enters into a relationship with objects, he tries to squeeze happiness out of these objects. Many times in the absence of these objects it is very painful for him as those objects are temporary. But without relationship there is no fulfilment of life.

Relationships are formed at different levels to fulfill different needs. Needs may be physical, psychological, emotional, social, financial, family and so on.

Whatever be the nature of the needs, we form relationship to fulfil our needs, otherwise the relationship will turn to bad. If an individual looks closely, then the needs within himself rise because of a certain sense of incompleteness which we experience deep within ourselves.

But, Hindu Upanishad says, "Life is a complete entity by itself. One possible reason for incompleteness could be our ignorance or inability to explore life form to its fullest.

Life seeing 'life' via relationship leading to expectations at times are unrealistic that none of us can fulfill them even if we try our level best. The reason for this may be the expectations keep on changing with experiences. This can be realized if we try to understand the source of expectations and this may lead to form a beautiful relationship. While it is unhappiness that rules individuals. The meaning and reasons of unhappiness is followed.

Unhappines: An Overview

- It is not our enemies who are bothering and making our lives miserable, but it is our loved ones that are bothering and making our lives miserable in some way or the other.

  Hence, the unhappiness may be caused by the relationship of our own kith and kin family, or friends or whom you loved the most.
- People who care for each other and are concerned about each other are the ones who are making each other's lives miserable.

  Hence, it is not enemies care for us but our own people.
- This is the continuous practice for generations, since there is a strong belief that people need to be managed.

  Hence, people need to manage the objects or relationship.
- An individual is very selfish that he will not bother to manage the others. Rather he should seek how to include the other person, without bothering to understand everything about the person.

  Hence, one should try to manage other persons.
- There is a danger in understanding the persons fully, his thoughts, behaviour and so on and the moment we try to understand everything, the person may start feeling threatened.

Hence, understanding a person also leads to unhappiness.

Nobody likes to be managed by others we all need to understand. The moment people realize that you are managing them they will give you unhappiness in so many different ways and try to make your life more miserable.

So, people around us whom we claim to know are not looking for our understanding though they claim for understanding in fact they all are looking for inclusion. People look for inclusion in relationship and not understanding.

Ways and Means to Happiness

The ultimate truth of one's happiness lies in oneself only. Self-understanding, consciousness of mind and heart, inner voice, inborn qualities and so on are some of the components of self. It is believed that one can fool everybody, but not his or her conscience. Conscience speaks truth and will not function with the vested interest. Disliking, hating, unhappiness, jealousy, anger, etc., are the driving forces of the mind, but not the conscience. That is the reason; the mind will suffer with stress and strain and absence of the conscience.

Spiritual belief is that your body, the mind, the intellect are not "you", in reality, but only the shells covering you. They are not 'you', but other than you. That is why, you say as "my mind, my body, my thoughts or intelligence and so on. These are all the instruments for you to use. They should be rightly used as though they are the vehicles to reach the destiny safely without accidents. They should therefore should be maintained in good condition to promote happiness.

To maintain good condition, there is an example to learn, as a "flower blossoms only then bees come, so we need to open up and blossom only then people will have relationship with us."

It can be simplified by giving explanation like "most of us are closed buds calling bees to come to us, but they won't come unless we open ourselves and when we open ourselves they eventually will come". For this one should understand and practise appropriately the four level, they are:

(i) **Physical Level:** Keeping the body healthy and maintaining it with all cleanliness, healthy food habits' "Body is like a temple and should be maintained and cleaned properly."

(ii) **Mental Level:** Root cause for happiness and unhappiness is mind. Mental attitude is a key of other level. Mind is a power house, which gives strength, direction, decisiveness and control of body and action. It is **storage of knowledge, commander of thinking, leader for creativity.** The mind is directly linked with the happiness. For example : when someone meets us, when we are happy he feels great and holds us high and he wants to be joyful with us. On the contrary when someone meets us, when we are not happy, he feels the other way round and wants to move away from us and which may create unhappiness to us. At the same time when we achieve our goal or desire, we feel happy without anyone. Hence, "self" is the root for the happiness.

(iii) **Emotional level:** Emotions are one's feelings which may be instinctive such as love or fear. Emotions may be situational or occasional. Emotions are always guided by thoughts. Emotion may also be introvert or extrovert. Hatrade, fear, anxiety, love, enthusiasm, interest, intelligence, etc., are some of the components of emotions. When we employ our emotions to reach the ultimate nature of our very being, then we are using our devotion. Emotions may lead to positive or negative, good or bad. It is one's intelligence and sense to use the emotion on an appropriate way in the appropriate situation. People with high degree of emotions may not be encouraged by others; as such people may create good or even bad in circumstances. Emotions with control, knowledge, intelligence and within the limited boundaries are always safe.

(iv) Energy level: Energy is the strength of action both for mind and body. Energy is the driving force in putting the things in action. Energy of an individual may be a guiding force to many activities. It is the capacity for activity, force or vigour. It is also capacity of matter or radiation to do work. It is believed that an energetic person is strong and positive. Such person's approach is clear, unambiguous, strong and stable.

Hence, to achieve happiness or promote happiness one should understand self and follow four levels like, **physical, mental, emotional** and **energy.**

If we enhance at all the above four levels, then surprisingly every other person would want to have relationship with us. Instead of enhancing ourselves, at physical, mental, emotional and energy level, we are trying to manage these levels which does not work.

Hence, "we need to enhance and not manage ourselves".

Advantage of enhancing one "self"

- Stray relationships will create with continuous enhancement.
- Growth of intelligence and knowledge will be strong.
- Individuality and individual identity through understanding of self.
- Imagination, innovativeness, integrity, inner-understanding and inter-relationship between body and mind.
- Connect, commit, contract and control are another actions of enhancement.

What is "Enhancement" and how to achieve it ?

"Enhancement" is the inner journey to understand self deeper and deeper. It has spiritual relationship which creates a strong will power to withstand in any sort of situation. It is "self" understanding and inner engineering. It has the power of managing physical, mental, emotional and energy level.

Enhancing ourselves to ultimate levels is, keeping ourselves in aligning ourselves with body, mind, emotion and energy."

Nobody wants to be in the company of weak people. If we keep ourselves low at any of the levels be it physical, mental or energy wise, then nobody wants to be with us, forget the relationship, we will be burden to others.

As human beings, we should always focus on enhancing our way of being, then every other thing gets naturally managed which may be our profession or relationships. As people get educated, they think they are more modernized, but in fact they tend to have more problems in having good relationship.

Education, in fact, should widen and broaden our horizon and scope of life, but it has compressed it in such a way that getting along with other people is become difficult.

Enhancement focuses inclusiveness and should be powered by knowledge and education.

The opposite of enhancement leads to exclusiveness. Modern societies encourage exclusiveness, and that leads to **depression.**

Suicides, drug abuse, alcoholism, crime, etc., are some causes of exclusiveness.

Despite high levels of comfort and convenience, people are more depressed as they cannot get along with others, as they have become too exclusive.

Hence, inclusiveness means "relationship." "Exclusiveness" means "depression".

Relationships long for inclusiveness, and if we approach others as such and include others as part of ourselves irrespective of what they are, and how they are and they will be wonderful with us.

Without our inclusiveness in any relationship almost nothing seems to work, as our approach is to manage them, in that case whichever way they are, they are almost impossible.

When we include someone as part of ourselves without seeking anything from him, then we are a joy for the other person and things work for the betterment.

Relationship should not be used as a medium to fulfil our expectations rather it should be used to express happiness and feeling of joyfulness. This means, we make our life an expression of joy and not a pursuit of happiness.

Happiness can be pursuance and not just expressed. It should be carried through the life of an individual with consistency. Yoga, meditation, relaxation techniques, spiritual understandings, etc., are the various means to pursue happiness. Through these means, the relationships will naturally become wonderful. These techniques train an individual to express the joy without any expectations from anybody. In fact the needs of an individual are gone and now his happiness is on "self" starts. Here, the individuals reach the stage of "giving-end" and "not receiving-end".

There need to have a strong mental power to practise this. Muscle, money and material are compared to will power. A strong will or mental power can be attained only through mental related exercise. This will develop the personality. Personality may be focused on two different things, namely, inner and outer. Outer personality is influential and situational. But inner personality in consistent and constant. There should be growth of inner personality for happiness. There need to be co-relation between body-physical, mind-psychological. Both are natural existence. The mind, the psychological, is derived and developed from the society. Sum-total of all bodies like mineral, plant, animal and human may be called "cosmic–body". Sum total of all intelligence may be referred to as cosmic intelligence of "cosmic–consciousness".

Consciousness is the self and inner voice which lives in each and everybody. One should strengthen this self or conscience to enhance happiness. Which may also result in pleasure, power and protection.

The power of yoga, meditation, cosmic energy and spirituality enhances conscience which needs vigorous and continuous practice every day for enhancement of happiness.

The following diagram shows how self is the centre for every other source of happiness.

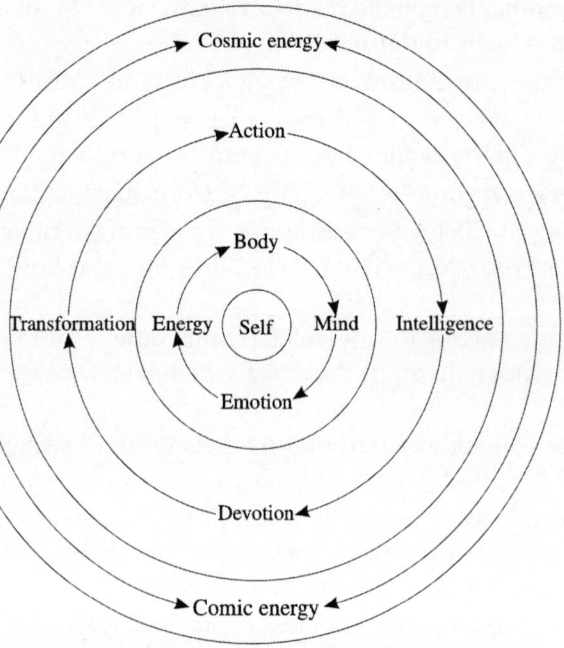

"Self" as the centre of "Happiness"

So, it is expected as, "choose good man for emulation, bad man for correction and no man for imitation". So, be yourself.

KARMA YOGA

Karma in Sanskrit means "to do". In other words it is the 'action' of an individual. And 'yoga' refers to union. Yoga is in other words means to be a science of life. Thus Karma yoga is literally translated to the path of union through action. Whereas in the vedantic philosophy, karma means both action and the effects of such action. Karma yoga is not only action but also thinking and willing to act. This is to orient oneself towards realization by acting accordance with one's duty which may be known as dharma. The duty of an individual is focused on dharma, with consideration the personal and self-centred desires, and both liking and disliking. The duty or action can be performed without attachment and also to attain supreme.

The Karma yoga is explained in the philosophy of Hindus, known as the *Bhagavad Gita*. *Bhagavad Gita* gives a summary of Karma yoga process. The *Gita* is one of the chapters from the epic *Mahabharata*. Gita is a dialogue between the prince Arjuna and his friend and chariot driver Lord Krishna. The conversation between the Arjuna and Lord Krishna prompted by Arjuna as he is engulfed by sorrow and misgiving the oncoming battle in which he has friends and relatives on both the sides. In reply, Krishna then elucidates upon a number of philosophical yoga system and practices, one of them being Karma yoga. The philosophical yoga system is indeed continuous fight on righteous principles.

In Karma yoga, it is explained that work done without expectations, motives, or anticipation of its outcome purifies one's mind and gradually makes an individual fit to see the value of reason. *Gita* says, that it is not necessary to remain in external solitude, or remain action-less, in order to practise a **spiritual** life, since the state of **action** or **inaction** is primarily determined in the mind.

In order to achieve perfection of life *Gita* explains, that it is important to control all mental desires and tendencies to enjoy pleasures of senses. The practice of Karma yoga in daily life makes an individual fit through action of meditation and devotion. It sharpens an individual's reasoning power, develops the intuitive power acquiring knowledge and to transcend the mind itself.

UNDERSTANDING KARMA YOGA

Karma yoga is based on a general understanding of **karma** and **reincarnation** (Sanskara). This is one among the various philosophies of Hinduism. It is believed that a man is born with certain tendencies known as **Sanskaras,** both positive and negative, from previous lives, which push him towards performing certain actions in his present life. This process continues until the individual attains a zero balance (no karma remaining), wherein one achieves liberation. According to the great saint, Shankaracharya; "By practising Karma Yoga, one's mind gets purified".

CLASSIC YOGAS

There are different types of classic yogas like, Raja yoga, Jnana yoga, Karma yoga, Bhakti yoga, Mantra yoga and Tantra yoga. Among all these Karma yoga is appropriate for common persons. Students, professionals, academicians, managers, management gurus and so on are different group of people to follow for better understanding and better results of their work or action.

Its philosophies and the insights Kama yoga are intended to reach beyond the scope of religion and to humanity as a whole. It is at times referred to as the "manual for mankind'. It has been highly praised by not only the prominent Indians like Mahatma Gandhi but also by Aldous Huxley, Albert Einstein, J.Rober Opperheimer, Ralph Waldo Emerson, and Herman Hesse.

The other meaning of Karma yoga is **"selfless action without attachment to results".**

In modern interpretation, it can be viewed as duty-bound deeds done without letting the nature of the result affect one's action. It one of the ideal paths to realize the truth. Karma yoga is not focused on renouncing the work, but the purpose of the work. According to *Bhagavad Gita* following verses emphasise the path to Karma yoga:

- Perform your prescribed duties for the satisfaction of others and in that way you will always remain away from bondage.
- Action should be right and never expect any fruit out of it and let not the fruit of action be your motive, neither let there be attachment in your action.

- Fixed in yoga and do the work, abandoning attachment, with an even mind in success and failure, for evenness of mind.
- With the body, with the mind, with the intellect, even merely with senses, the yogis perform action towards self-purification, having abundant attachment. He who is disciplined in yoga, having abandoned the fruit of action, attains steady peace.
- In order to achieve true liberation, it is important to control all mental desires and tendencies to enjoy pleasures.
- The object sense is from the mind, which produces attachments. From attachment springs desire and from desire comes anger.
- From anger arises bewilderment, from bewilderment, loss of memory, and from loss of memory, the destruction of intelligence and from destruction of intelligence, the individual perishes.

Karma yoga for present society (Modern view)

Karma has become a sectarian term which umbrallas the entire collection, both conscious and subconscious of human emotionality. The **modern** view of karma, devoid of spiritual exigencies, obviates the need for an acceptance of reincarnation in **Judeo Christian** societies and attempts to portray Karma as an universal psychological phenomenon which behaves predictably, like other physical forces such as gravity.

It is said, like gravity, karma is so basic we often don't even notice.

This view of Karma yoga as an universal and personally emotional constant, correlates with Buddhist and Jungian understanding that volition or libido (created from personal and cultural bases) is the primary instigator. Any conscious thought, action or word arising from a cognitively unsolved emotions results in Karma.

According to Sadh-Guru, Isha Foundation

"You don't have to watch your actions, you are not getting anywhere. It is the thought process which creates the volition, the intention. If you do something with strong volition, either positive or negative volition, both ways you build Karma. If you are looking for just create a little more pleasant atmosphere for yourself to live in, then you try to create good Karma, but being on the spiritual path is not about making life pleasant. It is about seeing how to transcend both the pleasant and the unpleasant."

"You have had enough of both the pleasant and the unpleasant; now you want to just drop this bag and go beyond this present dimension of existence. So this must always be understood. Karma is not in terms of what you do and do not do. Karma is only in terms of what you desire to do. It is attributed to Gautama Buddha, he said, people can exist without desire."

"Karma has gathered in you in so many ways. This Karma that is recorded either on the level of your body, mind or physical energies is an accumulation, but once your awareness comes to a certain point, all of this happens separately from you. In *shoonya* (maya/empty), do you see, the mind is happening separately and you are happening separately. This can go so deep into you that if you sit here, everything that is not you and that which is you are separate. Once you are like this, it is all done. Your tape-recorder where everything is recorded is there, and you are here. Whatever noise it makes has no impact on you. You are free from it in a moment."

The present generation should learn the Karma yoga, without creating tension, they should perform their duty or action without any attachment or desire. This may attain fullness and stress-free, happy work life.

Karma yoga can be practised with the mind setting and with determination. Concentration, selflessness, devotion, detachment are some of the means to attain Karma yoga.

- Popular methods like meditation techniques, metacognition, counselling, psycho-analysis, etc., may help individuals to enhance emotional self awareness and thus to avoid negative Karma. This results emotional hygiene and reduces Karma impacts.
- Permanent neuronal changes within the amygdala at and left prefrontal cortex of the human brain attributed to long-term meditation has been proved scientifically.

This process of emotional maturation aspires to a goal of **self-actualization.**

Such peak experiences are hypothetically devoid of any Karma.

Emotional Honesty

Emotions refer to a intensity or sensibility. It is a strong instinctive feeling such as love or fear.

The simple meaning of honesty is truthfulness. Honesty is also absolute or chastity. It's fairness and straightforwardness of conduct, adherence to the facts, namely, sincerity. Whereas emotions have two vitally important purposes for human beings. Emotions are a form of communication. Our feelings are one of the means by which we define ourselves. The interaction of our intellect and our emotions determines, how we relate to ourselves.

Healthy guilt is what we feel, when we violate our own value system. It is an important intuitive component for maintaining a healthy, honest relationship with ourselves. Guilt helps us to be aware of areas that need more healing – behaviour that is a reaction to old wounds. It is generated by our spirit when we have acted in ways which we need to make amends for our humanness.

An individual can feel happy for healthy guilt like when he says for himself, "When I catch myself worrying then I know that I am not being emotionally honest with myself. Worry is a symptom that tells me I am avoiding some feeling."

Understanding Emotional Honesty

Honesty like any other arena in recovery is not a black and white issue. There is a multitude of levels of honesty, of perspectives in which to view the concept of honesty. **Emotional honesty** is related to intellectual honesty with ourselves. It is necessary in order to become emotionally honest.

Hence, emotional honesty may be defined as "a truthful or straightforwardness of conduct of an individual with a strong instinctive feeling, which may be positive or negative."

It is necessary to start seeing ourselves with more clarity in order to recognize the attitudes, beliefs and definitions dictate our emotional reactions. Once we start achieving more honesty in our perceptions then we can get more clarity in our emotional process. **Relationship** is another key for emotional honesty.

Attitudes, definitions and beliefs determine perspectives and expectations dictate our relationships—to ourselves, to life, to other people, to great spirit or even to goddess energy. Our relationship to our own emotions, bodies, gender, etc., are dictated by the attitudes, definitions and beliefs that we hold mentally and intellectually. And we require those mental constructs, ideas, concepts in early childhood from the emotional experience, intellectual techniques, and role modeling of the beings around us."

The process of recovery is a journey to larger perspectives, higher contexts in which to view everything. Consciousness raising or enightenment is a process of peeling away layers of denial to get to higher consciousness or expanded perspectives or deeper levels of honesty.

Why Emotions and Honesty?

Emotions can be referred to as energy in motion. i.e.,

Emotion = energy + motion.

In this feeling emotions are energy. **So emotions are energy.** Emotion = energy in motion. It is supposed to be in motion and it is meant to flow.

Emotions have a purpose, a good reason to even those emotions that feel uncomfortable. Like fear, anger and tear. Whereas:

Fear is for warning

Anger is for protecting

Tear is for cleaning or releasing.

From the above three we can see that negative act. But these so called negative acts help an individual to come out of his feelings and free from tensions. Warning, protecting and releasing are the acts of an individual which make him to understand himself more and more in any given situation.

Emotions are important for human beings. Interaction of our intellect and emotions are how we relate to ourselves. This relation forms the energy. Emotional energy is not only supposed to be in motion, to glow, it is also the energy that gets us in motion. It is what drives us, and propels or pushes us forward through life. When emotional flow is blocked and suppressed it does not go away. Energy cannot simply disappear. It can transform but it cannot disappear.

Emotions may be both positive and negative. Worry is a form of emotions. Worry is negative fantasy. When a person catches worry it is very important to judge himself. He needs to be patient and compassionate towards himself.

Worry is not a feeling but it is a reaction, an negative emotional state, that is created by the perspectives of a belief system that empowers illusions like failure.

Emotions do not have value in and of themselves. They just are. What gives emotions value is how we react to them. There must be balance between emotional and mental action. Blame has to do with attitude, with buying into the false beliefs, it does not really have anything to do with the process of releasing the emotionals.

So, we need to strive for emotional honesty with ourselves for ourself. Being honest with ourselves is what works best to help us see ourself.

Paying attention, confrontations, discerning strategy and letting go, recovery are some of ways being emotional honesty.

The best way is to be "being yourself and true to yourself".

PROACTIVE

Proactive is taking initiative. The use of proactive action is limited to the domain of experimental psychology. It is "impairment or retardation of learning or of the remembering of what is learned by effects that remain active from conditions prior to learning". Proactivity is being anticipatory and taking charge of situations.

In organizational behaviour and industrial or organizational psychology, proactive behaviour by individuals refers to anticipatory, change oriented and self initiated behaviour in the workplace. Proactive behaviour involves acting in advance, rather than just reacting. It means taking control and making things happen rather than just adjusting the situation or waiting for something to happen. Proactive employees or individuals generally do not need to be asked to act, nor do they require detailed instructions.

UNDERSTANDING PROACTIVE

Proactive is an extra action and intention of an individual to take decisions for implementation. Most of the individuals who are positive, energetic, intelligent follow the path of proactive. Organizations, society, family and individuals should be proactive rather than inactive or reactive.

Proactive behaviour can be contrasted with work related behaviour, such as proficiency. This may be fulfilment of predictable requirements of one's job, or adoptivity, the successful copying with and support of change initiated by others in the organization. In regard to the latter, where adoptivity is about responding the **change**. Change and poactivity is to **initiating change.**

Proactivity is not restricted to **extra role performance** behaviour. Individuals can be proactive in their prescribed role. Behaviours labelled as organizational citizenship can be carried out proactively or passively.

According to Alain P. Martin, in his book in 1983 titled *Think Proactive: New Insight into Decision Making* there are four horizontal dimensions comprising four interventions:

(i) Laissez-faire.
(ii) Focus on relationship (symptomatic intervention in medicine such as pain killer).
(iii) Focus on substance or problem solving (etiologic intervention in medicine such antibiotic injunction to cure bacteria).
(iv) Focus on hybrid intervention integrating both the substantive and the rational choice (oral antibiotics sweetened for children who would resent the etiologic intervention noted in (iii) above).

For each of the above interventions, four generic and ethical groups of options can be explored, namely:

(i) Wait and see option: Going for the status quo and remaining purposely and consciously inactive or adopting wait-and-see attitude.
(ii) Compliance option: The compliance is to do only what is necessary to get it. It an also be a temporary strategy to deal with sudden crisis.
(iii) Active option: This is to play the game, adopt the best practice or do what is normally expected or commonly accepted in the organizations.
(iv) Proactive option: The proactive stand and builds on foreknowledge (intelligence) and creativity to anticipate and see the situation as an opportunity. This is regardless of how threatening or how bad it looks, and to influence the system constructively instead of reacting to it. The proactive stands consider the contribution each stake-holder can make to the issue. Even in situations where the issue is irrelevant, the proactive stand is to find ways to benefit from riding on the issue.

PROACTIVE STEPS FOR PERSONAL ETHICS

This is also referred to as preparatory ethics. Some of the tips are:

(i) Role model for moral behaviour: Developing consistency in creating goodness and practising good, correct and just. According to Mark Twain "Always do the right thing, this will surprise some people and astonish the rest."
(ii) Moral advisor should be hired and associated and consulted frequently.
(iii) Introducing stress standards for mental health and to promote values, culture, standards, etc., to prevent ethical problems.
(iv) Time and devotion: devoting more time for moral training, to build strong leadership, initativeness, risk management and time management.
(v) Setting up of ethical stamina: Developing self-consistency and incorporating individual standard of stamina towards ethics.
(vi) Construction of appropriate proactive steps. Like:
    (a) Determination of salient facts and ethical norms.
    (b) Focus on the objective only.
    (c) Identify the problem in setting up of ethical norms

(d) Reflect on the ethical problem.
(e) Take action as early as possible.
(f) Evaluate the outcome and the process.
(g) Setting up of the activity for the continuous improvement.

Keys to personal ethics by various religions

Truth

- Buddhism – 'Him I call a Brahmin who has truth and love for all life'.
- Christianity – 'The truth shall make you free'.
- Hinduism – 'Be sincere and truthful'
- Islam – 'Speak the truth'
- Judaism – 'They love him who speaks what is right'
- Taoism/Confucianism – 'He who knows the truth is not equal to him who loves it'.

Righteousness

- Buddism – 'Him I call a Brahmin who never asks what life can give, but only what he can give to life'.
- Christianity – 'Blessed are those who hunger and thirst for righteousness'.
- Hinduism – 'Give freely and control the senses'
- Islam – 'Perform what you promise'
- Judaism – 'The righteous man walks in integrity'
- Taoism/confucianism – 'The man of honour thinks of his character; the inferior man thinks of his position'.

Peace

- Buddism – 'Him I call a Brahmin who is never angry and is free from the chain of fear'.
- Christianity – 'Peace be with you'.
- Hinduism – 'Be fearless and calm'
- Islam – 'Keep your heart free from malice towards anyone'
- Judaism – 'A man of understanding is of a calm spirit'
- Taoism/Confucianism – 'To a mind that is "still", the whole universe surrenders.'

Love

- Buddism – 'Him I call a Brahmin who has the power of love no army can defeat'.
- Christianity – 'Love one another'.
- Hinduism – 'Be loving, and show goodwill to all'
- Islam – 'Do you love your Creator? Love your fellow-beings first'
- Judaism – 'What is desired in a man is kindness'

- Taoism/Confucianism – 'Love the world as yourself, then you can care for all things'.

Non-violence

- Buddism – 'Him I call a Brahmin who has renounced violence towards all creatures'.
- Christianity – 'Love your enemies'.
- Hinduism – 'Don't harm any living creature
- Islam – 'Withhold your hand from striking'
- Judaism – 'If your enemy is hungry, give him bread to eat'
- Taoism/Confucianism – 'All men have a mind which cannot bear to see the suffering of others'.

Guidelines for personal Ethics

- Be humble, be harmless. Be gentle and forgiving of any hurt you receive.
- Be personally harmonized. Make sure your thoughts, words and actions match.
- Purify your mind and heart because purity is indispensable to your spiritual growth.
- To rid yourself of the pain and suffering that drags you down, spiritualizes your life.
- The fundamental goal of all spirituality is to know the Atma, the soul, the True Self Within.
- Do not see yourself merely as this body-mind complex dependent on external, worldly things.
- Balance your life by giving more than you receive; without giving is stealing.
- Stop assuming that you can avoid pain and only experience pleasure. Pleasure and pain go together, asking for pleasure invites pain. Always.
- The sweet fountain of eternal happiness flows only from the Atma, the True Self within. The cessation of your present pain and sorrow depends on how well you know this.
- Live your life and do your work in a particular attitude, a general mood of adoration. The act of loving in itself is a spiritual experience of knowing and being divinity.

Source: R. Nandagopal and Ajith Shanker (2010)

Case Study 2

Spirituality and Human Values at Work

1. APJ Abdul Kalam: The Launch of Agni

Presented the excerpt from *Wings of Fire*, the autobiography of Dr. APJ Abdul Kalam, the former president of India:

'The Agni team was comprised of more than 500 scientists. Many organisations were networked to undertake this huge effort of launching Agni. The Agni mission had two basic orientations – work and workers. Each member was dependent on the others to accomplish his target. Contradiction and confusion are the two things most likely to occur in such situations. Different leaders accommodate concern for workers while getting work done, in their own personal ways. Some shed all concern for workers in order to get results. They use people merely as instruments to reach goals. Some give less importance to work, and make an effort to gain the warmth and approval of people working with them. But what this team achieved was the highest possible integration in terms of both the quality of work and human relationships.

Involvement, participation and commitment were the keywords to functioning. Each team member appeared to be performing by choice. The launch of Agni was the common stake not only for our scientists, but for their families too. VR Nagaraj was the leader of the electrical integration team. Dedicated technologist that he is, Nagaraj would forget basic requirements like food and sleep while on the integration gig. His brother-in-law passed away while he was at ITR. His family kept away this information from Nagaraj, so that there would be no interruption in his work towards the launch of Agni.

The Agni launch had been scheduled for 20 April 1989. This was going to be an unprecedented exercise. Unlike space launch vehicles, a missile launch involves wide-ranging safety hazards. Two radars, three telemetry stations, one tele-command station and four electro-optical tracking instruments to monitor the missile trajectory had been deployed. In addition, the telemetry station at Car Nicobar (ISTRAC) and the SHAR radars were also commissioned to track the vehicle. Dynamic surveillance was employed to cover the electrical power that flows from the missile batteries within the vehicle and to control system pressures. Should any deviation be noticed either in voltage or in pressure, the specially designed automatic checkout system would signal 'Hold'. The flight operations would then be sequenced only if the defect was rectified. The countdown for the launch started at T-36 hours. The countdown from T-7.5 minutes was to be computer controlled'.

This is an example for individual and work ethics.

2. St Joseph Health System

St. Joseph System – Sonoma Country (http://stjosephhealth.org), headquartered at Santa Rosa, California, is a non-profit catholic helathcare system that exists 'To continually improve the health and quality of life of people in the communities we serve' with a vision to 'bring people together to provide compassionate care, promote health improvement and create healthy communities. In their foresight, the parent organisation, The Sisters of St. Joseph of Orange, developed a plan to continue their legacy through a program called 'Mission and Mentoring'. This initiative trains organisational leaders to increase their understanding of the core elements of mission and values integration so that participants can lead and support this integration at all levels. It also helps the leaders to increase their understanding of the elements of spirituality so that participants can be more effective spiritual leaders. It includes nine sessions in retreat throughout a year, culminating with a final project on values integration.

The organisation has thoroughly integrated its mission with a Quality of Work Life Policy, which states: 'We respect each person as an inherently valuable member of the human community as as a unique expression of life. This policy permeates all of HR programs and practices at St. Joseph Health System. In addition to its work-life policy, the organisation has also developed a Quality of Work Life Team. Candidates are screened through value-based competencies. For instance, during performance reviews, employees are evaluated in two dimensions: 'What they do' (learned skills and performance) and 'How they do it' (their demonstration of core values). The organisation believes in fair wages in a country where the cost of living is very high. Furthermore, they are committed to establishing the practice of reflection as an integral to their culture. All meetings begin with a relevant reflection (a poem, quotation, etc.) to allow staff to reflect inwards as well as to connect with each other and the topic before moving on to the business of the day.

The Life Learning Center (LLC) is the organisation's education department which endeavours to balance personal and professional development by integrating mind, body and spirit in all its programmes. At St. Joseph Health System, this is just another way to further their mission and nourish the human spirit of their employees through offerings such as mindfulness meditation, yoga, pilates, guided imagery, healing and the arts, cooking, flower arranging, cultivating joy, therapeutic touch, preventing compassion fatigue and more. Many of their programs are a collaborative effort and taught by internal subject matter experts. The LLC is also the training and development arm of HR.

Occasionally, in this quiet and tranquil state, they meditate on some words of wisdom, which are read out aloud several times. Some such examples are: 'The self is one, unmoving it moves, is far away yet near' ; 'Only if you put yourself in the light, can you see your shadow sides' ; and 'The word of eternity is only to be heard in silence.' Alternatively, a colleague may read aloud a poem or a story based on our shared values. Thoughts born of these moments of meditation are then shared.

Van Ede cultivates an attitude of contemplation and seeks the spiritual meaning of all phenomena in creation by 'taking them to heart'. People in the company find that this attitude results in an incredible highness of being, coming forth out of constantly being encouraged by colleagues to set their own personal priorities at any time. An amazing environment to work in ! The boundary between life and work becomes permeable and dissolves.

The above is an extract from the international center for 'spirit at work' (www.spiritatwork.org), a not-for-profit organisation that support global transformation by integrating spirituality and the work place.

3. Abdul Kareem : A Seed Sent from Heaven

'It is dark at noon. A thick, wet leaf pile squelches underfoot. Often the way is blocked and one must crawl under branches or take detours. The silence of the forest is sometimes unnerving. Every now and then you are lost and can't tell the way.

Abdul Kareem, in front of you, wends and weaves through the thicket with a proud case. But then he has been around here, in fact, for 25 years. He has seen the 32 acres of a lateritic hillside grow into this wild forest. He had simply dreamt it, willed it, kept vigil, stood guard, ran a few errands - and the forest happened. And is still happening; it's a work in progress. Abdul Kareem has created and saved forever a piece of wilderness for India.'

The Pull of Kaavu: Abdul Kareem is one of India's midnight children. He was born in 1947 at Nileswar, a small town on the NH7 between Kasargod and Payyanur in Kerala. His father Abdullah was a small time businessman. After passing his high school and a year in college, Kareem decided to venture out to India's Big Apple - Bombay ! He worked in a private dockyard as a labourer to learn the ropes. Just when he thought he had found himself a vocation, he was shaken by parochial riots in 1969. Back in Nileswar he taught himself book-keeping and typewriting with assistance from the Muslim Waqf Board. He began to earn a steady income as an itinerant accountant. Marriage followed and also some good fortune.

The Persian Gulf boom began in the early 1970s and Abdul Kareem sensed opportunity. He began a travel and placement agency for the thousands of Keralites eager to flood the Gulf. These details are relevant, for, we have so far no indications of the man he would become. His wife came from the village of Puliyamkulam, about 20 km from Nileswar. He would often visit there with her and spend some weekends. And that's how he came by his hill.

'I would walk around the area and see barren hillsides,' he says. 'It was heartache of a sight and yet the pull on me was strong. I suddenly realised that I had often - though only for brief moments - dreamt of the Kaavu of India's collective memory. They were the sacred groves that every village had once upon a time. I had been told of them as a child. I think I had subconsciously yearned for one.'

So, on an impulse he bought 5 acres of barren rock with a pathetic well. And instantly became a laughing stock. The well would yield about five litres a draw and one then waited for it to slowly recharge. During the next monsoon he stood on his land and was nearly washed away by a roaring flood along the rocky laterite surface. Yet, the well just blinked and had no water to show.

Gut Steering: Kareem was a man who was neither lettered nor connected to any source of information that would help him. He trusted his guts. He was a man haunted by his desire for a Kaavu. After about a year of helplessly watching his property, he began to plant mature saplings of wild trees in spaces between laterite rocks. During the summer he would fetch water in cans lashed to his motorbike from a source a kilometre away. The reasonably successful travel business was seeing all its surpluses flow into this impossible dream. Landowners nearby found in Abdul Kareem an exit route. For decades their rocky spreads had produced nothing and here was a crazy man willing to buy them. As his family watched in panic amazement, Abdul Kareem bought 32 acres of a rocky slope.

For three summers, he nursed his plants with water ferried from afar. And then nature sent him feedback. 'In the third year, when my plantation was but of young adult trees, the water level in the well rose!' he says. 'That itself seemed an end for me and I began to plant the whole extent in a frenzy.' He chose a variety of plants plucked from the wild and let nature do the rest. He learnt that, "you enable nature, not direct it". Birds began to arrive and discharge all manner of seeds. Weeds grew and amidst them rare herbs and medicinal plants - none chosen' by Kareem. Water levels in Kaliyanam, Varranjnyur and other villages within a 10 km radius rose. The once barren hill was now a water sponge.

He has never weeded his acres, never lopped a tree, never swept the leaves, never hunted game, never selected a species and of course, never used a chemical of any kind. 'My rewards are the highly mineralised, herbalised water, the fragrant air, the daily walks through the woods, a healthy life and enormous peace,' he says. He has, for over ten years, lived in a house built in the forest. Not a shred of plastic or paper is seen anywhere. They are a part of his long list of 'no-no's along with cars, noise, smoking, fire or partying.

Notices and Needs: Recognition has been trickling in. Environmentalists and the media noticed of this self-taught man. The 5-litre well of yore filled to the brim and spilt over for weeks after the monsoon subsided. Hare, fowl and other small game colonised the forests. Beehives the size of a sack - emerged. There was a dry inherited tank on the land. He says that today he could pump a 100,000 litres out of it at a go and the level would bounce back in a few minutes. 'The forest is actually producing water!' he exclaimed. The water was almost like a meal. The soil under a thick, wet, leaf pile crawls with soil animals that were almost angry at being disturbed.

His children have grown and the growing family has its monetary needs but Abdul Kareem having put his entire nest egg in this forest had no cash. He now hoped to strike a balance between preserving his growing dream and his growing responsibilities. He talked of marketing the water for the table. With a sensitive business partner, the acreage would be a great eco-destination. Nileswar railhead was a comfortable motoring distance. It would also be possible to aid Kareem if academics with grants wished to spend time researching his forest. A small eco-school was another possibility. GoodNewsIndia appealed to its readers to connect this man with an opportunity. He was willing to discuss any sensitive proposal.

We were about to part ... 'Deep inside every one of us is a call to the wild,' he said broodingly. Then, in simple words, he added: 'Much of the impatience, discontent or violence around us is due to lack of opportunity to reconnect with where we came from. For sanity and generosity of spirit, we should be able to witness nature in its unceasing, rejuvenating form.'

He waited for us to leave. In a moment, he would return to his forest, his soul.

The above story sets an example for individual ethics with the strange believer of positivity, consistence and proactiveness from the nature.

4. Value-Based Leadership in Bhagavad Gita

Bhagavad Gita is a an important scripture which includes many important issues about leadership. It summarizes the instructions given by Lord Krishna to Arjuna when he was in a dilemma. It supports the value based notion of leadership style. In literal terms, the *Bhagavad Gita* means Song of God. While many believers date the text to over 5000 years ago. Originally written in Sanskrit, the earliest English translation was done in 1785.

One of the major characters in this discussion at the battle of Kurukshetra was Prince Arjuna, who was a member of the Pandava clan and had to fight to regain the land unetically grabled by the Kauravas. Arjuna asked Lord Krishna to raise him up above the battlefield so that he could see the forces on both sides. When he saw his relatives, teachers, and friends on the opposite side and reflected on the death of those people. He was hesitant to engage in battle, even though he knew he will win the battle since he had Lord Krishna on his side. Arjuna questioned Lord Krishna on the value of war, even when the outcome was known to be victorious, when the death of relatives will result. Lord Krishna explained to Prince Arjuna why he must fight and how his actions must be considered in the larger context of his role. The *Gita*, contains eighteen chapters which can be divided up into three parts: karma yoga or selfless action, jnana yoga or self-knowledge, and bhakti yoga (Hee 2007). The *Bhagavad Gita* represents the many struggles, or battles, modern-day leaders face and their responsibilities to multiple stakeholders. Some have even proposed that the *Bhagavad Gita* is useful for a better understanding of specific managerial issues such as quality management (Sharma and Talwar 2004).

Gita says about compassion, kindness and forgiveness. These qualities are essential for sound leadership. A responsible leader is a devoted and dedicated master. In *Gita* Krishna values knowledge and wisdom. Many great civilizations have been destroyed by foolish, selfish, and greedy leaders. Anyone who is sincerely devoted to his own duty is successful. Anyone who is honest to his duty can attain perfection. And to be honest to his duty he must know the values that can help him to practise a good leadership style. Sri Krishna explains that one should always try to understand his own character, abilities, and capabilities and that all duties should be undertaken according to one's own character. One should not abandon his own duty and attempt to do duty of others. If one abandons his duties and takes up the duty of another, there will be serious disorder in society. Good and bad are two values that we project on to circumstances according to our viewpoints.

Bhagavad Gita teaches that service is the highest of all actions, for it leads to liberation. Leadership can be described as a set of principles that can be learnt and applied. No one can deny that there have been many leaders in the past, like Adolf Hitler, who effectively mobilized and mesmerized many followers towards the pursuit of distant goals. However, most of the people would disagree to consider such leaders as someone to follow in the long run or to remember him with respect and passion. We are sure that he is not a leader who is worthy of emulating. We have a sense that leadership in not only its form, but also its function, is governed by moral imperatives. Leadership which conforms to these principles in terms of its form is effective leadership and authentic, as well.

With great power comes great responsibility. Those who do not lead in accordance with these principles, intentions notwithstanding, are guilty of misleading. *Bhagavad Gita* describes these fundamental universal principles, the underlying framework of the universe that reflects the purpose of the universal architect. Leaders who align their practices with these principles will be effective leaders. Leaders who align their goals and the goals of the organizations they steward with these principles will be authentic leaders. Leaders who are empowered to create a better world. Leadership is absolutely crucial. At this present moment in time, with so many social and environmental indices tottering toward the red line, the world is crying out not just for effective leadership, but for authentic leadership. *Bhagavad Gita* contains the timeless principles that will empower leaders to be effective and authentic leaders. The greatest need at this point in time is for those people who have been called to lead to step forward and take up the service of leadership.

In the language of Stephen Covey, the Directive leader is all about efficiency getting people moving up the hill. The Strategic leader is all about effectiveness, making sure that the team is moving up the right hill. The Directive leader is about engagement - engaging himself or herself, and engaging others in the task at hand. The Visionary leader is about detachment - stepping back and looking at the bigger picture. The two are generally complementary roles, and a person is generally better at one or the other. The Strategic leader enables the Directive leader by providing him or her with strategic vision and direction. This is very valuable to the Directive leader as it ultimately makes him or her more effective. In classical terms a Directive leader is known as a Ksatriya and a Visionary leader is known as a Brahmana. Kshatriyas would act as kings, and they would maintain an advisory staff of one or more Brahmanas who would act as strategic input to their decision-making process. The predominance of his brahmana nature - the Strategic Leadership capability - means that he is not satisfied simply doing things - he has a deep need to teach others to do things, accompanied by the capacity to understand the theoretical underpinnings that affect action. The strength of his Ksatriya nature, his secondary leadership ability, weakens his ability to act as a pure Strategic leader, who deals with the really bigger picture issues. This combination makes him uniquely suited to be a military advisor and teacher. He is a person who has a highly developed theoretical understanding of execution, greater than that of a pure Directive leader, combined with a personal drive for execution that allows him to earn the respect of Directive leaders.

In today's scenario, organizations generally lack vision. It takes no time for very big organizations to lose sight of the bigger picture and get lost in the minute implementation details. Leaders have to constantly restate the vision to keep it fresh and vibrant. It is being observed that the leaders have started gaining the tendency of micro-managing things in their organization, thereby losing valuable time to have visionary approach for their systems. Directive leaders excel is casting vision, but crafting vision is especially the area of strength of Strategic leaders. They have a highly developed ability to "feel" the future. To inspire people, a vision must be compelling. In order to be compelling it needs two things: first of all, it needs to include the people. Secondly, it needs to be felt by the leader. The compelling vision of a leader is not simply an idea of what could be - it is what should be. It carries with it a moral imperative that is felt by the leader. When vision is aligned with eternal universal principles it is beneficial for everyone, and not simply for one particular group at the expense of others. Aligning vision with eternal universal principles must be a primary concern of authentic leaders. *Bhagavad Gita* is an exposition of those eternal principles, and persons with leadership ability who study these principles will be empowered to provide authentic leadership.

Researcher Jim Collins, author of "Good to Great", led a team in a six year research effort which investigated the causative factors that distinguish good companies from so-called "good-to-great" ones, an arbitrary distinction created by the research group of a sustained, significant performance improvement that was so stringent that only 15 companies made the cut in the entire US economy over a 40 year period. Among a handful of significant factors was the finding that the good-to-great companies had a relentless focus on what the researchers termed: "First Who, then What". They use the analogy of a bus to explain this concept. Leaders in the good-to-great companies focused first on getting the right people onto the bus and making sure they were on the right seats, before deciding where to drive the bus. They were prepared to leave a seat empty for as long as it took to find "the right person", rather than settle for someone who was less than ideal.

Leaders in the comparison companies, in contrast, would often start out with the idea of where they wanted to go, and then get people on board to go there. Getting the right people is fundamental. Both Duryodhana and Arjuna spent a lot of time and energy recruiting for this battle. Sun Tzu, in his classic treatise the *Art of War* states leadership as one of the five essential factors that determine ultimate victory.

Truly great leaders, however, surround themselves with the brightest people they can find, and empower them to do their best work. They provide a working environment in which leaders are able to reach their full potential, and provide opportunities for them to do significant work. By doing this they secure the loyalty of their staff. Real loyalty comes when a leader has made an investment in the development of the people they lead, when they have empowered those persons and helped them to become more effective.

Krishna had vowed not to fight in the battle, but to join one side of the conflict. His army, however, would fight on the other side. Duryodhana chose Krishna's army, and Arjuna chose to have Krishna on his side. Krishna is the enunciator of the fundamental universal principles described in *Bhagavad Gita*, and as He will explain later, their source. The inner meaning of His appearing on the side of the Pandavas, which was substantially weaker in strength than Duryodhana's side, is that leadership which is lacking in effectiveness, in efficacy, due to a lack of understanding of the principles of practice is preferably to leadership which is lacking in alignment with the principles of purpose. For all the efficiency of modern western civilization we see a number of alarming statistics, among them rates of violent crime, suicide, divorce and other indicators that efficiency is not everything.

Bhagavad Gita is an extreme case to prove a point. We can see how Duryodhana is an extreme archetype of the self-absorbed, manipulative leader. Arjuna is about to demonstrate the other end of the spectrum. However, just how extreme a case Bhagavad-gita is will be fully revealed after this, when Krishna shows how even Arjuna's current level of leadership falls short of what is required of an authentic leader. Arjuna's concern for this is a symptom of his compassion, and an indication that he has the character needed to be an authentic leader. Arjuna demonstrates through his concerns that aside from the legality of the succession, he is more the indicated person to sit on the throne than Duryodhana. However, Arjuna's compassion, while admirable compared with the mentality of Duryodhana, is still insufficient to elevate him to the position of an authentic leader. Krishna is about to enlighten Arjuna to fundamental principles that will illuminate the way forward for him, and empower him to be an authentic leader, acting in knowledge selflessly in the service of the people.

Krishna was a visionary leader and he says to Arjuna that he should not think about the instant results. He should think about how result will affect people in future. He explained Arjuna that he is actually not fighting for himself. He is fighting for the entire society and for Dharma (or ethics and values). Basically, Lord Krishna identifies follower's strengths and weakness so that he can recognize their pure potential and capabilities and transform their strengths to perform their duty. Qualities of leaderships are self-realization, self-control, humility, simplicity, purity, honesty, spirituality, and absence of false ego, power, determination, resourcefulness, and courage described in *Bhagavat Gita*. Krishna in *Bhagavat Gita* had all these qualities. Lord Krishna changed his leadership style according to the situation recognizing the people and their potential. He clearly knew what appealed to whom and how to get the work done.

Lord Krishna is a cosmic power but his role on a real world platform is a benchmark for leaders. His eternal words (from *Bhagavat Gita*) nurture our minds, blossom our hearts and purify our spirits so that every one can feel eternal love as well as bliss. His every action creates new form of art. At that time when Krishna was in Mathura and Brindavana he was a leader accepted by everybody, but without crown or authority. His leadership was based on ethics and value. He led people to establish Dharma in society. In teen age he killed Kamsa , who was a promoter of wrongdoings in Mathura.

Lord Krishna tells that knowledge is supreme. So it is the right of everyone to acquire knowledge and a duty also for spreading this everywhere for wellness of all living entities. Krishna was the versatile genius. When Arjuna denied to fight, Lord Krishna started his dialogue with Arjuna. The essence of this management dialogue was divided into eighteen chapters in the *Bhagavad Gita* (1) Despondency of Arjuna. (2) The way of discrimination. (3) The way of action. (4) The way of knowledge. (5) Renunciation of action. (6) The way of contemplation. (7) The way of knowledge and realisation. (8) The way to supreme spirit. (9) The way of royal knowledge and royal secret (10) Meditation of the divine glories. (11) The vision of the universal form. (12) The way of devotion. (13) Discrimination between nature and soul (14) The separation of three gunas. (15) The way to supreme person. (16) The distinction between divine and demonical attributes. (17) The separation of the three kinds of faith. (18) The way of renunciation.

After completing the dialogue, Arjuna says that his delusion is destroyed and he has gained his memory through Lord Krishna's teaching, he is ready to fight battle, free from doubt, about his duties will be carried out at Krishna's command. This clearly shows the management and development of individual (self) in right direction taught by Lord Krishna to Arjuna which made Arjuna do his duty selflessly by fighting the historic Kurukshetra war and winning the war was his goal.

He was a charismatic leader. His graceful appearance spread divine energies and opulence in the universe so that waves of happiness and true love can stabilize everywhere.

A leader should set example of his power and intelligence before of his followers. So that followers can get motivated by remembering their leader's doings. Lord Krishna was a continuous warrior even from his twelfth year. He entered the place of sacrifice in Dhanuryajna performed by Kamsa and broke the great bow. Then Krishna killed him and relief the kingdom from wrongdoings. Krishna fought bravely with Jarasandha, emperor of Magadha and Kalayavana, who was the father-in-law of Kamsa. He invaded Mathura seventeen times; Krishna drove out Jarasandha every time. He fought with Bana, the thousand armed king of Sonitpur. Krishna's son Aniruddha had secretly married Bana's daughter Usha and was living with her. Bana was informed of this. He imprisoned Aniruddha. Krishna fought with Bana and cut off his arms and returned to Dwaraka with Aniruddha and Usha. Thereafter, he killed Paundra, king of Karusha who denied Krishna's divinity and assumed Vishnu's conch, discus, club and lotus and declared him to be the real Vasudeva. The wicked Sisupala challenged Krishna in Yudhisthira's Rajasuya Yajna. Sri Krishna threw His Chakra at Sisupala and cut off his head. Similarly, he slew Dantavaktra also. Salva, king of Saubha and friend of Sisupala, waged war with Krishna to avenge his friend's death. Salva was put to death by Lord Krishna.

Sri Krishna was a great statesman. The world has not witnessed a greater statesman than Sri Krishna. He was a companion of liberty and a peacemaker. He had wonderful foresight and held positively liberal views. Even when he was a boy, he taught people the essentials and the true significance of religion, when he rose against the popular worship of Indra for getting rains. Krishna was the greatest of the political heroes. He was the greatest statesman of all time. He was a king-maker. He was the founder of the city of Dwaraka. He was a great historical person. He was the spiritual leader and of mankind. He had gone as the peacemaker to stop the civil war that was to be fought between the Kauravas and the Pandavas. Sri Krishna's political insight and wise statesmanship were admired by the ablest rulers of his time. His wise counseling helped the kings and rulers.

Conclusion

Bhagavad Gita is an embodiment of knowledge that defines the character of a leader. A manager or leader should perform some duty. Lord Krishna did all his duties perfectly at that time. Firstly manager should decide on a goal. And Krishna had clear goal which he taught to Arjuna: (a) Paritranaya Sadhunaam Welfare for Saints, (b) Vinashaya Dushkritaam - Destroy Evil. Secondly a manager should have motivational skill. When Arjun reached the battlefield, he lost his determination to fight when he saw that among the opponents were many of his relatives young and old and that he was going to kill them for the sake of kingdom. He resisted from fighting and dropped arms. Krishna motivated him by his speech and Arjun recovered and decided to fight. Thirdly, managers must have skills to build strategies to achieve target. Pandavas and Kauravas had soldiers and warriors strength in the ratio of 7:11, Pandavas having 1.53 millions and Kauravas with 2.41 millions. With this count it was clear that the battle could be won only with effective strategies. The fact that Pandavas won the battle proves that Krishna was successful not only in building strategies but in implementing them to achieve success. Fourthly, good managers must have leadership quality. When Krishna asked Arjuna and Duryodhana to choose between him and his army, the choice was, in fact, between a leader and his resources. While a good leader can gain from limited resources, a bad leader will lose even with vast resources. Knowing his excellent leadership qualities, Arjuna requested Krishna not only to lead the entire mission but to personally lead him by accepting to be his "Saarthi" (charioteer), guide him and lead him to success. Lastly, manager should have sound direction and controlling power. *Bhagavad Gita* is an important text for leaders to understand value-based leadership and imbibe these characteristics in day-to-day operations and dealings. These values will help gain a visionary outlook and will prove to be very useful for their organization.

Source: Gitalichoudary, "Integrating Spirituality and Organisational Leadership (2011).

Philosophical Understanding of Ethics of Virtue

Some moral philosophers and theologians have argued for an ethics of virtue, being, character, or ideals in opposition to the ethics of duty, doing, action, laws, principles, or rules. Our so-called new morality seems to favour the former. The issue may be understood as follows. As we have seen, there are two kinds of moral judgments, deontic and aretaic. Our actual morality–and most ethical theory–recognizes both kinds of judgment. Ross and Kant, for example, do this. It is often said, however, that aretaic judgments are primary in the morality and ethical theory of the Greeks, while deontic ones are primary in Christian and modem morality and moral philosophy. Whether or not this is historically true, it is possible to hold that deontic judgments should be regarded as primary in morality and aretaic ones as derivative or dispensable, or, alternatively, that aretaic judgments should be regarded as primary and deontic ones as derivative. If one holds the former, one has a deontic ethics or ethics of duty; if the latter, an aretaic ethics. But aretaic ethics is not necessarily an ethics of virtue which insists that moral judgments about actions. What is basic in morality are judgments such as "Be just" or "Be sincere," or, more accurately, "Justice is a virtue" or "Sincerity is morally good."

It should also be noticed that, so far, we have been proceeding as if the ethics-of-duty approach is correct; this is because most modem moral philosophers, both teleologists and deontologists, have taken that approach. The utilitarians studied earlier are as much committed to an ethics of duty as the deontologists. But an ethics of virtue can also be either teleological or deontological; roughly, an ethics of virtue would be teleological if it holds that benevolence is the whole of virtue, deontological if it denies this and insists that there are other moral virtues as well, such as honesty or chastity.

Instead of adopting either an ethics of virtue or an ethics of duty that has a place for virtues and aretaic judgments, which is what philosophers have usually done, one might argue that a fully adequate morality should consist of two parts: an ethics-of-duty part for one sphere of life and an ethics-of-virtue part for another sphere of life, one sphere being subject to the call of duty, the other being outside or beyond that call. Such a view has a good deal of attractiveness-among other things, it makes it easy to find a place for saints and heroes and might be worked out in a variety of ways.

Plato and Mayo are great philosophers and their views on virtue ethics are discussed below.

The Virtue of Justice and Ethics by Plato

If the case is put to us, must we not admit that the just State, or the man who is trained in the principles of such a State, will be less likely than the unjust to make away with a deposit of gold or silver? Would anyone deny this?

No one, he replied.

Will the just man or citizen ever be guilty of sacrilege or theft or treachery either to his friends or to his country?

Never.

Neither will he ever break faith where there have been oaths or agreements?

From "The Republic," in The Dialogues of Plato, *3rd ed., trans. Benjamin Jowelt (London: Oxford University Press,* 1892)).

Impossible.

No one will be less likely to commit adultery, or to dishonour his father and mother, or to fail in his religious duties?

No one.

And the reason is that each part of him is doing its own business, whether in ruling or being ruled?

Exactly so.

Are you satisfied then that the quality which makes such men and such states is justice, or do you hope to discover some other?

Not I, indeed.

Then our dream has been realized; and the suspicion which we entertained' at the beginning of our work of construction, that some divine power must have conducted us to a primary form of justice, has now been verified?

Yes, certainly.

And the division of labour which required the carpenter and the shoemaker and the rest of the citizens to be doing each his own business,' and not another's, was a shadow of justice, and for that reason it was of use?

Clearly.

But in reality justice was such as we were describing, being concerned however, not with the outward man, but with the inward, which is the true self and concern of man: for the just man does not permit the several elements within him to interfere with one another, or any of them to do the work of others, he sets in order his own inner life, and is his own master and his own law, and at peace with himself; and when he has bound together the three principles within him, which may be compared to the higher, lower, and middle notes of the scale, and the intermediate intervals, when he has bound all these together, and is no longer many, but has become one entirely temperate and perfectly adjusted nature, then he proceeds to act, if he has to act, whether in a matter of property, or in the treatment of the body, or in some affair of politics or private business; always thinking and calling that which preserves and cooperates with this harmonious condition, just and good action, and the knowledge which presides over it, wisdom, and that which at any time impairs this condition, he will call unjust action, and the opinion which preserves over it ignorance.

You have said the exact truth, Socrates.

Very good; and if we were to affirm that we had discovered the just man and the just State, and the nature of justice in each of them, we should not be telling a falsehood?

Most certainly not.

May we say so, then?

Let us say so.

And now, I said, injustice has to be considered.

Clearly.

Must not injustice be a strife which arises among the three principles —a meddlesomeness, and interference, and rising up of a part of the soul against the whole, an assertion of unlawful authority, which is made by a rebellious subject against a true prince, of whom he is the natural vassal, what is all this confusion and delusion but injustice, and intemperance and cowardice and ignorance, and every form of vice?

Exactly so.

And if the nature of justice and injustice is known, then the meaning of acting unjustly and being unjust, or, again, of acting justly, will also be perfectly clear?

What do you mean? he said.

Why, I said, they are like disease and health; being in the soul just what disease and health are in the body.

How so? he said.

Why, I said, that which is healthy causes health, and that which is unhealthy causes disease.

Yes.

And just actions cause justice, and unjust actions cause injustice? That is certain.

And the creation of health is the institution of a natural order and government of one by another in the parts of the body; and the creation of disease is the production of a state of things at variance with this natural order?

True.

And is not the creation of justice the institution of a natural order and government of one by another in the parts of the soul, and the creation of injustice the production of a state of things at variance with the natural order?

Exactly so, he said.

Then virtue is the health and beauty and well-being of the soul, and vice the disease and weakness and deformity of the same?

True.

And do not good practices lead to virtue, and evil practices to vice?

Assuredly.

Still our old question of the comparative advantage of justice and injustice has not been answered: Which is more profitable, to be just and act justly and practise virtue, whether seen or unseen of gods and men, or to be unjust and act unjustly; if only unpunished and unreformed?

In my judgment, Socrates, the question has now become ridiculous. We know that, when the bodily constitution is gone, life is no longer endurable, though pampered with all kinds of meats and drinks, and having all wealth and all power; and shall we be told that when the very essence of the vital principle is undermined and corrupted, life is still worth having to a man, if only he be allowed to do whatever he likes with the single exception that he is not to acquire justice and virtue, or to escape from injustice and vice; assuming them both to be such as we have described?

Yes, I said, the question is, as you say, ridiculous ....

COMMENTARY ON PLATO

R.C. Cross & A.D. Woozley

About the fourth virtue, justice, [Plato] does speak at slightly more length. Attempts, such as were made in Book I, to characterise justice in terms of a man's conduct are misguided and place the emphasis in the wrong place, for conduct is only a sign or "image" of character. A man is just when the three elements of his soul are in their correct harmonious relationship under the overall rule of the rational element. Such a relationship will manifest itself in just conduct. Conversely, the practice of just conduct, through moral training and example, will serve to produce and maintain the relationship, but should not be confused with it. In this contrast between conduct and the character of which it is, or should be, the expression, Plato is underlining a distinction which is central to ethics. Some of our moral judgments are judgments about a man's conduct, regardless of his motives or his reasons for acting so; and to this sphere belong especially words like "right," "wrong," "ought" and "obligation." We say that a man has done what was right if his action conforms with what we accept as moral rules, wrong if it violates them. For example, in the ordinary situation where no problems arise over which there is reason for moral disagreement we may say that a man has done what was right if, having made a promise, he keeps it, that he has done wrong if he breaks it. If one man keeps a promise out of respect for the sanctity of promises, and another keeps his promise because he thinks it will pay him to do so, or that he will suffer loss if he breaks it, we do not say that the first man's action was right, but the second's was not. If it is right to pay taxes and bills when they are due, to tell the truth when giving evidence under oath, to obey traffic lights when driving a car, to report for duty when called up into the army, etc., then your conduct is right when it is of the prescribed kind. In judging that what you did was right, or judging that you have done what you ought, we are judging you for your conduct, and are not interested in your motives or reasons. We shall not withdraw our assertion that you did what you ought, if we discover that your reasons for so acting were much less reputable than we may have at first supposed. But belief and knowledge about your reasons will determine a different kind of moral judgment which we make, judgment about you as a man, or about your conduct in relation to you as a man. And this is the sphere to which the "virtue" (and "vice") words belong: the general words like "good" and "bad" and the more specific virtue words like "generous," "honest," "courageous," "conscientious," etc., and vice words like "mean," "malicious," "untrustworthy," These are the words which we use in describing and assessing a man's character, and in appraising his conduct when we are not simply judging it externally by its conformity with (or violation of) a moral code of behaviour, but are judging it in relation to the man's reasons and motives for so acting. We approve of a man keeping his promise. whatever his reasons may be, but we shall not admire him if we know that his sole reason was fear of the consequences to himself of being caught breaking it. Plato's point is that in right conduct as such there is no virtue. If a man sticks to his job, or stays within his class, he is acting justly, but he is not on that account a just man: he may be sticking to his job because he can make more money out of it than at any other. because of fear of unemployment if he leaves it, because he will lose his house if he leaves it, or because it has been made a legal offence to leave it. He will be a just man, or his conduct will display justice, only if it is the manifestation of his inner self or character, and only if that inner self consists of the three elements in their correct relationship; real justice, then, characterises, not a man's behaviour, but the state of his soul, which will naturally manifest itself in his behaviour.

From Plato's Republic *(London: Macmillan & Co., Ltd.,* 1964; *New York: St. Martin's Press,* 1964).

ETHICS OF VIRTUE VS ETHICS OF PRINCIPLE

Bernard Mayo

Duty and Virtue

It has been said that the whole of Western philosophy is a set of footnotes to Plato. This is a pardonable half-truth for, say, metaphysics, but it is very far from true of moral philosophy. The philosophy of moral principles, which is characteristic of Kant and the post-Kantian era, is something of which hardly a trace exists in Plato. Plato speaks at great length of goodness and the good; we also speak of the word "good" as a moral word, but, . . . it is an evaluative and not an imperative word, and is less at home in the context of moral principles than are such words as "right" and 'wrong." These words, on the other hand, do not occur in Platonic ethics. Plato says nothing about rules or principles or laws, except when he is talking politics. Instead he talks about virtues and vices, and about certain types of human character. The keyword in Platonic ethics is virtue; the key word in Kantian ethics is duty. And modern ethics is a set of footnotes, not to Plato, but to Kant, and, more remotely, to the Old Testament and Roman Law.

Attention to the novelists can be a welcome correction to a tendency of philosophical ethics of the last generation or two to lose contact with the ordinary life of man which is just what the novelists, in their own way, are concerned with. Of course there are writers who can be called in to illustrate problems about duty (Graham Greene is a good example). But there are more who perhaps never mention the words duty, obligation or principle. Yet, they are all concerned—Jane Austen, for instance, entirely and absolutely—with the moral qualities or defects of their heroes and heroines and other characters. This points to a radical one-sidedness in the philosophers' account of morality in terms of principles: it takes little or no account of qualities, of what people *are.* It is just here that the old-fashioned word virtue used to have a place; and it is just here that the work of Plato and Aristotle can be instructive. Justice, for Plato, though it is closely connected with acting according to law, does not *mean* acting according to law: it is a quality of character, and a just action is one such as a just man would do. Telling the truth, for Aristotle, is not, as it was for Kant, fulfilling an obligation; again it is a quality of character, or, rather, a whole range of qualities of character, some of which may actually be defects, such as tactlessness, boastfulness, and so on. A point which can be brought out, in terms of principles. only with the greatest complexity and artificiality, but quite simply and naturally in terms of character.

If we wish to enquire about Aristotle's moral views, it is no use looking for a set of principles. Of course we can find *some* principles to which he must have subscribed, for instance, that one ought not to commit adultery. But what we find much more prominently is a set of character—traits, a list of certain types of person—the courageous man, the niggardly man, the boaster, the lavish spender and so on. The basic moral question, for Aristotle, is not, What shall I do? but, What shall I be?

These contrasts between doing and being, negative and positive. and modem as against Greek morality were noted by John Stuart Mill. I quote from the *Essay on Liberty:*

Christian morality (so-called) has all the characters of a reaction; it is, in great part, a protest against Paganism. Its ideal is negative rather than positive; passive rather than active; Innocence rather than Nobleness; Abstinence from Evil, rather than energetic Pursuit of the Good; in its precepts (as has been well said) "Thou shalt not" predominates unduly over "Thou shalt . . ." Whatever exists of magnanimity, highmindedness, personal dignity, even the sense of honour, is derived from the purely human, not the religious part of our education, and never could have grown out of a standard of ethics in which the only worth, professedly recognised, is that of obedience.

Of course, there are connections between being and doing. It is obvious that a man cannot just *be;* he can only be what he is by doing what he does; his moral qualities are ascribed to him because of his actions, which are said to manifest those qualities. But the joint is that an ethics of Being must include this obvious fact, that Being involves Doing; whereas an ethics of Doing, such as I have been examining, may easily overlook it. As I have suggested, a morality of principles is concerned only with what people do or fail to do, since that is what rules are for. And as far as this sort of ethics goes, people might well have no moral qualities at all except the possession of principles and the will (and capacity) to act accordingly.

Principles and Ideals

When we speak of a moral quality such as courage, and say that a certain action was courageous, we are not merely saying something about the action. We are referring, not so much to what is done, as to the kind of person by whom we take it to have been done. We connect, by means of imputed motives and intentions, with the character of the agent as courageous. This explains, incidentally, why both Kantians and Utilitarians encounter, in their different ways, such difficulties in dealing with motives, which their principles, on the face of it, have no room for. An Utilitarian, for example, can only praise a courageous action in some such way as this: the action is of a sort such as a person of courage is likely to perform, and courage is a quality of character the cultivation of which is likely to increase rather than diminish the sum total of human happiness. But Aristotelians have no need of such circumlocution. For them a courageous action just is one which proceeds from and manifests a certain type of character, and is praised because such a character trait is good, or better than others, or is a virtue. An evaluative criterion is sufficient: there is no need to look for an imperative criterion as well, or rather instead, according to which it is not the character which is good, but the cultivation of the character which is right.

Dispositions of the special sort applicable to human beings are . . . in an important sense "elastic"; that is, from the information that some one is timid we cannot rigorously deduce that he will be frightened on a given occasion, as we can rigorously deduce from the solubility of sugar that it will dissolve when immersed in water. Timid people sometimes act courageously, that is, as courageous people behave; in general, people can act "out of character." Acting out of character is interestingly different from breaking a principle. There are no degrees about rule breaking: the rule is either kept or broken. In terms of rules, all we are entitled to consider is the relation between an action (the subject of judgment) and a rule (the criterion of judgment), and the verdict is either Right or Wrong. But in considering action by an agent, we have to take into account as well a whole range of other actions by the agent, on the basis of which we form a judgment of character. Actions are "in character" or "out of character" in varying degrees. Further, we can never state precisely what a person's character is instead of the extreme simplicity of the moral judgment based on a moral principle and an instance of conduct which either does or does not conform to that principle, we have a double complexity. Corresponding to the moral principle (which represents the conduct of an ideally righteous man) we have, instead, the idea of a virtue (which represents the conduct and conduct-tendency of an ideally good man). But whereas a man's action can be compared directly with the principle and only two possible verdicts result (or three, if we include "indifferent"), it cannot be compared in this way with the standard of virtue. For we cannot say exactly either how far the action is "in character" for the man, nor how far the character of the man matches or fails to match the ideal. It is not surprising that moral principles, with their superior logical manageability, have proved more attractive than moral ideals as material for ethical theory.

No doubt the fundamental moral question is just "What ought I to do?" And according to the philosophy of moral principles, the answer (which must be an imperative "do this") must be derived from a conjunction of premisses consisting (in the simplest case) firstly of a rule, or universal imperative, enjoining (or forbidding) all actions of a certain type in situations of a certain type, and, secondly, a statement to the effect that this is a situation of that type, falling under that rule. In practice the emphasis may be on supplying only one of these premises. The other being assumed or taken for granted: one may answer the question "What ought I to do?" either by quoting a rule which I am to adopt. or by showing that my case is legislated for by a rule which I do adopt. To take a previous example of moral perplexity, if I am in doubt whether to tell the truth about his condition to a dying man, my doubt may be resolved by showing that the case comes under a rule about the avoidance of unnecessary suffering, which I am assumed to accept. But if the case is without precedent in my moral career, my problem may be soluble only by adopting a new principle about what I am to do now and in the future about cases of this kind.

This second possibility offers a connection with moral ideals. Suppose my perplexity is not merely an unprecedented situation which I could cope with by adopting a new rule. Suppose the new rule is thoroughly inconsistent with my existing moral code. This may happen, for instance, if the moral code is one to which I only pay lip-service; if its authority is not yet internalised, or if it has ceased to be so; it is ready for rejection, but its final rejection awaits a moral crisis such as we are assuming to occur. What I now need is not a rule for deciding how to act in this situation and others of its kind. I need a whole set of rules, a complete morality, new principles to live by.

Now according to the philosophy of moral character, there is another way of answering the fundamental question "What ought I to do?" Instead of quoting a rule, we quote a quality of character, a virtue: we say "Be brave," or "Be patient" or "Be lenient." We may even say "Be a man": if I am in doubt, say, whether to take a risk, and someone says "Be a man," meaning a morally sound man, in this case a man of sufficient courage. (Compare the very different ideal invoked in "Be a gentleman:' I shall not discuss whether this is a *moral* ideal.) Here, too, we have the extreme cases, where a man's moral perplexity extends not merely to a particular situation but to his whole way of living. And now the question "What ought I to do?" turns into the question "What ought I to be?" —as, indeed, it was treated in the first place. ("Be brave.") It is answered, not by quoting a rule or a set of rules, but by describing a quality of character or a type of person. And here the ethics of character gains a practical simplicity which offsets the greater logical simplicity of the ethics of principles. We do not have to give a list of characteristics or virtues, as we might list a set of principles. We can give a unity to our answer.

Of course we can in theory give a unity to our principles: this is implied by speaking of a *set* of principles. But if such a set is to be a system and not a mere aggregate, the unity we are looking for is a logical one, namely, the possibility that some principles are deductible from others, and ultimately from one. But the attempt to construct deductive moral system is notoriously difficult, and in any case ill founded. Why should we expect that all rules of conduct should be ultimately reducible to a few?

From Ethics and the Moral Life *(London: Macmillan & Co. Ltd.,* 1958; *New York: St. Martin's Press, 1958).*

A person's belief and attitude are notoriously difficult to change without there being a willingness to accept the message being offered.

Manuel G. Velasquez

3

Chapter

Ethics in Management

INTRODUCTION

Scientific management is based on practicability and realism. Today's management is human-centric, value-oriented and many of the activities are based on human values. Any activity without management amounts to vacuum and it leads to the most critical situation for the success of any organization. Management system is based on three areas, namely, (i) organisation, (ii) communication and coordination and (iii) human values and relations. The system is also surrounded by the various environments, namely, natural, economical, social, and political. Management is expected to set up the goal, standard of living and standard of life to the society. It is related directly to employees, consumers, members and finally to the society. It is to assure safe and smooth running through powerful innovative force in the organization. Many times it as a tool for effective governance and also contributes towards wealth of the nation.

Ethics in management determine the values in the functional and other areas of organisation. "Ethics in management may be referred to values-oriented holistic management." Business in the management need not to be taken as a unethical or materialistic factor. Rather this can be considered a sacred and it is a matter of attitude, approach and level of consciousness. The management is expected to meet expectations of all stakeholders like employees, customers, citizens, creditors, shareholders, etc. Profit is earned through service and satisfaction of all interested parties.

It is being increasingly recognized by academics, businesses, policy-makers, and other management gurus, that the business or corporate ethics in the global economy is simply too important to be merely left to chance. Many corporations such as McDonald's, Shell, Nike, Nestle and Indian giants like TATAs, Birlas, Infosys and others have realized to their cost the threat that perceived ethical violations can pose to their zealously guarded reputations. In 2002 a strict regulation was formed by **"Sarbanes-Oxley"** legislation that any company listed in the US must introduce "Codes of conduct"—ethics, policies and whistleblower hotliners. This brought a lot of significant implications among many corporates to introduce ethics in management.

Indeed, this has given rise to a multi-million Euro international business. Ethics "industry" with ethics managers, consultants, auditors and other experts are available to advise and implement ethics management policies and programmes in corporations across the globe. In respect of business ethics management, refferring to "Sarbanes-Oxley" legislation, "Corporations are wishing to learn ethics virtually overnight, and as they do so, a vast new industry of consultants and suppliers has emerged. The ethics industry has been born (Hyatt 2005). To connect this, in 2006 Wal-Mart, the world's largest retailer advertised for a new "Director of Global Ethics" to lead the company's global ethics strategy and to oversee its ethics related administration and training.

Ethics in management is determination of what is right, proper and just in the decisions and actions that affect other people. It goes far beyond simple questions of bribery, theft and collusion. But how can companies actually manage business ethics on day-to-day basis across the various national and cultural contexts, that they may be operating in.

It raises various issues related questions when the question of ethics arises in management like:

- Is it possible to improve ethical behaviour of employees so that they make right decisions every time?
- What should be the relationship with customers, shareholders, creditors, suppliers, distributors and society as a whole?
- What kind of management programmes are necessary to produce the level of information and impacts that various stakeholders demand?

The above questions are answered by analysing various factors relating to ethics in management. However, in this area in particular, there are a few definite answers, as the subject ethics varies from person to person, organisation to organisation, society to society and nation to nation. There are many ethical dilemmas in respect of cultural and cross-cultural activities in the management.

Ethics in Management

Ethics in management may be referred to managing any area of business, whether it is production, marketing, accounting, finance, human resource, or any other function. It constitutes a whole range of activities covering formal and informal means of planning, implementation and control. The most relevant aspects of the management of business ethics are those that are clearly visible and directed specifically to resolve ethical problems and issues. Hence, the following definition may render a clear picture on ethics in management.

"Ethics in management is a direct attempt to and for many or informally manage ethical issues or problems through specific policies, procedures, practices and programmes."

To realise the above definition into practical implications there need to have ethics in business and management to create values in management. The different components are essential to cover business ethics management like:

- Mission or values statements
- Codes of ethics.
- Reporting/advice channels.
- Risk analysis and management.
- Ethics manager, officers and committees.
- Ethics consultants.
- Ethics education and training.
- Auditing, accounting and reporting.

(i) Mission or Value Statements

Mission or value statements are popular statements of corporate aims, expectations, values and beliefs. The research study reveals that such statements frequently include social goals of one kind or another and often specify a commitment to operate in an ethical fashion. Some of the examples like: The British retailer "Marks and Spencer" aims to be the most trusted retailer, "Whereever they trade they demonstrate a clear sense of social responsibility and consistency in their decision making and behaviour. As another leading Indian company Infoyses expresses its mission and value statement as "Powered by intellectuals and Driven by Values". The Swedish furniture giant IKEA suggests that its corporate vision is to "create a better everyday life for every one". Whilst virtually all large and many small and medium-sized organizations now have a mission statement of some kind, there is little evidence to suggest that they have much impact on employee behaviour" (Bartel 1997).

(ii) Code of Ethics

Code of ethics is understood as "voluntary statements that commit organizations, industries or professions to specific beliefs, values and action and/or that set out appropriate ethical behaviour for employees and other stakeholders."

A code of ethics simply cannot be drawn up by an individual or a small group of the top management without studying the various frameworks of stakeholders' position. It needs to have a lot of discussion on what type of conduct is desired and expectations of stakeholders from an ethical point of view within the organization or management.

Ethics is too complex a question to be dealt with. Many times such codes will lack the credibility among the employees. Hence, it draws up a long task involving discussions at different levels. Some companies introduced code of ethics in seventies. Whereas some companies have a long history of ethical conduct and a testament coming from its founders which successive generations have endeavoured. TISCO in India is a good example of a company for best practices and ethical conduct in business. However, it is it a Herculean task in setting up standards and preparing code of ethics in management for long sustainability.

(iii) Reporting or Advice Channels

Effective management is to gather information on ethical issues which is important for the growth of organization and providing stakeholders with appropriate channels for reporting and receiving advice regarding ethical dilemma. This may be a vital means of identifying potential problems and resolving them before they became public. Some of the organizations have introduced ethics hotlines or other forms of reporting channels specifically dedicated to providing a mechanism for employees to notify management of ethics abuses or problems and to seek help and guidance or solutions. One of the recent UK surveys reported that something like 50 per cent of large firms had instituted channels of this kind (Weblay and Lejeune, 2005).

(iv) Risk Analysis and Management

Managing and reducing risk is one of the key components of business ethics management. A key attention of business ethics is not merely financial risks but risks involved in the areas related to stakeholders also. As one of the researchers suggests that, the language of risk assessment has enabled business ethics to "show its bite" by spelling out the risks that firms run by ignoring ethics, and measuring these risks in momentary terms, such as fines, damages and sanctions that courts can impose (Alego Jose Sison, (2000). This has been proved in the US, with Foreign Corrupt Practices Act, which gives greater attention to unethical business practices such as bribery and accounting malpractices.

Managing business ethics is identifying areas of risk, assessing the likelihood and scale of risks. This will mitigate or prevent such risks from harmony business. However, many companies have not yet developed an approach to risks and ethics. This is the areas of continued development and a greater range of ethical problems such as human rights violations, corruption, climate change impact and so on.

(v) Ethics Managers, Officers and Committees

Ethics and its implications are calculated in the organization, a specific individual or groups are appointed to co-ordinate and/or take responsibility for managing ethics in organizations. Designated ethics officers under various titles are appointed. A separate association called "Ethics Officer Associations" was set in 1992 in the US with 1000 and above members. Most of the members in this association are from Fortune 100 companies. The Sarbanes-Oxley legislation has tightened the regulations to be followed. The appointment of ethics officer and training on ethics and ethical practices are becoming common phenomenon among the corporates. In Sept. 2001 the European Business Ethics Network (EBEN) was launched by the "Ethics Practitioner Forum". A website for reference 'www.eben.org' was opened. A large number of corporations now have an ethics committee or a CSR committee which oversees many aspects of the management of business ethics. For example, the pharmaceutical giant "Astra Zeneca" has a Non-Executive Director with responsibility for overseeing corporate social responsibility within the company, and has also established a global corporate responsibility committee with members from across a number of corporate functions. The responsibility of this committee is implementation and review of the company's approach to corporate social responsibility, setting of priorities and planning of future activities.

(vi) Ethics Consultants

Ethics consultancy is yet to become popular. The ethics consultants may also be referred as 'ethics advisers'. These advisers could occupy staff positions in the organization and their major function being to oversee ethical concerns. Individuals occupying such positions would review decisions for their ethical content in an attempt to improve the overall ethical climate of the organization. Initially, these consultants or advisers were driven from environment consultant who tended to offer specialist technical advice, but as the social and ethical agenda facing companies has developed they also extended to research, project management, strategic advice, social and environmental auditing and reporting, verification, stakeholder dialogue and others.

(vii) Ethics Education and Training

Ethics education and training, like all other ethics programmes, is a part of a larger efforts to instill ethical behavioural culture in the organization. Furthermore, it is just one of many parts of the puzzle designed to instill an ethical culture that will benefit the company in the long run. Ethics training includes the subject like codes of conduct, top management practices and strategy, culture, values, and so on. Subject on business ethics and corporate ethics and CSR has been introduced by the universities and colleges. Formal ethics training has tended to be more common in the US than in Europe. The US army announced a move to provide ethics training to its troops in Iraq in 2006 following the alleged murder of civilians. (BBC 2006 – Ethics lessons for US troops, BBC News, June, www.bbc.co.uk/news). Many researchers and academicians have stressed the need for more ethics education among business people, not only interim of providing them with the tools to solve ethical dilemmas but also providing them with the ability to recognize and talk about ethical problems more accurately and easily. The training may provide the following awareness among the managers of ethics.

(a) Identifying the situation where ethical decision-making is involved.
(b) Understanding the culture and values of the organization.
(c) Evaluating the impact of the ethical decision on the organization.

(viii) Auditing, Accounting and Reporting

Auditing, accounting and reporting are closely related activities that are concerned with measuring, evaluating and communicating the organization's impacts and performance on a range of social, ethical and environmental issues of interest to their stakeholders. European companies like Norsk Hydro, SBN Bank, body shop, shell and so on are very popular in this area. However, there is rapid development in this field across the globe, the recent survey suggests that 52 per cent of the worlds 250 largest companies now produce separate CSR reports, an increase of 7 per cent since 2002 (KPMG 2005). There is a provision for internationally comparative standards for aspects of auditing, accounting and reporting. But corporators should grow relatively by enhancing the area of corporate accountability for good governance.

For effective and efficient implementation of ethics in management there need to uphold an appropriate stakeholder theory and practices. This is possible only through adoption of the various principles related to human values, marketing practices, environmental issues, financial transparency, social responsibility and so on. According Clarkson (1999) there are nine principles to adopt in building the stakeholder relationships like: (1) Acknowledgement, (2) Monitor, (3) Listen, (4) Communicate (5) Adopt, (6) Recognise, (7) Work, (8) Avoid and (9) Acknowledge conflicts.

The above nine principles are discussed below under various headings like Ethics in Human Resource, Marketing, Financial Management and Ethics in Profession.

ETHICS IN HUMAN RESOURCE MANAGEMENT

Human resource management is one of the pillars which support stability of the organization. Human resource management attempts to integrate the long-term policy and planning of an organization with the development of its human resources. It includes personnel management, knowledge management, industrial relations, total quality management, talent management, stakeholders management, especial employees management and planning, and controlling of human resource.

Most of the organizations have realized that people with diversified skills, behaviour, attitude, perception, innovation are the major strengths. The organizations are formulating strategies, based on the multidimensional values and skills of the employees in the organization to meet the competitive advantage. Though in the recent past the organizations have downsized their operations, push down their structures due to the recession or otherwise. Implementation of TQM programmes information technology, implementation of an appropriate ethical programme for good corporate governance, gradually brought back the reinstalling of human resources and their management. It is also proved through the research studies that effective human resource management has positive impact on productivity and financial performance of the companies. Thus, understanding diversified human behaviour, unify it in accordance with organizational requirements and direct it towards organizational strategies are necessary not only for efficient human resources management but also for the success of organization.

Human Resource Management and Ethics

The main principles of management is to make the things to do for others or organizations. Human beings are assets in the organization. Yet "human assets" are virtually never shown in the balance sheet as a distinct category, although a great deal of money is invested in the recruitment, selection and training of people. To give more weightage to HRM the ethical practices towards the employees are developed. This can be focused with the different groups or systems.

(1) HR system approach: This is the approach where the human resources are considered to formulate various policies and programmes. This requireds a system design consistency of:
- Performance management
- Recruitment system and profiles
- Retention strategy for key performers.

HR helps in managing interpersonal conflicts and makes employees better team players. It also helps them in dealing with cultural differences. Clear communication content and channels are customized to address cultural differences.

HR also deals effectively with the integration issue. Effective employee communication plays a key role. Questions about job security, relocation, changes in benefit programmes and new reporting relationships are answered by the HR only. Keeping a check on rumours, anxiety, resentment and loss of talent, has also to be dealt with.

Many times a sense of insecurity arises among employees in the organization. HR in such situation, makes people retain their faith in the organization. The best HR can do is to retain the confidence of employees and assure them job security.

Two fundamentals of human relations are related directly to employees. The best ethical practices towards employees by the business houses are:

(i) Providing with a fair salary and wages.
(ii) Providing good working conditions.
(iii) Satisfaction of security needs and job satisfaction.
(iv) Providing opportunity for career development.

or

Providing opportunity towards sustainable employment.

(i) Fair wages and salary

Right to fair wages is one of the fundamental expectations of any employee in an organization. Most of the wages and salaries are protected legitimately in the law. This certainly applies to lower incomes in many of European and Eastern countries like India where there are a statutory minimum wages. However, the assessment of what is fair wage becomes more complex when we place wage levels of those at the bottom of the organizational hierarchy in comparison with those at the top level.

The basis for determining fair wages is commonly the expectation placed on the employees and their performance towards goals, measured hours worked, prior training risk involved, responsibility for assets and meeting of targets.

There is a 'broader issue of performance-related pay (PRP)' and other contingent systems of reward. It is rewarding those at the top for good performance, but when such procedures are introduced for those at lower levels, further ethical problems can arise. According to Edmund Heesy (2000), there are two main problems: "risk and representation."

Risk PRP introduces greater risk into remuneration, that means salaries and benefits for employees become less secure, and potentially open more to arbitrary and subjective management decision making.

Performance PRP also tends to individualize employees pay bargaining restricting the influence of collective representation of employees' interest and thereby weakening employee power.

Of course, there are also good opinion in support of PRP, as Heery (2000) indicates, the ethical appeal of such payment system often depends on how they are developed and implemented. Such arguments typically depend upon notions of justice, in that fair processes and outcomes should accompany pay schemes, regardless of mechanism used.

Fair wages and salary depend on:

- Public support that society provides to the worker.
- Social security, unemployment compensation.
- Medicare, public education, welfare, etc.
- Freedom of labour market.
- Contribution of the worker.
- Needs of the workers.
- Competitive position of the firm.

The following are the factors to determine wages and salaries

- **Minimum wage law:** This is compulsory as per the provision of the labour laws.
- **The nature of the job:** This is to refer to the nature and expectations of the job. Like greater health risks, less security, skills, training technical education and so on for higher salary.
- **Firm's capabilities:** These may reflect through higher profits and it can pay to the workers.
- **Labour market in the industry and the area:** Here the labour market is an industry and area may be manipulated or distorted. However, it provides rough indicators based on wages.
- Fairness of wage negotiations.
- Restricted negotiations otherwise it will lead to fraud, power, ignorance, etc.
- **Relation to other salaries:** Workers who do similar work should receive similar salaries.
- **Local cost of living:** Goods and services that a family needs to meet their basic needs.

The fair wages to be balanced by striking both employer's interest in minimizing costs and employee's interest in providing a decent living for themselves and families.

(ii) Providing good working conditions

This is one of fundamental rights of the employees. There is a lot of legal emphasis on enforceability of providing good working atmosphere and safety of the employees. The working conditions can be discussed under the headings as:

- Health and safety
- Job satisfaction

Health and safety are referred to protecting the employees' health and safety in the working atmosphere. There are many hazards in the workplace like:

- Mechanical injury
- Extreme heat and cold
- Burns and boilers heat
- Radiation and glare
- Textile fibre dust
- Chemical flames
- Skin and eye irritants
- Noisy machinery
- Rock and stone crushing dusts
- Mercury, lead, beryllium, arsenic, corrosives, poisons.

There are legal actions taken on some of the giant corporations for causing health problems. For example, IBM was prosecuted for causing health problems from chemical exposure at its plants in East Fishkill, New York. Nearly 128 former chip workers have sued since 1996. But companies like IBM, Motorala and Seagate insist that their plants are safe. The semiconductor industry has also been subject to litigations regarding job safety.

Semiconductor manufacturers tend to portray their industry as clean, free of smokestacks, with no visible pollution or health risks. Workers, according to the manufacturers, have to wear "head-to-toe bunny suits" and work in sterile 'clean rooms', where air is filtered to remove particles down to $1/100^{th}$ of the width of human hair. This image however, is being challenged by occupational health experts, government scientists and chip workers.

The right to healthy and safe working conditions has been one of the very first ethical concerns for employees, right from the early part of the industrial revolution. Charles Dickens, a novelist brought social reforms and Robert Owen, a pioneer who brought co-operative movements, sought a light on working conditions faced by those working in mines, factories and mills at the time. The various issues related to working conditions were addressed in early nineteenth century. This made a change by formulating a legislation in Germany as Bismarck's Social Laws, as well as motivating to create voluntary paternalistic activities.

At present most industrialised countries, specially European Union, have implemented a broad network of health, safety and environment regulations that companies should compulsorily follow and which are also imposed through various related laws. To practise some of the companies may cut corners as health and safety through negligence or in contempt of regulations, e.g., Union Carbide Ltd. This is the responsibility of the employers to impose on employees to use the safety measures, wherever necessary and actually police worker compliance with regulations. A common example is the signs, typically found in the toilets of pubs and restaurants, which instruct members of staff to wash their hands (or wash your hands now!) after using the toilet. It is a pressing issue in developing countries where companies are not forced by law to impose strict standards. This will be difficult in certain jobs that include a risk on health and life. Working on an oilrig, doing research in nuclear technology or working as a stunt person in action films, working in gas filling and so on are all directly or indirectly related to certain hazards. The organizations should adopt the "principles of informed consent". No worker should be exposed to these factors without precise information about the risk involved. Consequently, any damage to the worker's health is the result of his or her deliberate decisions perhaps to effectively 'trade' exposure to health risks for higher compensation.

The organizations are facing new risks, most commonly in the form of new diseases and new technologies. In fact, some diseases even owe their names to the company where it first occurred, such as 'pseudo-krupp', a lung disease first discovered among workers and neighbours of the German steel mill 'Krupp'. One more example the recent new diseases and a threat to human lives is the rise of AIDS epidemic. Employers are found themselves in dilemma that, on the one hand, they want to provide their employees with a reasonable level of protection, on the other hand a company does not want to discriminate against employees or customers (i.e., patients) infected with the disease.

New problems are emerging in the context of new technologies like computers. The long-term consequences of extended computer work for eyes and other parts of body are also emerging. The new ethical issues arise in the context of:

- Excessive working hours and presenteeism.
- Flexible working pattern
- Job stress.

(a) Excessive working hours and presenteeism

An increasing threat to employee's health and well-being that is receiving considerable attention now is excessive work hours, and its influence on the employe's overall state of physical and mental health. One of the studies found that 84 per cent of managers claimed to work in excess of their official working hours with the average being between 50 to 60 hours a week (Simpson, 2000).

'Presenteeism' refers to the phenomenon of being at work when you should be at home due to illness or even just rest and recreation (Cooper 1996), is a common cultural force in many organizations. The implicit assumption is only those putting in long hours will be rewarded with career progression and other rewards. Presenteeism appears to particularly affect the middle and upper levels of management, and in particular is likely to disadvantage women in career progression since they tend to have more responsibilities for childcare, home making and so on at home (Simpson 1998). As such, the whole issue of "work life balance" has come very much more to the force in recent years.

(b) Flexible working patterns

Changes in working patterns have also led to more 'flexibility' which can enhance opportunities for women and other disadvantaged groups, but it can also have a major downsize for those marginalized from 'standard' work and working conditions. Karen Legge (1998) suggests that, flexibility can just be another way of saying that management can do what it wants. Pressure towards deregulation of labour markets in many parts of Europe brought on by intensification of global competition, and rapid market changes, has led to the emergence of a large constituency of workers on 'non-standard' work relationships. This includes part-time work, temporary work, self-employment and teleworking (Stanworth, 2000). The status of such employees is weak in the organization with less job security. These employees suffer from poor working conditions, increased insecurity, lower pay, exclusion from training and other employment benefits, as well as other possible disadvantages.

This sort of problems are acute among low-skill service industries such as retailing, the hospitality industry, health care industry industrial cleaning and in call centres. These are the areas with greatest growth in jobs in recent years. Such workers are offen expected to have work at 'unsocial' hours, with working hours often unpredictable. For instance, fast food companies in Europe commonly insist that workers should work round the clock during busy times to compete with all-night cleaning "parties". Work intensification in such service industry has become common. Flexible working is common especially in the organization where there is a contract for 'zero-hours'. These issues have become ethical issues as there is no guarantee of minimum hours, no stable level of earnings and prevent employees from planning even the basic elements of their lives (Stanworth 2000).

However, the study shows that the flexibility will boost competitiveness and provide for a strong economy. It also provides more opportunities for women and other groups. However, flexibility hits basic protection for employee working hours. On the other hand understanding flexible contracts can be considered as unfair when it is compared with the core workforce.

(iii) Satisfaction of security needs and job satisfaction

An organization's efficiency and effectiveness depends to a large extent on the satisfaction of its employees. Behavioural and social science research suggests that job satisfaction, security needs and job performance are positively correlated. (Bowran and Todd, 1999). In recent years job satisfaction has suddenly received as a topic for academic research, thanks in large degree to insights brought to it from the field social psychology (Clark, 1996; Rose, 2000). One reason for the renewed interest is the increasing concern with individual well-being. The study says that job satisfaction is an important ingredient for personal happiness. It also led to exploring job satisfaction, its different dimensions, its organizational relationship with factors like high stress fatigue reduction, burnout, role of culture and other organizational variables.

Workplace issue is a major ethical issue under corporate ethics. Workplace issues include job safety, labour practice, workers' rights etc. Attempts have been made to have work standards across countries. A few companies have voluntarily changed their workplace environment. Many are subject to allegations and litigations. In addition, in recent years, sexual harassment has became an important workplace issue in countries like US, India and Japan. There are regulatory systems in force and voluntary attempts have been made by companies to reduce sexual harassment at the workplace. Since the 1980s, human rights issues have become increasingly prominent. Companies have faced litigations as well as boycotts leading to the formulation of both voluntary as well as international company guidelines.

Human beings deserve respect, and on the other side of the coin, are entitled to certain basic rights. It is therefore no surprise that the central ethical issues in HRM can be framed around the issue of rights and duties of employees.

The following are considered **ethical rights and related issues**.

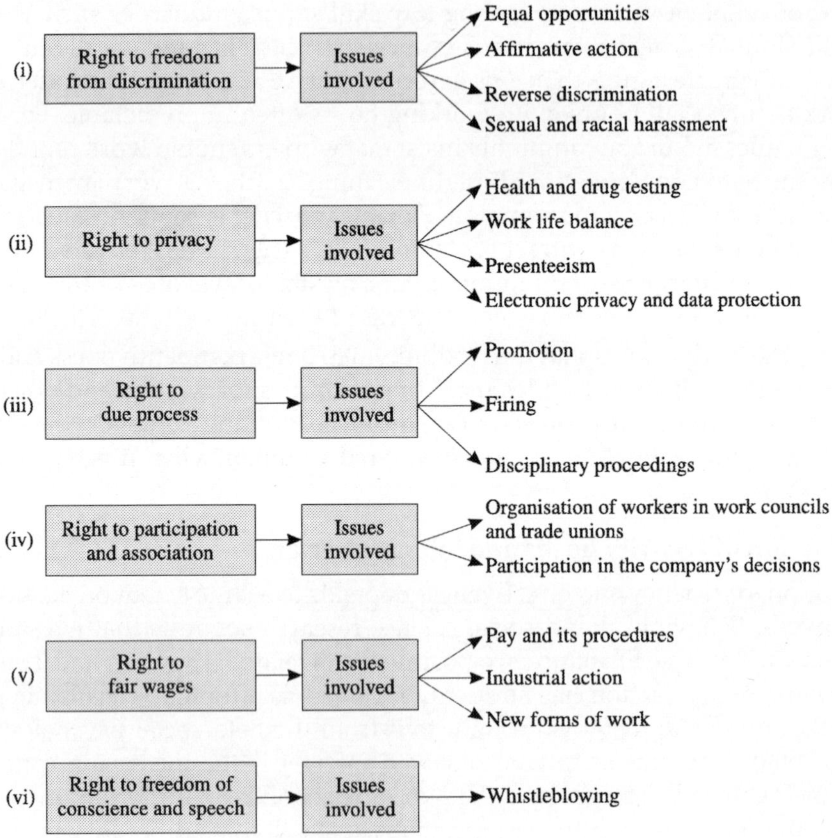

Employee duties and issues involved

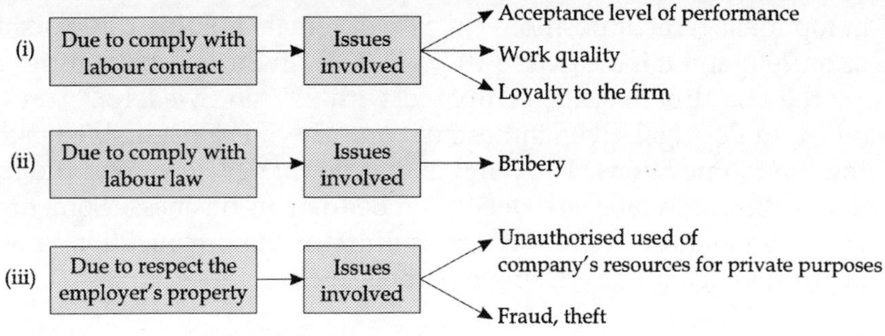

The organization should practise strong HR practices in order to protect the rights and duties of its employees. Major rights and duties as well as the issues involved are discussed in the follwing topics.

(a) Discrimination

Discrimination in the business and workplace occurs when employees receive preferences for some hidden reasons which may not be reasonable. It may not be related to quality and qualifications of the employees. The most common bases for discrimination in the workplace are race gender, age, religion, disability, job safety, and nationality. Job performance suffers due to discrimination. Employees marital status, physical appearance, sexual orientation or gender reassignment are different reasons for discrimination. There are inequalities between individuals. But the reasons for choosing one person over the other have to be based on qualification that in principle could be fulfilled by anyone. Making gender or race a criterion for a particular position would exclude certain people, and would clearly constitute an act of discrimination. However, there are certain factors and reasons which are debatable. Like, owner of an Indian supermarket in the UK was looking for a manager who can speak Hindi or Urdu fluently, who has reasonable knowledge of Indian culture, and had knowledge of current consumer preference in the British Asian products market. It may sound good but ethically wrong as it is specifically demanding for Indian managers. Racial discrimination is another important ethical issue. The European countries where the issues of immigration currently high on the social and political agenda are facing lot of ethical issues in HRM. In recent years a number of major multinationals have also found themselves in the ethical or legal spotlight regarding racial discrimination. In 2001, however, Coca Cola paid the world's largest settlement for racial discrimination a sum of nearly $ 200 m, for alleged problems in the home town of Atlanta. In an attempt to restore credibility and tackle the problem head on, the firm made the unusual step of directly linking director's pay to diversity targets.

Other discrimination issues are issues of disability and of age. Physical disability, sight disability or dyslexia are great issues. Employees across the world with health problems such as HIV/AIDS also face considerable discrimination and harassment from the fellow employees. In respect of age discrimination both old and young are the sufferers.

Another burning issue is gender discrimination. Women still, on an average receive lower wages for the same jobs as their male equivalents. Women are also still under-represented in top management positions. In case of female holding directorship was is only to 5.8% as on 2000 and it increased to 10.5% in 2005. In European countries only 29% women occupy the boardroom seats, compared with 23% in Sweden, 7% in Germany 2% in Italy and 0% in Portugal. Even in Eastern countries it is a negligible percentage of women holding the top positions. The point is that no matter how good the legislation is, many forms of discrimination are deeply embedded in business. Sometimes there is institutional discrimination where the very culture of the organization is prejudiced against certain groups, e.g., divorsed, single parents, etc.

(b) Sexual and racial harassment

A lot of discrimination in the promotion, pay, job opportunities, diversity like physical, verbal and emotional harassment female employees is faced in organizations all over the world.

Sexual harassment is unwanted conduct of sexual nature or other behaviours related to sex which affects dignity of women by men at workplace. The non-verbal conduct like gaping (i.e., continuously staring distasteful expressions, inappropriate facial expressions (blowing kisses, winking eyelets) inappropriate dresses (e.g., sexual remarks on T-shirts).

Some of the verbal conducts try to attract women by names like baby, sweety, honey sweetheart, etc., inappropriate sounds and comments, attempting to converse about sexual reference, fantasy sex life and spreading rumours and gossip which are irrelevant. Workplace harassment and sexual harassment are very common in film industry, airline industry, construction industry, garment industry and so on. The workplace harassment has become a matter of daily incidence in the European countries like Germany 93%, UK 73%. Netherlands 58%, Spain 40% Norway 41%. It is far more even in the Eastern countries like Japan, India, Arabian countries, etc. Many places sexual favours are requested for promotion or other rewards which stand as a unsolveable ethical issue. Mild forms of harassment are jokes or comments about a person's gender, race, sexual orientation, etc., that could lead to significant effects on working relations. According to the research studies, companies have introduced codes of practice and diversity programmes in order to tackle these issues and to define for the specific context of the company the limits of harassment.

To prevent sexual harassment at the workplace, following steps can be implemented:

- A strong code of conduct to be formulated in respect of discrimination.
- A separate redressal wing for female employee issues.
- Revision of existing HR policies favouring women employees and setting up of 'separate ethic department'.

Racial discrimination is another important issue in many parts of the world. In this respect there is no difference between rich and poor countries.

A suit against the Texaco involving racial bias resulted in a US $ 176 million settlement in 1996. The law suit alleging widespread racial bias at the Coca-Cola company was filed on

22nd April 1999 in a Federal court of Atlanta by four black employees. The suit contended there were massive disparities in salaries, promotions, performance evaluation and dismissals between black and white employees. Same black employees sought the help of the National Association for the Advancement of Coloured People (NAACP) before filing the suit the NAACP met the Coca-Cola officials but the company did not respond adequately. The suit alleged dramatic differences in pay at corporate headquarters. African-American hit a glass ceiling at Coca-Cola, with a few executives advancing to senior positions. Black employees also faced other barriers 'glass walls' that segregated the company into divisions where African-American leadership was acceptable, and divisions where it was not acceptable. Most black executives were channeled into non-revenue generating areas like human resources, external affairs and community relations. Other areas like marketing and finance were mostly reserved for whites. The class action included all salaried black employees who had worked at any time for Coca-Cola in the US since 22nd April 1995. Racial discrimination is increasingly becoming common in Australia, Canada, Africa, some parts of US and a few Asian countries.

(c) Freedom of conscience and freedom of speech in the workplace (whistle-blowing)

Freedom of speech with conscience may be referred to listening to the inner voice. This is generally referred as 'whistle-blowing'. Whistle blowing is an attempt by an employee or a former employee of an organization to disclose what he proclaims to be a wrongdoing in or by the organization.

According John R. Boatright, "Whistle-blowing is the voluntary release of non-public information as a moral protest by a member or former member of an organisation outside the normal channels of communication team, appropriate audience about illegal and or immoral conduct in the organization or conduct in the organization that is supposed in some significant way to the public interest".

Normally, the right to freedom of conscience and speech is a constitutional right guaranteed by the legislation and so individuals can usually count on the government to grant the right. However, within the boundaries there might occur situations where this right, especially the freedom of speech might face certain restrictions. This is the case with regard to speaking 'confidential' matters regarding the firm's R&D, marketing or accounting plans that might be of interest to competitions, shareholders or other stakeholders. In almost all cases this restriction of the freedom of speech is unproblematic, since most rational employees would find it in their own best interest to comply with company's policy and there is little reason to suggest that most corporate decisions need to be made public. When employee reveals such misdoing within the organization is referred to 'internal'. If he reports it to an outsider it is 'external'. If the matter concerns some harm done to the whistle-blower it is 'personal'. If it is at behest of others it is 'impersonal'. If it is done by a former employee it is alumni. It is understood that the entire field of whistle-blowing is one of the conflict of ethics. The conflict is between the right to privacy on the one hand and the ethics of trust on the other. Both possess values. Whistle-blowing is supported on the basis of absolute morality as:

(i) The whistle-blower has moral motive if not, he is being unethical.
(ii) The whistle-blower acts responsible for avoiding or exposing moral violations.
(iii) The whistle-blower has failed to get the moral error corrected, in spite of trying very hard.

There are however, some cases where these restrictions could be regarded as the restriction of employee's rights. For example, manager requesting for "creating an account which is not for the benefit of the organization, as an individual the employee will be in dilemma whether to accept or not. The problem here is that the third parties outside the organization cannot be asked to create anything which is not available. Otherwise it will lead to serious embarrassment, disruption and even possibly financial harm to the company. It may also be possible if employees decide to inform third parties about alleged malpractices within the firm, this external whistle-blowing may cause serious damage to the company. In such cases the following are the consequences:

(i) The whistle-blower perceives that the violation can lead to serious dangers.
(ii) The whistle-blower has enough evidence.
(iii) The whistle-blower's action has a reasonable chance of success.
(iv) Organisations will be in trouble if whistle-blowers are not controlled or an appropriate remedy is found.
(v) It reduces the cost of monitoring implementation of law.

The main problem for employees with whistle-blowing is the fact that it involves a considerable risk for them. As they violate confidentiality, which would normally be part of their duty towards the firm, they put their job and their economic security at risk. The risk can be high as being ethical and even if the allegations are right, the individual workers might find themselves in a critical situation and the only way is to escape is through legal protection.

The following are the usual subjects for the whistle-blowing:

(i) Industrial dumping of pollutants.
(ii) Adulteration
(iii) Defective vehicles marketed to unsuspecting customers.
(iv) Waste of government funds by the private contractors.
(v) Discrimination by age, race and sex.
(vi) Deceptive advertising.
(vii) Companies and campaign contribution.
(viii) Misusing of government power for private gain.
(ix) Corruption and bribery.
(x) Suppression of occupational diseases.
(xi) Monopolist price-rigging.

(xii) Proxy pricing.

(xiii) Misusing of pension funds.

(xiv) Misusing of stakeholder's fund.

Whistle-blowing as a concept is examined by absolute moral standards and by its consequences. Development of public institutions and laws to avoid the need for whistle-blowing is considered important. Currently, academicans are in support of whistle-blowing as socially desirable and are less concerned with developing public institutions and laws. These could reduce the need for whistle-blowing. Whistle-blowing in defence establishments is much more of an ethical dilemma.

(iv) Career development and providing opportunities for sustainable employment

Innovation and skill development are the basic needs for the present trend. Organisations should emphasise on career growth and development. The employees are to be given ample opportunities for exhibiting their talent and skills. Providing opportunities for sustainable employment is another important factor for the organization to grow effectively. Many times protection towards wages and good conditions for workers may have to be provided to encourage sustainable economic development and maintain employment. The organizations should respect the employees as human beings for conformity in contributions. There is a need to take care of social dimensional sustainability by focusing on long-term effects like lifestyle, health and well-being. The workplaces should create opportunity to establish social relationships and support with their families, neighbours and friends. To carry on this the organizations should address the following problems both in theory and practice:

- Re-humanised workplaces
- Wider employment.
- Work life balance.

(a) Re-humanised workplaces: The impact of technology, rationalized work processes and the division of labour means that many employees, simply repeat the same monotonous and stupefying actions over and over again, bringing, little real meaning, satisfaction or involvement in their work. Call centre jobs is series of meaningless 'Mcjobs' subject to intense management control and with little chance of real engagement or job satisfaction. Even the high level employees engaged in computer and technology related work are busy tirelessly rather than enjoying active, creative and meaningful work. No doubt the rational ways of organizing work can, and have brought the organization tremendous efficiency and material wealth but they have also created the prospect of impatience, monetary, dehumanized behaviour and deskilled workplace. The impact on the workplace is least contingent on variety of factors including work organization, managerial motivation and employee involvement.

There are numerous attempts over the years to re-humanise the workplace. Employees' empowerment, job enlargement like giving employees a wider range of tasks to do, and job enrichment like providing employees a larger scope for deciding how to organize their work may create re-humanised activities. Providing the opportunities for the group activities, partly autonomous, have been succeeded in team based working groups. The organization should give prominence to the employees. The organizations, with strong HR policies with 'humanised' approach proved best result.

(b) **Wider employment:** Modern employment patterns tend to create a line between those who have the highly skilled jobs which require long terms of work for high returns and those who are reduced to unemployment or at best a succession of low-skilled, poorly paid, temporary jobs. In recent years there have been a number of interesting efforts to tackle this problem of creating a society of the haves and the have-nots. One of the recent attempts of the French government is the introduction of "a 35-hour week". This made the same number employees with the same level of output. This ideas of reducing working hours is successful during recessions and many organizations attempted the same.

Another example at the corporate level is from Germany. In order to maintain a competitive cost structure, 'Volkswagen' a car manufacturing company was recently faced with the choice of either laying off large number of workers in its northern German operation or reducing working time and pay for existing employees. After long negotiations the 5000 × 5000 model was set up in early 2000. This allowed Volkswagen to keep 5000 workers with a reduced working time and fixed pay of 'DM 5000'. All parties involved saw that it would be more economical and socially substainable to accept this model rather than exposing an entire region to massive employment and economic recession. (Schmidt and Williams, 2002).

(c) **Work-life balance:** Work-life balance is a current topic which is focused, debated and studied in HR practices. The increasing threat of unemployment for some has been matched with almost exactly the opposite problem for others, namely the increasing incursion of working hours into social life. There has been growing pressure for long hours including travelling time at the workplace. Apart from some service oriented jobs like doctors or other professionals, it has been evidenced that even in other jobs the practice of long working hours is increasing. A healthy balance between work and private life or in other words, 'work-life balance' is difficult to maintain. Many employees including executives are not able to strike balance between work and life. The employees, especially women face problem with their children, couples face the delicate task of maintaining a long distance or weekend relationship and ultimately they land up by saying marriage is "not working" and break their relationship. Many of the IT employees along with others express that life is completely absorbed by work without any time or energy left to maintain or build up meaningful social relationships (Simpson 1998; Collier 2001). This is leading to a significant challenge for long-term economic and social sustainability. This is a great problem to resolve as it goes with individual perspective and every individual is unique in the organization. Any demands for less involvement in the workplace may ultimately be counterproductive to one's career aspirations and job security. Some jobs with specialty and high level concentration cannot be easily reduced or shared.

The study also revealed that employees with poor work-life balance might not be as effective in the long run, and such working patterns should not be encouraged. There are certain schemes that allow people in highly demanding jobs to take a period of time off to concentrate all those issues that have been falling by the wayside and thereby restore greater balance. Another important solution to the work-life balance is home-based teleworking. But this may lead to poor working conditions. Whereas tele-working may bring social benefits for the employee and economic benefits for the companies. Adding to this there is also ecological advantages, which may create road congestion and air pollution while commuting to the workplaces. Tele-workers are likely to use for fewer resources by staying at home and communicating remotely.

In respect of career opportunities an organization need to hire the right people at the right place at the right time and continue to develop. It needs them to introduce on going career development programmes or skill oriented training programmes. An investment in upgrading the workforce is one of the best investments a company can make when looking at the long-term growth. Hiring the people that are comfortable with the culture of the organization meaning that their values, principles, ethics and goals both subjective and objective, clearly match those of the company and then training as necessary will go a long way towards ensuring employee loyalty and retention. Organisations should also provide thorough orientation to help employees avoid feeling overwhelmed. Employees also like exciting and challenging work along with the recognition for their work. This can be used as career opportunities in order to encourage talented employees.

(d) **Job Stress:** Job stress is another important ethical factor in the organizations. The employees are forced to undergo both directly or indirectly, intentionally or otherwise the stress on their working, hitting their morale. According to the National Institute for Occupation Safety and Health, job stress can be defined as "the harmful physical and emotional response that occurs when the requirements of the job do not match the capabilities, resources or needs of the worker.

At present, job stress is often linked or equated with challenges. Challenges can be taken as both a positive or negative feeling of the employees. The positive side is like it motivates and energises psychologically and physically to learn new skills and help to master the new task which may lead to job satisfaction. A challenge is also one of the tools in the work environment to increase productivity. It may be taken as brighter side as 'a little bit of stress is good for you' in the other sense it is referred as "a little challenge is good for you".

Stress, on the other hand has negative side, when the job demand is not met, relaxation may turn to exhaustion, sense of satisfaction turns to tension. The employees are over taxed both psychologically and physically which leads to illness, injury, job failure, non-performance, frustration, disappointment and the result—low productivity.

A lot of research is going on in relation to HRM for the benefit of employees and organizational effectiveness. Hans Selye was one of the founding fathers of stress research. His view in 1956 was that "stress is not necessarily something bad – it all depends as how you take it. The stress of exhilarating, creative successful work is beneficial, while the failure, humiliation or infection is detrimental". Selye believed that the biochemical effects of stress would be experienced irrespective of whether the situation is positive or negative.

However, the following are the main causes for job stress:

- Infrequent rest breaks.
- Long working hours and demanding work shifts.
- Monotonous work and less scope for skill, creativity and mental exercises.
- Very poor management styles like lack of workers' participation in decision making. Poor communication and lack of family-friendly policies.
- Interpersonal relationships – poor social environment, lack of support or help from co-workers and supervisors.
- Work roles – conflicting or uncertain job expectations, too much responsibility, too many "hats to wear".
- Career concerns – job insecurity, lack of growth opportunity, rapid changes for which workers are unprepared.
- Environmental conditions – unpleasant physical conditions and work conditions.

It is a great ethical and moral responsibility of HRM to solve stress and stress related issues. A strong HRM should introduce a "stress management" as a separate wing in the HR department by stressing on two major divisions like:

(1) To improve worker's ability and capability to cope up any sort of situation. A good stress management training and techniques to be practised through "employee assistance programme".

(2) Organisational change by the company upon identifying stressful aspect or work and designing strategies and improving working conditions to reduce or eliminate the identified stressors. A good stress management and strong techniques will serve as a great tool for good governance towards business as well as health of the employees.

The following are the advantages of business management both towards business and employees' perspective.

Stress Management

Business Advantages	*Employees' Health Advantages*
Less absenteeism	Decreased stress related symptoms.
Reduced illness or accidents.	Improvement in mind resting and sleep.
Improvement in job performance.	Reduction in anxiety
Less stressful, more efficient workplace	Decreasing in using medications
Sound, positive and healthy working atmosphere.	Self-awareness and self-strengthening.
Improvement in employee attitude. Increase in stamina through relaxation techniques both mental and physical.	Self-balancing and improvement in self-esteem.
Increase in organisational efficiency.	

Moral relationship between organization and employees

The core of learning organisation's work is based on five learning disciplines. They include:

Personal mastery: Individuals learn to expand their own personal capacity to create results that they most desire. Employees also create an organizational environment that encourages all fellow employees to develop themselves towards the goal and purpose that they desire.

Mental model: This involves each individual reflecting upon, continually clarifying and improving his internal perspective towards the world, and seeing how they shape personal actions and decisions.

Shared vision: This involves individuals building a sense of commitment within particular work groups, developing showed images of common and desirable futures, and the principles and guiding practices to support the journey to such future.

Team learnings: Team larning involves relevant thinking skills that enable groups of people to develop intelligence and an ability that is greater than the sum of individual member talents.

Systems thinking: This involves a way of thinking about and a language for describing and understanding forces and interrelationships that shape the behaviour of systems. This discipline helps managers and employees alike to see how to change systems more effectively, and to act more in tune with the larger processes of the natural and economic world.

Team performance to attain the best

The following are researches based on employees' perspective towards leadership issue for best HR practices of team development process:

- Set the team's targets.
- Describe performance styles of team within the targets.
- Define information collection method.

- Fix the team leadership issue.
- Influence individual and team motivators.
- Prepare base for success through skills, techniques and team work.
- Manage equipment and technology procurement
- Manage confusion and tension.
- Invest a team maturity matrix and plot team growth.
- Learn how to hold team meetings.
- Examine external boundaries and how the team interacts with other teams.
- Monitor and measure team performance.

HUMAN-CENTRIC MODEL

Michael Spencer has rightly put it as "I've never known anybody who has lost because of consistent ethical practices" and it is true. The companies are expected to uphold individual and business values. This is possible only when the organization system has been supported and supplemented with human system. It can also, take further step that the organization, should be human centric. The following diagram clears the picture as human centric agent

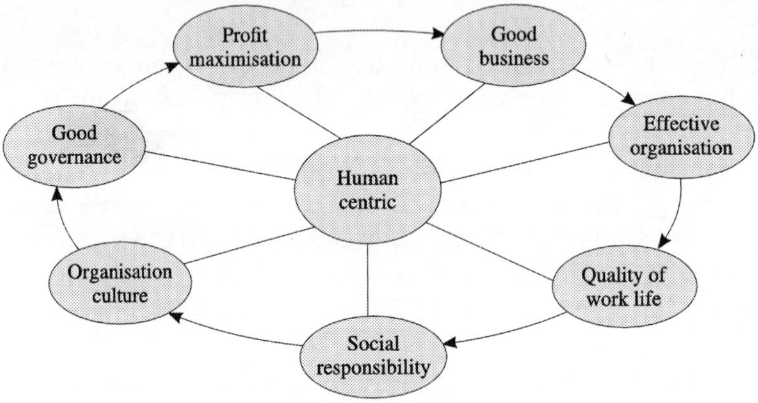

The model is based on the following principles:

- To practise the core value of business for innovative performance, total quality management, integrity, customer satisfaction and social well-being.
- To develop social responsibility and culture towards stakeholders.
- To be transparent and truthful to all the business activities.
- To recognize the concept of corporate responsibility in the widest sense with obligations to the community as well as customers and employees.
- To develop corporate mission, long-term vision, credo, for business considering customers, government and human relations, shareholders and society.

- To optimize the core values and good citizenship in organization.
- To adopt sound ethical business and marketing practices.
- To create organizational culture and good governance.
- To adopt sound ethical business and HR practices.

The above core principles can be successful when the companies or organizations practise HR and its development with "human-centric" model.

Consistent ethical practices for the future : Mission to the business world

Future rests with people. People with knowledge and competence hold the power to constantly shape the future. It has been realised that the people alone can build the business world through their creation, value, knowledge, skill and innovations. But many business/service sectors still lag behind in this context. They should understand survival will be achieved through excellence and this is possible through people alone. Excellence should be built through mutual collaboration, joint venture and connective leadership. Such that, understanding among the employees and close relation with management develope. This will also reduce the distance between company and the customers and result in opening new ventures and expand business.

In order to achieve global leadership the business organization should have strong HR policies. The policy should give empowerment to the employees. The management of business should adopt a change where people or employees are placed in one of the points of the organization as shown below.

Management model for transformation of change

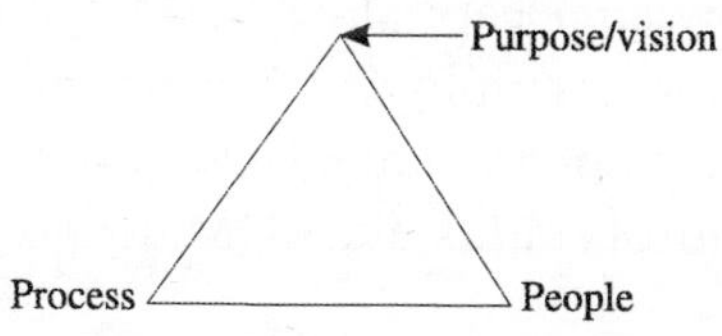

Future architect of organizations is based on vision and vision is the art of seeing things which are invisible. The business architect will evolve around the single most important resource, that is, its 'people'.

Business architect for the future – A macro perspective

The organization is ultimately based on key business drivers to connect to the customers. Key business drivers are linked with knowledge, intelligence, commitment and values and is based on people in the society. The society provides best people to the organization in the form of employees. The quest for achieving excellence through people for the future continues. To select, train, mould and create organisational values and ethics to practise the HR plays a paramount important role in the organization. Hence, the future HR must be "building relationship enterprise".

Relationship model

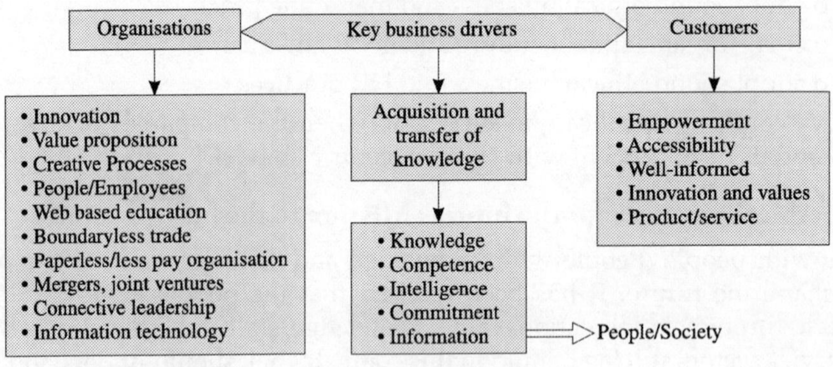

Suggestions for Ethical Practices in HR Management

- Best human resource planning.
- Fair and just selection and staffing.
- Quality training and development.
- Establishment HR research and development.
- Hand in hand employees and employers relationship to develop the organizational goals and objectives.
- National initiative to develop the workforce.
- Setting up of performance management system.
- Acceptable compensation and benefit.
- Enhancement of knowledge capital.
- Fair and just evaluation of employees' performance.
- Conduct return on investment analysis on important training initiatives.
- Introduce quality control stands like TQM, ISO or Six Sigma to identify needs and ensure quality.
- Encourage union/labour relation.
- Create ample opportunity for career development.
- Ensure individual performance improvement which will lead to organizational performance improvement.
- Establish talent and knowledge management.
- Encourage higher education and standard training programme.
- Setting up of knowledge based compensation management.
- Scope for 360° performance appraisal/360° feedback.
- Encourage team activities incentive/bonuses along with the individual incentives.
- Establishment of quality management system.
- Provision for coaching and maintaining along with the performance appraisal.
- Gradual application of global best policy of HR.
- Employment to deserving and loyal staff in decision making.

Exhibit

India is a place for greater contribution in management and human relation techniques through epics and upanishads. The following is an extract from such source and presented a paper at the International conference related to spirituality and leadership.

An Evaluation of Workplace Misbehaviour: Revisit to Indian Roots for Global Solutions

Misbehaviour in workplace has assumed high proportions in recent years due to a variety of factors. Globalization and the resultant stress levels and cultural complexities have significantly contributed to this malaise. Sexual harassment, growing levels of ambitions, fall in leadership qualities and lack of personal morals are the manifestations arising out of the decadence of organizational values. However, the work culture is ultimately determined by the value systems obtained in a country. This, in turn, has close affinity to the national ethos and can be gainfully researched from the traditional texts which have shaped the societal values. The relevance of studying literature for understanding managerial traits has been emphasized by Badaracco, J.L. (2006) amongst others.

This is to evaluate and to study the contemporary phenomenon of misbehaviour in workplace from the work culture and value systems portrayed in three ancient works of India namely:

- *The Ramayana* of Valmiki
- *The Arthasastra* of Kautilya
- *The Nitisatakam* of Bhartrahari

and examines their relevance to contemporary organizational situations. The reason for the choice of the above works is the long chronological span of about 4000 years which provides a wide time spectrum, when significant economic, political and cultural changes have taken place. Another factor is their widely divergent nature — a dramatic presentation of a story (*Ramayana*, circa 3500 B.C.), a normative approach to administration (*Arthasastra*, circa 320 B.C. and a moral high tone of a philosopher-king (*Nitisatakam* , circa 6th century A.D.), which adds depth to the study. Thus, this paper presents a temporal analysis of misbehaviour in workplace and tries to draw solutions.

Taxonomy of Indian Texts on Workpalace mis behaviour

Text	*Ramayana*	*Arthasastra*	*Nitisatakam*
Author	Valmiki	Kautilya	Bhartruhari
Period*	3500 B.C.	320 B.C.	540 A.D.
Nature	Epic	Political science	Moral science
Style**	Kaanta samhita	Prabhu samhita	Mitra samhita
Approach	Through characters	Ruler's role	Preaching

The dates are debatable **Style

- Kaanta = approach of a sweetheart
- Prabhu = approach of a master
- Mitra = approach of a friend

Definition

There is no uniform definition of the term workplace misbehaviour. At least six different terms are used such as organizational misbehaviour, workplace deviance, antisocial behaviour, workplace aggression, organization-motivated aggression and organizational retaliation behaviour (Robinson & Greenberg, 1998). Certain virtues such as courage, honesty, fairness, and empathy are considered as necessary traits for ethical behaviour (Covey, 1989). Their absence leads to workplace misbehaviour. This paper works on the general concept that workplace misbehaviour is any behaviour by a member or members of an organization that violates accepted norms of organization and/or society.

Causes of Workplace Misbehaviour

Such misbehaviour may be related to factors inside the workplace, as well as personal attributes and individual circumstances outside the workplace, such as family and relationship problems. Some of the main causes are:

- Training and career development. A failure to provide employees with opportunities for career development, and adequate training to enhance their employability.
- The conduct of the supervisors and the way the relationships are nurtured.
- Behavioural patterns arising out of transactional analysis and the basic 'mental models'.
- Work intensification, long hours, and tight deadlines.
- Poorly defined and designed work roles and tasks.
- Irregular / unpredictable work schedules,
- Poor work environment.
- An inadequate work-life balance.
- Unhealthy interpersonal relationships.
- Sexual and emotional harassments.

The 6-Step Analysis

The next part of the paper is devoted to an analysis of the Indian texts on this area under six broad heads namely:

1. Problem identification
2. Issues in solving workpalce misbehavious
3. Approaches
4. Processes
5. Roadblocks
6. Getting results

Problem Identification

(a) Identifying Work place Misbehaviour

WM may not be manifest in its early days, and a proactive management would do well to diagnose it early. **Kautilya** describes three ways by which a manager can ascertain what is happening around, namely:

(a) direct perception - that is what is seen by him directly;
(b) unperceived - that which is communicated by others; and
(c) Inferred - where he forms an opinion.

Professional managements use all of them together. Enhancing productivity requires problem identification through formal and informal sources, and diffuse crisis situations in advance.

Detailed Complexity and Dynamic Complexity

This is an aspect of management, which Peter Senge introduced. Dynamic complexity relates to situations where cause and effect are subtle, and its effects in the long run are not clear. Major things like profit-mix, quality design, capacity, etc., are related to dynamic complexity. But most of our tools and planning are directed at detailed complexity which deals with relatively more routine issues.

Identifying such differences can diffuse organizational disputes, and lead to greater efficiency. Such examples of leadership focused on dynamic complexity can be seen in a number of cases in the *Ramayana*. While all the others (Kausalya, Lakshmana, Dasaratha and the entire population of Ayodhya) look at the detailed complexity, as Rama has to go on exile, only he could perceive the dynamic complexity of the situation, and taking a long-term view, and the subtle nuances of dharma, he decides to leave for the forest. Long-term vision is often essential in solving workplace misbehaviour issues, where a lesser manager may be tempted to assess the detailed complexity alone and resort to short-term measures to buy peace.

Issues in Solving Workplace Misbehaviour

(a) Fickleness of Mind

Workplace misbehaviour is mainly related to attitudes, and often people act and react irrationally. The major problem confronting the executives, in their day-to-day affairs is the difficulty in carrying the team of executives together to achieve the desired ends. The problem is compounded by the unpredictability of the human nature which distorts the best strategies of the firm from reaching fruition. This attitude is aptly illustrated by Dasaratha who explains the fragile nature of mind. First, he suspects his own mind, and suggests that while his **citta** does not get perverted presumably as a result of persuasions by others, nevertheless adds that the human mind is fickle.

Calaa hi praaninaam mati-h

Subsequent events endorse his misgiving. The other side of it is the mind of the steadfast. **Nitisatakam** endorses the path of the latter. Come what may, the dheera purusha never strays from the narrow path. Supporting this broad concept, Shiv Khera (1998) attributes 85% of the success to attitudes, and only the remaining 15% to other qualities like knowledge of facts, figures, etc.

(b) Gender Issues

Workplace misbehaviour is often traced to gender related problems. Indian culture however has been largely immune to this and reverence to women is not new to our ancient thinking machine. *Manusmriuti* says 'gods rejoice where women are worshipped, and every work turns fruitless where they are not worshipped'. We have a list of women rishis like Gargi, Maitreyi, etc., who were venerated by the intellectuals. Kautilya provides for a reasonable livelihood for women who had none to support them. The spinning of yarn is left entirely to the domain of widows, crippled women, maidens and women who have left their homes. Besides, the payment of wages, which is to be fixed as per the quality of yarn produced, the women must be favoured with oil and myrobalan unguents and on festive days they should be honoured with gifts. Women – widows, crippled women, maidens and those living separately — who do not want to leave their homes either due to societal norms, security reasons or physical inabilities, should be given work by sending the female slaves to their places of residence. This is obviously a reflection of the society that existed during his period, which had great consideration for women in the workplace.

(c) Lack of Empathy

Many conflicts owe their origin to the absence of mutual trust and bonhomie. Valmiki highlights it effectively. Finding all his worthy words of counsel falling into deaf ears, and unable to bear the rude abuses of Ravana, Vibhishana, chooses to part company with him and with profound sorrow utters the following words:

"It is very easy to find people uttering pleasing words; but it is difficult to get somebody providing unpalatable, yet conducive words of advice. It is also difficult to find people who listen to such wholesome advice."

The above statement forcefully underscores the need for a personal chemistry in the face-to-face transactions of enterprises during workplace misbehaviour issues, as it ensures a sense of participation and pride and produces better results and mutual understanding. This process distinguishes managers and leaders for managers do things right, whereas leaders do the right thing (Bennis, W. and Nanus, B. 1985).

APPROACHES

(a) Bring them Together

Conflicts arising out of workplace misbehaviour are best addressed by meeting and discussing with all concerned parties. Kautilya supports the concept of meeting and prescribes a highly modern agenda for deliberations consisting of five elements namely, (1) the means of starting the process; (2) the excellence of men and materials; (3) proper selection of the place and time; (4) provision against failure and (5) achieving the target. This functional agenda embraces all the aspects of workplace misbehaviour debottlenecking, and is holistic in its coverage. Of particular interest to a modern executive is making provision for failures, which is considered an exclusively modern concept. The conceptualization of these techniques by Kautilya 2000 years ago, being viable in the modern context, is stunning.

(b) Fine Art of Mockery

Workplace misbehaviour may sometimes be addressed by subtle nuances. Pointing out some weaknesses (without malice) can contribute to solving intricate issues, particularly if the person administering the dose has a clean reputation. Rama decides to leave on exile, and advises Sita to stay back and take care of his parents. Her arguments to follow him fail to work. 'Finally, Sita scores over him by adopting sheer mockery. Says she, 'My father has got a female in a male's guise when he selected you as the son-in-law.' by these strong words, Rama yields.

(Rama Jaamaataram praapya striyam purusha vigraham)

In grievance redressal processes a cautious application of this subterfuge comes in handy. But subtlety is a double edged sword. Argyris (1990) explains how we contribute to the conflict by our own thinking by making sweeping generalisations. These subtle patterns of reasoning which cause our behavioural patterns, lead us to further trouble.

(c) Handling Egos

Dealing with members in a workplace misbehaviour issue, with preconceived ideas poses a serious problem. Ego-orientation gives rise to aggressive behaviour coupled with narrow self-serving interests. This type of aggressive behaviour appears to be driven by ego threat (Fast, NJ.; Chen, S. 2009) rather than personality traits. Bhartrahari advocates a panacea for this type of people (who are obsessed with their little knowledge) a consisting of association with scholars, which can melt their bloated egos. He also brings out the transformation that knowledge causes in the recipient. Limited and superficial knowledge creates vanity and pride. But the learning process in the scholarly ambience quickly melts the arrogance and the conceit disappears to be replaced by holistic knowledge. A philosophical expression of this phenomenon in the modern-day context makes interesting reading.

"Whether an organization, a group, or person, each entity needs at least a preliminary answer to the question "Who are we ?" or "Who am I ?" in order to interact effectively with other entities".

The ego-free mind alone can contemplate on the above lines.

PROCESSES

(a) Conduct of meetings

Kautilya discusses the manner of conducting meetings, providing for discussions individually as well as jointly. Thus, he could ascertain their views on various issues and the reasons for the divergent opinions, if necessary in private. He also cautions against counselling those who could harm or sabotage it and advises against prolonged deliberations. Provision for discussion by e-mail with those not physically present is made, even when such facilities were not so very sophisticated. The view of the majority shall be considered in all urgent matters (when consensus is not possible) and what is essential for the success of the work shall be undertaken.

(b) Constitution of Workplace Misbehaviour Teams

Regarding the selection of the members for such teams, Kautilya quotes the opinions of other experts. Visalaksa is of the opinion that he should consult a number of people mature in intellect and act according to their views. (This is broadly the practice in the government departments.) Pisuna is of the relatively modern opinion that councilors, when asked about remote undertakings, might give their opinion with indifference. Winston Fletcher quoting a HBR study reveals that an executive spends in committees every week three to hours on average. It consists of 8 members. Each member wishes that at least 3 of the rest 7 were not present. Besides about a full day is spent on informal conferences and consultations. This view presents a flip side of the attitude and team spirit of the members. Kautilya himself prefers a strength of three to four members.

ROADBLOCKS

(a) Mental Models

The way people react to situations and individuals is defined under this new concept called 'mental models'. Peter M. Senge calls this "deeply held internal images of how the world works, images that limit us to familiar ways of thinking and acting. Two people with different mental models can observe the same event and describe it differently, because they've looked at different details".

Workplace misbehaviour is mostly behavioural and cannot be solved by supercilious approach. Ravana's mental model is a case in point. Bossism marks many an act of Ravana. His approach to Maricha to take the deer's form to ensnare Rama away is a typical example. Ignoring the advice tendered by Maricha, he says with arrogance that one should speak to an emperor in words that are pleasing and in soft accent; and a king does not prefer even a wholesome counsel, when uttered in an insulting manner. He also makes it abundantly plain to him that he is not seeking his opinion on the merits and demerits of his argument or even what is advisable for him.

"Gunadoshau na pruchami kshemam caatmani raakshasa" but orders him to obey his command. Even more fatal for him was the way he deals with Vibhishana. He abuses the latter in no uncertain terms. Using strong words, Ravana says that even as wealth exists in cows, capriciousness in women, and tapas in Brahmins, peril exists in one's own kith and kin. Thus, Ravana accuses his well-meaning brother, of being jealous of the power and the adulation that he gets from the world.

The same issues are viewed differently by Ravana and Maricha in the first case and Ravana and Vibhishana in the second case, thus highlighting the role played by the mental models of the concerned individuals.

(b) Scanty Knowledge

Rastogi emphasizes the need for companies to foster knowledge and learning in a continuing manner. This tenet is advocated in a number of Sanskrit texts. **Bhartrahari** devotes considerable space to this and emphasizes knowledge of a holistic nature in his work **Nitisatakam**. Explaining the dangers of scanty knowledge, he laments:

"An ignorant person can be pleased (satisfied) easily; a very learned man can be pleased still more easily. But even Brahma (the creator) cannot please a man who is vainly proud of a smattering of knowledge."

Bhartrahari's concern is understandable as persons with a little knowledge tend to be obstinate. This is the attitude of Svetaketu in **Chandogya Upanisad** as he returns from his studies. The author of Nitisatakam also is concerned about people who do not follow the path of learning and emphasizes a life-long regimentation.

(c) Sexual Misbehaviour in Workplace

In these days where molestation of women in offices and factories has become familiar news and seems to be indulged in with immunity by men holding the highest offices, it is redeeming to note that Kautilya about 24 centuries back had provided specific measures for their protection. The women, who want to collect payments for the work done at home, may bring their products to the superintendent by early dawn. A lamp may be kept only for inspecting the quality of yarn brought in by them. If the superintendent of yarn looks at the face of the women or tries to indulge in conversation (obviously with ulterior motives) a fine is imposed. Higher penalties are prescribed for delaying the payment of wages and also for payment of wages for work not done — in order to win their favour. This is a laudable measure and is in line with modern legislation providing various security measures for the female employees in India and elsewhere. (It is a different matter whether these provisions are strictly adhered to or not.)

GETTING RESULTS

(a) Value-based Approach

A proper approach to workplace misbehaviour can bring positive results. Interests not only divide, but they also bring people together and produce homogeneous groups. This conflict is forcefully explained in Nitisatakam. It understands the divisive nature, but provides the ideal mix for persons with a noble bent of mind. The contrasts can be explained with a few examples:

- silence amidst valour
- restraint amidst knowledge
- humility for the learned
- forgiveness for one enjoying power.

The above are some of the attributes, which the author elaborates. A management focused on values shall hold aloft the three beacon lights as enumerated by Kant, namely, reason, feeling and deeds. Quoting Richard Morrill, Swami Tyagananda explains:

"To paraphrase and expand on Kant: Values without reason would be blind, without feeling would be impotent, and without deeds would be empty".

Their relevance lies in establishing a base for a society/organization to function with a set of codes in contexts where the ethics come under trial.

(b) Charismatic Leadership

Workplace misbehaviour is universal and is also inevitable (Blonder M.D. 2006). A powerful leader with charisma can exert a positive influence over the workforce, and motivate them for dynamic action. This can stop negative behaviour. The entire population of Ayodhya was afflicted by Rama's departure to the forest. They joined Bharata en masse on his mission to bring back Rama. This charisma is a characteristic of leadership qualities. The masses had not even experienced the potential royal qualities of Rama. But this ability to communicate to a large number of people is a trait seen in great many leaders of the day. This comes out even more clearly in the Kishkinda Kand. The subjects of Sugriva had not even the limited contacts that the inhabitants of Ayodhya had vis-a-vis Rama. But the enthusiasm with which they start for searching Sita is astounding. "Aham eko hanishyami praptham Ravanam ahave".

(c) Perseverance

Getting results in an exercise of this nature is not always easy. Some managements do not make a conscious effort at all, and stick to fire-fighting operations. Others start with vigour but half way down the line, give up the efforts. The nobler ones persist irrespective of all problems. **Nitisatakam** brands them respectively as Neecha (low calibre); Madhyama (medium); and Uttama (high calibre) managements; thus giving a 3-point matrix for assessing endeavours of entities in resolving workplace misbehaviour.

The Indian texts discussed in the paper not only indicate the prevalence of workplace misbehaviour in the ancient days but more importantly, provide the answers as well. In a nonglobalized economy, the complications are obviously less, but human nature being same across the chronological time span, it is wise to draw from the wisdom of the past. The study is limited to three works only, and future research may identify more such texts right from the Vedic days. Revisiting the cultural roots always throws light, and India, we can proudly say, is well equipped in this regard. The blend of dharma and karma has universal relevance and across-the-board sustainability. This is the outcome of this modest study.

Source: A.V. Rajagopalan, Shriram Venkataraman "Integrating Spirituality and Organisational Leadership (2011)

Case Study 1

Ethical Issue on HRM

(1) Operations of Nike in South East Asia (A leading sports company)

Nike is a leader in the sports shoe industry. The company had a sales of US $9.5 billion in 1998 with a 40% share of the American Sneaker market. The company also became a lightening rod for worldwide protests over alleged "Sweat Shop" conditions in factories across South east Asia. Phil Knight the founder of Nike and also CEO admits that "Nike product has become synonymous with stave wages forced overtime and arbitrary abuse". In less developed countries (LDCs), company is paying wages and imposes working conditions that are shockingly low by US standards and yet they operate well above the standards of local firms. Nike is a well known company, whose "Swoosh" logo is a symbol for the "Just Do It" spirit, come to be associated strangely with deplorable labour practices.

Phil Knight, an able administrator of the company, had a phenomenal success on account of his visionary strategy, developed from his student days visions at the Stanford Business School. His strategy at Nike involves outsourcing all manufacturing to contractors in low wage countries and pouring the company's resources into high profile marketing. One of the vice presidents expressed 'we do not know the first thing about manufacturing. We are basically good marketers and designers'. The central effort to Nike's marketing effort is placing the Nike "Swoosh" on the uniforms of collegiate and professional athletes. Nike enlisted such superstars like Michael Jordan (great basketball player) and Tiger Woods.

Nike started the operations in 1964, contracted with manufacturers in Japan when the wages were low in Japan. Later on they transferred their operations to Korea and Taiwan in view of the wage rise in Japan. By 1982, 80% of the Nike shoes were supplied from Korea and Taiwan. Again, the shift was to South East Asia as the wage raise was found in Korea and Taiwan. By 1990, Nike production was based in Indonesia, Vietnam and China. The Indonesian wages were low. Their women used to work at 15 cents an hour. Some of the experienced women who were working at Korean owned plants got a maximum of $2 for a 11 hour day. The Indonesian minimum wage was raised in 1991 from $1.06 for a 7 hour day to $1.24 (the government estimated $1.22 as necessary wage for "minimum physical needs"). The Korean managers acted brutal on Indonesian women. Koreans betrayed those women for failing to meet quotas and withheld pay to enforce discipline. Indonesian labour laws, lax to begin with, were flouted with impunity by contractors, since the government was eager to attract foreign investment for which workers suffered much. They toiled in crowded, poorly ventilated factories. Surrounded by machinery and toxic chemicals. Union activities in Indonesia to fight out justice was not in vogue and any labour strikes found were firmly suppressed by the army. The labour was exploited to the maximum.

When Nike was under growing criticism, it denied any responsibility for the practices of its contractors. Nike argued that it merely buys shoes from independent companies situated in those countries. Further, the workers are not employees of Nike and the salaries what they are getting is above the legal minimum and the prevailing market rate. Commenting on the labour unrest and poor working conditions in some factories supplying Nike, the GM of Nike incharge of Indonesia said that he did not know the causes and added I don't know that I need to know. GM defended his company by arguing "Yes, there are low wages. But we have come in here and given jobs to thousands of people who would not be working otherwise". He might have added that the company had also given additional employment to Michael Jordan whose reported $2 million fee in 1992 was larger than the payroll that year for all Nike production in Indonesia.

Q. Put forth your arguments of ethicality in favour of the following:

(i) Is company Nike going in the proper way, to offload manufacturing operations to countries where wages are low, e.g., Indonesia?

(ii) Why Nike received worldwide protests over alleged 'sweat shops conditions' in factories across South Asia?

(iii) Do you appreciate Nike's marketing efforts? Comment.

(iv) What are your feelings if one single person like Michael Jordan gets US $2 million whereas the wages of thousands of people in Indonesia put together will get less than that amount in 1992 ?

(v) Do you appreciate the arguments of GM, Nike incharge of Indonesia.

(2) Men in Distress

Women have made rapid strides in education and workforce participation, their economic and social indicators show considerable improvement over time. This narrowing of the gender, gap could lead to greater violence against women. This can be at least in the short run. We should therefore control the consequences of gender empowerment, chiefly dysfunctional families and relationships. The issue of how men can be helped to change their existing mindsets so that women's progress does not come at a heavy cost deserves more attention.

Women as workforce are patronized for their increasing skill levels, their willingness to take on jobs for less money, their commitment and sense of responsibility to certain kinds of work.

The feminist movement and the emergence of role models aided to the assertion of professional middle and upper middle class women, who made strong careers while managing their homes adorably. These successful women sometimes hide the stress of managing two sets of responsibility. But what happens when genuine role reversal takes place and women become defacto bread winners? Or when a woman puts family and personal fulfilment with equal footing?

Women who were married at 18 bore children, entertained in-labs and nurtured the husbands career before they finally went out and got a job, said. "I feel I'd rather be at work and get acknowledged for my efforts than work at home and be taken granted."

One comes across a variety of responses to the emerging challenges.

Sample 1: Woman A begins to bear the double burden of running home and house and her husband pitches in which neither, he refuses to become a house husband even though she spends a grueling day at work. They separate but leave the door open for getting back together later.

Sample 2: Woman B enters an arranged marriage. She soon realises they are neither intellectually nor emotionally tuned to each other. But two children arrive in the mean time and she stays in the marriage. She takes the brave step of going out and getting a job and carries on with all her responsibilities. From time to time, she wants to opt out of the marriage, but finding no support, continues. Money is not a problem but the husband resents her job, her independence the fact that she has a mind ticking away that he cannot deciper. Here it looks that the man develops an inferiority complex because he cannot share his educated and talented wife's flight into the wider world and begins to suffer from suicidal tendencies.

Sample 3: Woman C and her husband had a love marriage. Both are professionals. But somewhere along the line the husband turns jealous of his poised and talented wife. One day, he gets drunk and throws her out of the house, with their young child sleeping inside. With the abusive behaviour becoming a pattern, she decides to ask for a legal separation she decides to take charge of her own life, work and bring up her child by herself.

Sample 4: Women D has an affair with a colleague and when the husband discovers it, he initiates divorce proceeding? The woman pleads it was an aberration and asks him to take her back. Should he take her back, even though his manliness has been challenged and he is a cuckold in the eyes of the world?

While focusing on equality for women, we also need to develop new models of masculinity which will enable men to adjust to the new realities of women. The study of masculinities, a parallel idea of research which has grown in response to women's studies, needs to explore family and intimacy issues which couples as the above ones are trapped in the man can easily be condemned as a wife-beater, masochist, and perpetrator of violence and terror. But what makes him into what he becomes?

Questions

1. Do you find it ethical that a non-earning (and sometimes non-helping) woman have been thrown out of the house?
2. Does the man develop an inferiority complex due to reasons explained above? What are your comments in such cases?
3. Should the wife who understands that her husband is the way he is because of having grown up in a dysfunctional family try a softer approach? Discuss.
4. Should the man realise that he is a victim of pure role reversal (women always having been in the position of being cheated on earlier) and take his wife back if she wants to come back?

(3) Provocative Dresses Leading to Rapes

The provocative clothing worn by many women these days is also to blame for the vulnerable position in which women find themselves in the present-day society. The revealing costumes worn by cabaret dancers and vamps in the films of yesteryears seem to be in vogue today. The dresses showcased in the fashion shows these days can hardly be worn by an average Indian woman on the street. On the other hand, these fashion shows have a detrimental effect on the spectators. Especially, the male section, in that they arouse voyeuristic tendencies and sexual desires in them. Unable to control or give a proper vent to these urges they, in turn, pounce upon the unwary, hapless woman on the street.

Similarly, certain advertisements that are aired on television these days are in bad taste. The film star, in a tight orange T-shirt dancing to vulgar lyrics, is safe from molestation because she is famous. But what about her not-so-famous sisters on the street? The subliminal message that she sends across to the male viewers of the advertisement tunes their minds to viewing any woman as only a sex object and nothing more.

Also many women themselves are partly to be blamed for all this. A dress reveals a lot about a person's personality. About 40-50 years ago, when the present women were young, there were hardly any cases of rape. Women had definite codes of dress. The present trend of dressing by women does not augur well for the future. Just imagine, 20 years from now, what will their daughters be wearing? That is anybody's guess!

(4) Is Gambling Good?

The citizens of ancient Rome played dice once in a year, at the festival Saturnalia, in honour of the god of plenty (though the wagers were only nuts, not money). Gambling is often described in traditions mythology as an embodiment of the workings of the universe itself.

Scandinavian myths tell us that dice and runes, i.e. numbers and letters were given to human beings by Odin king of the Gods. The Gods are said to play at tables, a game whose moves are partly determined by dice, using golden boards that remain unbroken even after Ragnvok, the god's downfall: this suggests that the gods themselves are subject to fate: that number and measure rule all things. The word 'dice' comes from the Latin 'dates', meaning that which is 'given' by fortune.

Even in Indian epics, *Mahabarat*. Yudisthira played 'dice' and faced suffering. The game took place between two parties, i.e., good and evil to decide fate. Shakuni was a great deceiver in the game. He helped Duryodhana, the evil, to get him followed by 14 years of exile, One year Ajnanavasa, during which time if they are located, the cycle repeats. Further, they were so cruel they went beyond to win Draupadi, Yudishitira's wife and they humiliated her and wanted to undress her in the open house. Lord Krishna came to her rescue. At the end, the evil perished.

In the ancient world as per the western theory the forces of randomners were personified as the unpredictable will of the gods. The will of fortune and the mill of fate are images that reveal the unalterable cycles of change in the world embodied in the turning heavens as well as in the fall of the dice. The game board was seen as the four-quartered earth, with the players moves determined partly by the dice, i.e., by fate.

Gambling is depicted as a ritual that pits the human intellect against the unpredictable forces of chance that surround us. It is a concentrated form of the risk taking behaviour we carry out everyday. Gambling trains the mind to handle risk. It helps in taking real-life risks. But to put one's trust in fortune alone is the mistake of the addict.

Many gambling boards, dice and images of people playing games of chance and skill have come down to us from the ancient world. Board games, in particular, are known as the warrior's recreation and training him in the complex judgements. It needed in the choosing of battle when unpredictable factors interact with his skill and judgement at the breakneck speed.

A spectrum of skill runs from games of pure luck such as dice or the Lotto, the games of pure intellect such as chess. But even games of pure luck challenge our judgement. They test our ability to wager only what we can afford to lose and to know when to walk away with our winnings, or to cut our losses and stop playing a skill we need in more calculating ventures. Nobody can continuously win in gambling. "Do not put all your good aboard ship for trading" wrote the poet Hesiod in the 7th century B.C., "for it is a bad thing to meet with disaster at sea. Leave the greater part at home: Due measure is best in all things". Equivalent advice holds for those who play the stock market today.

(5) Tripura boy is 11 year old – Driver

A minor who is of eleven years from Tripura drives a loaded truck weighing 22 tonnes without a driver on the Assam-Agartala highway surprises anybody who happens to listen and physically see this. His name is Dilwar Hussain and he is hardly visible when he is at the wheel.

This boy has been helping his family of five by driving a heavy loaded truck on National Highway 44 that passes through hilly regions from past one year. Hussain was not a good student and averse to studies. This made his father Riazuddin to use him as a driver, made him an assistant first when he was 9 years old. This boy has now mastered the trade and has become a highly skilled driver negotiating sharp bends, comfortably and finding nothing to be worried.

The boy is driving the vehicle so smoothly and courageously all this time without getting involved in any accident.

Riazuddin at first considered that his son's service during his absence or driving at certain times would add a little more to his family's income. Fate on the other hand made Riazuddin to suffer from a severe massive heart attack some time back and he could not resume his work.

Hussain, took a bold step to become money earner for his family. He with much more vigour and enthusiastically continuing his work as a highway driver and is now the main bread winner of the family. Within a short span of time, the boy learnt driving fast with accuracy and considered a good negotiator in managing the deadly curves.

Riazuddin himself appreciates driving skill of his son. "I was aware of his interest in driving, but was surprised to see the ease with which he was doing it." He gets tears and wipes his face with affection to Hussain. Hussain, his young son says "I am not afraid of hills or difficult curves, but my only fear is about the police, because 1 don't have a driving licence. My father contacted transport department officials and tried to make them understand the excellence of my driving. But they refused to issue me a driving license due to the rules to be followed about the minimum age and other standard procedures.

This forced us to device some tactics to deceive the police he added. Abhijit Ghosh, a little more aged person, who has offered himself as an assistant to young Hussain. The former says he has no hesitation for this and he never finds it difficult to work with a driver who is younger to him .

Initially, Riazuddin allowed his son Hussain to drive the truck only on comfortable roads. But, now, the boy is highly comfortable even in the narrow hilly regions.

Hussain has satisfied many people including his father and Abhijit Ghosh in the last few months with his unimaginable skills and dexterity and has now become a full-fledged driver with high confidence.

Questions

1. On the ethical grounds, discuss driving of Hussain over such hilly roads, considering yourself in the positions of:
    - His father
    - As an assistant of young Hussain
    - As a strict law enforcer
2. Do you agree that such driving may be permitted to young boys who could be developed like Hussain? What would be the implications of allowing such boys on the roads as drivers? Comment after comparing Hussain, at the same time with some bad drivers who may be having valid driving licences but are not even half good as Hussain is, who do not provide safety?

(6) Bhopal Gas

More than twenty years ago, Bhopal choked over methylisocynate fumes from the Union Carbide India Limited (UCIL) factory. According to the Madhya Pradesh Gas Relief and Rehabilitation Department, over 15,000 lost their lives and 550,000 suffered serious injuries. The Supreme Court awarded a compensation package of $470 million in 1989, based on estimates of 3000 dead and 15,000 injured. The judgement absolved UCIL and its parent company in the US, Union Carbide Corporation (UCC), of criminal liability and appointed the Indian government as the sole representative of the victims, thereby ruling out individual suits against UCC and UCIL. Neither the Centre nor the State government has acted sincerely in that capacity. The Centre dragged its feet over carrying out a comprehensive medical survey as a result of which documentation of medical disorders, crucial to establishing the corporate's guilt, remains inadequate. Former UCC chief Warren Andersen, charged for culpable homicide is no more yet it is learnt that the then state government did not try to hold him back when he was here. Today, the $470 million has multiplied by way of interest to about $700 million, but courts have disbursed only $335 million. On July 14,2010 the Supreme Court ordered the immediate disbursal of the remaining sum. Over 5.5 lakh individuals have on an average received Rs. 25.000; the latest order would entitle each person to another Rs. 25,000. Is Rs. 50,000 per person a compensation or a pittance for a people economically and physically destroyed over two generations?

In 2001, Dow Chemicals acquired UCC and said it owed nothing to the Bhopal victims. It is high time the SC reopened the 1989 settlement in view of the unfolding magnitude of the disaster. The Bhopal chief judicial magistrate should summon Dow at the earliest. Class action suits in the US have led to huge compensations; the Indian system should allow for the same in an age of 'corporate accountability'. Dow and Indian Oil Corporation are reportedly working on a facility in Paradip, Orissa. The government should put a stop to any such exercises. Meanwhile, globalisation has altered the nature of transnational corporate operations. A present-day company covers the world in a spider-web of holdings rendering it impossible for laws of individual countries to pin it down. In the interest of world trade and business, episodes like Bhopal gas tragedy should be referred to an international court set up under the aegis of the World Trade Organisation. Faceless enterprise needs swift and neutral arbiters. Or else death will continue to stalk commerce as its shadow.

Questions

1. What are the unethical events that have taken place so far in the tragedy according to you?
2. What lessons on corporate governance lapses you find, two decades after the tragedy?

"I've never known anybody who has lost because of consistent ethical practices."

—Michael Spencer

4

Chapter

Marketing Ethics

Market and marketing activities are an essential part of everybody's life. All marketing activities should be based on legal foundation related to consumer and consumer's protection. It is understood that it is mandatory to follow law. It checks the external activities and ethics for internal values. But ethics is beyond law, which studies internal qualities. But ethics and law should go hand in hand. All business and business houses should follow ethical foundation in marketing.

As marketing and society are interwoven, the purpose of marketing goes beyond making profits, which will necessitate a different decision making guide. Marketing process tends to come under great scrutiny. It generates controversy and receives criticism with respect to potentially unethical business practices. In order to succeed in today's Indian and international markets, responsible managers must recognize and understand how ideas, values and moral standards differ across cultures and how these, in turn, influence decision making. This is appropriately put as "individuals who have strong sense of shame, are very conscious of what is improper or disgraceful and avoid behaving inappropriately (Schwartz 1992 and 1994).

Marketing Ethics

Marketing ethics is a standard set for marketing activities to judge the rightness not of action pose, but of action of one person relative to another. Marketing is a specialized process involving role relationship and interactions. Marketing is something, that people do as people, not merely as buyers and sellers, nor even just as economic men.

"Ethics in marketing is also understood as moral judgement, standards and rules relating to marketing decisions to avoid unfair behaviour, deception and suppressing the voice of the competitors in the marketing activities".

"Marketing is a process of engaging men completely with social entities."

Marketing ethics is defined as "a matter of social saction not of mere technical appraisal and ethics is not part of the promotion package, it's a nutrient that runs through the main stream of a business".

"Marketing ethics is being credible, being honest, taking credit for the things doing right, from caring marketing to community service, for fair trade and fair employment practices, taking responsibility when things go wrong and set them right whether it is a missed delivery, a bad-trade or an oil spill".

The purpose of business goes beyond making profit. So one will have a different decision making guide. Every marketer must be aware that:

- According to the customers; the purpose of a business is to provide goods and services that satisfy needs and wants.
- According to the owners; the purpose of business is to maximize wealth of its shareholders.
- According to the employees; the purpose of a business is to provide a good standard of living.

Robert Bartels (1967), in his *A Model for Ethics in Marketing*, says: "Marketing ethics is a part of general ethics in business, it is an attempt to construct a model for ethics in marketing, which may be logical framework."

Marketing is the functional area within business that interfaces with the consumer, it tends to come under the greatest scrutiny, generates controversy and receives criticism with respect to potentially unethical business practices. Eminent market researchers like Ferrell and Skinner (1998), Hunt, Chonko and Wilcox (1984), Mason, Bearden and Richardson (1990), Vitell (1986), Murphy and Lackzniak (1981) referred the marketing ethics as an injury into the nature and grounds of moral judgement, standards and rules of conduct relating to marketing decisions and marketing situations. For ethical decision making in marketing, the different situational variables taken into account are:

(a) Individual (include nationality, culture, religion, sex, age, education, employment and personality).

(b) Situational referred to groups, rewards and sanctions, codes of conduct, type of ethical conflict, organisational effect, industry and business competitiveness.

Among these variables culture has been receiving an increasing amount of attention in the marketing ethics literature. Culture is a fundamental determinant of ethical decision making. It directly affects ethical problems, alternatives and consequences (Hunt 1989; Vitell, 1992). In order to succeed in today's international markets, managers must recognise and understand how ideas, values and moral standards differ across cultures and how these, in turn, influence marketing decision making. Individuals are very conscious about improper and disgraceful activity and they will avoid behaving inappropriatly".

Moral Values in Marketing

More than a quarter century now, the subject ethics or moral values has received expanding affection in marketing literature. But only a few of the sources, in a vast literature on marketing ethics offer a definition of the term. The original meaning of the word "ethics", in the Aristotelian philosophy based on tradition in human actions from the point of view of the rightness and wrongness or body of principles, which could serve as an adequate guide for the wise choice. Marketing ethics could be considered a conduct based on standards and moral judgement applied to marketing practice, or a system or code of conduct or morals for the field of marketing.

Responsibility for ethics in marketing is attributed increasingly to the individuals on the higher management levels. Robert Bartels (1967) rightly puts: "it is assumed that the expectation of the participants in the respective marketing roles are known, and it assumed that ethics is a matter of social sanction, not of mere technical appraisal."

Social Responsibility and Marketing

The growing interest in broadening the concept of marketing seems to be confined largely to extending the application of the marketing concept rather than extending the orientation of the concept of marketing. The challenge of a humanistic perspective to current theory and practice in marketing has origin in the larger context of challenge and confrontation to all established institutions. A humanistic perspective would ensure the widespread practice of incorporating in the concern of social responsibility by the business houses. These should be concerned about something more than making money, they have responsibilities towards the community in which they work and to the society which has given them land, labour, and capital. The corporations are more than an economic institution and they have responsibility to help society to solve pressing problems both from the internal and external environment of the business.

Ethical Foundation in Marketing

The task of marketing is to convert social needs into profitable opportunities. In this course of action there are many ethical issues faced by the corporate, especially with the products, pricing, advertising and sales and distribution. Eminent market researchers like Chonko and Wilcox (1984), Farrell and Skinner (1998), Bearden and Richardson (1990) Vitell (1986) Murphy and Lackzniak (1981) and so on refer the marketing ethics as an injury into the nature and generate moral judgement and standards relating to marketing

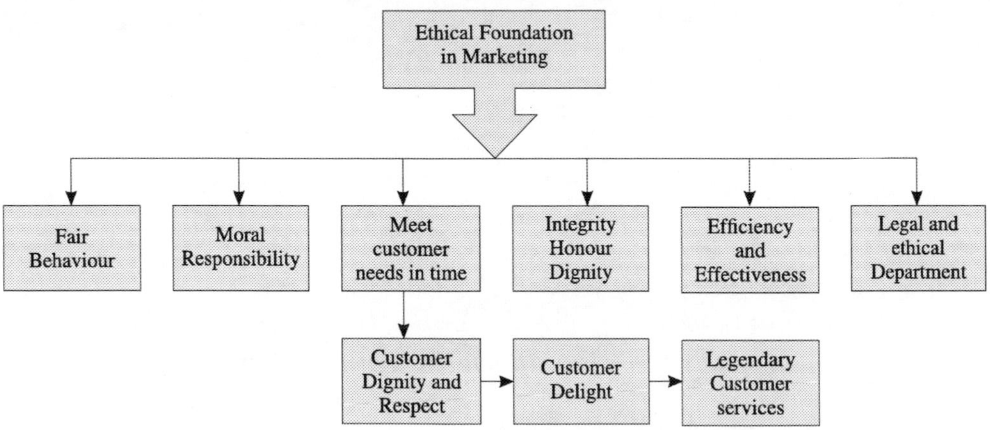

Business ethical foundation in marketing

decisions. However, there should be concrete ethical foundation in marketing with the building blocks like fair behaviour, moral responsibility, legal and ethical departments and so on. Ethical foundation blocks are shown in the figure in the prevoius page.

Efficiency of marketing activities is mainly based on 4Ps, namely, product, price, promotion and sales and distribution. The 4Ps of the marketing activities are the foundations of all other activities of marketing.

MARKETING OF PRODUCT AND ETHICAL ISSUES IN PRODUCT

"While great devices are invented in the laboratory, great products are invented in the marketing department".

Product

Under the old concept of marketing, product was viewed as a specific combination of physical characteristics, in other words a material or a thing. This emphasis on tangible aspects, however, prevented marketers from creatively understanding and responding to consumer needs and wants.

Kotler (1999) defined it as: "Product is anything that can be offered to a market for attention, acquisition, use or consumption that might satisfy a want or need. It includes physical objects, services, person, places, organization and ideas". Kotler (1999).

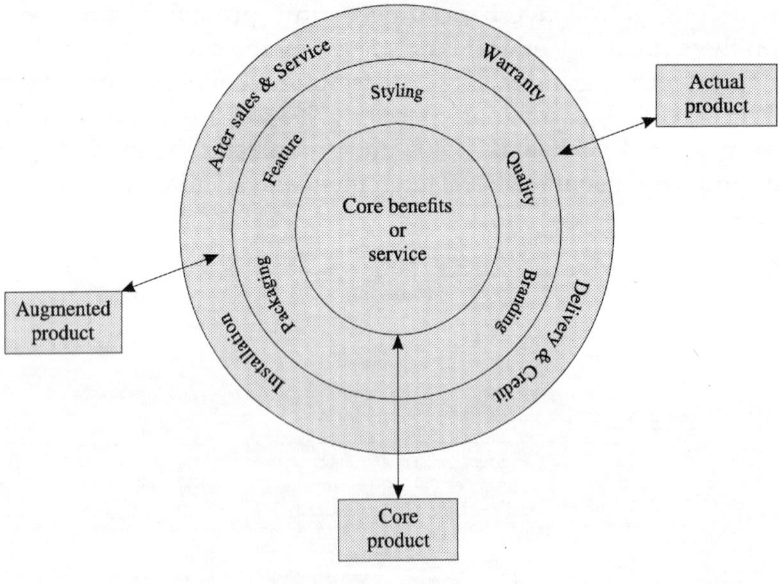

Product and its core benefit. Source: Philip Kotler (1999)

As product is for the consumer's satisfaction. It is considered a combination of psychological as well as physical benefits, and hence includes much more than just its physical or tangible attributes. Marketing is a process wherein the consumers are satisfied through the products, so, it is said that:

"In the factory, we make cosmetics, in the store, we sell hope, Industrial purchasing agents do not buy quarter inch drills, they buy quarter inch holes". **–Kotler (1999)**

An organization will need creativity to transform the ideas for its product into reality.

A product can be processed through three levels:

The product should meet customer satisfaction fully, which can be met only through customer service and by giving freedom to exercise their right.

Ethics and Product

All the marketing activities should be based on legal foundation and any product development and selling should follow the legal provisions. It is generally accepted that any activity based on law is ethical. But ethics is beyond law. When the product is meeting the customer's satisfaction and safety, such product is termed ethical. Some of the ethics in product are: product should meet total quality, relationship based on integrity and trust, meeting customer expectations, prompt service and reasonably priced. In addition to these the product should give way to the customers to exercise their rights against safety, right to choose, right to be informed and the right to be heard. The following figure shows ethics and product.

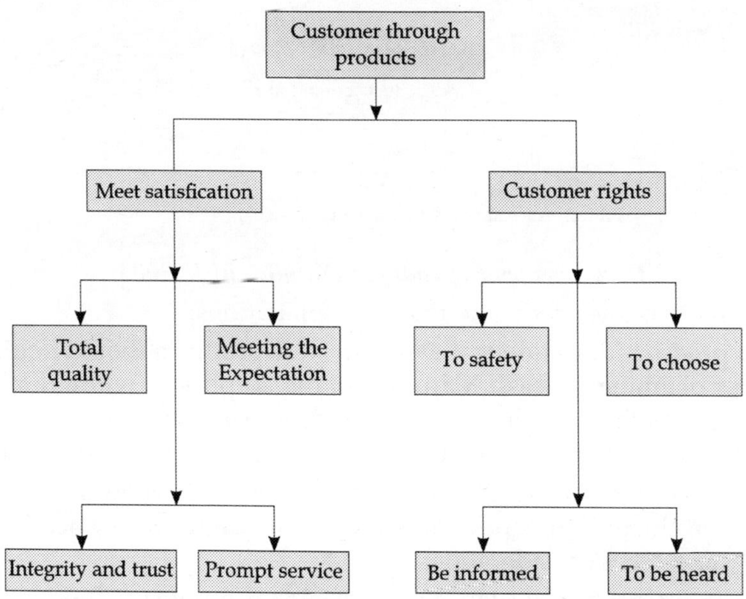

All the above can be practised when products are based on the above factors otherwise it will lead to customer dissatisfaction and unfairness, which are referred to as ethical issues in product.

Ethical Issues in Products

Ethical issues in products cause a lot of problems in business. This is a great hurdle in the long run of the marketing. The following diagram shows the various ethical issues in product.

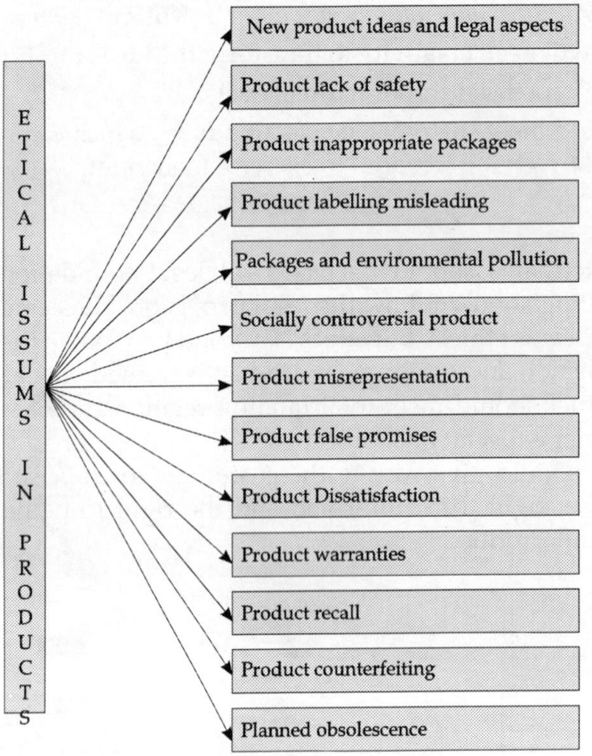

Ethical issues in products (Kamatchi p. 2003)

Ethical issues in products (Kamatchi P, 2003)

The ethical issues of the product with brief explanations:

(a) **New product idea and legal aspects:** New products should go through some sort of planning process. Many times the corporates will ignore law in conceiving the ideas and development of new products. This may lead to lack of safety. This may be identified as potential legal or ethical violations.

(b) **Product design and safety:** Product and product safety is an open-minded affair. Products require periodic study. New products may need guidelines for safety and other considerations.

Poor/faulty product design is responsible for product failure and many times customers consider more of product feature rather than product safety.

- Ethical issues facing organisations is the extent to which they *are* responsible for designing safety into a product. Such safety design would add to the price and consumers may not be interested in paying more prices.

- In children's products, especially toys, ethical issues raise to concern. Products with jagged edges could cause injuries, toys with small parts that can be swallowed and toys that have projection that can lead to eye injury, are all products which are potentially harmful to children.

(c) **Packaging:** Packaging component of a product refers to any container in which it is offered for sale on which information is communicated. To a great extent the customer's first exposure to the product is the package, and it is an expensive and important part of the marketing strategy. Packages provide important benefits for the manufacturer, retailer and ultimate consumer like communication benefits, functional benefits and perceptual benefits.

So, packaging provides communication, functional and perceptual benefits. The two emerging trends in packaging are the product warranty, environmental impact and safety of packaging materials.

Packaging includes activities of designing and producing the container or wrapper for a product (Kolter, 1998). Well designed packages can create convenience value for customers and promotional value for products. Some of the ethical issues under this *are* lack of safety concerns in connection with environmental pollution, raising the problem, like shortage of paper, aluminium and other materials, non-returnable glass containers, broken bottles and crumpled cans littering the streets and countryside. It creates problems of solid waste disposal. Some other ethical issues concerned with packaging are:

- Products which need no package include the cost of package in their prices (e.g., bolts and nuts).
- The cost of transportation increases because of unwanted and bulky packages.
- The costs of damaged goods are also included in price, which is a burden to the customers.
- Many times the packages may not contain accurate/adequate information of the product. The information may be exaggeration or deceptive.
- Consumers are kept in dark regarding the cost of packaging that is included in the final price of the product.

(d) **Labelling:** Labelling is a part of packaging. The label may be a simple tape attached to the product or an elaborately designed graphic that is a part of package. Some of the ethical issues in labelling are:

- The consumers are not aware of the nutritional value of the product.
- The consumers are unaware to face the conflicting evidence concerning things such as nutrition and environmentally compatible products and also to decide the same.

- The mere provision of a list of ingredients may not provide useful information for the average consumer.

In addition to the above, warning label is another factor to be taken under ethical issues. Warning labels are used to draw the attention to dangers that might exist with certain products. It should provide information to consumers to use the product safely, but for some of the products having dangerous features, warning label is necessary (Driver, 1987).

(e) **Environmentally incompatible products:** Environmentally incompatible products like aerosol spray cans, non-biodegradable packaging, chemicals and detergents that create pollution; medical wastes, etc., pollute environment.

(f) **Socially controversial products:** Some of the socially controversial products are cigarettes, firearms and alcohol. For these products, health warning is not adequate. They should be eliminated from the market.

(g) **Product dissatisfaction:** Products that lack quality give little benefit to the customer and lack of safety like:

- **Products lacking quality:** Some of the products which are used as fixtures like rattles, pins, loose buttons or missing knobs will be dented, mismatched sizes, static fluttering, leaking, etc., will always be inferior in quality.
- Products that deliver little benefit, for example, high nutritional value may be lost when they are delivered.
- **Product king safety:** Damaged appliances, carbon monoacid poisoning from room heaters, faulty steering in automobiles, etc.

(h) **Product warranties:** The final component for product consideration is a statement indicating the liability of the manufacturers for product deficiencies is warranty. Many times the sellers do not keep up the expressed warranties. The manufacturers do not maintain many of the warranty expressed through advertisement. Even in the implied warranties, some of the defects in case of packages, labellingm, etc., will not be looked into.

(i) **Product recall:** Product recall refers to when the company does not meet safety needs of a product and satisfaction of the consumers it can withdraw the product from the market.

As products may not fare well in the market specially some of the products that are inherently dangerous. Some of the products are harmful to consumers because of product defects, product tampering, and product misuse. When organisations ignore product safety issues, they risk serious and costly product liability damages, e.g., product recall (Procter and Gamble cost about 75 million dollars - The Product, Toxic Shock Syndrome, (1983) and Johnson and Johnson - Tylenol capsules (1986)).

(j) **Product counterfeiting:** The unauthorised copying of patented products trademarks and copyright is product counterfeiting. This costs US business billions of dollars every year (Harvery, 1988). The counterfeit is sold at the same price, though it differs in quality for example watches, shampoos, sunglasses, and liquors, etc.

(k) **Planned obsolescence:** They are products where the manufactures produce a product with an intentionally limited life. Ethical issue here is that the manufacturers have the capacity to produce a *battery* with lifetime working potential. Instead they produce batteries that have a limited life. It is a reality that consumers are purchasing limited life batteries for the cost of lifetime battery but the limited-life batteries are much less expensive per unit than the cost of the lifetime battery. Another example of planned obsolescence is *fashion typed products,* e.g., designer jeans, readymade garments, etc. Such products receive heavy promotion as trendy, upscale and stylish. But they go out of style the next year when the same promoters, promote next year's fashion in the same way. The ethical question here is whether consumers dictate fashion preferences or it is vice versa. The mobile phone industry is similar to the fashion industry in making old products absolute.

Another example is in *high-tech industry,* microcomputers are implicitly advertised as out of date, slower or having less memory, although, such claims may be true, there is some ethical concern about whether consumers need all of the extras by the next generation computers. Many consumers purchase computer upgrades because of pressures to have the latest in technology, whether or not a real need is being satisfied by that technology.

Global Marketing of Products and Related Ethical Issues

There are also other types of crises which may affect a particular product. These are product boycotts and product recalls. First, the general framework under which product or companies boycotts occur will be examined along with their nature, and the strategies used for handling such situations. Two cases in particular will be discussed—the infant formula case and Adidas products. The second aspect concerns product recalls. There have been three major product recalls in recent times–Johnson & Johnson's Tylenol capsules in 1982, Philip Morris' cigarettes in 1995 and Coca-Cola's beverages in 1999. In each case, the response was different. Many products are subject to litigation as well, particularly in the US. Some of these cases are described below.

Product/Company Boycotts

There is a rising trend towards consumer protests which are proving to be increasingly successful. Boycotts are the opposite of relationship marketing. Boycotted companies face negative results which affect their marketing efforts. For instance, the purpose of boycotting of tuna was to force companies to change their fishing practices and save dolphins. Boycotts may also have private motives, such as changing the behaviour of certain companies. At times boycotts are the result of the past behaviour of the companies targeted or the result of international animosity against some of the countries due to political reasons.

Products from a certain country may be boycotted because of that country's past behaviour, as for instance, World War II veterans in the US refused to buy Sony televisions because they remembered the Pearl Harbour incident. The boycott had nothing to do with the business practices of Sony.

Some of these animosities towards particular countries can result in indirect instrumental boycotts:

- Resentment against the Japanese occupation of Nanjing and the massacre of Chinese civilians during 1937-1938 was expressed through animosity in buying Japanese products in the area. This is an example of indirect, expressive boycott.
- US consumers showed resentment towards Japanese products as a result of the Second World War.
- Australian consumers showed their indignation towards French nuclear tests in the South Pacific through the boycott of French companies between 1995 and 1996.

A product's quality is usually the key factor in the evaluation of that product and determining its choice but as can be seen, in some circumstances, quality may not be the consideration, but animosity towards the country.

Framework of Boycotts

Boycotted companies face serious negative consequences, which require crisis management. There are different types of boycotts, but all are generally aimed at influencing a producer's behaviour. Klein et al. (1998) distinguish between direct boycotts which are due to a specific act by the producer, and indirect boycotts which are motivated by the actions of entities and not directly related to a producer. Another distinction is made between instrumental and expressive boycotts. The former is directed towards bringing about changes and the latter to express anger.

Some examples are given below.

(1) The Nestle Infant Formula Case

Activists found that breastfeeding was best for babies. Moreover, encouraging infant formula was also inappropriate in the Third World countries where hygienic conditions were often inadequate, and where the use of the formula would be unsafe. This issue became a public controversy in 1974 when a group called 'War on Want' used the slogan 'Baby Killer' Nestle. This led to clashes between the company and activists who boycotted Nestle products (Sethi and Bhalla, 1991).

In May 1981, the World Health Organization adopted an international code on the marketing of breast-milk substitutes in response to the concerns of several private and public groups over the sale of infant formula products in the Third World countries.

The code imposed restrictions on the marketing and distribution of breast-milk substitutes:

- Education and promotion: The code prohibits the promotion of infant formulae either directly or indirectly.

- Role of health workers: The code stipulates that industry should contact end-users only through local health workers. The industry should not give free samples or financial help for the purpose of promoting the product.
- Labelling: The code requires that a clear message out that breast feeding is superior to bottle feeding in all local languages should be put.
- Implementation and monitoring: There is a three-tier system of implementation. The primary responsibility lies with the governments to take the required legal and administrative actions. Industries and distributors are responsible for monitoring their own marketing practices in conformity with the code. WHO provides technical assistance to member governments in preparing the necessary legal and administrative actions.

(2) Adidas

The official balls for the FIFA World Cup 1988 were made in Morocco and Pakistan under strict supervision by company technicians and human-rights monitors. In June 1998, Adidas-Salomon AG stopped all its orders for soccer balls in China, following reports that licensees and subcontractors were having the balls made with Adidas and Official World Cup logos inside a Chinese prison labour camp near Shanghai.

Adidas's announcement coincided with an extraordinary World Cup conference held on 2 July 1998 organized by the global governing body of soccer, the FIFA, regarding the use of child-labour or prison-labour in the production of soccer balls or any other athletic equipment.

Since 1973, Molten, a subcontractor, has been manufacturing Adidas-branded items in China for export to Japan and North America, including Adidas soccer balls carrying the Tango and World Cup logos. The break-up between Adidas and Molten ended a 25-year licensing relationship between the two companies. Meanwhile, customs officials confiscated some 144,000 items of counterfeit merchandise, including soccer balls, associated with the World Cup which were manufactured in Pakistan, Taipei and China.

Adidas announced plans to speed up the creation of a full-time human rights department inside the company to centralize all future Chinese production in one location so as to avoid any possible diversion of production to prison labour camps.

(3) Tampax Corporation

In 1980, a link was found between tampon usage and deadly toxic-shock syndrome (TSS), threatening the survival of the Tampax Corporation in the US, although the company has been marketing tampons since 1936. The chairman immediately gave assurance to loyal Tampax users that risks were minimal. He requested the Centre for Diseases Control (CDC) to identify the causes of TSS. In addition, the corporation funded the Harvard Medical School to carry out research on TSS. Later the CDC found that TSS was also linked with Procter & Gamble's Rely tampon; P&G withdrew its product. The timely actions initiated by Tampax Corporation helped it avoid the problem of product recall (Hibbert, 1997).

(4) Johnson & Johnson

In 1982, Johnson & Johnson faced a major crisis due to product tampering. Cyanide was put into Tylenol headache capsules causing seven deaths in Chicago. The company's crisis management team withdrew stocks nationwide, though the tampering was done only in the Chicago area. Second, it redesigned the packaging and reintroduced Tylenol in the market. This was considered an example of successful handling of a crisis where one executive took complete charge.

(5) Philip Morris

Philip Morris recalled all its stocks of Marlboro cigarettes in 1995 fearing that the product would harm smokers' health. Later it was found that only one batch of filters had been contaminated with a chemical causing slight coughing and sneezing.

(6) Coca-Cola

On 15 June 1999, four northern European countries banned Coca-Cola products as a result of a health scare. The Belgian health ministry announced that 100 people had fallen ill in a week, suffering from stomach upsets, nausea and headache as a result of consuming Coca-Cola. Eight had been hospitalized. Belgium, Luxembourg and France immediately banned Coca-Cola, while the company itself withdrew from the Dutch market, and recalled its product produced in its Belgian factories.

The scare was an embarrassment for Coca-Cola, which prided itself on the quality of its product. It blamed two separate chemical problems at different plants. The Antwerp factory had used a batch of sub-standard carbon dioxide in the production of a small quantity of bottled Coca-Cola during the previous two weeks. The other problem was on the surface of some canned drinks from its Dunkirk factory, delivered only to Belgium. These had become contaminated as a result of fungicide sprayed on pallets used to transport the drinks, although the fungicide had not got into the drink itself.

The Coca-Cola company informed Belgium that these problems might cause 'discomfort' in people consuming affected products, but the concentrations of contaminants were too small to make them a danger to health.

Coca-Cola had to recall 17 million cases of its product costing the company US $103 million as a result of non-recurring charges and disposal costs.

The scare was similar to that caused by Perrier, the French manufacturer of sparkling mineral water. In 1990, traces of benzene were found in its product and the company was forced to recall every bottle. It is estimated that the incident cost Perrier about US $200 million; it took the company several years to reach to its earlier levels. By then the company was acquired by Nestle of Switzerland.

During May-June 1999, Belgium was faced with a food scare after cancer causing dioxin was found in poultry, eggs, pork and beef sold in supermarkets; all the items had to be subsequently removed from supermarket shelves. The scare helped to topple the government of Jean-Luc Dehaene during the mid-June 1999 election.

(7) Pfizer

The anti-obesity drug, Redux, widely used by slimmers, was withdrawn from the market in 1997 after it was found to cause potential heart valve problems.

In May 1998, Viagra, the world's first pill for countering impotence also faced a setback: six people died while taking the drug. The US Food and Drug Administration was not clear whether the deaths were caused by the drug. About one million prescriptions had been written for Viagra since its US launch on April 15 1998. Viagra had become America's latest fashionable drug, widely compared with Prozac, the anti-depressant, and Redux, the anti-obesity drug. Both drugs attracted a broader audience than intended.

Pfizer said that it had reported the deaths to the FDA as part of routine practice but added that the deaths suggested 'nothing unusual, nothing different from clinical trials. No change of label is contemplated.' The drug's label includes a warning that it should not be taken in conjunction with nitrates, a common heart medicine. Pfizer sent an emergency letter to doctors reiterating the warning in May 1998. Pfizer's stock price, which had surged on promising early sales of the drug, slid US $4 to US $105 in May 1998.

In June 1998, Pfizer began a wave of ads in the *New England Journal of Medicine*, the *Journal of the American Medical Association* and other medical journals. There is a risk in not advertising. Pfizer communicated plainly and repeatedly about the attributes and known risks of Viagra including the contraindications with nitrates. Viagra ads ran in about 50 medical publications and targeted an audience of doctors, including urologists, primary-care physicians, psychiatrists, cardiologists and those treating diabetes.

Pfizer expected that it would have to spend another US $60 million on advertising aimed at consumers. Competition was the primary reason which prompted Pfizer to advertise aggressively in spite of it being one of the fastest selling prescription drugs ever.

(8) Computer Tampering

A serious security flaw was discovered in popular e-mail programmes published by Microsoft and Netscape Communications, which would permit a malicious person to send a message containing a virus that could crash a computer, destroy or even steal data. The flaw existed in Microsoft's Outlook Express and Outlook 98, and Netscape's web browser, the Navigator, which was part of its communicator suite of the Internet programmes.

Microsoft was already providing fixes by July 1998, but these were not able to solve the problem. The company had already distributed about two million copies of the more seriously flawed Outlook 98 programme and at least a million copies of Outlook Express. Microsoft was already providing 'patches', i.e., small programmes that could repair the flaw in the e-mail programme of its Windows and NT operating systems.

Netscape posted a notice regarding the security flaw on its website noting that the flaw only affected the Windows and Windows NT versions of the Navigator and not those distributed for the Macintosh and Unix machines and that it would post a patch for its Windows and NT versions within two weeks.

Security experts say that both companies had distributed software containing a well-known type of programme-design error. The code that resulted in the flaw had been a widely documented problem for over 30 years.

(9) The Automobile Industry

There has been a spate of recalls by manufacturers of automobiles. Such recalls and lawsuits against defective products are common in the US. Some well known cases are given below.

Ford

On 16 July 1999, Ford announced its plans to recall up to 200,000 of its best-selling Focus cars after discovering component faults in its European-produced models. The recall covered the entire production run of Focus cars from their launch in September 1998 to March 1999.

The motive behind Ford's action was partly to avoid potential lawsuits both in Europe and the US over defective products. Ford blamed the problems on a defect in the car's alternator cap design which allowed water to leak into the electrical systems. All the cars involved were made at Saarlouis, in Germany, and Valencia, in Spain.

BMW

In June 1999 BMW of Germany recalled 250,000 of its 3-series models to rectify faulty airbag sensors.

General Motors and Ford

In the 1970s, a jury awarded damages worth US $128 million in a lawsuit (subsequently reduced to US $3.5 million) after finding that the petrol tanks of Ford's Pinto cars were prone to explode. Since then, there have been many allegations regarding air-bag design defects and the supposed unstableness of the sports utility vehicles.

In July 1998, General Motors had to recall nearly one million cars because of problems related to air bags. The recall primarily covered its Chevrolet Cavaliers and its Pontiac Sunfires, but also a smaller number of Cadillac DeVilles, Concours, Eldorados and Seville cars were also recalled. The problems centred around faulty deployment of air bags which required software adjustments.

General Motors also had to face litigation in the case of another product. Six people in a car crashed at a traffic light on Christmas eve when they were hit from behind by a car going at 112 kph. Their car exploded, with some of them trapped inside. The fact of the matter was that GM knew that if its 1979 Malibu were to be involved in an accident, its gas tank could explode. GM did not want to spend the money to prevent the consequences of this defect, and was accused of having no regard for its customers.

On 9 July 1999, a civil jury awarded US $107 million to the six people who had been badly burnt in the fiery crash involving the General Motors car. The jury also imposed so-called punitive damages of US $4.9 billion on GM.

Three days later, Ford got a US $295 million damages bill, from the jury in Ceres, California. In the case of Ford, the 19-year-old driver of a 1978 Ford Bronco swerved to avoid a collision. The vehicle spun and rolled over several times, and three of the six family members inside were killed.

In both cases, the plaintiffs said the companies knew of the potential structural weaknesses in the vehicles and had done nothing to correct them, charges which GM and Ford both denied. Before these incidents, there was a us $262.5 million jury decision in late 1997 against Chrysler over rear-door latches on its Dodge Caravan minivans. However, Chrysler recalled 4.1 million of its vans in the US in 1995 to repair the defective door latches.

(10) Other Auto Companies

There have been recalls of major products under the Clean Air Act in the US. This legislation requires that carmakers install special devices to monitor the level of hydrocarbon leaks, which are environmental pollutants:

- In 1995, General Motors had to recall and repair about 470,000 Cadillacs which government agencies said were equipped with illegal devices to defeat pollution controls; the company had to pay a us $11 million fine.
- Honda and seven manufacturers of heavy-duty diesel engines were similarly charged in October 1998. Ford and Honda also reached verdicts similar to GM's Clean Air Act settlements paying close to US $25 million in aggregate penalties. In Honda's case, 1.7 million Honda and Acura automobiles were involved. The company extended the warranty on all of its vehicle emission equipment to 14 years, or 150,000 miles, instead of three years, or 36,000 miles. Honda paid US $10.1 million in federal fines and US $2.5 million in state fines to the state of California. In addition, Honda paid US $1 million on federal environmental research and another US $3.5 million on environmental research to the state of California. The total cost of US $17.1 million was less than the company's proposed liability of more than US $42.5 billion.
- Toyota was pulled up in July 1999 by the US Justice Department (acting on behalf of the Environmental Protection Agency) because its computer monitoring system installed in its passenger car models had failed to alert the driver to the hydrocarbon vapour emissions from the fuel rank. The lawsuit covered all Toyota and Lexus car models of the years 1996 to 1998 sold by Toyota Motor Sales USA. The lawsuit potentially claimed up to US $58 billion for violating emission control laws. This was on the basis of a fine of US $25,000 to US $27,000 for each of the 2.2 million vehicles that allegedly failed to comply. The lawsuit demanded that the computer system be repaired, and that the company recall its cars until the system met US emission standards.

Toyota had rejected the earlier federal settlement offer that included a fine of US $75 per car making the cost in excess of US $150 million. Toyota contended that state and federal rules only required that the vehicles' warning lights meet the tests in laboratories. The rules did not give regulators the authority to conduct random checks on whether the vehicles actually performed on the road the way they did in the laboratory.

Source: S. Shivaramu 'Corporate Crisis Management' (2000).

PRICING AND ETHICAL ISSUES IN PRICING

"The real issue is value, not price"

—Robert T. Lindgren

1. **Pricing:** Pricing is one of the major decision areas in a firm. It is a process of determining price of the product with the object of profit orientation, sales orientation and status quo orientation in profit and sales.

Economic theory has traditionally regarded price as the marketing variable. Price is still another major component of the marketing mix. It looms considerably larger in certain market situations than in others, but all offers must ultimately be priced, and the price will affect the customer's response. Economic theory of price systematically relates price to both revenue and cost and hence profit serves as an analytical tool, and it is accepted as:

"Pricing is a water-testing process, You put your toe in and, If it is not too cold, the whole foot goes in"

– Robert Day

Broadly speaking, pricing objectives can be either profit oriented or volume-oriented. Pricing problems can decline in sales, prices higher or lower than those of competitors, excessive pressure on middlemen to generate sales, imbalance in the product line prices, distortion vis-a-vis the offering in the customer's perceptions of the firm's prices, frequent changes in prices without any relationship to environmental realities.

Price represents the value placed on a product by both the seller and the customer. From the seller standpoint, price represents what the seller feels the customer will view as fair value for the product or service purchased.

2. **Law and Pricing:**

"Ethics is beyond law"

—Moral theory

All legal provisions, which are connected to pricing, are the main basis for determining the price of a product. The Monopolies and Restrictive Trade Practices Act gives guidelines for determining the prices of the product. Unfair pricing, price discounting, price fixing, misleading prices and so on are some of the pricing activities against the law in India.

3. **Ethical issues in pricing:** As pricing represents the value placed on the product or service by both the buyer and seller, a key pricing issue concerns the setting of prices that are viewed as fair by both the buyer and the seller.

The ethical issues on pricing are shown below.

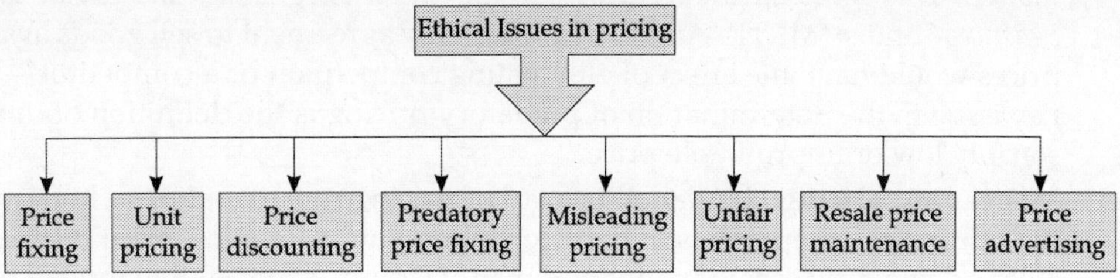

(a) Price fixing: Price fixing refers to maintaining of prices at a certain level by agreement between competing sellers. Price fixing is anti-competitive and therefore illegal. The marketers need to know the laws affecting price and make sure that their pricing policies are lawful. Many times the sellers set prices without taking competition into consideration and ignoring nature, purpose and effect of any agreement among themselves. This will lead to great disadvantage to the consumers.

(b) Unit pricing: Unit price is the price charged for each unit of goods supplied. This is common in grocery store retailing and other forms of retailing in which packaged goods are sold. The issue here is that the small and independent retailers are placed at a disadvantage. The issues raised under unit pricing are:

- The small retailers and independent retailers are placed at a disadvantage when compared to large retailer's abilities to install unit pricing system.
- The ability of consumers to process the additional price information is kept in dark. Retailers use different labelling approaches and different terminologies, making it difficult for consumers to assimilate all the pricing and product information. The consumer actually pays more for the product than marked on the product and often never discovers it.

(c) Price discounting: Price discounting would appear to be good news for consumers.

Retailers make promises concerning low price, competitive prices and matching prices, which is actually beneficial to the retailers.

- The price discounting will be beneficial to the retailers, and often gives customers a false sense of security.
- The discounting trend has made consumers more aware of discounting practices. Consumers are tempted to spend a lot of time on shopping and finally land up with disadvantages.

(d) Predatory price fixing: It is price fixation in which an organization reduces prices to a low level, to meet competitions and drive it out of the markets. They expect profits to increase when competition is reduced.

The ultimate goal of the predatory price fixing is to secure a monopoly in the market. This act is illegal according to the *"Restrictive Trades and Unfair Trade Practices"* under (MRTP) Act section 33(j) "Any agreement to sell goods at such prices would have the effect of eliminating competition or a competitor". The key issue in the determination of predatory pricing is the definition of unreasonably low or unprofitable price.

(e) **Misleading pricing:** It is another way of pricing where complete honesty is the minimum acceptable standard for marketing in making price decisions. Sales pricing, price comparisons and manufacturers suggested that retail prices have all been points of concern when it comes to retailers. Misleading consumers with the *"Sales every day"* and clearance sales have come under scrutiny as this misleads consumers. There is a legal guideline for misleading pricing.

The ethical issue concerns whether or not the consumer recognizes the new price, whenever there is a change in the price and when it is clearly given on the label in bold letters. Another form of misleading is comparative pricing, when the retailer compares prices of other retailers. Supermarket basket comparisons are one form of comparative pricing. Ethical issues involved here include how items for the basket. Any supermarket can usually find some items that are less expensive than those of the competitor. Here the consumers are given an impression that the store's products are all less expensive.

(f) **Unfair pricing:** A product must be fairly priced, as it is a major determinant of the market demand for it. Price affects competitive position and its market share; many of the retail prices are based on *"offers"* but not on the basis of real value of product. Many competitors determine the pricing on the market position, but it will not be customer oriented and product oriented. Many of the corporate focus on making profit decide the price, but as it reaches the consumers through retailers or other middlemen the price would have been doubled. It is a great burden on ultimate consumers. The corporates are expected to take the middlemen, retailers and other marketers in view in determining the price that may form a fair price.

(g) **Resale price maintenance:** This is known as vertical price fixing. The practice occurs when manufacturers specify the minimum and maximum price that a wholesale or retailer can charge for a product. In the US. The Sherman Act governs this practice.

The ethical questions that occurs here is when a manufacturer has an agreement with its dealers to terminate any dealer, who are viewed as price cutters. Here the consumers suffer with lack of services provided by the dealers and paying more for the product than marked on the product and often never discovers it.

(h) **Discriminatory pricing:** It refers to when the prices are changed with differences which may be favourable or unfavourable. Price discrimination applies when one person pays a different price than some other person for an identical goods or services. Discriminatory pricing is another issue. This is an issue in point of customers as, price discrimination applies with one person pays a different price than some other person for an identical goods or service.

(i) Price advertisement: Many times price advertising will not reveal the reality of the actual price of the product. There may be lot of differences between the prices in advertisement and the actual price. Advertisers use false comparisons and never disclose the real price, which mislead the consumers. This will lead to an ethical issue in pricing.

ADVERTISING AND ETHICAL ISSUES IN ADVERTISING

***"A person's belief and attitude are notoriously difficult to change without there being a willingness to accept the message being offered".* Manuel G . Velasquez**

Advertising

In the past decades, advertising was referred as *"keeping your name before the pubic"* or a salesmanship in print. But in recent years, advertising, as it is too often used, is a blanket term covering everything Charles (1994).

Advertising is a planned communicative activity in which messages are used to persuade customers to adopt goods, services or ideas.

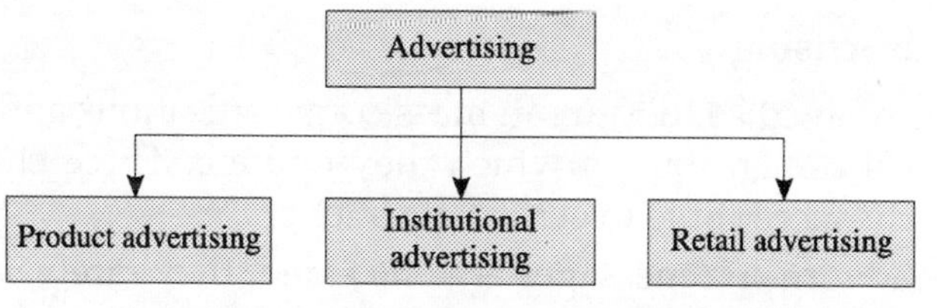

Source: Classification of Advertising, Kotler (1999)

- Product advertising focuses on selling of products.
- Institutional advertising focuses on the image of a product category, a company, a non-profit organization, or an industry association rather than a specific brand.
- Retail advertising is often considered to be a special type of advertising as it is directly connected with the society and product. Institutional or retail advertising can be pioneering, competitive or retentive.

The general features of advertising that distinguishes from the other form of communications are:

- It is paid for by the sponsored, rather than run at the discretion of the medium.
- It is non-personal.
- It identifies the sponsor of the message.
- It is carried by mass media.
- It is persuasive.

Corporate Social Responsibility on Advertising

India is a land of culture and values and hence, the advertisement should be based on culture and social setup. Advertisement is to reach the general public by promoting social values and modify the attitudes and behaviour. Unfair advertisement copy and the products *of* social abuses must be avoided. Children are a vulnerable group who cannot distinguish between fantasy and reality. Companies should avoid targeting them in advertisements. Television is an effective media of advertisement. At the same it is also used for unhealthy advertisement like excessive and irrational exposure of women, product for personal and private use and irrational advertisement copy. The corporates must be held responsible for misleading and deceptive advertisements.

Advertising and Ethics

Advertising is a dynamic public forum where business interests, creativity, consumer needs and government regulations meet. Ethical advertising decisions are often complicated because advertising agency and media representatives involved in those decisions, although ethical criteria advertisers face extensive regulations but everything is not covered under written rule. Decisions may be based on a variety of considerations, including the objective of the advertising company, the attitude of target audience the philosophy of the agency and the advertiser and legal precedent. Many decisions are based on ethical concerns. Ethical issues in advertisement are very common.

Ethical Issues in Advertising

Advertising people, involved as they are in mass communications and persuasion, must be aware of the ethical dimensions in which they operate. Three characteristics make advertising particularly susceptible to ethical questions.

1. Typically, advertising messages are one sided, they rarely say anything about the deficiencies of the product or service being advertised.
2. Advertising is usually biased.
3. Advertising is intrusive. It interrupts our television show, it splits articles in magazines and newspapers. It interrupts music.

(a) Advertising and Law

It is expected that any product advertisement must be based on legal foundation. The Advertising Standard Council of India is one of the regulatory bodies to check the activities of advertisement. According to the Advertising Standard Council the code of advertising practices are:

1. Advertisement must be truthful.
2. Advertisement should not contain any reference to any person, firm or institution.

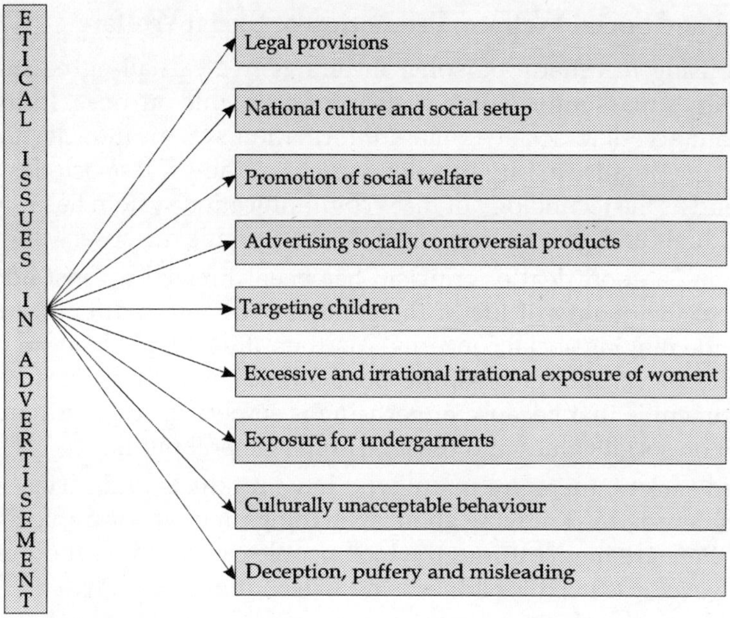

Ethical Issues in Advertisement (Kamatchi, P., 2003)

3. Advertisements shall not distort facts nor mislead the consumer by means of implications or omissions.
4. Advertisement statements should not mislead the consumers.
5. Products shall not be described as "free" where there is any direct cost to the consumer other than the actual cost of any delivery, freight or postage.

(b) Advertising and Culture: National Culture and Social Set-up

In contemporary India, persons are drawn through a variety of state and private media discourses through an imagined community of consumption, into the social status of the nation.

Advertising is aimed at a homogeneous group of consumers or would be consumers— who may be different in many other respects such as tradition, language, religion, etc. Advertising of a particular product is microcentred on potential consumers and seeks to get them to purchase and use that product. It takes consumers in that context and seeks to persuade them to change consumption habits with some products this could mean changes in lifestyles. But advertising itself the communication of a persuasive message and must therefore be understood by the target consumer. To do this advertising must be within the cultural frame of reference of the target consumer. Advertising in this way is in response to an existing cultural context and an attempt to change it.

(c) Advertising and Social Welfare: Promotion of Social Welfare

Although advertising has many personal meanings, we can all agree that it refers to the use of a society's mass information system for economic purpose. Individually or in groups, men want access to society's mass information system in order to give or gain information and eventually, to buy or sell a variety of things. As societies have become more complex and as the technology of mass communication system has improved, more and more individuals and groups have used it for economic purpose.

In recent years, a good deal of criticism has been directed against advertising and its contribution to the quality of life of the general public. It is difficult to find distinct categories for wide ranging social concerns. Another often heard criticism of advertising is its insensitivity to various groups, the poor ethnic minorities, the old women and others. The argument is that because advertising is so pervasive in and out of society it must have effect on social values and lifestyle of the general public.

In our mixed society, there are many who have products and services to offer and there are many interested in knowing about such things and who are able to buy them. In the free world, there are media through which people can reach each other. Techniques will change, however, the need for advertising will continue to grow.

It is true that any social group needs to assure itself of optional performance from its mass communication system which includes advertising. It is also true that this goal can be attained only on the basis of facts. Two types of facts are essential:

(i) We need to know the social, political and cultural preferences of a society.

(ii) We must also know the costs and benefit inherent in different organizational forms, the advertising institution may take.

(d) Socially Controversial Products

Advertisements should promote social welfare and well-being and modify the attitude and behaviour of the receiver of the message. But advertisement of products of social abuses may lead to negative results. All these years tobacco, gutkha and alcohol manufacturers are large advertisers. These products are subject to controversy. The effects of these products are not only detrimental to the health of individual consumers but also to the health of others.

(e) Targeting Children

Another ethical issue that advertisers face is advertising aimed at children. The following points explain why advertising to children is such an intense issue:

(a) Children are exposed to advertising of products that could be harmful to them if the advertising were to mislead, e.g., cereals with heavy sugar content.

(b) Some television techniques may be deceptive because children lack the ability to evaluate them properly, e.g., programme hosts or cartoon characters selling products.

(c) Advertising to children is bad because it exploits children, e.g., children have little sense of value, time and money.

(d) Long-term exposure to advertising may have adverse effects on the development of children's values, attitude and behaviour. Smith and Quelch (1993), Monko (1997).

(f) Excessive and Irrational Exposure of Models

Advertisement is self-regulatory. Some of the advertisements will hold no regulation in product promotions. But some advertisements are offended by the products and services themselves, others by the manner in which the advertisement is presented. These are seen in bad taste when sexual stimuli are utilised. The products of personal or private use, advertised continuously during prime time, are unhealthy to children and youth. Some advertisements based on excessive and irrational exposure of men and women and advertisement for undergarments are not Indian culture based.

(g) Puffery

Puffery sometimes called 'the permissible lie', is generally allowed in advertising. The other issue here is that would not stand on, *"Making promises that cannot be kept, Whatever your lips utter you must be sure to do"*, When we make a promise, we have to keep it. Unfortunately many advertisers seem to think that such statements are conditional, like" *I'll keep my word if, I profit from it"* or I'll keep my promises only if someone forces me to do so, in other words, they assess whether or not keeping a promise is to their advantage and if it is not (e.g. it costs money), they'll break the promise. Many advertisements promise more than the product can deliver, e.g., fruit juices that have come under fire for misleading the public about the amount of real fruit juice contained. But advertising and packages, although highlighting the word juice in a variety of ways, often contain small print that reads something such as *"Contains 100% real juice"*. Many products come in containers that are only partially filled, which leads the consumers to think that they are receiving full quantities, e.g., chips, cereals, coffee, etc.

(h) Deception and Deceptive Demonstration

The product and service advertised are evaluated for their relevance to the conveyed claims, failing in which leads to deception. Advertisement can be judged deceptive if it is perceived to have the tendency or capacity to deceive. Deception in advertisement is the primary issue.

This is another ethical issue where, often what you see in an advertisement may not be what you think it is. When a company runs an advertisement in which a product is demonstrated, that company is attempting to show that, in some way, their brand is superior to the brands offered by the competitors. One of the earliest and most well known demonstrations was undertaken by Colgate-Palmolive in which a brand of shaving cream was shown as being superior. In this advertisement, the shaving cream was applied to a sand paper and then the sand paper was shaved of, supposedly demonstrating the superior moisturizing capability of the product. In reality, sand paper will not be used. Instead, the advertisement used sand sprinkled on Plexiglas and this advertisement created impression that the consumer was seeing a real product demonstration. As the product was not real it is considered deceptive.

(i) Mock-Ups

It is an artificial alteration of product so that a very appealing photograph of the product may be taken, for example, ice cream, it is no real ice cream but smashed potatoes, beer foam is not real it is soap-suds. Soups are not really chunky but there are marbles in the soup so that the vegetables rise to the top. A mock-up may be considered acceptable, depending on the purpose of substitution and the product characteristics being demonstrated, e.g., smashed potato. The real ice cream cannot withstand the heat of the lights needed for proper photography. This substitution is acceptable if the purpose of the advertisement is to emphasise the texture of the ice cream or to claim that the ice cream melts at a slower rate than that of competitors then the substitution is likely to be considered deceptive.

Exhibit

Dear terrorist,

For so many months now, you've been indulging in quite activities. Whether they are right or wrong, you've been doing them. And you still are. You've been seeing the consequences, and perhaps facing them too.

And all this while, you've been seeing many weapons, piles of massacred bodies, deafening shouts and screams, wildfire and pitiful cries.

All this while perhaps you've never been yourself.

Dear terrorist, when was it you last slept peacefully, not restlessly? When was it you last smiled, not scowled? When was it that you last had sweet dreams, not nightmares? When was it you last saw flowers, not weapons? When was it you were last needed, not 'wanted'?

Now dear terrorist, give it a thought. Ask yourself. Who are you? Where have you come from? Where are you going? Where do you belong? What exactly are you doing? What is this name that you are called by? What is this caste and religion that you say you belong to? What is this place you call temple or whatever? What is this language that you love so much? What precisely are you doing? Why are you doing whatever you are doing? What is it that you've achieved? What is it that you are desired to achieve?

And dear terrorist, how long have you been here? How long will you be here?

For one brief moment, look back and see your present. Your future is with you, today. Not tomorrow. Think, but this time think for yourself. All this while you've never been thinking on your own.

See a flower. See a smile. See a dream. See a future. See yourself. See humanity.

Think of your mother. Think of your wife. Think of your children.

No weapons. No blood. No cries.

Your loving,

A human, like you.

Social Awarness Ad : Discouraging Terrorism.

Case Study

1. Lakme Girl

Revlon, the cosmetic giant in the West created a breakthrough in advertising by featuring a Revlon girl. Cindy Crawford, the well-known super-model, was now the Revlon girl. The face for many years was of a model, Lauren Hutton. In 1987, they created a .new campaign titled "The Most Unforgettable Women in the World." Renowned beauties like Imam were featured with Jerry Hall.

Lakme in India has also featured versatile as well as saleable faces - Yasmin (Miss India - 1966), Purnima Dixit, Maureen Keelan (now Wadia). Lakme's search for a model gave them a sophisticated face of Shyamolie Verma in 1981. Shyamolie was a corporate model for all their products for three years. Then followed an assortment of faces, some known, some unknown. (Juhi Chawla, Sonu Walia, Vidya Rao, Sabita Dhanrajgir, Poonam Gidwani, Anu Agarwal, Anu Ahuja, Mehr Jessia, Sherry Mehrhomji). However none of these faces could take on the whole gamut of products. Shyamolie surprisingly surpassed all her successors. Once again the search for a Lakme girl is on. Lakme Lever never took an unknown face. Besides, Lakme as a brand is bigger than the face. Aishwarya Rai in the 90's was their perfect face and screen. Bipasha Basu was their change in the mid-90's. To be Lakme face today, you don't have just to look good, you have to feel good.

Ethical Issues:

(1) Concentration on only models but not on range of product.

(2) Difference between Lux model and Lakme models recommendations.

2. Complan

- Formulated by Glaxo, UK as 'complete planned food.'
- Found its way into emergency rations for British soldiers during the Second World War.
- First positioning 'meal in a tea cup' for famished men in the army. 'Complete meal for soldiers.'
- Glaxo India's largest brand. Sales touching Rs. 60 crore.
- Launched in 1967 in India.
- Milk beverages market, currency estimated at Rs. 300 crore. 70% of the market is of white beverages. Complan's share is one-third of this market.

- Market has stagnated in the last four years. Complan has however managed a 10% annual growth rate.
- First positioning in India.

Ideal food supplement for aged and recuperating

Promotion: ethical

1971 Complete food aspect of the brand. 23 vital foods as against 9 contained in milk. Positioning fuzzy.

Targeting a too narrow segment.

1975 Larger targeting: Growing children. Make it tastier and appeal to kids. Chocolate variant made its entry.

Tasty nutrition drink.

Another flavour - cardamom saffron.

- Mass media campaign while continuing ethical promotion through chemists and doctors.
- Communication strategy:

To create a personality for the brand:

"I am a Complan boy; I am a Complan girl."

SP schemes to keep excitement alive.

1980 Plain Complan: low priced. Chocolate Complan: high growth segment. Cardamom Saffron.

1990 Started pushing one of its new flavours (mango) and promoting a new usage habit for it (mix with cold milk — milk shake). Best selling flavour for Complan after chocolate.

Ethical Issues

(1) It targets both: the children and the aged.

(2) It is not a food substitute.

(3) Issue of relationship marketing?

(4) Sales promotion, can play in affecting sales of Complan?

3. Lintas

Prakash Tandon, the ex-chief of Lever had remarked that Lever was a creative experience. Padamsee, the ex-chief of Lintas was greatly influenced by this, and decided to make Lintas a creative organisation in the best sense. But that did not mean that he wanted accountants to become creative. However, he did emphasise innovative accountants who could find new and better ways to do their work. Lintas was made new. The salary structure including the year-end-gifts (YEGs) also evolved to keep pace with this new Lintas. The organisation must break off the old JWT syndrome. When Padamsee took over, the copy and the art departments were separate. He paired them up. Creative Lintas were constituted. Copywriters and visualisers were made to work in close cooperation. It worked off excellent creativity. Padamsee formed mini-agencies, instead managing one huge one.

He introduced a managing committee of eight to nine well-informed, dedicated and intelligent people to run Lintas. They throw in ideas.

Many new ideas emerge in the meeting of the managing committee, e.g., small is beautiful. Lintas, Bombay was divided into Lintas Bombay and Lintas Bombay 2. Two MD's were appointed. Padamsee became the chairman of the BOD, rather than MD. The MD's set objectives, and MBO was introduced. Padamsee was left free to conceptualize by these arrangements. At the lowest rug, jobs are managed. Up scale, people are to be managed. At the top, concepts are to be managed. Padamsee at the top managed the concepts of what Lintas wanted to be. They put down a Lintas code. The code read: 1. We believe there is always a better way of doing things (innovation). 2. We believe in completing everything we start. To complete an idea, you must have an author or father of that idea or else the idea becomes a step child. 3. We believe that we should treat our colleagues as our friends, and not rivals.

Ethical Issues

1. Challenges involved in managing an ad agency.
2. An agency to position itself?

4. Dalda

There was a strong prejudice against Dalda, a hydrogenated vegetable oil. Many voiced apprehension that Dalda gave a tickle in the throat and led to stomach upset. Dalda was considered to be a culprit for all types of known and unknown physical disorders. In those days, Hindustan Lever's marketing director was Morris Zinkin. He was of the opinion that to ward off negative associations of Dalda it was necessary to project it as a superior product of international standards. It contained so many thousand units of Vitamin A which was good for skin and so many thousand units of Vitamin D and so on. They prepared a number of ads. One headline talked of Maya and the question of fats. It was about Dalda being rid of cooking fat. The ad explained how Maya would be strong and healthy because her mother used Dalda. It ran for about two to three years in a wide media mix. Later, the research showed that the prejudices against Dalda were as strong as they were before the campaign began. The most important lesson, therefore, in communication and advertising is that emotions play a great part in decision making. So far, the Dalda ads were only rational. While the decision to use Dalda is taken on emotional plane. Further research showed that even those housewives who were using Dalda tried to conceal the fact that they were doing so. They were ashamed of it.

A research study on this case has been undertaken. It was decided to do motivational research. Later, they formed a team. Padamsee, Gerson da Cunha (Lintas), Morris Zinkin, Dr. Rajni Chhada — a psychologist of Lever and Balwant Tandon — a Hindi copywriter were the members of this team. Rajni Chhada was able to cut the Gordian Knot. She said 'The reason people are saying that Dalda gives them all these aches and pains is they have transferred aggression from being deprived of ghee because of its price. It is falling into the substitute product." It was like a stepmother syndrome.

The team decided to fight fire with fire. They moved the ground from rational to emotional. Balwant Tandon came out with a brilliant line in Hindi: "Mamta ki Kasauti par Khara" - Dalda. They ignored 1000 units of this and that. The movement towards Dalda then began. Dalda became an acceptable product. If Ma accepts it, then who am I to reject it? Padamsee says that the lesson has never been lost on him. Even his public service campaigns are emotional.

Even as a theatre person, he never stages a play that is highly intellectual, but lacks in emotional content.

New Dalda

Sept. 2003	:	Hindustan Lever sold its Dalda brand to US-based Bunge Ltd., which specializes in agri-business. Bunge now wants to relaunch and revitalize the brand.
Plans	:	It was planned as the product, packaging, distribution and promotion will be reworked.
	:	HLL manufactured Dalda in a decentralized manner in 13 units spread across the country to save on the state excise tax. Burne will restrict Dalda manufacturing to just four units, out of which three are owned by it. This may result in increased excise outflow but will give greater control to Burne.
The Target audience	:	Were mothers in the Hindi-speaking belt of UP and MP where its usage is more.
The Health Platform	:	Was decided as some fat is necessary especially for growing children.
The Competitors	:	Were Sunflower, Sunflower Gagan, Rath and smaller regional players.

Issues

Rational appeals in advertising.

Emotional appeals in advertising.

5. Coca Cola

Year	:	Event/Remarks
1886	:	John Styth Pemberton, Atlanta, a pharmacist, brew a caramel-coloured syrup, the precursor of the modern Coca-Cola.

	:	Frank Robinson, his partner, named it Coca-Cola in a distinctive lettering style. Pemberton sold the drink through Jacob Pharmacy.
	:	Candler, an Atlanta druggist, bought Coca-Cola for $ 2300. In 1892, he formed the Coca-Cola Co. with four companions with a stock of S 100000.
	:	Coca-Cola was registered with US patent office. Coca Cola began selling at soda fountains for five cents a glass.
	:	Coca-Cola was bottled.
1899	:	Bottled regularly under a reigion-wise franchise system.
	:	Pepsi Cola, its first major competitor, opened a plant at Chattanooga.
1900	:	Another Pepsi plant opened in Atlanta.
1900-1920	:	Coca-Cola bottling plants crossed 1000.
	:	Six-and-a-half-ounce pale green bottle designed by Root Glass Co. of Terre Haute Indiana. An intrinsic part of the brand.
1919:	:	Robert Woodruff, acquired the company for $ 25 million and assumed charge in 1923. Coke, associated with sports events and Woodruff.
1928	:	Coke accompanied summer Sydney Olympics team of US.
Early 1940's	:	Brand described as 'the real thing' to distinguish it from other colas.
1939-1945	:	Second World War. Soldiers from the US had access to Coke at five cents a bottle in Europe which was being liberated from the Nazis. 64 overseas bottling plants.
1950's	:	Became daily consumption item stored in household fridges
1960	:	Fanta, an orange drink was accidentally made by Coke's German counterpart.
1961	:	Sprite, lemon-lime drink developed in the late 1950's was formally launched in the US.
1963	:	TAB, a one-calorie cola was launched.
1966	:	Fresca, a low calorie citrus drink was launched.
1980's	:	Pepsi targeted the new generation. Coke became 'fuddy duddy' brand.
1981	:	Roberto C. Goizueta took over as chief at Atlanta H.Q. He took equity in bottling plants. He got rid of weak businesses.
1982	:	Diet Coke, most successful brand extension was launched.
1985	:	Cherry Coke, cherry flavoured Cola was launched.
	:	New Coke to compete with sweeter Pepsi was launched but failed to satisfy the customers. Classic Coke was recalled.
1988	:	Break-mate, a Coke dispensing machine was launched.

1991 : Coke distributed advertising between McCann Erickson and Creative Artist Agency (CAA), a Hollywood set-up.

1992 : Colas witness a declining share (from 63.6 p.c. in 1984 to 60.4 p.c. in 1991). Nestea, ready-to-drink iced tea was launched.

: PowerAde launched as a sports drink.

1993 : Coke re-enters India after 16 years.

Ethical Issues

(1) Strategies followed in India.

SALES AND DISTRIBUTION : ETHICS AND ETHICAL ISSUES

"Virtually every human interaction involves personal selling of one form or another."

–Joe R. Mars.

Selling is not a new profession, in fact it may be considered to be world's oldest profession right from the stage of Adam and Eve. Even in India the *epics* speak about sales and business.

Selling is an art of approaching the prospect, creating an impression about the product and making the prospects into customers. Selling encompasses a whole variety of sales situations and activities, selling provides a mechanism for exchange and through this process, customer's needs and wants are satisfied. As Geoffrey S. Moss of Bausch and Lomb puts it, *"If Selling is identifying needs, evaluation of alternative means of satisfying those needs and then presenting the best solution to satisfy the need."*

Concept of Personal Selling

Selling is one of the many marketing components. In business, personal selling refers to the personal communication of information to persuade a prospective customer to buy something – goods, service, idea or something else — that satisfies that individual's needs. The concept of selling mentioned above, involves a person helping another person. The salesperson often works with prospects or customers to examine their needs, provide information, suggest a product to meet their needs and provide after-sales service to ensure long-term satisfaction. It also involves communication between the seller and buyer.

It is understood that in personal selling a salesperson can tailor the needs of an individual customer. Selling services offer excellent career opportunities; banks, hotels, airlines and travel agencies are industries that need professional sales people.

Distribution

The distribution element of the marketing mix particularly the management of physical distribution, has long been felt to be one of the areas in business where substantial improvements and cost savings can be made. The management of distribution has now been recognized as being a key part of the strategic management of a company.

Concept of distributions

Distribution is concerned with all those activities required to move goods and materials into the factory, through the factory and to the final consumer. Distribution strategies concerned with the flow of the object of distribution is to reach optional number of customers, at the lowest possible cost, while maintaining the desired control.

Retailing and wholesaling are the two major physical distribution functions in business, involved in bringing goods and services from the point of production to the point of use.

Ethical Issues in Sales and Distribution

Organisations are composed of individuals. These individual morals and ethical values help to shape those of the organisation. The moral principles and values that govern the behaviour of person or a group with respect to what is right or wrong. Many salespersons are in dilemma in determining the right and wrong as they have no proper training and orientation. They operate at the conventional level and would feel they must go along to get along, in other words, they go along to keep their jobs. At the most they only follow formula policies and procedures, to be boundary spanners to the corporation and not acting independently. The following figure shows some of the ethical issues in this area.

Ethical Issues in Sales and Distribution

(a) Relationship Marketing

Organisations target and present customers – the emphasis is shifting from selling to customers to creating customers for tomorrow. Thus, business is finally, beginning to think more long term than short term. This process is referred to as relationship marketing. In relationship marketing the seller contacts customers after the purchase to determine if they are satisfied and have future needs. Relationship marketing refers to 1:1 customer service wherein marketer and customer deal with many products. In this the focus is on the transaction making the sale along with the service after the sale the seller contacts the customer to ensure satisfaction with the purchase, hence it is said, *"The company practicing relationship marketing* is *ethically oriented"*.

(b) Boundary Spanners

It is exercised when corporations do not allow the salesperson to act independently. The force management must be ethical and legally considerate in giving freedom to the salespeople and try to attract and retain good sales personnel. On one hand, they are advocates of the products and services offered by the organization on the other hand, they are advocates of customers in that they attempt to match up their organization products and services with customer's needs and wants. Freedom from supervision and opportunities for personal development are characteristics of the salespersons. Selling

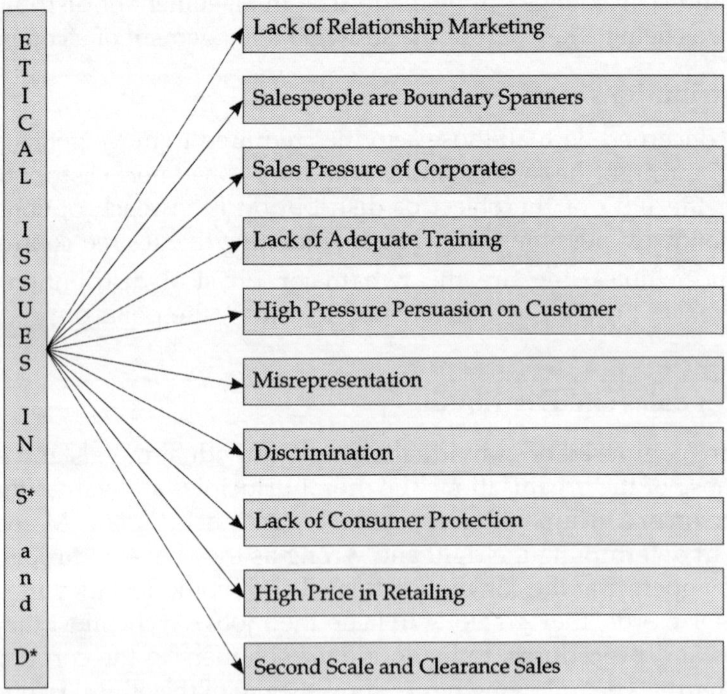

Ethical Issues in Sales and Distribution (Kamatchi P., 2003)

involves constant attempts at influencing other people. A high degree of self-management is necessary and *"Sales people are not to be made boundary spanners to the corporation and they should act in the interest of consumers"*.

(c) Sales Pressure

Many of the corporates make their salespeople to work under pressure.

A goal or target is set to meet with in a particular or limited time. This brings salespeople to achieve the goal and try to reach beyond the set goals for the incentives. This attitude will lead to the suffering of quality sales management and targeting innocent customers. However, the corporations/organisations must be realistic and set obtainable goals so that *salespeople under the pressure of corporates will not ignore the interest of consumers.*

(d) Training to the Salesperson

Most significant phase of the selling process also tends to be the most neglected one in many sales training programmes, which often focus primarily on product knowledge and sales. Although these are also important, new salespeople are frequently left to learn the skills of sale persuasion largely through experience. This is frustrating for salespeople as well as their customers. Inadequately trained salespeople struggle to master this most critical challenge of sales work. As a customer, Green (1985) rightly put it as, *"In the sales field today, adequate education is a must, refresher courses are helpful, and constant updating through trade journals and other material is necessary.* Hence, *"Sales people should generally receive very good training".*

(e) High Pressure Persuasion on Customers

Persuasion may be considered the core of the selling process. This is to help customers crystallise their awareness of specific wants or needs and persuading them to purchase products or services that can satisfy those needs. Persuasion must be conveying ideas and values created for the benefit of the customers. A prospective customer is moved to buy not only by the merit of the seller's ideas but also by the seller's motivation and this will turn to high pressure persuasion. Hence, *"The salesman should not exert high pressure persuasion on customers".*

(f) Misrepresentation

Most salespeople are unaware that they assume legal obligations with accompanying risks and responsibilities whenever they approach a customer. Honesty in selling goes beyond telling an outright lie. It includes being reliable and responsible for promises made. Salespeople cannot change their minds if the deal is not right. Salespeople to maintain the integrity, should be loyal to their promises. Intentional misrepresentation of products or services is considered fraudulent behaviour. *The corporates should supervise and see that the salesman do not misrepresent the product.* Sales representatives should not misrepresent the products to the consumer in order to improve sales, otherwise it will lend to unethical act.

(g) Discriminations

Customers are innocent, intelligent and experienced, they are the 'king' and 'goal' for many of the products. They should be treated equally. Sometimes salespeople provide more favourable treatment for one customer than another. Some customer may receive price reductions, promotional allowances and support while others do not. Individual salespeople or managers may practise price discrimination to improve sales and might show discrimination in treating the customers. Hence, the corporates must train the salesmen to treat the customers equally.

(h) Consumer Protection

Every salesman must satisfy customer's needs. The salesmen's expectations are rising without considering the right of the customer like the right to safety, right to choose. The salespeople will sell the product particularly products which are dangerous in nature. Many customers, unaware of the risk, purchase the product under the friendly persuasion of salespeople. Here the unethical act of the salesperson comes to picture. Every salesman should be aware of various legal provisions on consumer protection and be instructed to make the sale accordingly. Hence, *the corporates must create the opportunity in giving more attention on consumer protection.*

(i) Seconds Sales and Clearance Sales

It is another method of sales where the defective products are sold to the customers. The advantages of the seconds and clearance sale is through price reduction The big corporates will increase the price and show that 50% discount is made. Many of the products will misguide the customers with poor quality, size and colour and improper pricing. The practice of clearance sale is considered to be more unethical than seconds, as the chances of duping the customers are more. Thus, seconds sale is fair since the consumers know that the product has defects, whereas clearance sale is unfair where consumers are duped with the substandard products.

If the above ethical practices are not taken care of by the corporates, it will lead to ethical issues in sales and distribution.

A good corporate ensures customer satisfaction through its marketing activities. Again the marketing activities should be exercised ethically like fair behaviour, moral responsibility, meet customer needs in time, integrity, honesty and dignity, efficiency and effectiveness, protection of customer dignity and respect and customer delight. Job of marketing is to convert societal needs into profitable opportunities and these are to be met through product, pricing, advertisement and sales and distribution There are many issues in these aspects like product misrepresentation, lack of safety, socially controversial products and so on. With respect to pricing, misleading pricing, unfair pricing, price fixing and so on are some of the issues. In case of advertising, unfair advertisement copies, socially controversial products, excessive and irrational exposure women, deception, puffery and so on. Lack of relationship marketing, discrimination, lack of training are some of the issues in sales and distribution.

Exhibit

AMERICAN MARKETING ASSOCIATION'S CODE OF ETHICS

Members of the American Marketing Association (AMA) are committed to ethical professional conduct. They have joined together in subscribing to this Code of Ethics embracing the following topics:

Responsibilities of the Marketer

Marketers must accept responsibility for the consequences of their activities and make every effort to ensure that their decisions, recommendations, and actions function to identify, serve, and satisfy all i.e., customers, organizations, and society.

Marketers' professional conduct must be guided by:

1. Basic rule of professional ethics: not knowingly to do harm.
2. Adherence to all applicable laws and regulations.
3. Accurate representation of their education, training, and experience.
4. Active support, practice, and promotion of this Code of Ethics.

Marketers shall uphold and advance the integrity, honour, and dignity of the marketing profession by:

1. Being honest in serving consumers, clients, employees, suppliers, distributors and the public.
2. Not knowingly participating in conflict of interest without prior notice to all parties involved.
3. Establishing equitable fee schedules including the payment or receipt of usual. Customary, and/or legal compensation for marketing exchanges.

Rights and Duties of Parties in the Marketing Exchange Process:

Participants in the marketing exchange process should be able to expect that:

1. Products and services offered are safe and fit for their intended uses.
2. Information about the products and services are not deceptive.
3. All parties intend to discharge their obligations, financial and otherwise, in good faith.
4. Appropriate internal methods exist for equitable adjustment and/or redress of grievances concerning purchases.

It is understood that the above would include, but is not limited to, the following responsibilities of the marketer:

In the area of product development and management.

- Disclosure of all substantial risks associated with product or service usage.
- Identification of any product component substitution that might materially change the product or impact on the buyer's purchase decision.
- Identification of extra-cost added features.

In the area of promotions.

- Avoidance of false and misleading advertising.
- Rejection of high-pressure manipulations, or misleading sales tactics.
- Avoidance of sales promotions that use deception or manipulation.

In the area of distribution.

- Not manipulating the availability of a product for purpose of exploitation.
- Not using coercion in the marketing channel.
- Not exerting undue influence over the reseller's choice to handle a product.

In the area of pricing.

- Not engaging in price-fixing.
- Not practising predatory pricing.
- Disclosing the full price associated with any purchase.

In the area of marketing research.

- Prohibit selling or fund raising under the guise of conducting research.
- Maintaining research integrity by avoiding misrepresentation and omission of pertinent research data.
- Treating outside clients and suppliers fairly.

Organizational Relationships

Marketers should be aware of how their behaviour may influence or impact the behaviour of others in organizational relationships. They should not demand, encourage, or apply coercion to obtain unethical behaviour in their relationships with others, such as employees, suppliers, or customers.

ETHICAL ASPECTS OF FINANCIAL MANAGEMENT

Introduction

About three decades ago, the scope of financial management was confined to raise funds. Little significance was attached to analytical thinking in financial decision making and problem solving. As a consequence, study was structured around this theme and constrained description of the instruments and institutions of raising funds and of the major events, like promotion, reorganisation, readjustment, merger, consolidation and so on, when the funds were raised. In the mid-fifties the emphasis shifted to the judicious utilization of funds. The modern thinking in financial management accords a far greater importance to management decision making. The finance managers are in key position in top management areas and play a vital role in solving complex management problems. Since they are responsible for shaping the fortunes of the organizations, they hold moral and ethical responsibility towards the stakeholders. A strong foundation of ethics towards finance and financial management is sure to attain success and sustainability in the long run.

Ethics in Finance

Money by itself is not necessarily evil. Rather, it is something that is used to trade goods and services. We call it 'currency' and it allows us to do business between organizations. Unfortunately, that is the sterile dictionary type definition but it does not capture all the issues that are involved with finances. In business life just like many other realms money causes all sorts of problems. People make incredibly bad decisions because of money and plenty of people have gone to prison because of money-related crimes (ex.: Ramalingaraju of Satyam Computers). This is why people always approach money with a certain amount of uneasiness, Hence, there is demand for ethics and ethical behaviours is finance and financial management.

Ethics in general is concerned with human behaviour, that is acceptable, 'right' or not acceptable, 'wrong' based on conventional morality. As it is already known that general ethical norms encompass the truthfulness, honesty, integrity, respect for others, fairness and justice. They relate to all aspects of life, including business and finance.

Financial ethics is, therefore, a subset of general ethics.

Ethics in Financial Aspects

The current financial crisis was largely triggered when trust in financial market was destroyed by lack of transparency and evidence of the absence of ethical behaviours by many of the financial business. According to the global finance professionals from all over the world, through their prize winning conceptual ideas on finance, namely:

(i) The need for order in the disorder of finance.

(ii) Internalism, institutions and individuals: Systemic changes for a systemic ethical crisis.

(iii) Emotions, personal ethics and professional life – the lost link.

The above is to research are all focusing on the best return, but with the balance between risk and reward. It is suggesting the confidence towards financial professionals to trust with integrity and interest.

Why ethics is finance?

People who work in finance are placed in a fiduciary position of trust, by their employers, if they are not self-employed, but more importantly, by the members of the general public, over whose assets they are given control. Their daily business is directly working with other people's money or doing other things that are public's investment decisions. And if they are unethical people, their clients and the public, are at high risk for being cheated. Finance workers are entitled to reasonable fees for their services, but they are not entitled to engage in investment activity solely to generate more commissions for themselves, or engage in any other self-dealing while they are doing their jobs on behalf of their clients or customers and they have to exercise reasonable care when doing their jobs.

Given the many scandals of recent years, many companies have done their best to publish their code of ethics and to acknowledge their responsibilities to the public. These firms know that public confidence in their financial matters is a great concern. Unethical bahaviour of the firm means that people will stay away from that firm, and they may stay away from all the others as well. Ethical lapses may take down of the business.

If those lapses are even perceived as widespread, that perception can potentially destroy an entire industry, that is why ethics are not merely relevant but, as Michael Spencer says "I've never known anybody who has lost because of ethical practices". So this is given a sense they are vital to the existence of the industry. But they are not optional.

Hence, "if ethics is lost, the business is lost, and morality is lost, the industry is lost."

ETHICS IN FINANCIAL MANAGEMENT

It is widely accepted and understood that ethics is financial management which is a branch of the main management has a vital role to play. There are many firms framing individual code of ethics in dealing with financial matters as it is concerned with the public money. It is to promote honest and ethical conduct and compliance with applicable laws, rules and regulations, particularly selected to the maintenance of financial records, the preparation of financial statements and proper public disclosure.

Financial executives like chief accounting officers, controller, treasures and persons performing similar functions are various persons who are responsible for practising ethics in finance and financial management. There need to have obligation in practising ethics by setting up ethics policies and standards in business. The following are the expected financial principles (ethics) of an organization:

(1) **Promote honesty and ethical conduct:** Engage in and promote honest and ethical conduct, including ethical handling of actual apparent conflicts of interest between personal and professional relationship.

(2) **Act in good faith:** Act in good faith, responsibility, with due care, competence, prudence and diligence, without misrepresenting material facts or allowing one's independent judgment or discussions to be sub-oriented to ones personal interests.

(3) **Fair disclosure:** Produce full, fair, accurate, timely and understandable disclosures in reports and documents to the submitted to the Securities Exchange authorities and other regulators and in other public communications made by the company.

(4) **Measures to protect confidentiality:** Take reasonable measures to protect confidentiality of non-public information about the company and its customers and vendors obtained or created in connection with the activities and to prevent unauthorised disclosure of such information.

(5) **Application of Law:** Necessary steps to be taken to follow the law of the land fully, without violating any of the rules and regulations.

(6) **Prompt report on material deficiency:** Promptly reporting of any information concerning significant or material deficiencies or weaknesses in the design or operation of the internal controls of the company.

Any fraud, whether or not material, involving any member of the management or other employees who has a significant role in the financial reporting, disclosures or internal controls of the company.

Any other matter that could have adverse effects on the company or any of its subsidiaries ability to record, process summaries and report financial data.

The financial management should also facilitate the work of the independent auditors, auditors of the company and shall not directly or indirectly, take any action to fraudulently influence, coerce, manipulate or mislead the independent auditors.

Importance of Ethics in Financial Management

Ethics in financial management is also important because of history. Just say "Enron" and people either laugh or get very serious. The trouble with "Enron" was that every one was happy as long as the numbers kept looking good, however much mischief was afoot at Enron and the company was running fast and loose without ethical principles.

Enron is a textbook example of why financial ethics are important. Without ethics, there are truly no boundaries when it comes to organization culture.

Ethics are important because finances make people do some strange things. The accounting books and sheets have no conscience. The goal of working with them is to make the numbers add up in a way that is pleasing to the organizations and its constituents but numbers do not have soul. Unfortunately, people can move around numbers in all sorts of ways to make them add up 'correctly' because of this, companies adopt financial management ethics in order to have an outside source of guidance. People are aware that without a moral barometer anything wrong is possible on the accounting procedures and records.

Countries like the United States are built around many great things but there are dangers also. In a post-modern world, capitalism can quickly dissolve into greed, again companies that do not have any sort of moral code of ethics. Principles are really free to do whatever they want. Because shareholders and financial markets have impossibly high demands on certain companies and executives feel they are forced to give moral compromises. Before people know it, Enron appears again and again. As people are not clear on their own ethical viewpoints and they are left to make decisions based on a reactionary environment. Therefore, if people are serious about living life in a certain way, they must write a strict moral code of ethics and be willing to follow it, and no matter what happens in the financial markets. The business activities and finance in business should have **ethical stamina.**

Ethics as core activities of finance and financial management

In the recent past with various context references ethics began to play a vital role in finance and its management. The business houses found a new relationship between ethics and finance. For long and sustainable business activities, the dealing with public money need checks and balances. The role of ethics in the financial aspects were not spoken much in the past. Later realization began that finance will not exist without ethical practices for long run.

Accountants should present a 'true and fair view'. The picture, which accountants give can be either enlightening or misleading, depending on how he or she chooses to define it. In spite of various accounting standards and professional code of ethics, there is a lot of opportunity for "creative accounting", a phrase which is popularly associated with "cooking the books" in a way which is legal, although morally dubious.

The businesses and corporate houses generally undertake two divisions of financial activities namely.

(1) Financial markets

(2) Financial operations and services

Under financial markets it consists of commodity markets, currency markets and option markets.

Whereas the financial operations and services include financial plans, tax advisor, stock broker, insurance agents and so on.

Ethics and ethical practices in all aspects of financial activities need to have significant attention. Good ethics is good business. As huge amount is involved in financial dealings people invest their money with financial institutions to build a better life after their retirement. There need to have well developed and organized structure of ethics to ensure personal and organizational welfare.

In India, many of organizations have cheated many highly ethical people who trusted them and their companies. Many of the companies started booting money by cheating the public without care and vigilance by the public and the government. As finance covers a broad range of activities and most visible aspects of finance is financial markets related to Stock Exchange. These are closely connected with the commercial banks, investment banks, Mutual fund companies, pension funds, both public and private and insurance, and the other core area is financial operations of a corporation.

Individual code of ethics by the companies, accounting standards and government regulations and income tax law and practices, professional ethics codes of auditors and related officers and various other laws may be protecting the financial mismanagements in the organization. These are laws and guidelines which are violated by many of the business activities in making money and profit. Ethics is beyond law with and all above said procedures. There are a lot of ethical issues without violating the law. Ethical misconducts by the financial institution are well identified. As huge money is involved in financial dealings, there must be well developed safeguards in place to ensure personal and organizational ethics. A strong emphasis must be placed as the integrity of the finance professionals and on ethical leadership in the financial institutions. There need to have a strong principles on:

(i) Duties of fiduciaries (held in trust)

(ii) Fairness in sales practices

(iii) Securities markets

Ethical issues or unethical practices in finance and financial management

Ethical issues are based on the daily practices of the company's context and reality. The following ethical issues in finances, financial activities and financial management need to be identified and rectified to uphold the morale of the business.

(i) Deception: It is an act of deceiving somebody intentionally. It is one of the common practices in the business world specially in India and third world countries, since most of the people are vulnerable. It is to practise to strengthen the returns and minimizing the risk factors. Salespersons, agents and financial advisors deceive the public using misleading statements like tax free or 0% interest etc., they make public enable to make rational choices among so many alternatives, they will also confuse the public in accepting any financial activities to obtain personal gain. Insurance agents, for example, a financial adviser will help you in selecting an appropriate planning or offer a sense of investment choices or options among which to allocate your money like on:

- Private retirement accounts.
- College savings plans
- Charitable remainder trusts

In general, in deception, a person is deceived when that person is able to make a rational choice as a result of holding a false belief which is creating some claims made by another. The claim may be either a false or misleading statement or a statement may be confusing or incomplete.

(ii) Unsuitability: This is another unethical practice where the insurance agents and stock brokers and other salespersons influence the public by good impression on wrong and unsuitable products. The main intention of such agents is to do business without counting the customers future financial stability or benefit with sole purpose is to make profit. This may also be referred to as security fraud. The following are the common causes for unsuitability:

- Unsuitable types of securities: This arises when there is a recommendation on stock, e.g., when bonds would better fit the investor's objectives.
- Unsuitable grades of securities: When selecting lower rated bonds when higher rated ones are more appropriate.
- Unsuitable diversification: Which includes the use of margin or options which can leverage an account and create greater risk.
- Unsuitable trading techniques includes the use of margin or options. This can leverage an account and create greater risk.
- Unsuitable liquidity is in limited partnerships, e.g., not very marketable and hence unsuitable for customers who would like to liquidate the investment.

Investments are most often deemed to be unsuitable since they are involved with the risks. However, the risks are multiplied by the unethical act of the responsible persons in the financial markets or financial executive. There need to have consultation to give proper guidance to the customers.

(iii) Inappropriate and excessive trading: This situation arises when the broker is more intersted in commission rather than benefits to clients.

Since the control of accounts is in the hands of a responsible authority and chance of misappropriation. Here the unethical acts may take place. This is referred as 'churning'.

Churning takes place when excessive inappropriate trading is done for a client's account by a broker who has control over the account with the interest to generate commission rather than to benefit the client. Though churning occurs there is a disagreement on the frequency. Unauthorized trading and other abuses are rising sharply in the recent years.

Churning is a breach of fiduciary duty. Churning appears only when a client hands over control of an account to a broker.

Excessive trading depends on the character of the account, which are :

(a) A client who is a more speculative investor, willing to assume higher risk for greater return, should expect a higher trading volume.

(b) High volume is not the only factor, traders may choose even if the volume is relatively low.

(c) Churning might be indicted by a pattern of trading that consistently favours traders that yield higher commission.

(iv) Securities fraud and manipulation in markets: This unethical act appears commonly in the financial markets. The financial markets are expected to be fair and just in their dealings. Here the fairness is not meant by preventing losses rather it contributes to the efficiency. When a company fails to report proper information and manipulation of buying and selling of securities for the purpose of creating misleading impression about the price to misguide the investors to buy or sell the securities, is referred as fraud in the financial markets.

Manipulation involves buying or selling of securities in order to create a false or misleading impression, to induce other investors to buy or sell the securities.

(v) Unequal bargaining power: The fairness of bargained agreements assumes that the parties have relatively equal bargaining power. A trader who negotiates for a future contract that results in general loss has only himself or herself to blame. Unequal bargaining power can result from many sources like resources and processing ability. But the general principle is that equal bargaining power should be equal to all parties in the market.

(vi) Efficient pricing: Efficient pricing occurs when:

- Fairness in financial markets includes efficient prices that reasonably reflect all the available information.
- Volatility results from a mismatch of buyers and sellers in eventually self-correcting. Meantime great harm may result by inefficient pricing. The individual investors are harmed by buying at too high a price or selling at too a high price during the period of mispricing.
- Volatility also affects the markets by reducing investors' confidence and driving them away. The loss of confidence depresses stock prices.

(vii) Insider trading: Insider trading is the act of buying and selling a company's stock on the basis of inside information about the company. This is also an information which is not available to general public but kept as a company's confidential and proprietary information. Basically, inside trading is illegal and many companies have been prosecuted. It is also unethical not because it is illegal but because it is claimed the person who trades on insides information, steals the information and gains unfair advantages of information. It is also unethical as the information which is confidential and not available to general public outside the company have significant impact on the price of the company's stock.

The following are general views on unethical practices of inside viewer.

- The information that the trader uses does not belong to him.
- The executives, managers, employees and others who work inside a company and who are aware of inside events that will affect the price of the company's stock do not themselves own the company.
- The resource they work with including the information available to them are resources that belong collectively to the shareholders.

- Employees have an ethical duty to refrain from using company information to benefit themselves or them. This may also lead to reduce the size of the markets which will affect the markets and society in general.

(viii) Creative accounting (financial statements): Creative accounting refers to voluntary creation of buyer's accounts. Misappropriation, omission and commission of statements are various activities used for creative accounting. Some ethical issues regarding accounting practices are:

- Under-reporting income
- Falsifying documents
- Allowing or taking questionable deductions
- Illegally evading income taxes and otherwise engaging in fraud.

However, there are many more unidentified ethical issues rather unethical practices in the finance and financial management. Kickbacks, earnings management, misleading financial analysis, bucker shop, forex scams, executive compensation, bribery and facilitation payment are unethical practices.

Though there strong laws, policies and procedures checking of public or companies' finance, a lot more unethical practices are prevalent in corporate finance. Ethics in finance is far more than trust. The companies should be responsible in protecting the interest of the investors through ethical practices. Ethics in finance is an unavoidable activity as it is concerned with only the ethical problems of individual in a specific occupation but also with problems in financial markets and financial institutions.

Exhibit

Case Study on:

The BHEL Disinvestment

The decision of the United Progressive Alliance Government to sell off 10 per cent of public holding of equity in Bharat Heavy Electricals Limited (BHEL) is in direct contravention of its own promise. The National Common Minimum Programme made it clear that profitable public sector enterprises would not be privatised. In the case of BHEL, it had further explicitly promised that while it would be allowed to raise resources from the capital market, the government would devolve full managerial and commercial autonomy to such enterprises to strengthen them and enable them to become globally competitive players.

The decision to divest shares in BHEL–just like the earlier sale by the UPA Government of some equity in NTPC—completely disregards both of these important promises. This particular act of divestment would take place without the agreement of the parties providing outside support to the UPA, and indeed by overriding the decision-making power of the Board of BHEL which has clearly not been consulted either. Further, the expected proceeds from the sale of this equity-around Rs. 2000 crore to the newly created

National Investment Fund. This is supposed to finance health and education schemes and also provide funds for the revival of public sector units. In other words, this money is to go towards spending by the government, a move that is both unnecessary and fiscally irresponsible.

Unnecessary, because this amount of public resources can easily be found if the government really intends to. After all, more than Rs 30,000 crore was found as additional defence expenditure. And irresponsible, because the sale of equity from a profitable enterprise necessarily involves the loss of future revenue because of foregone profits. The sale of any asset implies a capital loss, which properly should only be balanced through some other change in assets or liabilities, such as through retiring debt. Using such money as a form of current revenue, which is in effect what is being done here, is completely illegitimate.

In the case of BHEL, the amount of foregone profits is not small at all, since one of the year alone, the total operating profits of the company (before depreciation interest and taxes) amounted to more than Rs 19,000 crore and even post-tax profits were more than Rs. 10,000 crore. Indeed, BHEL, like several other "navratnas" has been showing profits continuously for some years, but has not been allowed to spend the money for its own expansion and development. Instead, it has simply added to its reserves, such that its reserves currently amount to well over Rs. 50,000 crore. This is extremely wasteful, and it also denies BHEL and other such companies the opportunity to invest and restructure in ways that would increase their external competitiveness. Many profitable PSEs are currently in this position, whereby they are simply holding huge reserves because of constraints put upon them by the government. The fear is that if they are privatised, the private purchaser will then have access to these huge reserves that it can use to its own ends rather than in socially desirable ways. This was true, for example, in the case of both VSNL and Baleo, where privatisation allowed the private buyers access to the enormous built up reserves to further other investment plans of the purchasing company.

It should be obvious that such a strategy is not only unwise but also counter to any genuine attempt to strengthen the public sector. It is even contrary to proposals made by a committee set up by this UPA government to consider issues of autonomy delegation of financial powers and empowerment of central PSEs, chaired by Dr. Arjun Sengupta. The report of this committee ("Group of Experts on Empowerment of Central Public Sector Enterprises") was submitted in April 2005. Many of the points made in this report have a direct bearing on disinvestment of the type now being pursued. The Report points out that "the Ministry in charge of the company should recognise the fact that they are not the owners of the company but are only exercising the functions of ownership as a custodian on behalf of the government and the public at large."

The report recommends much greater autonomy and clearly defined powers for the Board of Directors, which should be fully responsible for the supervision and control over the management of the company. It should have full powers of pursuing new lines of business, deciding on suitable acquisitions and mergers, setting up subsidiaries, as well as other decisions regarding capital expenditures, joint ventures and so on. What this means is that the Board of a PSE, rather than the Ministry or Cabinet, should decide in the best interests of the company and keeping in mind its social objectives, how to use its resources, whether to issue shares for expansion, and so on. The report therefore proposes a whole institutional package towards strengthening the PSEs, making their management more professional and providing them some autonomy from their ministries in order to allow them to invest and restructure in ways that would strengthen their competitive position over time.

It is obvious that the disinvestment proposed for BHEL runs completely contrary to the recommendations of this report. Instead, once again the profitable PSEs are being treated as milch cows for a government strapped for cash regardless of what is in the best interests of the company itself and the economic activities it is engaged in.

Another very important recommendation of the report is that any decision to reduce government shareholding to less than 51 per cent should be taken only with the consent of Parliament in each case. But the recent action of the government suggests it is willing to ignore not only its own promises and the views of its allies and supporting parties, but also the recommendations made by committees that it has set up, if it does not suit its own temporary and short-sighted goals.

Questions

1. Is it ethical for the UPA Government to go back on its promises and not taking the consent of Board of Directors and the views of its allies and supporting parties and the recommendations by its own committees set up by themselves, in selling off 10 per cent of public holding of equity in BHEL. Give your views putting yourself in the positions of:
   (i) As the PM of Indian Government.
   (ii) As Chairman of BHEL.
   (iii) As a dignitary of this country.
   (iv) As a common man of this country.
2. What made the government to take this quick decision ignoring several decisions of its own. Do you find any motive behind It?

TECHNOLOGY ETHICS

The rapid growth in the information technology brought a sea change in the communication system and digital technology. Digital technology has no limit in its geographical boundaries nor the Internet users. Man has evolved from his original form from the past centuries. He has come through so many stages, has made so many discoveries, and invented so many things. Since the discovery of electricity, electronic devices have been the most fabulous one. In the 20th century Charles Babbage invented the digital technology or it is popularly called computer. Initially, it only made simple calculator and later it became a multi-purpose device.

A revolutionary change is occurring day by day in lifestyle and communication system of people and business. Both society and individuals are using technology and it has become a part of the daily life. The computer or digital technology are in greater use for creating, transmitting and storing the information in the electronic form. E-commerce or E-business are very common among the modern business world. In comparison to traditional print media, the accessibility of cyber space has torn down the traditional barriers between an individual and his or her ability to excel. The users who are popularly called "Netizen" can reach millions of people/customers through technology all over the world. Since there is no barrier or boundaries in creating, innovating and projecting the ideas and skills the digital technology users are enjoying the free entry without proper cheques and balances. Though there are laws especially for the information technology, all over globe the misusing and over-using of technology have recorded frequently. The ethical scanning has become unavoidable to protect the interests of individuals, corporate houses, business, government and society at large.

Ethics in Technology

Information technology is a great tool to connect and create relationship among people in the society. These are the technologies which are bringing the world closer and closer and leaving the impression that the 'world is small' or 'world is flat.'

Ethics in technology is a subfield of ethics addressing the ethical questions specific to the technology age. Some prominent works of philosopher Hans Jonas are devoted to ethics of technology. Technology itself is incapable of possessing moral or ethical qualities, since 'technology' is merely tool making. Ethics in technology refers to two sub-divisions as:

- The ethics involved in the development of new technology – whether it is always, never, or contextually right or wrong to invent and implement a technological innovation.
- The ethical questions that are exacerbated by the ways in which technology extends or curtails the power of individuals.

In respect of development of new technology, ethics related to computer security and computer viruses asks whether the very act of innovation is an ethically right or wrong act. Similarly, does a scientist or technician have an ethical obligation to produce or fail to produce a nuclear weapon. What are ethical questions surrounding the production of technologies that waste or conserve energy and resources. What are the ethical questions surrounding the production of new manufacturing processes that might inhibit employment, or might inflict suffering in the countries where the economy is poor.

Digital media is growing at an alarming rate. The technology industry is soaring. People should know that software is protected by copyright laws. The awareness as Copyright Act, Patent Right are not highlighted by the authorities. Vulnerable people make illegal copies of the software without the knowledge of law. The law directs that "Ignorance of law no excuse'. There are many people in the society found guilty for illegal copying without paying for it. As an ethical act, there need to be a proper education in giving proper guideline for Copy Right Act related to piracy.

In other cases related to bioethics, the ethics of technology quickly break down into the ethics of various human endeavours as they are altered by new technologies. In bioethics which is now largely consumed with questions that have been exacerbated by the new life-preserving technologies, cloning technologies and new technologies for implementation. Computer is one of the popular devices among technology innovations.

A computing professional must understand:

- Cultural, social, legal and ethical issues in computing.
- Responsibility and possible consequences of failure.

New technologies can contribute to all goals relating to intellectual, personal and spiritual growth towards the advancement of knowledge for the good of all and to serve to the local, national and global community. However, as they bring new levels of interdependence, they also bring unprecedented kinds of individual and collective vulnerability. As we respond to both opportunities and vulnerability as a community, we need to be more explicit and more intentional about our shared values and their implications.

Safety Under Internet

A learning community developed to the growth and flourishing of its members requires the safety both intellectual and physical, of its members. Intellectual adventurousness requires an environment of safety where we can freely speak our minds and explore possibilities. Emotional and rational self-discovery requires physical safety and well-respected privacy in the community. Correspondingly, each member of the community must respect and take care for the safety of all others. We must respect the freedom of expression of others.

Care Taking

Any community with shared resources upon which all depend requires all of its members to take care of those resources diligently. Shared electronic resources may not be as visible as library books or equipment, but the same respect and civility is required. Leave the resources as good as you found it – indeed, ideally, better than you found it and stay alert to the need to defend and protect it, and through it defend and protect the community. In particular, companies responsible to take care, not to open the network to slowdown or infection as well as to stay alert for ways in which the system can be supported and enhanced by individual users.

Originality

The organizations should aim to develop our capabilities to think and to discover new things, and ultimately to contribute to the world. Thus, a learning community is not concerned solely with the mastery of information, but also, and perhaps most fundamentally, with the originality of thought. One should honour the thinking of others, then taking care to give proper credit and compensation. Recognizing that it is increasingly easy to appropriate the work of the others, even unintentionally, as electronic text and other information became even more readily transferable.

Civility

A learning community relies on the civility of its members in order to achieve the desired environment that is necessary for its success. People may mistakenly assume a sense of detachment while communicating electronically and forget there is a person with feelings on the other end receiving the communication. People deserve to be treated with respect. Nothing should be communicated electronically that would not be said face to face. We need to honour each other in every way and that includes being courteous and respectful in all communications, electronic or otherwise.

Impact of technology in terms of Ethics and Ethical Issues

Ethical issues	Education	Impact
→ Privacy and Confidentiality	Teachers	Economy
→ Hacking/Spanning	Students	Society
→ Property/Copyright	Administration	
→ Netiquette		
→ Vandalism		
→ Access		
→ Accuracy		

Computer Ethics

Computer ethics is a branch of practical philosophy which deals with how computing professionals should make decisions regarding professional and social conduct. Internet ethics are related to hacking, information stories retrieval, copyright infringement, file sharing, Napster.

Since 1990s, the field has been integrated into professional programmes in academic settings. The conceptual foundation of computer ethics are investigated by information ethics, a branch of philosophical ethics established by Luciano Floridi. The term computer ethics was first coined by Dr. Walter Maner, a professor at Bowing Green State University. Computer ethics is a very important topic in computer applications and technology.

The applications of computers are increasing its speed and excitement in almost all the levels of the business world in particular and society in general, subject to a lot of ethical questions. Computer ethics was founded by NIT, professor Norbert Ware II, when he was helping to develop an aircraft cannon capable of shooting down fast warplanes. He along with some colleagues created a new branch of science called as "Cybernetics" – the science of information feedback system. By combining cybernetics with digital computers, he foresaw revolutionary social and ethical consequences. In his book cybernetics:

"Control and communications in the animal and machine," he said. "It has long been clear to me that the modern ultra rapid computing machine was in principles".

Computers are used to assemble, collate and store a large amount of data on a variety of subjects. The business interests rest primarily on such data collected and stored in computers pertaining to human beings as individuals, banks, hospital, educational institutions, government department especially Income tax dept., newspapers, magazine services, credit agencies, etc., collect and collate such data, which the subject does not know about, and has no way of correcting. Such erroneous data may affect the subject in harmful ways. Facts are not owned by anyone, and so even facts about ourselves cannot be owned by individuals. Data, as entered into computers, can be owned, and is the property of the owner of the computer. Facts are never untrue, but data can be true or false, because they are merely the interpreted information fed in the computer. Falsehood may be caused by mistakes in making the entry, or defective programme or any number of other reasons.

Privacy in computers is a very large and fertile area for moral discussion. Our society recognizes areas of privacy for the individual. Others have no right to penetrate into one's privacy unless very serious harm to others or society is threatened. We have right to keep our thoughts, ideas, skills and feelings private and that is a fact to open society.

If data are stored in various computers on different facts and activities of a person that is by itself, not immoral. If all these data collected in one computer, even that cannot be termed illegal. Facts about us do not belong to use. Collections or transmission or transfer of data, by itself, is not illegal, it is only when it is used to harm the subject and if no opportunity is given to set right the errors and false data, to the subject, it becomes illegal or immoral.

Managers need to keep the confidentiality of their employees confidential records, inviolate, just as they owe security of funds to their shareholders. Many of them have no idea how safe computer files are or how open to compromise. Privacy is a great threat in computers in almost all the fields of business. It is subjected to a strong legal protection of privacy in computer. Maintaining a strong policy on data privacy is an ethical act in business world. There is a judicial protection in protecting all over the world.

Law and Information Technology

In order to protect the interests of the society and particularly the individuals, who are regularly using the technology for their skills and professions, corporate and business world, a legislation was enforced in the year 1999 and 2000 namely Cyber Law, 1999 and Information Technology Act, 2000.

Cyber law is an important law enacted in India covering a wide variety of legal issues relating to information and communication technology. It includes use of the Internet as well as other form of computer or digital processing devices (DPD) which also covers the intellectual property, privacy, freedom of expression and jurisdiction. It covers the rights of citizens of cyber space. No definite and exhaustive definition or meaning was given to the term, cyber laws. However, it is a new phenomenon having emerged much after the onset of the Internet.

Internet or cyber space has no geographical boundaries. It can be referred to all legal and regulatory aspects of the Internet and World Wide Web (WWW). Anything related to legal aspects or issues concerning any activity of citizen and others in cyber space is known as "cyber law".

Cyber Law in India

The West pointing at East, especially India in respect of tremendous growth and change in information technology and became a great competitor to the growing nations. This rapid growth brought a sea change in the communication system and digital technology. Any person with an Internet connection has the potential to reach an audience of millions, which is absolutely free of cost. This has been misused by the Internet users by issuing of obscene postings, gambling, child pornography and fraud. These also raise the question of an intellectual property and individual rights. After the liberalization policy, India is witnessing a sea change in the Information Technology (IT). This also brought a few issues along with its advantages. These issues are covered under a special legislation known as Cyber Law. This is to protect the misusing of public funds in banking, business and economic activities.

The Information Technology Act, enacted in the year 2000, chiefly covers.

(a) E-Commerce in India.

(b) E-Governance in India

(c) Cyber contraventions

(d) Cyber crimes

The subdivision of the I.T. Act covers (i) Digital signature (ii) Electronic Governance (iii) Attribution, Acknowledgement and Dispatch of Electronic Records. (iv) Secure Electronic Records and secure Digital signature (v) Cyber crimes and so on.

It also protects the Net user in respect of intellectual property right, piracy, copyright, infringement of copyrights, hacking, cracking, bulletin boards, credit card fraud, E-mail scans, publicity of false digital signature and so on.

In spite of a stray legal protection through Cyber Law and Information Technology Act, there are lot of unethical acts in the electronic media. As law can protect external course of human action, the ethics is to protect the internal course of human action, and after all, "Ethics is beyond Law".

Global Trends in Cyber Law

Globally, the legal experts have shown greater interest in security, intellectual property and criminal aspects of cyber law. The security aspects have been looked into by countries on the guidelines adopted by the OECD (Organisation for Economic Cooperation and Development) in given below. The guidelines aimed at promoting the use cryptography and the suggestions are follow:

(i) Trustworthiness of cryptography must be ensured.

(ii) Choice of cryptographic method to be the user's right.

(iii) Standards to be developed at the national/international level.

(iv) Protection of privacy and personal data.

(v) Lawful access.

(vi) Liability and international cooperation.

Global Information Infrastructure Commission (GIIC) has recommended the current intellectual property laws of a different countries as:

(i) There should be balance between copyright holders and the users of the copyright product.

(ii) It is necessary to have a precise definition which remarks the lawful and unlawful use or activities regarding copy right material.

In 1976, the 12th conference on criminal aspect, of the Director of Criminological Research Institute of the Council – Europe was held, regarding the cyber crimes. Again the 8th UN congress on prevention of crime, was held in the 1990. In the year 1994, the 13th Plenary Meeting of the UN and the 1994 Manual of the UN as the prevention and control of computer related crimes has held. The amendments to criminal laws in the US are guiding as:

(i) Causing transmission of data/program knowing that such transmission will damage a computer network, data or program, or that such transmission will withhold or doing use of computer network, etc.

(ii) International, unauthorized access of computer to obtain financial information.

(iii) Willful unauthorized access to computers related to national defence or foreign relations.

(iv) Knowingly disturbing / discarding transmission of data/program to damage a network data.

(v) Unauthorized access of computer with intent to fraud.

(vi) Unauthorized access of computer of a government department or agency.

(vii) Unauthorized access of computer/computer data of federal interest with intention to fraud.

The Global Business Dialogues are set to come up with industry related solutions to issues affecting electronic commerce, such as, consumer confidence in e-commerce transactions, controversial contents such as pornography, data security, protection of intellectual property rights, liability for on-line contracts, content, on-line privacy, taxation, technical concerns, about the Internet, and who has jurisdiction over the Internet transactions.

Ethical Issues in Information Technology and Computers

In the transition from the Industrial Age to the Information Age, business is being transformed in all its aspects. Computers and information technology have changed the way offices are organized and the tasks are done. They have changed manufacturing, purchasing, marketing, finance and management functions. The ethical issues are therefore not simply issues that are involved in computer and their use in information technology but in the way business is done in the Information Age. There are four different kinds of ethical problems connected with the information technology:

(i) Ethical issues in the use of technology in business.
(ii) Ethical issues in the information technology.
(iii) Ethical issues dealing with the Internet.
(iv) Ethical issues in E-business.

The fundamental views to computer ethics are based on applied ethics in which a high degree of uncertainty, chances of unpredictability are intrinsically present. The complexities here are not simply technical but encompass intersecting and conflicting goals, interest, traditions, purposes and so on. In addition to it, the very mediation of action by computing technology is referred to the instrumentation of human action and which may give rise to ethical issues. It involves and assesses unreliability of software and the uncertainties inherent in the implementation of large-scale computing systems.

Computer ethics should be given a new beginning by thinking in new ways by referring to moral accountability, responsibility and risk. The intrinsic nature of computer technology and its logical reasoning generates even greater levels of complexity, unreliability and uncertainty. This coupled with the ever widening contexts of application, in turn, leads to greater scope for the operation of chance of moral luck. This leads to professional responsibility of computing professionals and the identification and attribution of praise and blame. This also emphasises the importance of computer ethics to professional education.

Common Ethical issues in Information Technology and Computers

Information Technology is a great boom to the modern economy. But it is gradually becoming a threat to the society. The diversity of IT applications and increased use of the technology have created many ethical issues. An attempt to organize these issues into a framework was undertaken by Mason in 1986. According to the study the ethical issues can be categorized in four divisions namely:

(i) Privacy
(ii) Accuracy
(iii) Accessibility
(iv) Property

Again ethical issues related to computers and IT have been further studied as :

Privacy: Which is related to:

(i) Computer creates a false sense of security.
(ii) People do not realize how vulnerable information stores computer are.

Property/(Intellectual Property)

This can be classified into:

(i) Physical property
(ii) Intellectual property, related to copyright and patent.
(iii) Data as property
(iv) Value of information

Access to information

(i) Access to computing technology

(ii) There are moral issues that need to be considered in regard to the collection, storage and access of data in electronic form.

Information Accuracy

Accuracy of information stored (i) hacking (ii) cracking (iii) virus creation and (iv) software piracy.

Privacy is a major issue. It can be defined as "the right to be left alone when you want to be, to have control of your own personal possessions, and not to be observed without your consent.

Privacy is collection, storage and dissemination of information about individuals. The term information may be referred to as both facts and data. These facts/data are misinterpreted in the computer causing a lot of loss to the individuals. The ethical question has to be raised when such data and facts are collected, assembled and stored in a quantity diversity of subject matter. The organization like banks, hospitals, internal revenue department, newspapers, magazines, income tax department, credit agencies, stock exchanges, etc., have a voluminous information of the individuals, organizations and society. Privacy is one of the largest issues facing organizations. Privacy issues reduce trust for business over the Internet. In order to grow business trust has to be established with customers and this begins with employees practising good ethics.

In the broader sense, massive accounts of data on individuals and organizations are used it for a variety of purpose like national security, tax collection, demographics, international geopolitical strategic analysis, etc. Corporations do the same for commercial reasons to increase business, control expenses, enhance profitability, gain market shares and so on. Technological advances both hardware and software have significantly changed the scope what can be amassed and processed. Massive quantities of data, measured in peta bytes and beyond, can be centrally stored and retrieved effortlessly and quickly. Seemingly disparate source of data can be cross-referenced to glean new meanings when one set of data is viewed within the context of another.

In the 1930s, and 1940s the volume of data available were miniscule by comparison and the 'processing' of that data was entirely manual. Had even a small portion of today's capabilities existed, the world as we now know it would probably be quite different.

The data access and privacy is a issue with both internal and external implications. All organizations collect personal data on employees, which if not properly safeguarded can result in **significant negative implications for individuals.** Information such as compensation and background data and personal identification information, such as social security number and account identifiers, all have to be maintained and accessed by authorized personal. Systems that track this data can be secured, but at the **same point data must be personal.** Systems that track this data can be secured, but at the same time data must leave those systems that are to be used. Operational policies and procedures can address their proper handling but if they are not followed or enforced, there is hardly any point to them. Organisations routinely share data with each other, merging data bases containing all kinds of identifiers.

Under privacy in relation to information technology, identity theft occurs when some one steals key pieces of personal information to gain access to a person's financial account, which includes all the details including passport number, driver's licence number and so on. Total estimation of victims are about 10 millions per year.

Theft of Privacy under IT

2004	2,46,000	Complaints were registered
2005	1,47,000	Consumers records data were stolen.
2005	3,00,000	Theft of information by hackers
2005	19 million	Records were stolen.
March 2005	1.4 million	Credit card data and personal information theft from DSW store warehouse stores
March 2005	1.2 million	Federal employees computer reports containing credit card account records were lost, disclosed by Bank of America.
June 2005	40 million	Hackers accessed credit card numbers for which card system solutions has been cancelled by Visa authorities of USA and American Express.

Sources: (1) http.wwww.compercialalert.org/issues/cultures.privacy/

Source: (2) http:/www.computerworld.com/security/story/10801, 101058,00 html.

Steps to Protect Privacy

- The use of information technology in business requires balancing needs of those who use the information against the rights and desires of the people whose information may be used.
- The information gathered from the people is to be stored, analysed and reported appropriately for better decisions. Organisations should collect basic information about customers to serve the people better.
- The object of the business is to collect the data on the basis of policies of the government and business norms.

It should be considered a key concern of the Internet users and the main reason is to avoid non-Internet users.

One of the earliest computer ethics topics to arouse public interest was privacy. In mid-1960s the American government already had created large database of information about private citizens like census data, tax records, military service records, welfare records and so on. In the early 1970s, major computer laws were passed in the USA. Ever since then, computer threatened privacy has remained a topic of public concern. During the past decade, commercialization and rapid growth of the Internet, the rise of the World Wide Web, increasing "user friendliness" and processing power of computers and decreasing costs of computer technology have led to new privacy issues, such as data mining, data matching, recording of "clock trails" on the web and so on Tavani 1999. As computer technology rapidly advances – creating new possibilities for compiling, storing, accessing and analyzing information philosophical database about the meaning of "privacy" will likely to continue.

Question of anonymity on the Internet is sometimes discussed in the same context with questions of privacy and the Internet, because anonymity can provide many of the same benefits as privacy. For example, if someone is using the Internet to obtain medical or psychological counselling, or to discuss sensitive topics like AIDS, abortion, gay rights, venereal diseases, political dissent and so on, among unity can afford protection similar to that of privacy. Similarly, both anonymity and privacy on the Internet can be helpful in preserving human values such as security, mental health, self-fulfilment and peace of mind. Unfortunately, privacy and anonymity are exploited to facilitate unwanted and undesirable computer aided activities in cyber space, such as money laundering, drug trading, terrorism, etc.

Privacy threats come in several categories:

- International, institutional use of personal information.
- Unauthorised use of release by "insiders", the people who maintain the infor mation.
- Theft of information.
- Inadvertent leakage of information through negligence or carelessness.

E-Policies

Companies must develop information management policies and organizations should develop written policies establishing employee guidelines, personal procedures and organizational rules for information.

Intellectual Property in Computers

Intellectual property covers several different areas, but they are all related to ideas and creators whether it is a work of art (or music or book) or something more technical. Copy-right Law protects skilled things by asserting the rights of composers, writers and others to the work they have created. Design Laws cover the way things look, whether its car, laptop or mobile phone. Trademarks offer protection to brands, especially their logos that make them stand out from their competitors. Patent laws cover the technical aspects.

But there are a lot of issues towards property which are created intellectually by the individuals like film studios invest millions in new movies and each one is a gamble. Some make large profits, others turn to a loss. But part of the income for them is from DVD sales. Piracy and illegal downloads are leading to the loss to these companies. In some countries like China it is found almost all products are imitated. Software especially CDs and DVDs are pirated, violating intellectual property rights. Again in case of pharmaceutical industries the piracy is very common. There is a deeper ethical consideration, in respect of protecting intellectual property in general and in computer space in particular.

One of the more controversial areas of computer / IT ethics concerns the intellectual property rights connected with software ownership. Some people, like Richard Stallman who started Free Software Foundation, believe that software ownership should not be allowed at all. He claims that all information should be free, and all programs should be available for copying, studying and modifying by anyone who wishes to do so (Stallman, 1993). Others argue that software or programmers would not invest weeks and months of work and significant funds in the development of software, if they could not get the investment back in the form of licence fees or sales (Johnson 1992). Today's software industry is a multibillion dollar maket. Software companies claim to lose billions of dollars per year through illegal copying through software piracy. Many people think that software should be ownable, but "casual copying' of personally owned programs for one' friends should also be permitted (Nissenbaum, 1995). The software companies all over the world claim that millions of dollars in sales are lost because of such copying. Ownership is a complex matter, as there are several different aspects of software that can be owned. There are three different types of ownerships like copyrights, physical property trade secrets and patents. One can own the following aspects of a program:

(1) The "Source Code" which is written by the programmer(s) in a high level computer language like Java or C++.

(2) The "Object code", which is a machine language translated of the source code.

(3) The algorithm, which is the sequence of machine commands that the source code and object code represent.

(4) The "look and feel" of a program, which is the way the program appears on the screen and interfaces with users.

A very controversial issue today is owning a patent on a computer algorithm. A patent provides an exclusive monopoly for the use of the patented item, so the owner of an algorithm can deny others use of mathematical formulas that are part of the algorithm. Mathematicians and scientists are outraged, claiming that algorithm patents effectively remove parts of mathematics from the public domain, and thereby threaten to cripple science. In addition, reserving preliminary "patent search" to make sure that your 'new' program does not violate anyone's software patent, which is a costly and time consuming process. As a result, only very large companies with big budgets can afford to run such a search. This eliminates many small software companies, stifling competition and decreasing the variety of programs available to the society.

Information Ethics

Information ethics focuses on information, because of its crucial importance to the cultures. In other forms of ethics, only animal and people deserve to be the proper centre of moral claim. However, with information at the focal point, the privacy, security, ownership, accuracy, and authenticity of information, as well as access to information, became values in themselves.

The rise in information ethics has not occurred in a vacuum. There exist biomedical ethics, nuclear ethics, and numerous other branches of ethics to coincide with two phenomena; (i) the challenges of new technologies and (ii) the breakdown of historical ethical traditions and common assumptions.

However, people grapple with thorny ethical issues daily in entertainment, news media, non-profit organizations, governments, businesses, and the population as a whole.

Caring and trust are essential values to develop in a society. In the field of information ethics, the word "trust" appears repeatedly. Trust is relying with confidence on something or someone. In a healthy society, people should be able to trust information.

Information ethics, deserve special attention because, of the human ability to view personal action, in the real world. Among the issues open to debate are exporting software, releasing viruses on the Internet, defining copyright and fair use, and combining data from global information systems with other databases, thereby pinpointing people in ways that were never before possible.

In information ethics, a moral agent is a person or artificial agent who works or participates in the information environment and could improve it. Whether any information process is moral or immoral is judged or how the process affects the essence of the information. Information welfare, in other words, is what ought to be promoted by extending information quantity, improving information quality, and enriching the level of information in general.

Until 1980s information ethics questions were only of interest of a few specialists. However, like a forest fire spreads by wind, information technology has spread throughout society. Its importance to national economics and individual careers grows and every one who uses it will need to make ethical decisions. The database is designed directly affects the retrieval of information that citizens want so see. A widely circulated e-mail message could affect people in other countries within seconds of someone hitting the send button. Ethics are laws racing to keep up with the changes that computers have introduced. Before there was e-mail or the Internet, individuals could not send unsolicited commercial messages to millions of people. Now it can be done in a process called spamming. This brings an intensive question on ethics. Information is treated as property of the individuals, with data, ownership and rights. The personal data like name, address, phone, medical history, image, e-mail, government data, etc., can be kept protected and securitized.

Process to Information

Access may be interpreted restrictively to refer only to open versus closed access of users. In the context of information ethics, access has a far wider application than libraries. Internationally the digital divide among and within countries in probably the most obvious aspect of the access issue. Some see the digital divide as one of the most serious ethical problems internationally in the information age.

Factors that influence the digital divide are socio-economic status (income, education), gender, life stage and geography. The number of Internet users has topped billions now.

As a cost saving many of the Internet users are switching on free software as from Microsoft to Linux. The number of access to information is spreading like fire and it is possible that the successor would become equally efficient, if one were aware of and had access to the program. As the company's contribution is negligibly small or non-existent, the employee does not owe the company the program he has made.

Exhibit

(1) Kumar, an employee creates a program by using the input of his Z company, where he is employed.

The company has not directed and paid him to develop nor allotted any company time to do so. Even then Kumar has left the program in the computer of the company and not taken anything from the company. The program in his head does not belong to the company any more than his experience, intelligence and skill as a programmer. Moreover, it is not a trade secret of the company. (Only in this event, that it is a company trade secret, he could not legitimately reproduce it for a competitor.) Thus, Kumar's rewriting of the program in his work for the new employer is legal and morally valid.

(2) There is different case from the above one, in that Kumar leaves behind the original program, but takes away a copy for use in the new company. Thus, company Z no longer enjoys the right of exclusivity to the program. The company gave its computer facility to Kumar (who worked on own time to produce the program) and the program was stored in its computer. Here, the inputs of the company and that of the employee have to be matched and an agreement has to be reached beforehand. If the company's resources involved in producing the program were greater, the company's claim becomes proportionately stronger. If the monetary value of company time is low, the employee's claims will be much greater. Kumar wrote the program on his own initiative, in his own time and only made use of company computer and in return, left the program for the future benefit of the company. He is, therefore, within his rights to take a copy of it for his use. The same problem can be looked in another way. Suppose a company makes a policy that no programmer should make at in improvement in his work unless he makes over the improved program to the company. No programmer would have the initiative or be inclined to make improvement in his program. The result would be poorer work performance from the workers. Such a policy would undermine the interests of the company and workers. This policy might prevent a competitor from getting the use of better programs.

It is also pertinent to find out whether the cost of copying (on paper, or a floppy disc, or a print-out) is minimal, as is usually the case with office stationery. Unless there is a clear policy to the contrary. Kumar can copy his program legitimately. Secondly, Kumar might leave the program in the company's computer, but yet no one will know it is there or what it does, without Kumar providing them with the necessary documentation. If the company insists on documentation every time, it will be disincentive to producing the program. Unless there are clear guidelines from the company, the employee has the right to the copy of the program he produced.

The first instance may now be examined in the light of the above reasoning. Kumar might not leave the documentation necessary to access his improved program, and without it, the program will not be useful to the company. As such, Kumar can take away the original (not to speak of its copy) by erasing it from the computer. If Kumar sought the company's permission for taking the program (it was significantly expensive), it implies that he conceded that the company has a right over it, and has to abide by the company's decision. If on the other hand, the supervisor did not even know of the program and its use by Kumar, there would be no need for permission. As such, a company should clearly set forth its policies on the development of new programs by its employees on company computers but on their own time in the following manner: whether the new program (i) belongs to the employee; (ii) belongs to the company wholly; or (iii) belongs in part (to be specified/decided) by the company. In the absence of such clearly stated policy, it is possible to assume that the employee has full rights to what he produces on own time.

Kumar wrote the program on company's computer and on company's time. Being job related, it can be considered as part of his job. The program rightly belongs to the company, and his leaving it in the company's computer is proper. But when he recreates this program in the new job, is he copying? If the program is copied, it is morally prohibited. If the algorithm is being used, since an algorithm cannot be copyrighted or patented, his work is not illegal or immoral. An algorithm is a logical formula and cannot be owned by any one and hence Kumar is within his rights, unless the algorithm is defended by the company as its trade secret, and the rules for trade secrets become applicable to the case.

If the basic program were one of considerable complexity, and Kumar modifies it somewhat, the basic program is not his, even though it may not be the original program. He somewhat, the basic program is not his, even though it may not be the original program. He clearly has no right to take the original or the copy with him. But the question remains how much change must be made before a program becomes a new program and remains no longer the original (copyrighted) program. This is a difficult issue as yet unanswered.

In the light of the above discussions, it is clear that a firm will be wise and far-seeing if it establishes the ground rules and issues guidelines governing computer use and programs before any problems arise.

India and E-commerce

In the Draft National Policy on Information Technology it was stated that the Indian IT industry would be worth at least US $ 120 billion by 2010. For the year 2008, the targets were laid down as follows: software Export $ 50 billion; Domestic software $ 20 b; other IT industry $ 30 b. Total : $ 100 billion.

India has developed the National Information Technology Policy (NITP) and has enacted laws bearing upon the use of the Internet. Providing and improving the infrastructure for the Net are fast paced. Many private ISPs (Internet Service Providers) have come into the field; credit card systems are gearing up their services; electronic funds Transfer (EFTs) have been given the legal approval. A fast mechanism for the redressal of grievances such as a Dispute Resolution mechanism is the need of the hour. The successful implementation of the Internet activities can be done only by having due regard to the following aspects:

(1) The contract aspect

(2) The security aspect

(3) The intellectual property aspect and the criminal aspect. The disputants can be any user or server of the Internet such as telephone provider companies, regulatory agencies, personal computer companies, ISPs, software companies, universities, schools and colleges, or any individual or group who have established their presence on the Net. Broadly speaking, Cyber Law is in the domain of commercial law (but surely overflows it). It is still in its infancy in an undefined but all-pervading area, which is going to divide how we cope with the challenging world of virtual reality thrown by the Net.

Accuracy (Information Accuracy)

Business has always had a love/hate relationship with accuracy. Effective decision making is driven by accurate information but quality control comes with a cost both in terms of currency and productivity.

In a bygone era, there was less data to work with and the only quality assurance that needed to be performed was on data. Operations and procedures were manual, so it was the output of those functions that was most critical. Technology has enabled vastly more complicated and interconnected processes, such that a problem for upstream in a process has a ripple effect on the rest of the process.

Accuracy is considered to be a costly affair as it needs adequate perfection in decision making. A accuracy is responsible for data, integration, reliability and integrity. There is always conflict between legal liability versus ethical liability. Although there is a wide realm of information available on the net. There is no agency monitoring "truth or accuracy of information". There is no restriction on false information. Accuracy is mandated or demanded in the following fields: (i) business (ii) environment (iii) health (iv) education (v) journalism (vi) nuclear science (vii) product designing (viii) information technology (ix) law (x) working condition.

Computer Viruses

Viruses are software written with malicious intensity to create or to cause annoyance or damage. Computer viruses are great threat to the information technology ethics. A computer virus is a small program that impairs or simply destroys computer ability to function properly. Most viruses are designed to spread among themselves through the Internet especially through the e-mail programs, before they inflict harm on their host computers. Many times the computer hackers use viruses to create holes in a computer network's security system. Again these holes are used to get deeper inside in the network. It is expected that there is harm in opening e-mail attachments from the people you do not know other e-mail attachments can be dealt with caution.

As computer viruses are small software programs that are designed to spread from one computer to another and to interfere with computer operations. Viruse program are unethical acts, they have serious consequences and cause systems to crash and organizations to cease operating for certain periods. One of the most conserving consequences of such action is when viruses interrupt the smooth functioning of an organization such as a hospital which could in extreme cases even cause people to die. Logic bombs are also sometimes planted.

There are obviously a lot of anti-virus software in the market now which helps to deal with ever-growing problems.

Globalisation and Ethics in Computers

Computer ethics is rapidly evolving into a broader and even more important field, which might reasonably by called "global information ethics". Global networks like the Internet and especially the World Wide Web are connecting people all over the earth. For the first time in the history, efforts to develop mutually agreed standards of conduct, and efforts to advance and defend human values, are being made in a truly global context. (Gornik-Kockowsha, 1996). So, for the first time in the history of the earth, ethics and values will be debated and transformed in a context that is not limited to a particular geographic region, or constrained by a specific religion or culture. This may very well be the most important social development in history. Yet there are few issues related:

(i) **Global Cyber Business:** The world is very close to having technology that can provide electronic privacy and security on the Internet sufficient to safely conduct international business transactions. Once this technology, is in place, there will be a rapid expansion of global "Cyber business". Nations with technological infrastructure already in place will enjoy rapid economic growth, while the rest of world lags behind. Cheating or fraud is rapidly growing with cyber business.

(ii) **Global Laws:** Every country has its own laws based as applicability and usage. There is no common law to control computer crime globally.

(iii) **Global Education:** For the first time, nearly everyone on the earth will have access to daily news from a free press, texts, libraries, documents or museums of the world. But there is a great doubt that the poor countries will not able to reach to these facilities due to lack of infrastructure.

(iv) **Information Rich and Information Poor:** The rich countries enjoy more information, educational opportunities, employment, medical service done to the cyber space compared to the poor countries. This bring a gap between rich and poor.

Technology Ethics Adopted Worldwide

- A separate institute, unique of its kinds has been set up in 2004 by philosopher Nick Bostrom and bioethicist James Hughes called The Institute for Ethics and Emerging Technologies (IEET)
- Federal Ethics Committee on Non-Human Biotechnology – This is from the Gene Technology Act and the Swiss Federal Ethics committee on non-Human being enforcement of legislation.
- Ethics and Emerging Technologies, at the University of the West of Scotland, by Prof. Andy Miah.
- Techno ethics (TE), a research unit / area concerned with all moral and ethical aspects of technology in society.
- Ethics of artificial intelligence – addresses a number of moral and legal issues and also related to scientifically powerful technology.
- Information ethics – Touching the various ethical issues related to information ethics from the development and application of information technologies.
- Information and computer ethics : Program on emerging technologies and substantial contributor in field of Information.
- The ethics and policies of technology by Lucas D. Introna, Prof. of organization, Technology and Ethics at the Lancaster University of Management School.
- Computer Press Association: An Organisation formed in 2000, to prepare code of ethics for technology and journalists.
- Public population project in genomics – Related to different discipline in the area of and related to genomics, including epidemiology, law, technology and biomolecular science.
- The Association for Computing Machinery (ACM) and the Institute of Electrical and Electronic Engineers (IEEE) established code of ethics, prepared curricular and accreditation requirements to computer professionals.
- ACM code (1992) says :
  - (i) General moral imperative
    - (a) Avoid harm to others
    - (b) Be honest and trustworthy
  - (ii) Specific professional responsibilities
    - (a) Acquire and maintain professional competence.
    - (b) Know and respect existing laws pertaining to professional work.
- **IEEE Code: Principles**
  - (a) Avoid real or perceived conflicts of interest whenever possible.
  - (b) be honest and realistic in stating claims/estimates based on available data.

The ten commandments of computer ethics have been defined by the Computer Ethics Institute

(i) Thou shalt not use a computer to harm other people.
(ii) Thou shalt not interfere with other people's computer work.
(iii) Thou shalt not snoop around in other people's files.
(iv) Thou shalt not use a computer to steal.
(v) Thou shalt not use a computer to bear false witness.
(vi) Thou shalt not use or copy software for which you have not paid.
(vii) Thou shalt not use other people's computer resources without authorization.
(viii) Thou shalt not appropriate other people's intellectual output.
(ix) Thou shalt think about the social consequences of the program you write.
(x) Thou shalt use a computer in ways that show consideration and respect.

Ethics of technology is a sub-field of ethics adding the ethical question specific to the technology age.

Ethics definition "the discipline and practice of applying value to human behaviour, resulting in meaningful conduct".

Important Views

- Internet offers great riches for the future, but poses many threat.
- Technology requires vigilance.
- Considerations regarding information ethics influence personal decisions, professional practice and public policy.
- Information systems are very complex and have many components to as very vulnerable to many hazards. There are lots of threats in the information systems which are subject to safety and security.

Some of the threats are: (i) computer abuses, (ii) computer crimes, (iii) loss, (iv) theft of equipment, (v) theft of data, (vi) equipment malfunctioning, (vii) environment hazards (flood, power failure, storms, earthquake and fires), (viii) destruction from viruses, (ix) errors in handling and usages of data.

Steps for Practical Solution to Face With Ethical Issues

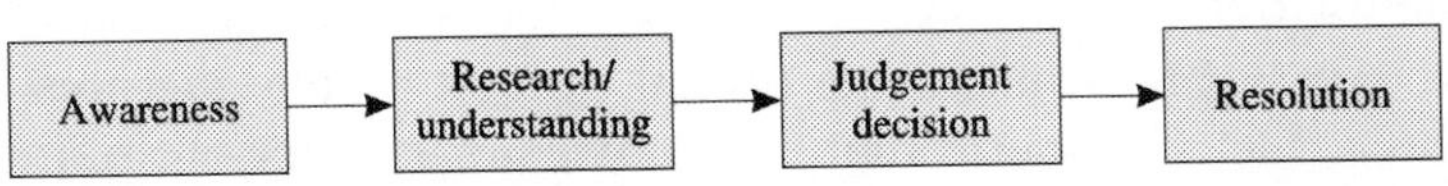

1. **Awareness/recognition:** Make the issue "official". Define clearly the boundaries and objectives.
2. **Research/Understanding:** Gather the facts, identify the variable, ignorance is not an excuse.
3. **Judgement / decision:** Decide what is and is not ethical for company.
4. **Resolution (of an incident):** Finding the proper balance, learning from it.

Some suggestions towards IT ethics

- **Preparation** is the key.
- **Be open** and honest about issues – Avoiding issues always magnifies the problem.
- **Make ethical decisions acceptable:** Within your group and throughout your company. No correct answers or right opinions. It is good business to do so.
- **Make these discussions professional:** Provide guidelines for ethical discussions. Purpose is to better the company.
- Avoid the personal crusades (not on company time)
- **Stay focused:** Only deal with issues that wrote to the company. Do not attempt to solve the greater issue. If individuals must pursuer the greater issues, they should do that on their personal time.
- **Seek qualified legal advice:** This may be difficult and expensive. Do not expect a Yes – No answer. Do not let it dominate the ethical discussion.
- **Plan for an effective corporate initiative:** But avoid the Dilbert syndrome.

Organisations formed on Professional codes of Ethics in IT

The following organizations have framed their own code of ethics in information technology.

ACM	–	Association of Computing Machinery.
DPMA	–	Data Processing Management Association
DAMA	–	Data Management Association Institute
AIIP	–	Association of Independent Information Professionals
IEEE	–	Institute of Electrical and Electronics Engineers
ASIST	–	American Society for Information Science and Technology
SCIP	–	Society for Competitive Information Professional.

Unethical act in using technology for Children

Situation/context gist of cases

Highlights of the incidents

(1) Jack's class has been using the digital camera to take pictures for the school year book. Jack has found that he can use a computer program to change the photographs. He has used the program so far to make himself look like the tallest boy in the class, to blacken out the front tooth of his best buddy who will think it is funny, and to give his teacher slightly crossed eyes.

While this example may seem different and even like "good fun", integrity is a serious issue which even young writers and photographers need to be aware of deliberate distortion of events whether through words or pictures may harm both those involved in the event as well as the reputation of the reporter. The purpose of a equity photo album is to make a record of the activities and appearance of individuals.

It is an appropriate use of technology for an unethical act.

(2) John, a ten years old boy, fills out a survey form as a computer game web page. The survey asks for his email address, mailing address, and telephone number which he fills in the following weeks he receives several advertisements in the mail as well as dozens of e-mail messages about new computer games.

Obviations

In this case the privacy of John is at risk. Children and young adults need to understand that businesses and the organizations use information to market products. Sometimes this information is collected without a person's permission or awareness that it is being collected. Information given to one organization may go to others. Her interesting discussion can revolve around how much a person would like a company to know about him or her.

This case of misusing privacy which questions ethics in technology.

(3) Computer Games: John borrows Ben's game disks for Master Truck Rally II and installs them on his home computer. He says he will erase the game if he does not like it, or will buy the game for himself if he likes it.

Observation:

The customer need to know that computer software is protected by Copy Right Law. It is unlawful, as well as unethical, to make copies of computer programs without permission or payment of the product of those programs. It also needs to be understood that when purchasing software, one is usually, only purchasing the right to use of software. The ownership of the code that comprises the program stays with the producers, which mean no alternation or selling of the software can be made by others.

This is the act of purely violating the law as well as totally unethical.

Ethical dilemmas in organization development

1. A business consultant sells his services to an organization based on his education/training. but associates with conduct the consulting job.
2. A manager obtains unfavourable information about a supervisor from an attitude survey and the management effectiveness report and uses this information in a performance evaluation against the supervisor.
3. At the first stages of a consultation, a management team determines that the consulting effort will not be successful, and reduces support and funds to minimum the risk of greater harm or failure.
4. A consultant informs the organisation that he can no longer provide consultancy services to the organization due to a value conflict with current management philosophy.

5. The management team of an organization asks various business consultants to bid on a project and submit a proposal, although there is a possibility that complete funding and approval may not be available for the later stages of the project. This information is not shared with the consultants who have submitted bids.
6. During the course of a consulting job a consultant refuses to continue the consulting job until an agreement can be reached concerning specific organization departments and consulting goals.
7. Line employees of an organization engaged in a highly successful consulting job are required to attend work group development sessions against their will.
8. A company official, when receiving project bids for a consultancy project, selected a personal who was one of those consulting bidding on the project. All of the proposals were roughly the same in cost and strategy.
9. After the first stages of a consulting job a consultant refuses to allow company training personnel a greater role in conducting group meetings with employees based on the consultant's perception of the lack of skill, background and experience of company training personnel.
10. A management team involved in a companywide consulting job requires the consultant to use techniques which the consultant feels are inappropriate.
11. A company official requires that a consultant uses the data gathered from a previous consulting job to design group development training for the company; the consultant refuses to continue with the current consulting job unless new data are gathered.

World Centres for Business Ethics

Centre for Ethics and Business

Loyola Marymount University, Los Angeles, CA

- **The Institute for Business and Professional Ethics**
  De Paul University, Chicago, IL
- **Society of Actuaries**
  Schaumberg, IL
- **Centre for Ethics and Religious Values**
  University of Notre, Dame Mendoza College of Business, Notre Dame, IN
- **Centre for Business Ethics**
  Bentley College, Waltham, MA
- **Program in Business, Society and Ethics**
  Carlow College, Pittsburgh, PA
- **The Institute of Business Ethics (IBE)**
  London, England.
  International Business Ethics Institute

- **E-Business State University Fort Collins, CD**
- **Council for Ethics in Economics, Columbus, OH**
- **Council of Ethical Organizations**
  Alexandria, VA
  Center for the Study of Business in Society
  California State University, Los Angeles, CA
- **Emerson Centre for Business Ethics**
  St. Louis University, St, Locuis, MO
  http/www.vanderbit.edu/centerforethics/othercenters.html#business.

Ethical stamina is essential for all activities of management especially with the core functional areas for better, success and continuous progress in the organisation. Hence, consistent ethical practices are demanded for long survival of the organisations.

"Nothing can be greater than a business, however small it may be that is governed by conscience, Nothing can be meaner more petty than a business, however large, governed without honesty and without brotherhood."

—William H. Lever

5

Chapter

Corporate Social Responsibility

INTRODUCTION

Business contributes to man's happiness and his material needs. Business organisations, apart from being economic utilities, are also considered to be social institutions. Business today is no longer only to maximise profits. They exist and operate for a number of reasons. One among them may be to meet welfare of the society. Business is not an end in itself. It is only a means to achieve an end. That end is the man himself and meeting of individual needs and satisfaction. Business organisations have tremendous impact on society and also on individuals working within them. There has been increasing concern about the ethical boundaries within which such organisations function. These concerns have been heightened by the increase frequency with which scams and instances of legally suspect and ethically doubtful behaviour emerges. Again every business needs society's approval in order to function with better understanding between self and society. Business and society interact with each other and are mutually dependent. Business exists within social framework and requires social sanctions.

In order to understand better the relation between business and society along with the various other aspects, Keith Davis (1973) explains under the heading "Interaction between business and society" as shown in the figure below:

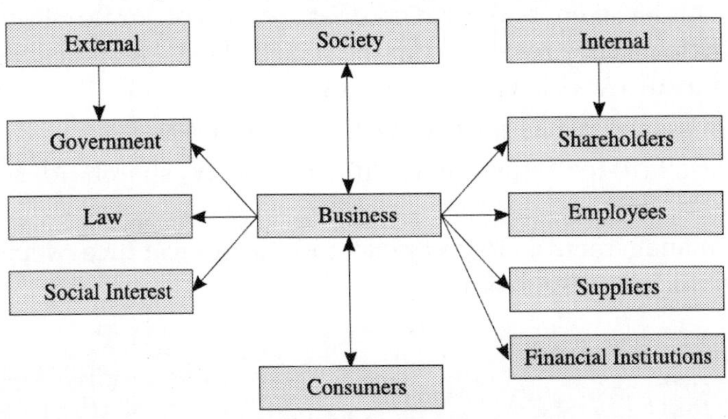

The above figure explains, the business is being the centre and it surrounded with various factors both internal and external which are unavoidable. These two factors ultimately are related to consumers and society.

According to Newman's Peery. Jr, in his book "Business, Government and Society" explains society is the centre of any activity. The same is shown below under the title. "The Threefold Society."

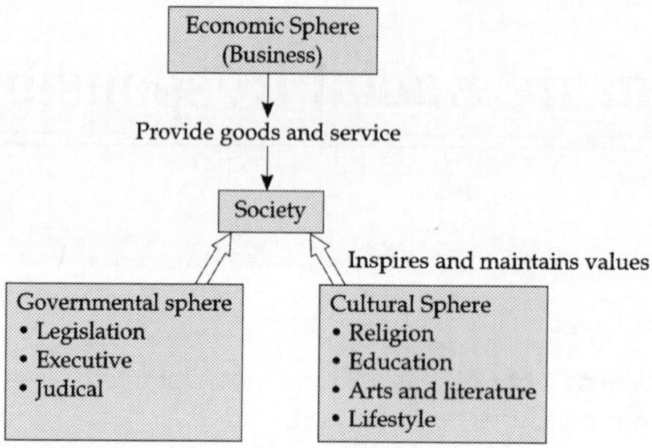

The threefold society shown in the above figure shows the economic sphere on top of the society. Everybody wants to live by fulfilling needs of the individuals. The economic sphere paves way in providing goods and services. Business is the major institution of the economic sphere and its key role is to provide the goods and services needed to maintain the standard of living within society. In a market oriented society, businesses compete with one another to satisfy the needs and demands of customers. Hence, it is the responsibility of the business to act responsibly towards society, which may be termed corporate social responsibility.

Understanding the Social Responsibility of Business

Social responsibility of business or corporate social responsibility, whichever way it is called, herein after referred to as CSR is also considered a subject which received greater attention and was sufficiently dealt with advanced countries already. Many research works have been undertaken and proved that every corporate should return back moderately that whatever they receive from the society. Social responsibilities of business emphasises certain features which are as follows:

(1) The business today has manifold responsibilities as

(i) to itself (ii) to its customers (iii) workers (iv) shareholders (v) community and state.

Task of management is to reconcile and harmonise these separate and sometimes conflicting responsibilities.

(2) The social responsibility of business can best be assumed in an atmosphere of freedom with the least possible restraint on healthy competition.Concentration and monopoly have to be watched and guarded and wherever necessary it is to be dispersed.

(3) Every business has an overriding responsibility to make the fullest possible use of its resources both human and material, as has each individual. The management has the responsibility to provide security of employment with fair wages and equal opportunity for personal growth and advancement in the business, which is a requirement of justice and the means of secruing efficient management. Responsibility to the consumers means setting up and maintaining standards of quality, service and price. These are best achieved by the business itself or through trade associations, failing which the state may intervene.

(4) Self-regulation is preferable to legislation. But self-regulation may encourage inappropriate situations.

There are four principles laid down by Ex- President Wilson of USA for the proper conduct of business: They are:

(i) The rule of publicity: Let the public know what is going on. Suspicion, false conjecture and misunderstanding arise out of secretiveness.

(ii) The equivalent service: Let the public receive service fully equivalent to the money paid.

(iii) The conscience in business: To emphasise that the rule of business gains must be of a higher order than those of the ordinary gains, sustained by the moral judgements of honourable men.

(iv) The spirit of service: To see that the thing that you do for the public and get money for it is the best thing of that kind that can be done.

The above declaration, like the rule of publicity, the equivalent service, the conscience in business, and spirit of service have paved the way for suggestion and recommendation towards social responsibility. Business brought the evolution of new idea and principles. Business began merely as an institution for the purpose of money or profit making. So long as a man made money and was accepted by public, he was considered successful. He felt no particular obligation and acknowledged no responsibility to the public. As the man was the owner of his business he thought that he had a perfect right to do with it what he pleased. Gradually, the word "service" became the slogan of innumerable business clubs and associations. And at the same time leaders all over the world were becoming increasingly conscious of the fact that the public was an integral part of general business scheme. In India TATA and Birla groups realised this and started showing responsibility towards business. The sense of service brought to quality and modified the greed for profit. It is now increasingly recognised that what is not for the public good is not for the good of the business. Economic order came to recognise social order as its basic foundation.

Social Responsibility: Indian Perspective

The concepts, notions and expressions of social responsibility in the business community in a traditional society are bound to be different than those of an individual society. Large part of Indian business in villages and small towns is still living in the old traditional way. That is a fact which must be clearly borne in mind while dealing with the economics and sociology of Indian business. Its disregard has made the necessary co-relation between offence and justice, difficult in India. There is more social injustice in a poor society than in an affluent society. Business cannot be larger, higher, better or any different than that society at large. In case of society business relationship, the public servant, the consumer, the worker, their habits and outlook are all linked in the above chain. Discharge of social obligations cannot be a one way traffic. It is necessarily a mutually interacting process where actions produce reactions.

Hence, there is a proactive action by the business houses to hold their responsibility towards society. A detail study on corporate social responsibility is disussed below.

CORPORATE SOCIAL RESPONSIBILITY

Corporate social responsibility is an obligation of the organisation to act in a way that serves both its own interests and the interests of its many external communities. There are multiple stakeholders in the external environment of business organisations including customers, suppliers, employees, stockholders/shareholders, competitors, labour unions, political parties, federal state and local government, educational institutions and others.

A good example of the benefits of social responsibility was provided by the Johnson & Johnson's response in the wake of the discovery that cyanide has been maliciously placed in capsules of Tylenol. Following the philosophy of social responsibility reflected in Johnson & Johnson's creed, both corporate and local level managers decided, independently, to remove the product from store shelves. Even though it was discovered that contamination occurred after the shipments had left J&J's manufacturing and distribution centres. J&J's commitment told them that it was right to do to protect consumers.

Definitions

Different authors have described the concept of social responsibility in different dimensions of the business.

According to Carroll (1979), "the social responsibility of business encompasses the economic, legal, ethical and discretionary expectations that society has of organisation at a given point in time".

Sethi (1991), Shivaraman (2000), "A good corporation is one which voluntarily shares its market power and resultant pecuniary gains and thereby yields accountability for its actions and performance with those groups who have been adversely affected by the power".

Again Sethi expreses "Social responsibility is a sense of obligation and duty. It might also mean to incorporate the notion of answerability.

Devi's Blomstorm (1975), "It is the obligation of decision makers to take actions that protect and improve the welfare of society as a whole along with their own interest, protecting and improving are two aspects of social responsibility".

Keith Davis (1960), "Social responsibilities refer to the businessman's decisions and actions taken for reasons of least partiality beyond the firm's direct economic or technical interest".

Adolph A. Berle, (1963), "Social responsibility is the manager's responsiveness to public consensus. This public consensus would be determined in each country by its customs, religions, traditions, its level of industrialization, norms and various other aspects".

Kenneth R. Andrew (1971), "By social responsibility, we mean the intelligent and objective concern by the welfare of the society that restrains individual and corporate behaviour from ultimately destructive activities, no matter how immediately and leads in the direction of positive contribution to human betterment variously as the later may be defined".

In early 1970s it was a controversial topic, but now it is a widely accepted concept among business houses.

The systematic reasoning about a conceptual framework for corporate social responsibility (CSR) started in the US half a century ago (Carroll 1999). During this time many different concepts and principles have been aired and debated in relation to CSR.

The following are a few reasons which also stand as case study or example as:

(1) Corporations perceived as being socially responsible might be rewarded with extra and or most satisfied customers. Otherwise the corporates may face the product boycotts or undesirable act from the customers.
Eg: Exxon Mobil and Nestle.

(2) To build confidence among employees and parenting care towards employees, CSR acts as a great tool to the corporators.

(3) Corporates through their social actions and programmes will impress legislation, through which they will be ensured a greater corporate independence from the government.

(4) Making a positive contribution to society might be regarded as a long-term investment in a safer, better educated and more equitable community, which subsequently benefits the corporates by creating an improved and stable position to do the business.

(5) Corporations cause social problems (e.g., pollution) and hence have a responsibility to solve those they have caused and to prevent further social problems arising.

(6) All corporate activities have social impact of one sort or another whether through product or services, the employment of workers or some other corporate activity. Hence, the corporations cannot escape responsibility for those impacts, whether positive or negative or neutral.

(7) Corporations rely on the contributions of a much wider set of constituencies or stakeholders in society (such as consumers, creditors, suppliers, local communities) along with the share holders and hence they have the duty towards social responsibility.

Feature or Nature of Corporate Social Responsibilities

Features of corporate social responsibility have been highlighted initially by Archie Carroll (1979) and subsequently refined during 1991 and 2000 by both Carroll and Buchholtz. According to them there are four dimensional responsibilities held by corporates which is shown as under.

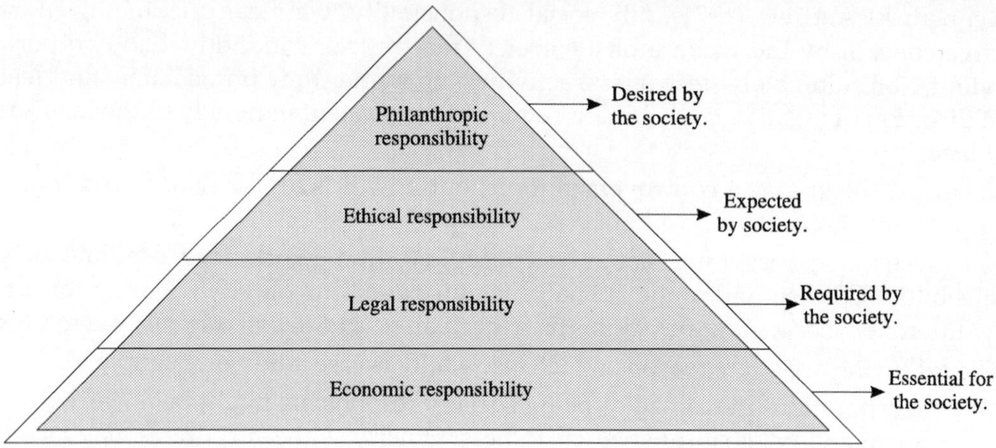

Source: Carroll (1991)

Based on the above model, developed by Carroll who regards CSR as a multi-layered concept, which can be differentiated into four interrelated aspects like economic, legal, ethical and philanthropic responsibilities, shown in the form of pyramid and ultimately every aspect is related to society. The factors related to model are explained briefly.

Economic responsibility

Larger economic responsibility is extended towards the country. This is the responsibility related to both internal and external environment of the business. Economic responsibility consisting of shareholders, employees, customers, etc., have shareholders who demand a reasonable return on their investments, they have employees who want safe and fairly paid jobs and they have customers who demand good quality products at a fair price, etc.

Based on these demands the businesses are established and each and every activity of the business is related to the society. Hence it is the first and foremost responsibility of the business to function effectively and profitably to stay in the business for long run. This is a solid basis through which the satisfaction of economic responsibilities can be fulfilled.

Legal responsibility

All economic activities and businesses are to be based on legal formalities. As law is supreme, the law relating to corporations and various business activities should be based on law. Laws are the code of conduct and also codification of society's moral views. Any corporate should work within the purview of law and also be aware of their legal restraints, which is not confined to the Articles of Associations, but also to business activities. The laws and regulations established by the government set the minimum standards for ethical behaviour. Law represents the values of a society, which have the force of formal authority of threat and punishment, if they are broken. This makes everybody to follow law compulsorily.

Ethical responsibility

Ethical responsibilities are the acts of the corporations to do what is right, just and fair even if they are not compelled to do so by the legal framework. But ethics is beyond law, though ethics and law should go hand in hand. Corporates are morally responsible towards society. It can be related to environment, stakeholders and any issues relating to marketing, human resources, crisis and so on. The organisational principles should be focused on public responsibility. The outcome of corporate behaviour should be constructed with society like creating social impact, social programming and social policies.

Philanthropic responsibility

It is the least responsibility, where corporates can act upon with option. It is expected that the corporates love mankind. Corporations are considered artificial persons whereas, let anybody whether artificial or natural being, "first let them be human beings".

As William H. Lever put it "Nothing can be greater than a business, however small it may be that is governed by conscience, nothing can be meaner more petty than a business, however large, governed without honesty and without brotherlihood".

Hence, philanthropic responsibility is the fourth level of model, which may insist upon improvement in quality of life of employees, local communities, and ultimately the society at large. Charity and other philanthropic activities are not new in India. The age-old corporations like TATA, Birla and newage, Wipro Infoysis are corporations where a number of activities are undertaken for the welfare and well-being of the society.

Aspects of Corporate Social Responsibility (CSR)

Corporate Social Responsibility (CSR) is essentially a concept whereby companies integrate social and environmental concerns in their business operations and in the interaction with their stakeholders on a voluntary basis. It is understood that the companies are more than economic institutions, they have a responsibility to help society to solve pressing social problems, both internal and external of the business atmosphere. Through the voluntary commitment to CSR, companies send a positive signal of their behaviour to their various stakeholders, namely, shareholders, employees, creditors, Customers, suppliers of goods, government and society at large.

Understanding Stakeholders (Concept)

A stakeholder in an organisation, any group or individual who can affect, or is affected by the achievement of the organisation's objectives. The term "stakeholder" in business was first noted in the 1960s and Edward Freeman developed an theoretical approach on stakeholders in 1980s. According to Stark (1994) "the stakeholder theory of the firm is probably the most popular and influential theory to emerge from business ethics". Unlike the CSR approach, which strongly focuses on the corporations and its responsibilities, the stakeholder approaches starts by looking at various groups to which the corporation has a responsibility. The stakeholders theory also emphasies on legitimate interest in the corporation.

Stakeholder theory studies in two ways like "affects" and "affected by". This can be understood as (1) The principle of corporate rights. (2) The principle of corporate effect.

The first point demands that the corporation has the obligation not to violate the rights of others and the second says the companies are responsible for the effect of their actions on others.

The following is the model towards corporate social responsibility related to stakeholders.

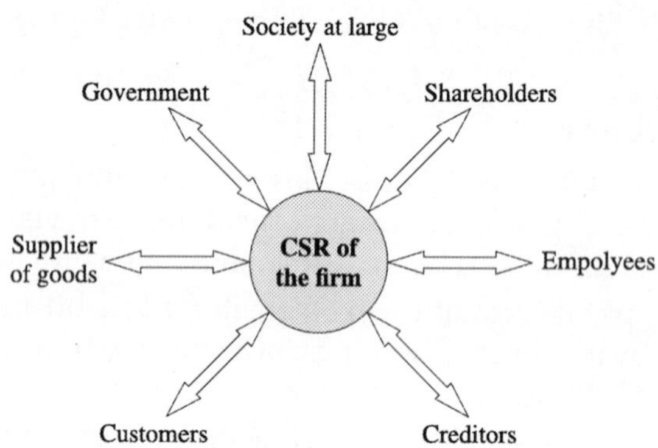

A model of CSR Kamatchi P. (2003)

From the above figure it is understood as, the stakeholders are one group among several others. The company has obligations not only to one group but also to a whole variety of other area that arear affected by its activities. The corporation or the firm is thus situated at the centre of a series of independent two-way relationships. Each of the variables is discussed briefly.

(i) Responsibility towards shareholders

It is the first and foremost responsibility of any corporate to hold a direct responsibility towards its shareholders. Shareholders are partly owners of the company and they cannot be treated as just investors of the company. The company should hold moral behaviour towards them, since they are bringing the finance to the business, which is normally considered the life blood of the business. The responsibility towards shareholders are:

- Investment into profitable scheme.
- Timely payment of dividends.
- Providing requisite information.
- Informing progress of the business.

(ii) Responsibility towards employees

Basically, the companies are to produce wealth with meaningful planning and execution. The employees are the main instruments in producing profit or wealth of corporations. The employees must be given all opportunities to grow individually.

They must be given identity and dignity to bring the best result of products production both qualitatively and quantitatively. Based on the corporate missions, companies do take various welfare measures for their employees, including endeavours by way of providing welfare measures like housing facilities, medical facilities, family related activities, power, water supply school, etc., and to lead a quality work life. The following are the core areas of responsibility towards employees:

- Providing with a fair salary and wages
- Providing good working conditions
- Satisfaction of security needs
- Providing opportunity for career development.

(iii) Responsibility towards creditors

Creditors are the backbone of any financial and finance related aspects. The banking, and financial institutions are great supporters and form integral part of the corporations. The following are the responsibilities towards creditors:

- Determination of proper terms and conditions of loans.
- Proper utilisation of debt capital
- Regular payment of interest and advances
- To provide with requisite information.

(iv) Responsibility towards customers

Corporates' main objective is to meet customer satisfaction through their products and services. Consumers are obviously one of the most important stakeholder of the company. Though there are a various consumer forums or councils to protect the consumers' interest through the Consumer Protection Act of 1986.

Again consumer's rights rest upon the assumption, that the consumer dignity should be respected. It is one of the main duties to treat consumers as ends in themselves, and not only as means to the end of the producer.

The following are the core areas of the responsibility towards customers:

- Determination of fair prices
- Making available goods and services

- Providing the quality goods
- Satisfaction and solution to customer complaints in time.

(v) Responsibility towards suppliers of goods

Suppliers are another mainstream of the corporates. Suppliers may be treated as partners which may go a long way to promote success of the firm. Suppliers provide input which the company transforms into higher value outputs. The interaction should be based on integrity, honesty, fairness, mutual respect and care. The responsibility towards suppliers of goods are:

- To pay fair prices in reasonable time
- Purchases on reasonable terms and conditions.
- To inform about the change in demands and preferences.
- To promote healthy competition.

(vi) Responsibility towards government in return

Corporate bodies are gradually becoming part and parcel of the government. The contribution of the business is a great booster for economy to any government through payment of taxes. Government is expected to provide profitable and stable economic environment for business to act, and business is expected to pay taxes, create jobs and economic investments.

The following are the responsibilities towards government:

- Timely payment of taxes and duties.
- Keeping away from politics of business.
- Following legal provisions pertaining to the business
- Cooperation with the government during times of crisis and emergency.

(vii) Responsibility towards society

Business and society go hand in hand the duties which the company and the society owe to each other are reciprocal. Social perception of business has undergone a genuine shift and expectations on its role have been high. The company can make environment improvements through contacting various local bodies. The welfare and growth of the society depends upon the business and at the same time survival and profit of the business based on the society. Hence, all businesses are integral part of society and cannot survive without the other. A firm or corporation carrying positive image in the society has a very strong probability of lasting growth vis-à-vis others having poor social image. The following are the areas the corporations can show their responsibility towards society:

- **Health services:** This may cover health programmes, donations to the hospitals, family welfare, health awareness programmes and health camps in the rural communities.
- **Educational services:** Can cover promotion of education, promotion scientific research, and technical education. Donation to school construction and building up of distance education.

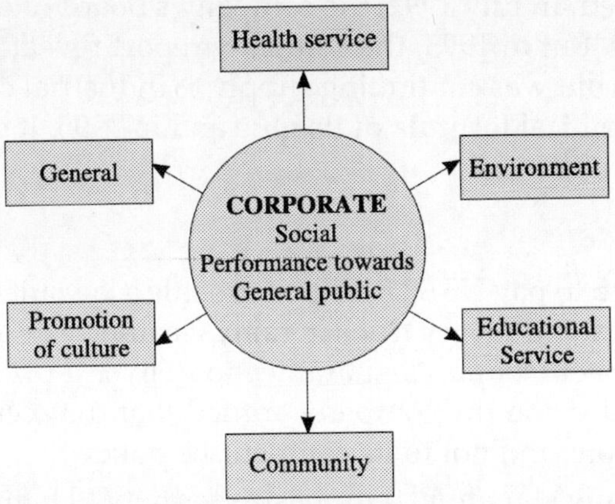

Corporate social performance towards society at large. – Kamatchi, P. (2003)

- **Community development:** The corporate can take up rural development, welfare of women and children and community services.
- **Environmental protection:** The corporations are involved directly in protecting the environment and physical conditions of the society like afforestation, conservation of nature, protecting ecology and environment.
- **Promotion of culture:** Culture of any nation is the wealth of the people who practise and maintain it. Care should be given to heritage and arts, religion and values, and promotion of art and culture.
- **General coverage:** The various activities which are directly related with day-to-day functions, practice or hobby can also be protected by the corporation. Like proper awareness in respect of road safety, promotion and funding of sports activities, giving hand to government in conducting safety week, anti-terrorism activities, etc.

CASES ON CSR IN BRIEF

1. H.B. Fuller and the Street Children of Central America

In the early 1990s, a newspaper article focused on the street children in Latin American cities. Toluene-based glue which was used as an ingredient in adhesives was being used by these children to inhale, resulting in many casualties. Inhaling the glue also produced many disorders including severe neurological dysfunctions, brain atrophy, loss of liver and kidney functions, loss of sight and hearing, leukaemia, and muscle atrophy.

H.B. Fuller was distributing its adhesive products in Central America through its subsidiary, Kativo Chemical Industries. There was pressure by child advocate groups on H.B. Fuller. A ban was imposed in Honduras in March 1989 prohibiting the import of solvent-based adhesives which did not contain mustard-seed oil. However, the company argued that the problem was due to 'social conditions' and that it was not responsible for the way its glues were used. In July 1992, the company's board of directors voted to stop selling Resistol adhesives. But in 1993, the company report revealed that it had stopped selling its glue to retailers but was continuing supply to industrial customers. In 1994, the company changed the chemical formula of its glue and in 1995, it claimed that it neither produced Resistol nor sold it.

2. Domino's Delivers

In May 1993, Domino's had to pay US $2.8 million to settle a lawsuit with Susan Wauchop, who was killed by a Domino's delivery truck in rainy weather. The allegation was that the driver was speeding to meet Domino's guarantee to deliver a pizza within 30 minutes. This guarantee was popular and the company argued that the accident occurred due to weather and road conditions and not to its competitive policy.

Although the company's manual emphasized safety, Domino's introduced the 30-minute guarantee in 1984. However, this guarantee started attracting increasing criticism. In 1989, the National Safe Workplace Institute claimed that Domino's drivers were involved in 100 accidents resulting in 10 deaths in 1988 and the institute started publicizing the accidents in 1989 and 1990 showing that they were increasing.

In 1990, Domino's introduced a 14-part safe-driving programme for its drivers, but, drivers testified that those who were able to meet the 30-minute deadline with four pizzas in one hour got a bonus of one per cent on those sales. Domino's had also installed a toll-free number so that people could report on any Domino's employee driving recklessly.

3. Social Responsibility vs Profit
A Case Study from SAIL

Large public sector enterprises geared to the infrastructural development of India, like the steel plants, were started in the early fifties as economic development projects and, simultaneously, as social service agencies. Gradually, however, as population pressures increased and social demands grew, the social purpose of these enterprises began to take priority over the economic objectives. Increasing employment, providing total welfare, including housing, education, medical care, recreational facilities and so on and so forth, became more important than operating efficiently and profitably. With the new stress on a market driven economy, SAIL faces a dilemma: efficiency or social service, profits or welfare.

In the early 1960s and through the 1970s, there was a lot of debate, especially regarding "corporate responsibility." Prof Theodore Levitt of Harvard Business School stated that "Corporate Social Responsibility makes good sense if it makes good economic sense – and not infrequently it does. But if something does not make economic sense, sentiment or idealism ought not to let it in the door." The other school of thought supported the view that the corporate sector should fulfill a wider responsibility towards society in general.

Social Responsibility as a Prime Factor

In India, there has been very clear thinking on the issue since the first five-year plan. At the conceptual stage itself, the steel industry was envisaged to fulfill much more than the basic economic role of producing steel for building the nation. It had the additional responsibility of developing the backward regions of this country by creating opportunities for employment and better standards of living for the inhabitants. That was the need of the nation at the time. This is a responsibility which Hindustan Steel Limited and, thereafter, SAIL, have consistently tried to fulfill.

In the early years, the emphasis was on recruiting unskilled manpower from the area, training and imparting skills to them to develop the people and, thereby building up the industry. At the same time, for the convenience of the persons recruited, the plants took on the responsibility of building houses and roads, providing water, electricity and all basic amenities to make life comfortable. This soon extended to building schools and hospitals so that a better future might be assured to the employees and their families. The plants even supplied breeze coke to the employees to be used as a fuel for cooking, as no other fuel was easily available.

Gradually, the social responsibility extended to providing parks, gardens, community centres, clubs, stadia, etc. SAIL has even taken on the responsibility for encouraging higher education through support to local colleges and professional bodies, encouraging sports by the recruitment of budding talent and by organizing tournaments.

The total cost of these social contributions to the public for the year 1989-90 was more than Rs 500 crore. This includes canteen facilities, recreational and cultural activities, concessional transport, training and development, holiday and retirement benefits, etc., and a sum of Rs 180 crore just for township maintenance and development.

Today SAIL runs hospitals, each of which compares with the best in the country. Besides treating the employees, this facility is extended to local government officials free of cost, and to other people at a subsidized rate. Over 600 doctors are on the rolls to render services to the employees and the community in general.

There are 220 schools being run by the company, and about 2 lakh students are being educated in these schools. SAIL employs 5500 teachers. In addition to primary and secondary education, SAIL plants extend help and facilities to local colleges and institutes of higher education.

Besides these, in the last five years, SAIL has made substantial investment of financial and managerial resources for the protection of the environment and the safety and occupational health of the employees. Messrs Kinhill, world renowned environment consultants, were engaged to advise in improving the environment in and around the plants through better pollution control and environment management. In the area of safety and occupational health, SAIL has taken help from Arthur D Little and Posh Consultants to identify areas which needed improvements.

New Expectations – Profits and Efficiency

However, in recent years, the nation's expectations from the steel sector have changed. Earlier, the social motive was stronger than the economic. Today there is a more competitive environment and, within this, each sector is expected to make profits and contribute to the national exchequer.

In 1986, SAIL set an objective to become self reliant. At the same time, to remain competitive, SAIL had planned to become one of the largest and best steel producers in the world by the turn of the century. Therefore, modernization and upgradation of technology in three of the oldest plants, Rourkela Steel Plant (RSP), Durgapur Steel Plant (DSP) and Indian Iron and Steel Co (IISCO), was imperative. This needed an investment of approximately Rs 15,000 crore. RSP and DSP have already started investing in modern equipment. To get optimum returns from this heavy investment, a detailed planning exercise has been undertaken by SAIL. The main component of the planning is human resources planning. This shows that RSP would need only 29,809 employees after commissioning the new equipment. DSP's need would be 29,155, and when IISCO is modernized as envisaged, it would need only 14,398 persons. As against this, the figures (as on 31.06.91) were 31,445, 29,012 and 20,647, respectively.

Moreover, the quality and skill-mix of the employees required to operate the more advanced technology is entirely different from the existing composition of the workforce. New technology needs better qualified and more skilled people to operate and maintain the equipment. Even with relaxation of the minimum qualification required for skilled and highly skilled categories, RSP has only about 6750 such employees and DSP about 3500 against the requirement of 12,000 and 15,000, respectively, after modernization.

Realizing its social responsibility to the nation, SAIL has not planned on any retrenchment. Emphasis has been placed on educating, training and redeploying the existing personnel. An attractive voluntary retirement scheme has been offered to help attain the optimal manpower requirement. The question is to what extent this social responsibility can be extended without compromising the broader national objective of efficiency and generation of profits. SAIL has a responsibility towards the existing employees which it is willing to fulfill. But, given the economic demands today, the question is: should SAIL be obliged to recruit additional manpower to alleviate the unemployment problem of the country? When education is a must for operating the sophisticated technology that we are investing in, should there be pressure on SAIL to recruit unqualified labour so as to develop peripheral areas of the country?

The Dilemma

The steel plants are islands of prosperity in the areas where they are situated. Therefore, there is constant and increasing pressure on all plants to recruit additional manpower. The situation in the near future is not likely to improve. Should the corporate sector then become responsible for providing employment at the cost of its own performance? The earlier results of continuous increase in manpower should be taken as a lesson to avoid such situations in future. It is after a lot of planning, communication with employees and discussions with Unions that SAIL has been able to arrest the trend of increasing manpower. The manpower in SAIL has, in fact, been reduced by about 20,000 over the last six years through normal separations, voluntary retirement, etc. SAIL has been recruiting every years but only to the extent of its actual needs for maintaining the age-mix and the skill-mix, and to fill shortages in critical categories. However, pressures all around the plants are mounting. This is a dilemma most public sector corporations are facing today.

Investment in Ancillaries

The steel plants have helped in the growth and development of many ancillary industries around the plants. The demand for continuing such investment is still there. In the initial days, it was an obligation to promote development around the plants. Therefore, these industries were supported financially and otherwise. But today, they should gear up to face competition and produce efficiently. Why should it be the responsibility of the steel plants to subsidize inefficient producers on a continuous basis?

The company's contribution to these industries can be to train and develop their personnel so as to promote all round efficiency. This will help the steel plants also to get better components and service from these ancillary industries. Development of the ancillary industries may also provide an avenue for channeling some of the surplus manpower from the steel industry. But the time has come when the public sector should be allowed to adopt Prof. Theodore Levitt's philosophy.

If a company functions in such a way as to make profits, it will also be in a better position to fulfill its obligation towards its employees; the people living in the neighborhood and the whole of society.

The new Industrial Policy has provided an environment for competition in the steel sector by delicensing and decontrolling the industry. Further, each industry is expected to generate through exports the foreign exchange needed for its operations and growth. No more can the public sector industries make losses in the certitude that they will be made good by payments from the exchequer. This is equivalent to imposing an additional tax on the people to maintain an inefficient public sector unit and to pay its employees. Today, the social and ethical responsibility of the steel sector as well as all other industries is to become internationally competitive and to generate the much needed foreign exchange for the nation.

Social Contribution to Nation

The steel plants were designed to produce types of steel which are of strategic national importance. Rourkela Steel Plant produces electrolytic tin plates used for building armoured tanks and bomb shells for defence. It also produces electric resistance weld and spiral welded pipes mainly used for transportation of oil and water. Durgapur produces items for the railways: wheels and axles, fish plates, sleepers. Bhilai steel plant makes rails. Production of many of these items is unprofitable at the sale price fixed by the government. No private steel plant would produce these items under such conditions.

Yet, they are of vital importance to the nation and SAIL has been producing them for over three decades at the cost of its own economic performance. Today, when competition and efficiency are the hallmarks of the new Industrial Policy, artificially controlled prices should be removed.

The other contribution SAIL is expected to make is to provide employment in order to help the nation to contain the pressure of unemployment. In the 1960s and 1970s, SAIL continuously recruited even though there was little need for it. Manpower in BSP, RSP and DSP grew by 22 per cent, 23 per cent and 25 per cent from mid-60s to the early 80s. A large part of this addition consisted of unqualified and unskilled employees. In 1984, SAIL had about 2,50,000 employees producing only 5 million tonnes of steel. Labour productivity was as low as 49 T/man years and SAIL was making losses.

Though excess manpower was not the only malady, it was an important reason for the overall downfall in performance. In today's context, providing employment cannot be the overriding objective of any company.

Having stated all this, SAIL is not turning a blind eye to the people around the townships. Investment and effort to contribute to the larger society is continuing.

Peripheral Development

SAIL has spent about Rs 114.31 lakh in the development of its periphery and the plan for the year 1991-92 was about Rs 240 lakh. This includes vaccination and health care of neighbouring villages, providing roads and drinking water, building schools, maternity and childcare, etc. In line with the nation's demand, adult education is being given a thrust in all the townships. In RSP alone, it is planned that each secondary school child will teach at least five adults. Adult education classes are being run in the company schools in the evenings.

Development of Women

For women, in and around the township, the plants help by opening various cooperatives. In RSP, BSP and BSL widowed and destitute women are engaged in making soap, stitching uniforms, hand gloves, etc., which are supplied to the plants. For this the plants provide them with the basic infrastructure, raw materials, initial investment capital as well as adequate remuneration.

The women employees of SAIL are provided with all opportunities to develop and grow within the company. Today SAIL employs more than 300 women managers in various positions. Every year this number is growing. The senior-most lady executive is in the rank of Deputy General Manager. Women are engaged in every field right from the shopfloor to the computer room, in marketing, purchasing and personnel, holding key positions.

Cultural Contribution

Art and culture of the local region are carefully preserved and promoted. In all the principal functions held in the plants, local music, folk dance and folklore find a place.

Some of the local professional groups are financially helped by the company. A classic case is that of Ms Tazan Bai, who was originally spotted and encouraged by the local management of Bhilai Steel Plant. She has become famous not only in Madhya Pradesh but also in the whole country. She has gone on to win a Presidential Award in 1988. BSP employed her about 10 years ago.

Promotion of Ethics

Industrialization of any region influences the values of the society in the region. The management's ethics get transmitted to the employees and then to the society.

Through its honest dealings with its employees, the state and central governments and the public, SAIL has promoted a society which, by and large, desires and strives for honesty. Incidents of corruption and underhand dealings, therefore, get widely talked about and are scorned in the steel plant cities. SAIL's stated objectives are to discharge its responsibilities faithfully and "constantly strive to deserve and enjoy the highest measure of public trust and esteem."

SAIL believes that its human resource department is its greatest asset. Concern for others is a value actively promoted by the company. Sensitivity to human problems, the human touch in interpersonal relations, concern for family life are part of the culture the company has been promoting throughout. The executives regularly visit employees who are hospitalized or ailing, and give support and help to their family members. Marriages and other ceremonies are occasions when everyone participates, irrespective of levels and hierarchy.

Despite all this discipline is of paramount importance in SAIL. This encompasses personal, organizational and technical discipline. Through various HRD initiatives, SAIL has tried to promote discipline amongst its employees. This is not confined only to the plant. Discipline in the township and harmonious living are encouraged. The management has taken steps to counsel family members and individuals in their homes so as to curb regular absenteeism, alcoholism and such problems.

Above all, SAIL plants are good example of national integration. People from all parts of the country, irrespective of caste and creed are working together and living harmoniously. Management gives equal treatment and opportunities to all. The reins of the company have been in the hands of individuals who have hailed from different corners of this country.

With a certain degree of justifiable pride one may say that, despite the handicaps under which it works as a government controlled company, SAIL, one of India's largest business enterprises, has striven to meet its changing social and ethical responsibilities, so as to create a healthy and progressive society.

Source: Mathias, *Corporate Ethics* (1994)

Corporate Social Performance

This has been studied since mid-1970 particularly in US. Corporate social performance is a business organisation's configuration of principles of social responsibility, processes of social responsiveness and policies, programs and observable outcomes as they relate to the firm's societal relationships (Wood, 1991, quoted Shivaramu, 2000). There are three levels of principles where corporate social responsiveness is developed. The first level is the perspective of business as an economic institution, referred to as *legitimacy*. The second level is the organisational level of an enterprise, referred to as *public responsibility* and the third is that of individuals in an organisation where the principle is *managerial discretion*. This is understood in the following Figure

Principles of Corporate Social Responsibility

Institutional Principle → Legitimacy

Organizational Principle → Public Responsibility

Individual Principle → Managerial Discretion

Process of Corporate Social Responsiveness

Environmental assessment

Stakeholder Management

Issues management.

Outcomes of Corporate Behaviour

Social Impacts

Social Programmer

Social Policies

Corporate social performance model

Source: Wood (1991), quoted Shivaramu (2000).

Indian Scenario from 1960 – 1980 Towards Social Responsibility

The Indian business scenario started changing towards slow progress.

Even as the cynicism and malpractices continued, a contrary trend became visible in the 1970s, which indicated that business attention was shifting from purely charitable behaviour measured in money terms to one where charity was only one aspect of socially responsible behaviour, and in which development of communities was considered important as charitable giving through trusts and establishment of prestigious institutions. The fast deteriorating image of the business community was responsible for the first, while global trends, mounting social problems, proactive chambers and the correct and strick policy of the government led to the latter. These factors are considered in more detail below.

Status of business community

The business community had further fallen in public esteem after the findings of several inquiry commissions set up to probe the state of affairs in the private corporate sector were made public. The Vivian Bose Commission on the administration of the Dalmia Jain

Companies, the Monopolies Inquiry Commission (1965), the Dutt Industrial Licensing Policy Enquiry Committee (1969), and the Wanchoo Committee (1972), all pointed to several unethical practices adopted by some large houses such as preempting capacity, multiple applications in different names, interlocking of funds, and violations of trust laws and tax concessions.

The state of affairs caused much anguish among the more enlightened and responsible business leaders. Not all businessmen were unhappy with the socialistic policies of the government, conscious as they were of the dangers of unprincipled expansion unmindful of social needs. Not were they happy with the deeds of the less scrupulous members of their own community. As early as 1957, SS Kanoria, a former president of FICCI admitted as:

"We have failed to win the confidence of the people and identify ourselves with the awakening of the masses to the consciousness of poverty and degradation and the insistent demand for a better life. The general impression we have made on the masses is that we are intoxicated with power and wealth, indulge in its vulgar show, and that our sole aim in life is to amass fortunes for ourselves regardless of national interests".

On another occasion, commenting on the co-existence of private wealth with corporate penury, and the fact that private wealth was being used for conspicuous consumption rather than employed in industry due to a pernicious tax system, he said:

"Our weakness is that there is no broad based, informed public opinion in our favour. On the contrary, criticism of private business, however irrational and ill informed, seems to evoke wide public approval".

In his address to the annual session of FICCI in 1963, Nehru referred to the Vivian Bose Report and the business community's criticism of the poor performance of the public sector and said:

"We want both to progress but it is clear that if an impression gets abroad that the private sector is not maintaining the moral standards or physical standards that one expects of them, it is that sector (rather than the public sector) that will suffer in public estimation. On the other hand, if it does maintain them, it will advance and grow".

One of the businessmen indicted in the Report of the Vivian Bose Commission was President of FICCI that year, but he did not step aside. It led to the exit of the Tatas and Mafatlals from FICCI in protest. Tata's disagreement with FICCI policies went beyond the Dalmia case. They believed that business must become politically active, openly espouse the virtues of free enterprise, and ostracise any anti-social elements in the community.

Responsibility of business community

The credit for bringing social responsibility into the business community's consciousness goes principally to Kasturbhai Lalbhai, JRD Tata, Arvind Mafatlal and Ramakrishna Bajaj. All believed in the trusteeship ideals of Mahatma Gandhi and in sound business ethics, and were worried about the deterioration in the latter. As champions of free enterprise, they also feared that irresponsible behaviour by the business community would lead the government to encroach on its freedom more and more.

At a time when money-making was all important, Kasturbhai stressed the need for moral leadership and social responsibility. Speaking at the Indian Merchants Chamber in 1963, he said:

"The businessman is ideally fitted to make an important contribution to this end. He should, therefore, actively participate in every worthwhile movement directed towards preserving for our country a sound social and economic structure".

He added:

"Industry and trade have to discharge many responsibilities to the community. They should provide—moral, personal and financial support— to institutions or causes which make their towns and villages better for living and which are intimately connected with our spiritual heritage. We should advertise what we produce and sell, but in doing so, also convince the public that free enterprise exists to serve the community by improving social and economic standards. We should also provide leadership to the community".

At the same time, he defended profit-making, saying as:

We must also impress upon the people that no business can for long exist without profits. Profits are a measure of effective, efficient operation and should be worn as a badge of accomplishment and of honour.

Practice of Trusteeship

Meanwhile, Gandhi's mantle as the moral guide of India had fallen on Vinoba Bhave who had launched the *gramdan* (gift of a village), the *bhoodan* (gift of land), and the *sampattidan* (gift of wealth) movements to put Gandhi's ideas of trusteeship into practice. Vinoba wanted businessmen to interest themselves in humanitarian, cultural, educational and other beneficial social activities; to adopt fair trading practices, and to consider their business as a social mission.

The end goal of Vinoba's campaign was not charity but the creation of an equitable society through voluntary and peaceful means.

Vinoba's work had the backing of the very political leaders who had opposed to trusteeship before Independence because, in spite of legislation based on the socialist rhetoric, there had been little dent on inequalities, and the government needed the financial support and administrative skills of the propertied and industrial classes for achieving the goals of economic and social development. Moreover, it could cope with only so many problems at a time. It was clear to Nehru and other leaders that encouraging class struggle and raising expectations of the depressed classes without the means to meet them would only be to invite trouble.

The socialist approach is based on the premise that the 'haves' will not voluntarily relinquish their wealth sufficiently enough to make a significant difference to the poor because it will thereby jeopardize their own position in the socio-economic structure. The philanthropic or charitable approach, on the other hand, does not upset the social structure, because charity cannot continue unless there are poor who are dependent recipients of this charity, and there are those who have a surplus to give.

The trusteeship theory therefore was seen as a safer way of bringing about social transformation without a violent social upheaval. It reinforced the traditional concepts of charity and thereby the viability of the old social structure, while simultaneously trying to promote the socialist ideal of a classless egalitarian society. It was therefore supported both by the capitalists and the government, through many paid only lip service to it.

Responsibility of Business Community

Vinoba's message was carried forward by Jai Prakash Narain. In 1965, he was the moving spirit behind an international seminar on social responsibilities of business, organized in Delhi by the India International Centre and the Institute of Gandhian Studies, Varanasi.

Narain's opening speech and much of the discussion at the seminar concentrated on Gandhi's concept of trusteeship and whether it was practical; what could be done by voluntary means to enforce it; whether a voluntary code of conduct was sufficient or whether the state should step in and regulate business; and whether labour and shareholders also had a responsibility.

Some of the participants were against the concept of trusteeship as being negative and impractical. It was pointed out that social responsibility should not be taken to mean charity. They felt it was necessary to spell out the goals and the kind of institutions that should be evolved, instead of simply leaving it to individual conscience and moral persuasion. Moreover, the concept of voluntary trusteeship would not make much headway because, due to poverty and illiteracy of consumers and the absence of consumer associations, there was no pressure on business. It was necessary to build in social audit as part of the concept of social responsibility.

One of the results of the conference was the declaration of the social responsibility of business, spelling out the need for it and pointing out that the concept was broader than charitable giving for community affairs. It included:

- Justice and fair play in all dealings
- Making serious attempts at growth and development of all factors or constituents of business from owners to consumers
- Utilization of surplus primarily for the above two purposes
- Utilization of surplus, if at all left over, for any other social purpose deemed fit for assistance such as education, health, research, etc.

The Delhi seminar was followed by a seminar at Calcutta in March 1966, addressed by Jai Prakash Narain. At its end it set up a study group to prepare a set of business norms for adoption by the business community; to examine the hurdles in the way of implementation of these norms; and to recommend remedial measures. The study group was chaired by Justice PB Mukharji. In its report, it examined responsibility under five broad heads: towards consumers, the community, employees, shareholders, other businesses, and towards the state. Several recommendations were made to encourage responsibility in each category. Among these were:

- Lightening the tax burden
- Introducing a policy of incentives on one side and the institution of social audit on the other
- Reduction of bureaucratic control
- Formation of Better Business Bureaus and Fair Trade Practices Associations and consumer groups
- More effort by chambers to introduce self-discipline.

One immediate fallout of the conferences was that JRD Tata, Ramakrishna Bajaj and other businessmen launched the Fair Trade Practices Association in Bombay in 1966 to codify and implement fair business practices. The Association elected Arvind Mafatlal as its first President. Its objective was to improve the public image of business by inculcating self-discipline as an alternative to government regulation.

Ethical way by JRD TATA and evaluation of change

But delivering the Anantharamakrishanan Memorial Lecture in Madras in 1969, JRD Tata, who always laid a great lead of emphasis on moral values, unhappy, admitted that the adoption of a code of conduct and membership of the Association had not had a significant impact on the public mind. He said:

"Today, let us face it, the reputation and image of private enterprise is far from being commensurate with its massive contribution to India's industrial and economic development during the last half century. To those of us who believe in private enterprise and are anxious to work for the economic revival of our country, such a state of affairs is a source of deep concern and frustration. A more serious consequence, however, is that as a result of the suspicion and hostility which this image of the private sector has generated in the minds of the government and Parliament, it is being increasingly denied the opportunities to play the full part of which it is capable, along with the public sector, in developing the country's economy".

He put down the cause of suspicion and hostility to low ethical standards adopted by some selfish members of the community who indulged in unrestrained acquisitiveness, tax evasion, black marketing, illegal foreign exchange transactions and conspicuous spending, and pleaded for responsible behaviour.

In order to redeem its image, JRD wanted Indian companies to go beyond conducting themselves as honest citizens. He pointed out that there were many ways in which industrial and business enterprises can contribute to public welfare beyond the scope of their normal activities. He advised:

"Apart from the obvious one of donating funds to good causes which has been their normal practice for years, they could, as some of the companies with which I am connected have done, use their own financial, managerial and human resources to provide task forces for undertaking direct relief and reconstruction measures. This form of public community service could be expanded by the cooperative effort among members of various industries".

In his advocacy of responsibility, JRD was joined by Ramakrishna Bajaj, grandson of Jamnalal Bajaj, who had inherited the family's devotion to Gandhian ideals regarding fair business practices and philanthropy. In a speech at the Maharshtra Chamber of Commerce in 1970, he pleaded for introspection by the business community and a sharing by the businessman in the responsibility for the well-being of the community where he operates. According to him, if business develops and implements specific norms of business behaviour in a conscious and convincing manner, it would earn popular recognition as a responsible partner in the common endeavour for attainment of national goals. This would also make government controls unnecessary. After all, he said:

"The business community is an essential ingredient of our democratic society and it has a duty not only to create wealth but also to promote the ethical and social goals of the community. Unless it fulfils both these functions and thereby plays its due role as a responsible section, it will not be able to ensure its own survival".

Arvind Mafatlal, Chairman of Mafatlal Industries, also pleaded for more social responsibility on the part of business but pointed out that it was a larger concept than philanthropy and went beyond giving funds to more normative issues such as self-discipline, quality control of consumer goods, fair trade practices, avoidance of vulgar display of wealth and ostentatious consumption.

It was not only a concern with ethics which made business shift from building institutions to becoming concerned with grass-roots issues at the community level. The shift was in keeping with global trends which had led to the emergence of the concept of managerial trusteeship after widespread social unrest in inner city areas and campuses due to increased unemployment and inadequate state provision for social welfare threatened not only the profitability but the very survival of companies. Though the contexts were different, a more constructive engagement with poor communities and national goals by Indian companies was similarly a response to the grim social situation in India.

Social and Unemployment Crisis

Population had increased alarmingly by 23.5 per cent during the decade 1950 – 61 as per against 14 per cent during 1941-50. The uncontrolled growth was a drag on economic development, and poverty resulting from over-population was sent to have a social cost for industry as well as the public exchequer.

The government's professedly socialist policies, with their emphasis on poverty removal through reduction of economic power rather than through expansion of production and employment, had little effect on income disparities or absolute poverty. In spite of steeply progressive taxation, disparities in income had widened so that the top 10 per cent of the population accounted for 30 per cent of the national consumption and the bottom 40 per cent for only 20 per cent. Almost 40 per cent of the population was estimated to be still below the poverty line, unable to afford the minimum intake of calories required for existence. Clearly, the trickle down approach—premising that if growth is taken care of, the results will trickle down to the poorest—had failed.

Growing unemployment, especially educated employment, had become an urgent social problem which boded ill not only for the government but also the business community. The industrial structure was not being diversified rapidly enough to absorb the new technical skills that were being developed at great cost, leading to unemployment of technical personnel. Society was exposed to dangerous pressures from a frustrated educated class.

During the Fourth Plan (1966-71), the actual rate of growth of national income, measured in 1960-61 prices, fell below the targeted growth rate of 5.5 per cent annum. The per capita income in constant prices fell from Rs. 348.6 in 1970-71 to Rs. 235 in 1972-73. Apart from domestic troubles, unfavourable external factors, such as escalation in petrol prices, and maintenance of 10 million refugees after the Bangladesh War, contributed to the dismal performance. The Draft Fifth Plan (1974-79), which had envisaged a national programme for minimum needs in rural areas and an extended programme of social welfare, amongst other objectives, never took off and after the elections of 1980; the Sixth Plan was launched instead.

The unprecedented labour unrest in West Bengal during 1969-70 and the Naxalite movement of the 1970s in particular, showed how deep and dangerous the social malaise was. There was social and political unrest in other parts of the country as well. It threatened the very stability of society.

It was not only a law and order problem but had its roots in a terrible sense of deprivation on the part of local communities. The anger was directed particularly at big busineses which, it was felt, had cornered all the benefits of development without putting anything back into society. While there had been massive investment in building up the country's industrial infrastructure, little attention had been paid to social amenities like schools, dispensaries and drinking water.

It was realized by society's leaders that more direct intervention on the poverty front was necessary to take care of imbalances in income distribution. But government seemed unable to grapple with the problems effectively.

Apart from an impatience with the accepted model of planning and government's slow and ineffective functioning, the intelligentsia was equally unhappy with the apathy and dependent mentality of the masses who waited for the government to solve their problems rather than take action themselves. It led to a tremendous increase in the number of private voluntary organizations (PVOs, also referred to as non-governmental organizations or NGOs) working for development outside the government framework. There was also a paradigm shift in thinking about the role of charity in social change and development.

Social Consciouse of Voluntary Sector

The need for relief in the wake of several calamities in the 1960s had brought a lot of people into the voluntary movement, anxious to assist their less fortunate fellowmen. In the 1970s, the growing social consciousness among the educated and especially among professionals—engineers, doctors, economists, lawyers—brought a new band of activities to the voluntary sector to try and solve problems of poverty and exploitation directly. They realized that charity was not enough. 'Development' had to replace charity handouts for 'welfare'. The emphasis among voluntary organizations, therefore, shifted from charity to promoting self-reliance and later to 'empowerment' of the disadvantaged.

To the older charitable welfare organizations and Gandhian and missionary agencies working for rural reconstruction were added new organizations relying on modern management methods and techniques.

The growing social consciousness was aided by the traumatic changes taking place in the political environment of the country. In mid-1974, Jai Prakash Narain (JP to his followers), the Sarvodaya leader associated with Gandhian and Sarvodaya organizations, launched a movement for a 'total revolution' which did much to awaken people to the need to bring the poor and oppressed into the mainstream, politically and socially, as well as economically.

At the same time, the declaration of an Emergency by Mrs. Indira Gandhi then Prime Minister and suspension of civil rights in 1975, in response to opposition to her government, brought many intellectuals into the voluntary sector and radicalized it. The decade of the 1970s saw voluntary organizations change from being 'welfare'-oriented to being 'change' or 'people'-oriented. It was regarded not merely as a question of income generation but of attitudinal and value changes which needed a reorientation of the social and political structure. There was, thus, more emphasis on people's participation in development, on public education, legal literacy, and on protest against socio-political abuses.

Simultaneously, women's issues came to the fore after 1975 was declared the Women's Year and the following decade as Women's Decade by the UN. The publication of the Report of the Committee on the Status of Women created a stir by showing how badly women fared in terms of all indices of development such as life expectancy, access to health, education and employment, quite apart from being subject to sexual harassment and violence. It led to the formation of many women's NGOs to tackle these issues, as well as to a focus on women in development programmes.

High Standard in Business Policy

Meanwhile, the government itself was waking up to the fact that its development strategy had not worked; that, by contrast, private voluntary action had been able to come up with innovative solutions to some problems and to target benefits to the most needy because of its local and flexible approach, and dedicated workers; and that industry could contribute more to the nation building effort. It therefore began to exert pressure on, as well as offer incentives to industry to conform to broader social and economic goals accepted by the country and to support voluntary agencies working for development. It frequently used the annual sessions of apex chambers for the purpose.

Nehru's last message to the Federation of Indian Chambers of Commerce and Industry (FICCI), before his death in 1964, was to "consider the larger good of India" and to work towards that end. It led the Executive Committee of FICCI to issue a statement urging the business community to run their industrial enterprises and business in the context of wider public policy, to exercise self-restraint, and to observe high standards in business practices.

Simultaneously, the government dangled the carrot of tax concessions to motivate industry to itself take up developmental work as well as to assist the growing voluntary sector. In 1977, Section 35cc was introduced into the Income Tax Act to provide for 100 per cent deduction to a company in respect of expenditure incurred by it on approved programmes of rural development, which included construction and maintenance of rural roads; drainage and sanitary systems in rural areas; construction and maintenance of hospitals, dispensaries and family planning centres; drinking water facilities; and so on. This induced many companies to enter the field of rural development. However, pleading misuse, the tax incentive was withdrawn in 1983-84, and along with it those whose reasons for community involvement were purely mercenary also stopped their contribution.

Leadership in Business Community Towards CSR

It was self-evident to sensitive business leaders that unless the business community contributed to basic development needs, its very survival would be threatened and it was in its own interest to participate in the nation-building effort.

One of the first to articulate this was JRD Tata. Anguished that the vision he had as a young man of a fast developing India free from poverty, misery and ignorance had not as yet materialized, JRD nevertheless did not give up hope and enthused his colleagues with the words:

"However disappointed some of us may be, let us never forsake that great vision of fail to do what we can to bring it to reality, for the day will surely come when the people of India at long last reap the fruits of their centuries of toil, patience and sacrifice".

Pointing out the need for industry to contribute more to community development, JRD said:

"In every village, large or small, there is always need for improvement, for help, for relief, for leadership and for guidance. I suggest that the most significant contribution organized industry can make it by identifying itself with the life and the problems of the people of the community to which it belongs and also by applying its resources, skills, and talents to the extent that it can reasonably spare them, to serve and help them".

He was also mindful that many enterprises were located in a town or city and had no rural connections. In his opinion, their contribution to the community must take a different form "for it would be difficult and probably ineffective for them to attempt direct activities of the kind for agricultural communities." Since the needs of a town or city may be great or even greater, he wanted private business and industry to make a significant impact on the problem by pooling their financial, technical and managerial resources and cooperating actively with the official agencies.

And as always, he led by example. He committed all the Tata companies to ethical behaviour and programmes of community development by amending the articles of association of the Tata companies to include a clause which stated "...and the company shall be mindful of its social and moral responsibilities to the consumers, employees, shareholders and the local community."

In committing his companies to social responsibility programmes, JRD Tata emphasized the principle that had underlain the work of the Tatas right from inception: that wealth is held in trust for the people and must be used exclusively for their benefit. What comes from the people must go back to the people many times over.

The article merely translated into a legal obligation what the company had undertaken to do ever since its inception in 1970. Long before he passed away, the founder of the House of Tatas, Jamsetji, had laid down community welfare as its policy, and instructed his heirs and successors to constantly bear in mind and implement it in letter and spirit.

JRD, like many other business leaders, was trying to reconcile in his personal and business life the contradictions between the individual and society, egoism and altruism, and a life governed by reason and one driven by passion. The ethical dimension of wealth creation and the vision of a moral and just civil society were what drove him and many Indian business leaders to the times, such as Arvind Mafatlal, to efforts at improving grass-roots communities.

Arvind Mafatlal belonged to the third generation of the family business established by his grandfather, Mafatlal Gagalbhai, in 1873. Under his leadership, the original textiles group had become one of the largest in the textile industry and had expanded also into non-textile business, especially chemicals and petrochemicals. In 1979, the family split and the brothers separated and continued to build and expand their own companies.

Arvind, the most philanthropically inclined of the brothers, had carried forward his family's charitable tradition ever since he became Chairman of the group at the age of 33. But in 1964 there was a change in his perspective. He saw that the social infrastructure had become more adequate and there were many institutions around. On the other hand, there were regular occurrences of famine, in spite of all the development that had taken place. In the mid-1960s, therefore, Mafatlal decided that instead of giving donations for institutions they would manage charitable funds themselves and ensure that they went to the right people.

It was during his work with JP Narayan during the Bihar famine that he saw poverty first-hand and came to understand its causes. But it was his meeting in 1968 with Ranchoddasji Maharaja, a saintly man who became Arvindbhai's guru, which was to change his entire life and outlook. At his guru's instance he organized famine relief operations in different parts of the country. This made him determined to convert crisis into opportunity, and took him from relief to rehabilitation.

He couched his arguments for business involvement in community development in terms of corporate self interest:

When a majority of the population is struggling for their survival, how can we keep quiet and plan for our progress and prosperity! If our customers do not have the buying power, how can we build up our business?... The corporate sector cannot continue to prosper, unless the economy of the common people is improved.

Mafatlal's exposure to rural poverty had made him realize that even more important than a monetary donation is the contribution of management skills to the task to development—a belief which led him, when he came into contract with Manibhai Desai, an eminent Gandhian, to partner the Bharatiya Agro Industries Foundation (BAIF) started by him. Mafatlal gave BAIF funds and management inputs by sending his staff to work in it for rural development through improved agricultural and animal husbandry practices. Today, BAIF is recognized as one of the best and most professional NGOs in the field of rural development.

Arvindbhai was also instrumental in setting up the Sadguru Sewa Sangh (SSS), the implementing arm of the Sadguru Foundation, with its headquarters in Madhya Pradesh, the home of his guru. The SSS is actively engaged in promoting income generating activities, literacy and health programmes in villages in MP. According to Mafatlal, philanthropy should promote long-term development work in the three 'A's—Anna (food), Akshar (literacy), and Arogya (health).

Chambers of Commerce and its Proactiveness

Apart from the leadership given by individual businessmen, chambers of commerce and industry also began to play a more proactive role to make business more socially responsible.

Chambers of Commerce and Industry had been formed as early as 1836 when the Bombay Chamber of Commerce came into being, but most were exclusively British till the 20th century. The first indigenous Indian business association was founded only in 1885 when British and Indian business interests began to diverge sharply.

Till Independence, FICCI and the other indigenous chambers functioned as nationalist watchdogs on many momentous developments affecting the whole nation, and not merely that of business. But the concerns were mostly political or economic.

After Independence, business had to function within a framework of a new set of goals and policies, and, again, most of the dialogues between government and business concerned economic matters such as planning, the industrial policy, export promotion, regulation of industry, taxation, and so on. But beginning in the 1960s, the chambers, led by FICCI, began to put social issues on their agendas, particularly problems of agricultural and rural development, and population growth. Partly they were prodded by the government to do so, and partly business leadership itself was awakening to the problems of the communities in which they lived and operated.

Massive

One of the first issues during this period was that of population growth. Though the country's income had gone up by 70 per cent, food production by 60 per cent, and cotton textile production by about 90 per cent, there had been hardly any perceptible improvement in the country's standard of living because of the runaway growth in population.

JRD Tata was one of the first to alert the nation to the dangers of uncontrolled population as early as 1951. He called for national efforts to contain the population explosion, and worked tirelessly towards this all his life, rallying his business colleagues and prodding government to act. JRD was joined by SP Godrej, Dr. Bharat Ram and others in a campaign for population control, and they together set up the Family Planning Foundation in Delhi for research and funding of family planning activities. It was one of the first examples of collaboration by several business houses who generally preferred to work individually and set up something in their own name.

FICCI presidents Madan Mohan Ruia in 1960, Dr. Bharat Ram in 1964, and Ramnath Poddar in 1966 also used the Annual Sessions of FICCI to highlight the dangers of unchecked population growth and appealed to FICCI members to take a direct interest in the solution of the problem and to initiate an intensive and vigorous family planning drive. As early as 1965, at a seminar "Better Calcutta", Sookamal Kanti Ghosh, the president of the Indian Chamber of Commerce, Calcutta, for that year said:

That large businesses, and groups of smaller ones, should establish family planning centres. To oversee the implementation of the drive, a family planning subcommittee was constituted in 1967, and in 1969 a separate family planning department was established for awareness of the problem and promotes action.

Many regional chambers followed suit, similarly urging their members to establish family planning clinics and undertake programmes of population control.

As a result, a large number of companies set up family planning clinics for their workers and supported public education and family planning camps for the larger community.

I have always felt that the Chambers of Commerce should not function in isolation but should be a part of the community life in which they operate. It is with this objective that we have tried to make the Chamber's functions more broad-based and I am sure that in course of time we will able to achieve better results" - President, ICC.

A City Affairs Department was established in ICC in order to continuously study the problems of the city. But the problems were not amenable to quick solutions, and there was little sustained interest by the business community.

Drawing attention to this indifference, ICC's president, GKB Bhagat, at the 1968 conference on Calcutta titled, 'Calcutta – A City in Crisis', reminded the members that,

"The improvement of the city is obviously not only the responsibility of the government at the centre or the state, but also of every citizen. In particular, all those who are better placed have a greater responsibility towards its improvement. In whatever way possible we, the business community, should help in improving the facilities for education, health and recreation."

Bombay and other chambers similarly pleaded with their members to take a greater interest in civic improvement.

From 1974 onwards, there was a debate on social issues at every annual session, and many chambers instituted annual awards for excellence in social, as well as economic endeavours. FICCI had instituted annual awards in 1967 to recognize individual, corporate an institutional initiative in economic, social and scientific areas. In the mid-1970s, it expanded the fields to include family welfare, research in science and technology, rural development, training and placement of disabled persons, environment conservation and pollution control.

Similarly, the Indian Merchants Chamber, Bombay, instituted 19 awards starting in 1969, endowed by different business houses such as Godrej, Bajaj, Arvind Mills, Birlas, and so on, for outstanding contributions in the field of rural development, family planning, control of environmental pollution, consumer protection, rehabilitation of handicapped persons, and so on. In its Platinum Jubilee year, it created a trust to recognize and reward any individual or institution in India for their outstanding contribution towards alleviation of human suffering or any other socially desirable cause, including family planning and rural development.

In sum, the chambers tried to awaken their members' conscience and to make them aware of a horizon beyond profit making. In a speech before the Punjab, Haryana, and Delhi Chamber of Commerce in April 1973, Charat Ram, President of FICCI that year, commented on this slow but steady metamorphosis in the attitudes of the business chambers:

"Time was when spokesmen of our Chambers betrayed an instinctive allergy to the government's socialist policies and egalitarian postures. But of late, the Chambers are realizing the futility of attacking the basic politics and programmes approved by the Parliament and have begun to avail themselves of opportunities to persuade the government to adopt the positive aspects of socialism, and to avoid the negative ones".

Rural Development

Rural development became the next thrust area as industry realized that it could not ignore the needs of about 80 per cent of the population which lived in villages in abysmal conditions.

FICCI brought rural development on to its agenda when Jagjivan Ram, the Union Minister of Agriculture and Irrigation, pointed out in a letter to FICCI's president in October 1975, that while some developmental programmes were being undertaken in rural areas by a few big business houses, these programmes could become more effective and purposeful if there was proper coordination of the efforts. First, a subcommittee, and then a rural development cell was set up in 1976, which drew up a plan of action which could be implemented by member companies, and organized several seminars on rural development and the role of industry. It also advised its members that business involvement in rural development should be treated as a normal business activity and not charitable work, and should be undertaken irrespective of the income tax relief's being offered by the government.

Other chambers also began to interest their members in rural development and some even began projects themselves. For instance, in 1977, the Association of Indian Engineering Industries, as the Confederation of Indian Industries (CII), was then called, adopted Khandagram village in Birbhum district of West Bengal for comprehensive development, and villages in the northern and western regions were identified for the express purpose of promotion of small rural industries. In 1978, it set up its Central Rural Development Commission to act as a resource body to coordinate the work of its subcommittees on rural development, and organized workshops and seminars to focus attention on the issues.

Alarmed by the Naxalite movement of the 1970s which highlighted the need for more direct engagement by industry with anti-poverty programmes, Calcutta-based companies and Calcutta Chambers also made an effort to take up rural development programmes. The Indian Chamber of Commerce, for instance, set up a trust in 1978, to finance rural development in 18 villages in the Krishnachandrapur area of the 24 Parganas district in West Bengal to improve rural area though as a proportion livelihoods, the actual implementation was left to the Vivekananda Trust, a voluntary arm of the Ramakrishna Mission. The Bengal Chamber of Commerce and Industry similarly adopted a cluster of villages in a West Bengal district for rural development.

City Development

Acute shortage of drinking water, inadequate transport facilities, congestion on roads, lack of housing and opportunities for recreation, growth of slums, and prevalence of insanitary conditions were endemic problems in all the major cities of India at the time and business leaders as well as chambers began to direct the attention of the business community to these problems.

Business Community Response

The cumulative result of all these influences was distinctly visible in the actions of many business houses. Of the total, the number of those with social responsibility programme was still extremely small, it was nevertheless an encouraging beginning. The issues addressed by them were mainly the three mentioned above, viz. population growth, rural development and city improvement. One exemplary programme was that of the Tatas.

The community development and social welfare programme of the premier Tata company, Tata Iron and Steel Company (TISCO), was started long before the concepts of 'social responsibility', or rural development, became fashionable or were adopted by other companies. It commenced in as early as 1949, covering a small *Adivasi* population round Jamshedpur. By 1970, the TISCO programme covered several villages apart from the town of Jamshedpur. It provided for training in technical trades and allied occupations, scholarships for education of women as well as men, and a midwife training programme.

The programme was implemented through a separate autonomous body called Tata Steel Rural Development Society for community services in 32 villages around Jamshedpur. Today, the Society operates in 600 villages in eight districts of Bihar, Orissa and MP for undertaking construction of roads, water sources for drinking and irrigation, promotion of rural sanitation and other welfare programmes for which it receives a grant of Rs. 30 million from TISCO. However, it is not dependent entirely on the Tatas for funds and attracts funds from other sources as well. Though no return was expected from the venture, clearly the company stood to gain in terms of improved industrial relations, rapport with tribal leaders, international exposure, and an image as a good corporate citizen.

TELCO too had begun its community development in seven bustees of Jamshedpur, with an initial thrust on health care, education and building roads to link remote villages. The work was steadily expanded to more villages and more themes like family planning and watershed management. Its Pune unit had also begun a massive effort at wasteland development through afforestation. These efforts were only formally recognized by the amendment of the articles of association which brought in the uninitiated companies.

The Tatas again made history when they conducted the first social audit in 1979 to find out whether the objectives laid down in the above clause had been implemented. Conducted by a team of three independent experts the audit concluded that, by and large, TISCO had fulfilled its obligation. Though many other companies have taken up community development work in the last few decades, such as audit remains, unfortunately, the only one of its kind.

Partly because the need was so evident, and partly because of tax incentives, a large number of other business houses initiated rural development and family planning programmes during this period. The house of Bajaj, for instance, which was already unique for its pro-rural work, now systematized and expanded its rural development work through its trusts and through group companies.

In Ahmedabad, the Kasturbhai Lalbhai group likewise set up the Narottatm Lalbhai Rural Development Fund (NLRDF) in the 1970s to undertake several programmes of development in family planning, forestry, rural industries, sanitation and so on. In 1984, another trust, the Lalbhai Group Rural Development Fund, was started to serve as a training, research and documentation centre.

Though the Birlas contined their ecletic mix of traditional and modern philanthropy, building several new temples (most notably at Hyderabad and Jaipur) and prestigious institutions such as the Sangeet Kala Mandir, the Sanskrit Sagar and the Birla Academy of Arts and Culture at Calcutta, alongside the JD Birla Institute of Home Science and Birla Institute of Scientific Research, they too began to experiment with pilot projects for rural development. In1978, BM Birla established the Birla Rural Development Association with the objective of improving the life of villagers. It undertook several programmes of rural industrialization and economic development in Uttar Pradesh. To demonstrate improved agricultural practices, the Biral Agricultural Farm was set up at Ropar in Punjab, and finally the Newata Mandal Village Project near Jaipur in 1979, whose objective was to provide employment and basic health and education facilities. Though the project was physically successful and changed the face of the area.

The 1970s also saw the professionally managed multinationals, who had contributed very little to Indian social development so far, entered the picture.

The India Tobacco Company (ITC), in India since 1910, made its first major contribution to society by establishing in 1977, the ITC Sangeet Research Academy in Calcutta to preserve an rejuvenate the *guru-shishya parampara* or traditional style of music training, and to undertake research and documentation of Indian classical music.

The case of Hindustan Lever Limited (HLL) is interesting because it illustrates most clearly how corporate self-interest is served by supporting social development.

Hindustan Lever had been in India since the late 19th century, first as a purely commercial concern, and then after World War I, as a manufacturing company making detergents and other consumer goods. The founder of the parent company in Britain, Lord Leverhulme, had established a major foundation in Britain committing to it a large portion of the company's shares. But in India, it did not set up any trust or foundation, nor did it contribute much to building up the social infrastructure apart from helping establish Breach Candy Hospital in Bombay in the 1940s. This was largely out of self-interest, because its Indian managers had no access to quality medical care, the high class hospitals of Bombay at the time being open only to white expatriates.

Its entry into community development was equally fortuitous. Around 1964, it was decided to set up a dairy plant in the backward region of Etah district in Uttar Pradesh to make processed dairy products. But despite considerable investment of money and men, the dairy failed to take off. On the verge of selling off the plant, the company was persuaded by the state government to stay and make a success by removing the root causes of the problem of poor productivity. Thus began Hindustan Lever's involvement with rural communities which included educating farmers in improved dairy farming, provision of interest-free loans, R & D for rural problems, demonstration of improved practices in oilseeds production, and introduction of new income generating activities such as poultry farming, cultivation of herbs for industrial and perfumery oils, training in sewing for women, and so on. All trainee managers were required to work in the Etah project for two months to get a first-hand knowledge of rural India.

The company put in very little of its own money but helped leverage funds from government schemes and nationalized banks. The results were gratifying. The prosperity of the area improved dramatically, as did the milk yield; so much as that the factory had to be upgraded. With increased prosperity, HLL's consumer products also sold more, proving irrefutable that it pay to give!

For Hari Nanda, founder of escorts, it was a lost election which triggered his entry into the field of rural development, as well as into institutional philanthropy. As a Swatantra Party candidate for the 1971 election, he had a chance to see at close range the poverty and hopelessness of India's rural poor. In his book, *The Days of My Years*, he mentions that little had changed since he was a child playing in the village fields. "There was no electricity here, no doctors, no drinking water, and no hope." The India of the towns, by contrast, presented an entirely different picture of comfort and affluence. He decided then to "forget about politicians and their pompous promises forever and to use my resources to try and make whatever little difference I could."

He began by establishing a chain of Ayurvedic hospitals under the Charak Ayurvedic Trust attached to his factories in Faridabad, Patiala, and Bangalore. In 1977, during the 'rural development wave.' Escorts began adopting villages for rural development to provide sanitation, drinking water, primary schooling, and so on. The Escorts Rural Development and Uplift Division were established for the purpose. Its efforts were recognized when FICCI in 1971 selected Escorts for outstanding activities in village and rural areas.

A number of medium-sized companies too had become socially conscious and introduced programmes of rural and community development, either through trusts or directly. Among them were Atlas Cycles, Amar Dye Chem, Deepak Nitrite, and Development Consultants Ltd (DCL). The experience of this last company illustrates well the difficulties faced by corporations in the unfamiliar terrain of human resource development in poor communities.

DCL was started in 1950 by Sadhan Dutta, a technocrat trained abroad. A first generation industrialist, he observed during his training in America that people there were eager to get involved in social causes in order to give meaning to their life. In India, on the other hand, there were many opportunities and causes to respond to, but very few affluent people caring about larger social problems.

Dutta's own awakening to social need came in the 1970s when the Naxalite movement forced him to think about employment opportunities for the educated unemployed. Conscious that his own company could recruit only a limited number of engineering graduates, he began by offering informal consultancy to unemployed engineers to help them start their own business. The enormous demand led him to enlarge the work by creating the Economic Entreprenurship Development Foundation (EEDF). It helped young engineering graduates to form into consultancy groups and to get contracts from the newly established Calcutta Metropolitan Authority. The informal groups were also trained by him in management, accounting and other business practices, apart from being given help in kind in the form of site stores. A group was also set up and trained in office catering. These efforts lasted for five years and helped about 500 unemployed graduates. The banks were approached to fund the scheme by giving loans to these groups, with DCL acting as the intermediary.

The next step was into rural development in the villages surrounding Calcutta, first by getting experts to look at rural problems like sanitation, drainage, irrigation, crop loans, etc. and then by approaching banks to fund individual projects.

With experience, it became clear to Dutta that it was not easy for a business individual or groups to do community work. Often motives were attributed to them: "they are trying to sell their product", or "they are politically motivated". There was also a tendency to get as much out of the donor as possible. Village politics in particular was difficult to handle, with moneylenders and state-level politicians creating obstacles. This led DCL to work through the Ramakrishna Mission and withdraw from direct engagement in rural areas, though it continued with its public health project in Calcutta.

During the Naxalite period, private health practitioners were being threatened for charging high fees. At this time Dutta conceived the idea of offering graduate specialists the infrastructure if they would work for the poor. But the project was to be self-sufficient, without reliance on public donations. Fees were therefore charged to all according to ability to pay. Today, this medical centre in a poor locality has grown into a modern health care centre.

Other first generation entrepreneurs like Kantibhai Shroff from Kutch who set up Excel Industries, an agrochemical firm, also became drawn to rural development. The company by then was making good profits and Kantibhai felt it was time to repay his debt to society. In 1976 he set up the Vivekananda Research and Training Institute in Kutch for water harvesting, health promotion, and education of the villagers near Mandvi in Kutch. Crafts marketing was also taken up to provide income for women. In 1978, he endowed the CC Shroff Self Help Centre in a Bombay slum with the objective of setting up *balwadis*, distributing nutritive food, and to promote adult education. Later, an innovative programme of garbage recycling helped take care Bombay's urban wastes and simultaneously provided fertilizers for the city and rural areas.

The Apeejay Group too, through its trusts, began to build schools, libraries, and sports facilities in Calcutta and around its tea estates in Assam.

Several others, too numerous to mention in detail, also became sensitized to their responsibility and started contributing to community development in big and small ways.

The many companies which took to rural development mainly to avail of tax concessions during a high tax regime stopped their programmes once the concessions were withdrawn in 1983 – 84, but many of them retained their humanity and stayed on.

However slowly, it began to be accepted, at least in theory, that business had to share a part of the social overhead costs of economic development if it wished to share in its fruits. Traditionally, it had discharged its responsibility to society through benefactions for education, medical facilities, and scientific research, among other objects. The important change now was that industry accepted social responsibility as part of the management of the enterprise itself.

A second change was a perceptible shift in beneficiary and issue focus from urban to rural areas, and from education to concerns like population control, agricultural improvement, employment skills for women, and so on.

Though several companies opted for direct operation of community programmes, the newly revitalized voluntary sector had opened up a possibility for supporting social development through NGOs, an option encouraged by the government which had provided tax incentives for the purpose. Many therefore opted for this route.

For the first time it was the poorer communities located around company units which were directly and systematically targeted through anti-poverty programmes.

Moreover, newer and smaller groups with no previous traditions of philanthropy joined established houses to take on this new responsibility.

But clearly, social consciousness was still confined to a small minority. Prime Minister Morarji Desai, addressing the annual session of FICCI in 1978, pointed out that in response to his appeal to industry to undertake rural development, only 70 business house had come forward, whereas the potential was much greater, given industry's managerial capacity and the resources it commanded.

Building institutions in an urban setting was something business leaders were familiar with, in fact, their aptitudes particularly fitted them to create such new projects. But human resource development in poor rural and urban areas was a new terrain full of pitfalls and uncertainties. There was neither precedence nor special aptitude. Moreover, the new type of philanthropy offered no scope for memorializing dear ones or for direct and perpetual publicity afforded by an institution named after the donor, whether an individual or a company. It is to the credit of many that they ventured forth nevertheless.

Courtesy – Pushpa Sundar (2000)

Issues in respect Corporate Social Responsibilities

Issues are the differences between perception and practices. Many time corporates' promise to the society and may not materialise. The following are broader issues and are known as the general issues

(i) Environmental issues
(ii) Issues in Corporate Governance
(iii) Issues in Marketing
(iv) Issues in Human Resource Management
(v) Issues in Finance
(vi) Issues related to decision making
(vii) Issues related to the general public at large

Each of the above issues has been discussed in detail in the proceeding chapter.

Exhibit

Corporate social performance on different aspects of social responsibility

In response to the research study (2003), the extract of research finding, on corporate social responsibility and corporate social performance are given below. And also the following are the perceptions, opinions and the real practices of corporates belonging to private sector, public sector and multinational companies.

The stakeholders like shareholders, employees, creditors, customers, and suppliers of goods, government and society at large are different aspects of the business environment and also the corporate social performance (CSP) on different aspects of social responsibility.

The outcome of research study follows:

- Customers are placed in a relationship parallel to that of close relatives to the business hence the customers should receive considerable concern and attention that goes beyond simply not harming them and some of the businesses do seem to have adopted the value of treating customers like nuclear family members (Donal P. Robin). This is evident with the statistical results of corporate social performance towards customers. Customer care and concern are very high (93.5%), this view is supported by some of the corporates for instance *"Customers are kings"* (Mysore Sales International Ltd.), *"Our pride is to satisfy the customers and we stand as a role model"* (Hindustan Petroleum Corporation), *"Nature and customer friendly products which are to be produced"* (Asian Paints), *"Business cannot be made at the cost of customers and society"* (Akai), *"Customers are kings and customer education is very important"* (Indian Telephones Industries) and the like.

- Shareholders and employees are other aspects of social responsibility, where the corporates show a high performance level and this is supported by the opinion as, *"welfare activities create a sense, a work is fun among the employees training to the employees"* (Sushrid Devasharma), *"ethical training to the employees, ethical behaviour in the organisation are essential"* (Dileep Ranjekar) training to the employees to become entrepreneurs by Wipro (Business World). Supporting this, the statistical results show the corporates high performance towards shareholders (87.8%) and employees (86.4%) and this is supported by some of the corporates expressing their practices like *"we follow the philosophy of team spirit which is driving the employee to top level and there is self motivation and self responsibility"* (L.G), *" we are 100% conscious in taking care of our employees and we give training towards safety measures"* (Shahi Exports), *"Meeting and developing a direct contact with the employees is beneficial and Premji is meeting 5000 employees, and delivers a $3^1/_2$ hours speech on motivation continuously, offering 40% stock option, and showing that every year we are rich on paper"* (WIPRO). *"There is education within the organization"* (IBM). *"There is transparency to the employees for over 50 years"* (TTK). *"Opportunity to the employees to become shareholders"* (Gokuldas Exports). *"Meeting employees needs and salary even when there was a factory fire in 1996 and assuring them of job security"* (Asian Paints). *"Direct recruitment from schools is encouraged, no foul language to be used among the employees"* (Arvind Mills).
- The corporate's social performance towards society at large is not very much encouraging (46.6%). However there are some corporates who show their concern towards society by involving in *"community service"* (Hindustan Petroleum Corporation), *"helping orphanage and the young mind programme for government school children"* (WIPRO), *"Community programme"* (Britannia Industries), *"Temple construction"* (Micro Nova), and the like.
- Though multinational companies and public sectors both stand closely in the high performance levels, they differ slightly with respect to shareholders, employees, government and society at large. Multinational companies give more importance to shareholders and the government, comparatively with that of public sectors as one multinational company expressed that *"we are tenant in this country, we must be careful with government and people"* (IBM), but with respect to employees and society at large, the public sector companies show high performance level than the multinational companies.

- Private limited companies and public limited companies are found to differ on some aspects like shareholders, employees, customers and society at large. The private limited companies are keen on customers and governments and they show high performance level than the public limited companies. With respect to shareholders and employees, the public limited companies show high performance levels than the private limited companies.
- However, the public limited companies, private limited companies and multinational companies all show equal performance levels towards creditors, and all the corporate sectors show equal level of performance towards the supplier of goods.
- Multinational companies show high performance with regard to their responsibility towards society at large, this performed more by multinational companies with regard to work like deforestation, ecology and environmental issues (IBM), de-sanitation for environment (Smith Kline and Beecham). This is more than the public sector companies. But with respect to donations to hospitals, scientific research, rural development, technical education the public sector companies show more performance level than multinational companies. This may be supported with some of the reactions from public sectors companies who say that the company has development human resources, they act as universities, set-up colonies, townships in addition to employment. Exclusive plants were set up called "Udaya Welfare Association" for the disabled and the destitute (Hindustan Machine Tools), *"we conduct periodic health camps, blood donation camps, adopted the village called, Shivanahalli, E-mobile dispensary services, nearly 10,000 saplings for plantation were planted near Devanahalli and we have around Rs. 20 crore budget on social responsibility. Every year scholarship is awarded for 10 school children who are handicapped and there is scholarship for Scheduled caste students"* (Hindustan Petroleum Corporation), *"we conduct health programmes, we give importance to higher education and grant educational loans"* (Karnataka Soaps and Detergents Ltd.)
- Between public limited companies and private limited companies the performance with respect to health programmes, scientific research, technical education and environment protection, is high by the public limited companies. These are supported by their clear conviction as expressed here, *"The WIPRO young minds program is conducted for government school children from Karnataka and Andhra Pradesh. We give free education from 10th standard to graduation for those children whose parents income is around rupees 1000 per month and we have technology for social work, helping the orphanage meeting their basic necessities" (WIPRO) "Adoption of village in Gujarat, we have school programmes towards environment as 'Save the Tiger' and we promote art and music by conducing a festival called Britannia Classical Music Festival for the last 25years in Mumbai" (Britannia Ltd.), "we have effluent treatment and environmental protection"* (Bata India), than the private limited companies. The private limited companies show better performance

with respect to welfare programmes for women and children and other community services than the public limited companies.

- The performance levels of different corporates like public sector, public limited, private limited and multinational companies with regard to social responsibility towards society at large are more or less the same.
- The corporates show more concern with respect to environment protection like deforestation, conservation of nature, ecology and environment. Some of the corporate conduct environment program (IBM), De-sanitation for environment (Smith Kline and Beecham), effluent treatment and environmental protection (BATA India), *"Ours is an environment friendly product."* (Asian Paints), *"We are environment friendly and our corporate office is green and our product is nature based."* (LG).
- Health service is another area where many corporates especially pharmaceuticals companies show interest, and they do practise in their respective fields. Services like setting up of health centres, conducting of diabetic detection camps (MICRO Lab), *"we conduct health programmes and donate to Sindhi Charitable Hospital"* (Gokuldas Exports), Mobile Dispensaries (Hindustan Petroleum Corporation), health check-up for hepatitis is conducted by Karnataka Soaps and Detergents Ltd.
- Corporates are also involved in another area of social commitment, namely, educational services. Some corporates show their concern to the promotion of education like *"scholarship for handicapped and scheduled caste students"* (Hindustan Petroleum Corporation), *"Conduct school programs on awareness to Save the tiger"*, (Britannia), *"conducting educational programs to develop creativity, a beautiful film is screened to the children in their respective schools to develop the idea of creativity"* (Coats India). *"Technical education like invention of education in I.T distant education, establishment of computer centres at Bangalore, Bhopal, Delhi, Bombay. The course material for hardware and software is supplied thus education is created within the organization"* (IBM), *"we also give the girl child education"* (WIPRO).
- Another important area is the promotion of culture; even in this area some of the activities relating to heritage and arts, religion and values and promotion of art and culture are some of the programmes of the corporates. One of the corporates has expressed that *"We follow our tradition and culture since the past 75 year"* (Kwality Biscuits), temple construction to satisfy the local people (Broun and Burk), *"workshop in the schools to promote our culture and slow down westernization"* (Coats India).
- Community development is another area in which some of the corporates are involved like, *"adoption of villages as a part of the rural development program, community services are some of the activities under the community development programmes like construction of community hall, welfare scheme for the weaker sections"* (Hindustan Petroleum Corporation), donation of books to rural children and development services by some community development programmes of the corporates.

- With respect to other activities like road safety, sports some corporates show interest in this area like the, *"setting up of the Britannia Amritraj Tennis Association, sponsorship to promote cricket and putting up traffic sign boards towards road safety"* (Britannia Ltd).

CORPORATE GOVERNANCE

Corporate governance is a system of structuring, operating and controlling a company with a view to achieve long-term strategic goals to satisfy its shareholders, creditors, employees, customers, suppliers, and society at large. It aims to comply with the legal and regulatory requirements along with environmental and local community needs. It is related to policies and procedures adopted by a company to achieve its objectives in relation to its shareholders, employees, customers, suppliers, regulatory authorities and the community at large.

Background of corporate governance

In the late 1980's a new concept of privatisation by the conservative government in UK gave rise to the opportunity for rapid financial gains to top management. This made to increase in salaries and granting of share options to the management utilities were seen as unfair by the general public. This brought the observations that: (1) Perceived excesses were contrasted against the minimal pay increases. This were granted to working junior staff, and their use of brutal reorganisations fallowed takeovers. (2) The workers or employees suffered a lot in change of organisation with the alternate regions and then were not able to work again. (3) The employer uncared for towards disadvantages created by the employees. (4) This created a lot of discrepancies in the accounting standards and many companies exploited the weaknesses in the accounting standards to inflate profits and understate liabilities. (5) Emphasis in the original roles of Chairman and the Chief Executive became gradually combined, thereby resulting in concentration of greater financial power and authority in a lesser number of individuals.

The above issues were talked through the formation of the "Cadbury Committee" under the chairmanship of Sir Adrian Cadbury to report on the Financial Aspects of Corporate Governance. Another committee called Green Bury Committee was formed in the year 1994 to investigate the allegedly huge salaries of some senior executives, choose the safe way and requested that compliance with the "Code of Practice" be made mandatory for listed companies. It was hoped that the companies would use the recommendations to create a more transparent corporate structure without the need for legal enforcement.

In India, the question of corporate governance has come up mainly in the wake of economic liberalisation and deregulation of industry and business as well as the demand for a new corporate ethics and strong compliance with the legislation. In this context, where the financial institutions hold substantial stakes in companies, the accountability of all the directors, including independents, has come into sharp focus. Therefore, good governance demands that a company must have a responsibility to set exemplary standards of ethical behaviour, both within the organisation as well as in their external relationships. By virtue of which the company can achieve "value addition" in terms of stability and growth, confidence, reductions of perceived risks, realisation of cost capital, stability and long-term substance of stakeholders relationship, position of pride. Both in the interest of stakeholders and the economy where the corporate governance has become necessary.

Moreover, India has been pushed to the centre of the sweeping changes. This took place in the economic and business scenes. Lifting of the trade barriers has shrunk the world to a sizeable market. Corporates have now access to opportunities worldwide. But they also faced with threats of their own survival with the entrance of global players in India. Resources are becoming scarce. More attention needs to be given to the development of skills.

Reforms in India

Corporate governance in India has evolved a wide range of institutional and corporate initiatives. The following are some of the reforms:

- Improving functioning of capital market.
- Ensuring more effective protection of minority investors through promotion of greater transparency of operations and higher standards of information disclosure.
- Reforming company board structure and operational systems to make the board of directors more accountable to shareholders.
- Reforming governance mechanisms of financial institutions, etc.

Concept of corporate governance

A corporate may be referred to a legally united body to act as an individual, whereas governance is control or direction. Corporate governance is referred to a good corporate management, responsible for all corporate activities and activity related to stakeholders.

Corporate governance provides twofold effect namely:

1. The long-term relationship which deals with checks and balances, incentives for managers and communications between management and investors.
2. The transactional relationship which involves dealing with disclosure and authority.

Corporate governance should function on the basis of principles of **business ethics, corporate ethics, organisational values, culture, individuals** like Board of Directors, shareholders and managers value, as well as **corporate social responsibility.** Corporate governance is rightly understood as putting people at the forefront of business, because business must be fundamentally a matter of people rather than machines, products or even money.

In corporate governance people-oriented management is highlighted which means that people must be given the highest respect and consideration. As it is the people who are employees, consumers, customers, suppliers, vendors, dealers, creditors, bankers, directors and members of the board. And it is the people who are represented by government and it is the people who will be affected by changes in environment and the policies of the corporation. Good corporate governance has been sought to be implemented by attending to long-term strategic goals, employees, community and environments, customers and suppliers. Good corporate governance will also comply with laws and regulations, will give equal shares to all parties, activities and functional areas of management in making decision making. The idea of corporate governance to present every part of the organisations of the company and make it reflect with good corporate governance.

Understanding Corporate Governance Though Definitions

"Corporate governance is vital for providing an economical, legal and institutional environment for both Indian and foreign firms in the years to come. The concept of governance is aimed at maximising the long term value for shareholders"—CII. (India)

"Effective corporate governance ensures that long-term strategic objective and plans are established, and that the proper management and management structure and in place to achieve these objectives. While at the same time making sure that the structure functions to maintain the corporation's integrity, reputation and accountability to its relevant constituencies". The Institute of Directors (UK)

"Corporate governance should be recognised as a set of standards which aims to improve the company image, efficiency, effectiveness and social responsibility. —B.H. Alagatti (2003)

Hence, through corporate governance the corporate should turn from the status of more legal entities to corporate social responsible entities.

Corporate governance and value creation:

Value based companies have proved to be successful in the recent past. After globalisation policies, the companies are open to competition and the society is watching every role of the companies.

The companies cannot just deal with the laws and internal and external factors of the businesses into their hands. They need to exercise transparency and measurable checks and balances for long-term sustainability. The following are the expectations of shareholder/stakeholders from the corporation, for good corporate governance:

Stakeholders Expectations

(a) Shareholders
- (i) A fair and steady rate of return (dividend) on investment;
- (ii) Increase in the future earning of the company;
- (iii) Increase in the market capitalization of investment.

(b) Employees
- (i) Recognition of service by providing fair remuneration as also incentives;
- (ii) Stability of employment;
- (iii) Help to improve standard of living.

(c) Customers	(i) Provide quality goods or services at a fair price and on fair terms; (ii) Restraint from restrictive practices or unfair practices.
(d) Competitors	(i) Restraint from adopting any strategy to elbow competitors out with unfair or restrictive practices or through violation of competition law norms.
(e) Creditors	(i) Ability to pay the principal and interest as per contractual obligations.
(f) Government	(i) Behave as responsible and good corporate citizens; (ii) Non-evasion of taxes and dues to the government; (iii) Involvement in social cause, e.g., charities, donations, etc.
(g) Community	(i) Growth in employment generation to secure good local employment; (ii) Protection of environment.
(h) Public at large	(i) To hold the board accountable for: (a) Limiting senior executives compensation: (b) Full environment protection: (c) Avoidance of fraud within the company: (d) Caring for employees.

Source: Subhas Chandra (2009)

MODELS OF CORPORATE GOVERNANCE IN INDIA

The basic need for corporate governance arose due to agency costs. As the shareholders are partly owners of the public limited companies and are scattered throughout the country they themselves have no direct access to the company affairs. The shareholder interests are mainly like in getting reasonable return, based on the risk profile of the company, year after year without any hindrance, whatsoever. The company is run by the managers who may stand as agents to the investors. These managers will be interested in their salaries, remuneration or other amenities, rather than focusing on the organisational development. This brought a lot of issues and anomalies among the stakeholders. To cover up this, the managers or board of directors used to indulge in window-dressing of operational results of the company by fudging the firms account.

More so all societies run by human beings to be properly governed. Corporate governance is concerned with the process by which corporate entities, particularly limited liability companies are governed with the exercise of power over the direction of the enterprise, the supervision of executive actions, the acceptance of a duty to be accountable and the regulation of the company within the jurisdiction of the country where it operates. In order to implement the good corporate governance three types of models are adopted by the corporates, all over the world.

Corporate Model

Generally, only two types of corporate models are discussed in the literature of corporate finance like

(a) Anglo-American model

(b) German-Japanese model

South Asian countries including India, have a corporate model based on ownership pattern of companies. The difference is mainly because of the fact that the Indian-South Asian corporate model comprises three types of owners like (i) Promoters and shareholders generally controlling one-fourth to three-fourths of the total share capital of the company, the remaining contributed by (ii) individuals and (iii) mutual funds and financial institutions, where also individuals may not be contributing more than one-third of the share capital generally. Hence, it is understood as three types of models shown below.

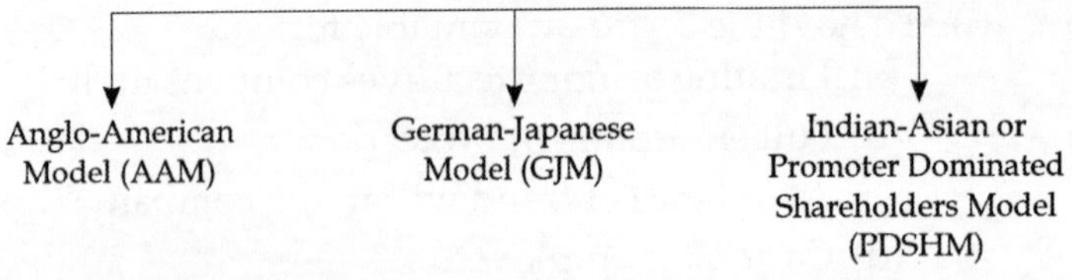

(1) Anglo-American Model (AAM)

In many countries corporate governance is rooted in Western practices, culture and ideologies. In most cases, it has followed the tradition of Anglo-American Common law by the countries like Australia, Canada, Hong-Kong, Malaysia, New Zealand, Philippines, South Africa, Singapore, USA, UK and so on.

Single-tier Board Structure – Anglo American Model

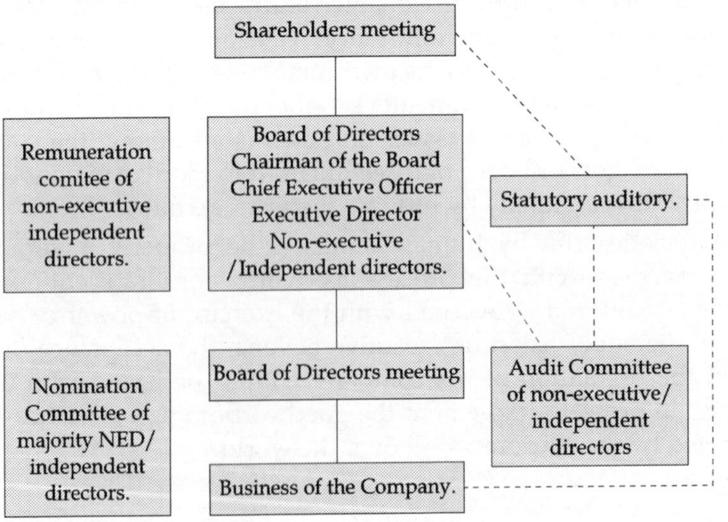

Source: Subhas Das (2009)

Primarily, corporate governance is concerned with the functioning of Board of Directors its structure, style, processes their relationships, roles activities, etc. It is also concerned with the roles of company stakeholders like shareholders, institutional investors or large shareholders, auditors, banks and others. In this the practice of corporate governance varies a with number of factors. The capital markets tends to be a strong factor that readily allows for merger and acquisitions and hostile takeover.

1. Distinctive Features of Anglo-American Model

(1) Pre-1990 period ownership pattern was dominated by a large number of retail shareholders scattered all over the country. There used to be full divorce between ownership and management with the agency problems.

(2) Post-1990 period ownership of the companies which is generally evenly balanced between both individual and institutional shareholders, with agency problems.

(3) Companies run by professional CEO's and managers with negligible ownership stake except in the form of Employees Stock Option (ESOP), thus, there is a clear divide between owners and managers.

(4) The institutional investors are generally portfolio investors like banks and mutual funds which are interested in quick exit after booking profit at the right time.

(5) The model is referred as a "high tension model, as the CEO has to ensure adherance to all regulatory authorities, capital market, money markets and threats to takeover.

2. German-Japanese Model (GJM)

This is another type of model where there is a two-tier board system consisting of a supervisory board and a management board. In respect of supervisory board, workers are allocated 50% of the seats and the major banks, financial institutions are also represented in this model.

German-Japanese model, although not altogether similar, shares the following common features:

(i) In both the countries the institutional investors (banks and financial institutions) are long-term investors and play quite an active role in management. Their keen interest and monitoring help in toning up companies' performance, and in protecting retail shareholders interest.

(ii) In both these countries the disclosure norms are lax and checks on insider trading is neither comprehensive nor effective. Similarly, hostile takeovers are generally unheard of.

German-Japanese model is based on "regulatory and macroeconomic circumstances" under which governance is exercised. In this model capital markets have tended to be relatively weak and hostile takeovers are unheard of.

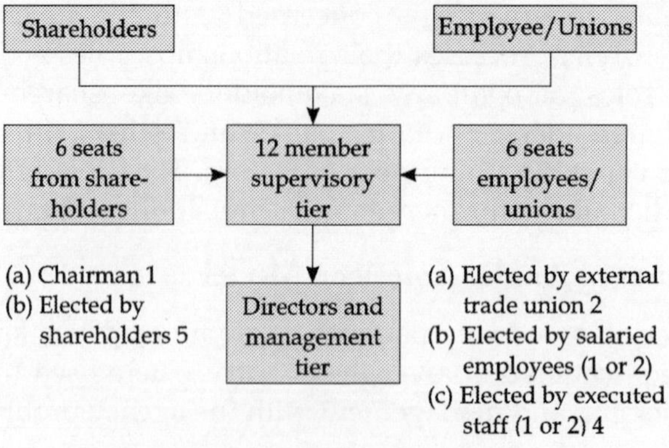

Two-tier Board Structure: GJ Model

3. Indian-South Asian Model

This is also known as Indian-Asian or promoter dominated shareholders model. In this the promoters are also shareholders. This is the model with combination of above said two models. This is again based on ownership pattern of the company. For example TATA Steel (as on 30.06.2003):

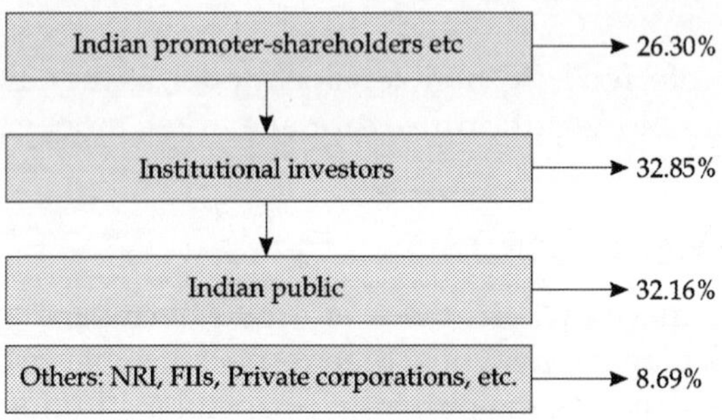

The models is based on the promoters, institutional investors and Indian and public and so on. General observations on this model are:

(i) Many time promoter-shareholders are dominant owners owing 33 per cent to 86 per cent of total share capital.

(ii) The promoter group head is also generally the Chief Executive Officer (CEO) of the company.

(iii) The principal agent is thus, considerably diluted in this model as the interests of promoters coverage with retail shareholders, at least theoretically.

(iv) The distinction between owners and agents (principal and agent) is blurred, resulting in altogether different remedial measures to protect interests of common shareholders.

(v) Capital market regulators (SEBI in India) are thus, required to take additional safeguards for protecting the interests of common shareholders.

(vi) Principal-agent relations obtaining in the model is not such as may generally create a clash of interest between the promoter-shareholders and retail .

The above three models explain the different factors and different people involved in good governance. There are different studies on stakeholder model for good corporate governance. In this model the central focus are the 'care', 'responsibility', 'ethics', 'transparency' and 'accountability'. This is also refered as "ethical stakeholder good corporates governance model," which is shown in the following figure:

Ethical Stakeholder Good Corporate Governance model

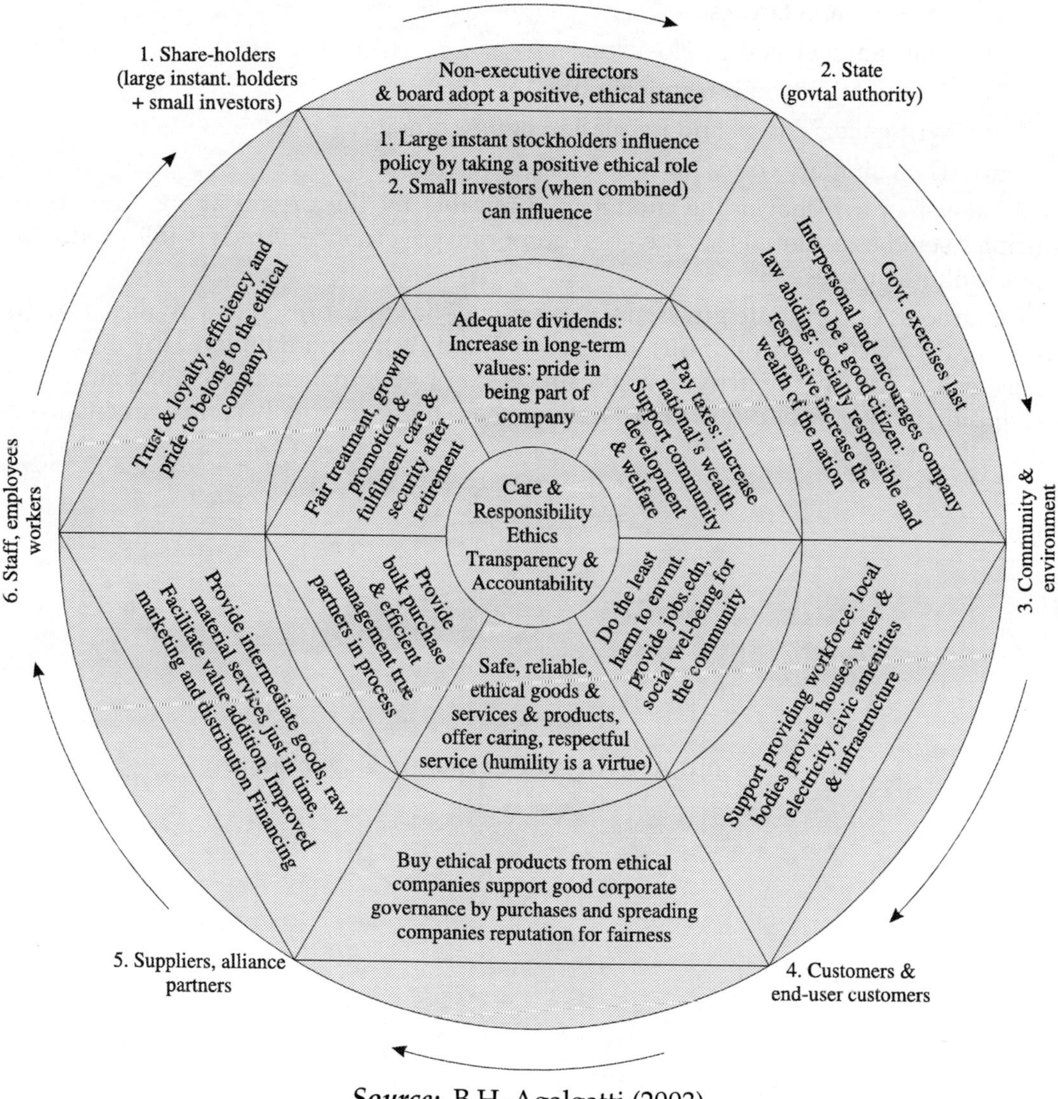

Source: B.H. Agalgatti (2003)

Shareholders, state or government authority, community and environment, customers and end use customers, suppliers and alliance partners, staff or employee or workers are all the main people contributing for ethical stake-holder good corporate governance model. This mode explains the various areas or activiites that each stakeholder is responsible to act individually.

Principles of Corporate Governance

Corporate governance principles based on interrelated segments. The principles may be the milestones of the company, which are as follows:

(1) Integrity and fairness
(2) Transparency and disclosures.
(3) Accountability and responsibility.
(4) Written legislation and regulation of the company
(5) The voluntary codes for best business practices

Whatever or whichever the model is applicable by the organisations, the above principles stand as essentials for the good corporate governance, which is followed with an appropirate process.

The process of corporate governance essentially has four principal activities, viz., (i) direction, (ii) executive action, (iii) supervision, and (iv) accountability. However, in a unitary board system, the activities and processes of governance and management get overlapping unlike the two-tier board system where these are totally compartmentalized in the following figures.

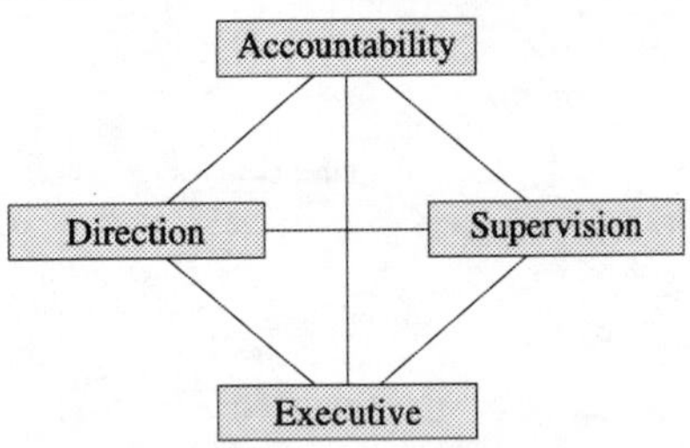

Processes and Activities of Corporate Governance

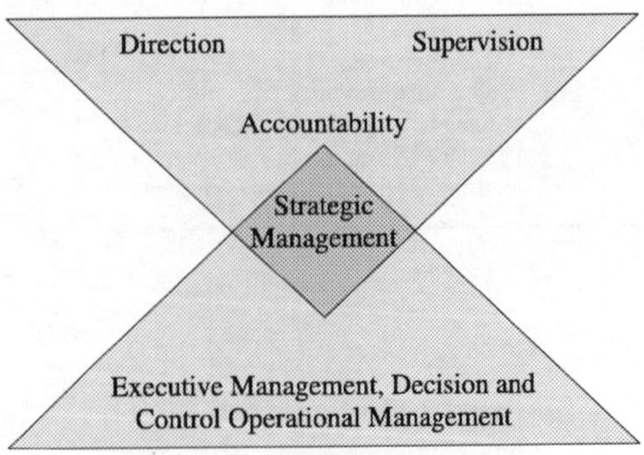

Processes and Activities: Governance and Management Compared

Source: Subhash Das (2009)

For the best strategy towards future, there need to be a blend of both governance and management which is shown in the above figure. For the understanding the following shows variation between management and governance.

Management Vs Governance

Both corporate governance and management are referred to the context of legal doctrines and regulatory activities based on the rights and responsibilities in the two-dimensional relationship between boards and senior management.

The core distinctions are:

Management	*Governance*
• Managers operate within the hierarchy of the delighted responsibility and authority.	• Board members are jointly and individually responsible with equal rights and duties
• Manager's task is to run the business.	• Board responsibility is to govern the company.
• Management focuses on internal matters.	• Governance has an external focus.
• Management assumes a closed system.	• Governance assumes an open system.
• Management is task oriented.	• Governance is strategy oriented.
• Management is concerned with getting things done.	• Governance is concerned with "where the company is heading".

Committee Towards Corporate Governance

In order to understand and to practise the best corporate governance, there are various committees formulated all over the globe. These committee recommendations are adopted by the corporations.

(i) The Blue Ribbon Committee (1998)

(ii) Kumar Mangalam Birla Committee (2000)

(iii) Reserve Bank of India – Report of the Advisory Group on Corporate Governance (2001)

(iv) Naresh Chandra Committee (2002)

(v) N. R. Narayana Murthy Committee (2003)

(vi) J.J Irani Committee (2005)

Good corporate governance should fulfill both mandatory and non-mandatory requirements.

Mandatory requirements are:

1. Board of Directors includes
   - (i) Composition of Board
   - (ii) Non-executive Directors Compensation and Disclosures.
   - (iii) Other provisions as to Board and committees
   - (iv) Code of conduct.

2. Audit committee includes:
   (a) Qualified and Independent Audit Committee.
   (b) Meeting of Audit Committee.
   (c) Powers of Audit Committee.
   (d) Role of Audit Committee.
   (e) Review of Information by Audit Committee.
3. Subsidiary Companies
4. Disclosures include:
   (a) Basis of related party transactions
   (b) Disclosure of Accounting treatment
   (c) Board Disclosure – Risk management.
   (d) Proceeds from public Issues, Rights issue, Preferential issues
   (e) Remuneration of Directors
   (f) Management
   (g) Shareholders
5. CEO/CFO Certification
6. Report on Corporate Governance
7. Compliance

Non-Mandatory Requirement:

(1) The Board
(2) Remuneration committee
(3) Shareholders' right
(4) Audit qualification
(5) Training of Board Members
(6) Mechanism for evaluating non-executive Board members.
(7) Whistle-Blower Policy.

Cases Study

In order to highlight a few cases on both Indian and international corporate governance are discussed below.

1. Governance – Reliance

Reliance's corporate governance principles uphold its global standing at the forefront of corporate governance best practices. Reliance continues to review its corporate governance practices to ensure that they continue to reflect domestic and international developments to position itself to conform to the best corporate governance practices. It takes feedback into account in its periodic reviews of the guidelines to ensure their continuing relevance, effectiveness and responsiveness to the needs of local and international investors and all other stakeholders.

Reliance's corporate governance practices focus on the following main principles.

Recognizing the respective roles and responsibilities of Board of Management. To establish an effective mechanism for overseeing the affairs keeping in view the Company's size, complexity, geographical operations and corporate tradition and culture, Reliance's framework is designed to:

- Having a Board of appropriate composition, size and commitment to adequately discharge its responsibilities and duties.
- To ensure effectiveness of the Board, facilitating efficient discharge of duties and adding value in the context of the company's circumstance; the Board periodically reviews its composition and size for ensuring a strong element of independence and commitment.
- Enable the Board to provide strategic guidance for the company and effective overseeing of the management.
- Define the respective roles and responsibilities of senior executives and officers to ensure accountability; and
- Ensure a balance of authority such that no single individual has unfettered powers.

Accordingly, the Board is structured in such a way that:

- It has a proper understanding of, and competence to deal with, the current and emerging issues of the business and the benefit of a variety of perspectives and skills.
- It has the appropriate mix of executive and non-executive directors ensuring Directors' commitment and time to participate in the affairs fully.
- It can effectively review and challenge the performance of management and exercise independent judgement.

The Directors are elected by the shareholders. However, the Board plays an important role in selection of candidates for shareholders' approval. Reliance's policy does not prescribe any term limit for Directors, as the term limits, while enabling induction of fresh ideas and viewpoints of new entrants, suffer from the disadvantages of depriving the Group of the valuable contribution of directors who, over time, have developed insight into the Company and its affairs.

Independent verification and safeguarding integrity of the company's financial reporting. To ensure the truthful and factual presentation of the company's financial position, the company has put in place a structure of review and authorization apart from strong internal audit process. For this purpose, the Board has also constituted on Audit Committee, which is charged with paying particular attention to the management process supporting external reporting, the performance and objectivity of the internal audit function, and the performance and independence of the external auditors.

Timely and Balanced Disclosure of all Material Information Concerning the Company.

To give investors an equal and timely access to material information, and to ensure that company announcements are factual, balanced and in compliance with the applicable provisions of law, the company has put in place a mechanism to ensure that:

- All investors have equal and timely access to material information concerning the company including its financial position, performance and governance.
- Company announcements are factual and presented in a clear and balanced way, disclosing both positive and negative information.

Highest Importance to Investor Relations. To ensure long-term shareholder value creation and promote shareholder participation in corporate affairs, Reliance has established and maintained communication strategies, including a policy for clarity in notices of meetings. Reliance also maintains its corporate website www.ril.com for convenient access by the shareholders to all the material information about the company. Reliance's endeavours are to empower its shareholders by:

- Communicating effectively with them.
- Giving them appropriate information about the company.
- Making it easy for them to participate in General Meetings.

System of Risk Management and Internal Control. To establish and maintain a system of risk management and internal control, the company has set up a policy which includes a review of the risk management system, and maintenance of a risk profile (both financial and non-financial risk). Reliance has set up an effective internal audit function, independent of the external auditors, to review the effectiveness of the risk management systems. This system is designed to:

- Identify, assess, monitor and manage risks.
- Inform investors of material changes to the company's risk profile.

Fair Review, Active Encouragement and Management Effectiveness. To ensure consistent effectiveness of the overall management, the performance of the senior executives and officers is subject to review. This includes equipping individuals with the knowledge and information they need to discharge their responsibilities effectively, and reviewing individual and collective performance regularly. Performance evaluation process is fair and transparent and uses both measurable and qualitative indicators.

Efficient Executive Remuneration Policy. The company has adopted a remuneration policy that attracts and maintains talented and motivated executives so as to encourage enhanced performance of the company. The remuneration policy envisages a clear relationship between performance and remuneration, including the link between remuneration paid and the overall corporate performance.

Remuneration of managing directors and whole-time directors is determined by the remuneration committee of directors within the permissible limits under the applicable provisions of law and is approved by shareholders. Non-executive directors are paid sitting fees within the limits prescribed under law.

Corporate Ethics Reliance has a defined policy framework for ethical business conduct by its personnel.

The Ethics Policy sets forth, inter alia:

- Our Values and Commitments
- Our Code of Ethics
- Our Business Policies
- Our Code of Conduct for Prevention of Insider Trading
- A detailed programme for Ethics Management at Reliance.

These policies support the consistent Endeavour to enhance the reputation of the company.

The "Values and Commitments" policy document states that Reliance believes that any business conduct can be ethical only when it rests on the nine core values of Honesty, Respect, Fairness, Purposefulness, Trust, Responsibility, Citizenship and Caring.

These values are not to be lost sight of by anyone at Reliance under any circumstances irrespective of the goals that are intended to be achieved. To us, the means are as important as the ends.

In pursuit of these values outlined in the "Values and Commitments" policy document, we are committed to an ethical treatment of all our stakeholders: our lenders and other investors, our suppliers and the government. A firm belief that every Reliance team member holds is that the other persons' interest count as much as his own.

The "Code of Ethics" and the "Business Policies" are in alignment with Reliance's values and commitments. The essence of these documents is that each employee should conduct the company's business with integrity, compliance with applicable laws, and in a manner that excludes considerations of personal advantages.

The "Code of Ethics" policy document contains policy on the following:

- Conflict of Interest
- Payments and Gifting
- Receipt of Gifts
- Purchases through suppliers
- Appointment of full-time agents, consultants and representatives
- Political Contributors

The "Business Policies" document contains policy on the following:

- Fair Market Practices
- Inside Information
- Financial Records and Accounting Integrity
- External Communication
- Work Ethics Personal Conduct
- Health safety and Environment
- Quality

The "Code of Conducts for Prevention of Insider Trading" contains policies prohibiting insider trading.

2. Corporate Responsiveness

(i) **Air Crashes:** The example of air disasters given here includes a description of the response from TWA and Swissair.

- Korean Airlines flight 007 was shot down by a Russian jet fighter in 1983. There has been no further news on the incident from the airline since.
- PanAm handles the crisis following its 1982 crash in New Orleans better than its subsequent crash in 1988. It had procedures and a senior manager in charge at the time of the first crash, and regular rehearsals had been held. Its 1988 flight 103 was blown over Lockerbie in Scotland on 21December 1988 killing 270 people. Though PanAm was known for its crisis management earlier on in the decade, it failed in 1988. PanAm was not able to get control of the information process and was reluctant to own up responsibility. Although the airline approached a consultant, it took eight days after the event to have its name protected, by which time it was too late. The disaster subsequently led to a decline in the airline's bookings and in 1991, Pan Am filed for chapter 11 bankruptcy.
- Both TransWorld Airlines (TWA) fight 800 in 1996 and Swissair fight 111 in September 1998 plunged into the sea off Nova Scotia. Neither accidents left any surviours nor were they ever fully explained. Two disasters provoking two differing reactions, which are described below.

(ii) **TWA:** TWA flight 800 crashed off Long Island in 1996. The airline was accused of incompetence and insensitivity for the way it responded to the needs of the victims' families. The result has been lasting damage to its reputation.

- The airline refused to produce a passenger list until it had determined the exact number of victims and notified their families only later, which took a full day
- There were complaints that calls made to special toll-free telephone numbers went unanswered
- The flow of information was inadequate
- Insufficient attention was paid to family members' travel and accommodation
- News headlines became critical of TWA and portrayed the company as one that could do nothing right.

The families of the victims became very angry with the airline and the crash investigators. President Clinton and his wife flew to New York to try and smooth things over. Complaints included refusal by the airline to make public the passenger list; delays in identifying the bodies; the ineffectiveness of the so-called special toll-free 800 numbers which could not be reached and the fact that information was issued to the press before it was given to the grieving relatives.

(iii) Swissair: Swissair flight 111 crashed on the night of 2 September 1998. The airline earned praise for its efficiency and compassion. It not only retained passengers' confidence but enhanced it.

- Without hours, a passenger manifest had been put out
- Fully functioning hotlines were set up
- Hundreds of crisis counsellors arrived in New York, ready to receive the grieving families
- Flights to take relatives to the crash site at Peggy's Cove were put into effect immediately
- Relatives were grateful for the way Swissair kept them informed of events and appreciated the airlines' pay-off of US $20,000 to each family to cover immediate expenses.
- Favourable headlines and praise for the airline
- Friends and relatives were full of praise for how the airline and the investigators accommodated their needs as best as possible
- Swissair's US partner Delta Air Lines put 1000 volunteers at its disposal for its crisis team
- Several hundred of them formed the backbone of an early response team at New York's Kennedy International Airport and later in Halifax
- Delta employees had received training in everything from grief counselling to media relations to the mechanics of releasing passenger lists and contacting relatives
- Swissair recruited their own volunteers and assigned them as caregivers to look after each family
- A special phone system and Website to help the families was put in place as dawn broke the morning after the crash
- The airline's president, Jeff Katz, joined some of the European families on a special flight from Zurich, then met with most others as they arrived in Halifax
- The airline immediately made US $20,000 available to every family for travel, burial and other expenses
- It took care to brief family members at least once a day before giving out any information to the media

Investigator found evidence of fire and electrical arching in the wiring of Swissair flight 111's in-flight entertainment and gambling system, and the airline agreed on 29 October 1998 to shut down the system on its other planes as a precaution.

Swissair and the Canadian Transportation Safety Board said that there was insufficient evidence so far to determine whether the wiring has played a role. The Canadian Board said that it was possible that the damage was 'merely the by-product of other events'. They wanted to take a new look at the video and gaming systems with touch-screen control that gave passengers a choice of up to two dozen movies, video libraries, Internet access, news stock quotes, hotel reservations and even gambling for money on some non-US routes.

3. US Legislation Regarding Crashes

A crash is a 'defining moment' for an airline. It can destroy the airline's reputation in a matter of seconds. The first 24 hours are therefore critical for the airline involved. Subsequent to the disasters the Aviation Disaster Family Assistance Act in the US requires that domestic carriers file detailed plans for providing accurate passenger manifests, issuing toll-free telephone numbers, returning a victim's personal effects and helping families with their travel and personal needs. This legislation was not in place before TWA's flight 800 went down. As a result of the disaster, TWA has been twice bankrupt, and today it is a relatively small carrier. The air disaster led to a change in US aviation law. The National Transportation Safety Board in charge of coordinating assistance to families of crash victims requires all airlines operating in the US to have an approved family assistance plan. In December 1997, this legislation was extended to all foreign carriers serving in the US.

Lessons to be Drawn

- Airlines should rehearse for the worst and often
- No expense should be spared in helping the families of victims (Tomkings, 1998)

Compariason between Japan and US towards a good business

On February 13, it happened again. Allegations of still another political payoff surfaced. Last month, a Japanese trucking firm was accused of channelling funds to politicians.

Instantly, the charges became one more in a succession of scandals in Japan that highlight major differences in business ethics with the U.S.

In late 1980s nearly all of Japan's leading politicians were implicated in the Recruit bribery scandal. Then last year several Japanese securities firms were revealed to have compensated their biggest customers for stock losses in 1990. And eight food-wrap manufactures were punished for forming a cartel to raise prices.

Remarkably, so many Japanese greeted the scandals with no more than a shrug of resignation that one tends to conclude that favouritism, influence-peddling, price-fixing, and other unfair practices must be a normal part of business life in Japan.

What does this portend as more Japanese companies set up shop in the U.S. to manufacture goods and to provide financial and other services? Will the Japanese abide by U.S. ethical standards or, with their economic clout, become more aggressive and confident that they can do business anywhere on their terms?

Breaches of ethics in the U.S. are pretty much isolated occurrences – Ivan Boesky, Michael Milken, the illegal Treasury bids by Salomon Brothers. But "in Japan it's part of the system," privately confessed a director of Hitachi Ltd. Shortly after his company was implicated in the 1990 securities payoffs.

Tak Wakasugi, professor of finance at the prestigious Tokyo University and co-director of the University of Michigan's School of Business Administration, blames rigid regulations for the securities compensation scandal. The rules make it impossible for securities firms to reduce their commissions for customers who trade stocks in large lots, so the firm devises other ways to keep their customers happy.

The Japanese government is preparing new laws to outlaw compensation for stock losses. And the Japan Securities Dealers Assn. (JSDA) is promising to more closely supervise its members' activities. Leading JSDA's efforts is Shogo Watanabe, who was brought out of retirement last year to replace the JSDA chairman who resigned in the symbolic gesture of responsibility for the securities scandal. Mr. Watanabe talks of a return to higher ethical standards.

Yet Prof. Wakasugi suggests unethical behaviour is a long-standing problem with origins deep in Japan's social and cultural tradition. "Loosely speaking, the Japanese think that [whether] one does business in a fair way or not is up to oneself," he observes.

Many Westerners who have lived and worked in Japan attribute Japanese tolerance of questionable practices to the nation's lack of a codifying religious morality. Japan "is not a Judeo-Christian country," remarks Thomas W. Whitson, a partner and auditor at KPMG Peat Marwick in Tokyo. Everything [in Japan] seems pretty situational. If I would compare the countries where I've worked – the U.S. Taiwan, South Korea, and Japan – the general quality of [accounting] work is best here. On the other hand, if...somehow the company decides to cook the books, there's nothing that says, 'No, that's wrong.' [Rather], they say, 'well now, what's the recipe?"

The recipe the securities companies followed was to label customer-compensation payments as entertainment expenses to hide the fats from potentially troublesome shareholders. But the companies got into trouble when they told Japanese tax authorities that their accounts were false. Marking that revelation may seem strange, but Mr. Whitson says the normally meticulous Japanese can be remarkably clumsy when they try to cheat. "Maybe they're hoping that even if people check, they'll understand somehow" why it was necessary to break the rules, he speculates.

Understanding another's "necessities" is one of the most important aspects of successfully doing business in Japan – whether the understanding is among companies belonging to the same corporate e-group or between companies and the government. Indeed, upon retirement many Japanese government officials take lucrative advisory posts in the companies they previously regulated'. Communication between companies and the government in Japan is, not surprisingly, "very, very good," notes Prof. Wakasugi.

In fact, communication is so good on the inside that often it's difficult for outsiders to figure out what is going on. For example, although Japan's Ministry of Finance issued a directive in the spring of 1990 instructing securities companies to stop reimbursing customers for trading losses, unofficially the ministry may have verbally indicated payments could continue. For public consumption, the Ministry reacted with surprise many months later when reports of the compensation surfaced.

The fact is that blatant contradictions between tate-mae, the public face, and hon-ne, the underlying truth, are an everyday part of life and business in Japan. What seems like lying to an American is, to Japanese, an acceptable way of avoiding an unpleasant situation. "Japanese people have an amazing capability to accept contradictions," states Mr. Whitson. "And as long as you don't rub their face in it, they're able to live with it, and things go along in a relatively placed way."

Few, if any, Japanese are fooled by the apologies government officials and business leaders usually proffer along with their resignations in the wake of a scandal. Still, they expect the ritual to be performed. The reality is that disgraced executives may be moved only sideways into advisory jobs in their influence – and even rebuild careers – after resigning in apparent disgrace. For example, involvement in the Recruit scandal did not keep Kiichi Miyazawa from being selected Japanese Minister – though it had forced his resignation as Finance Minister a little more than two years earlier. Similarly, Ryutaro Hashimoto, who resigned as Finance Minster after the stock-compensation scandal, was one of the leading candidates to succeed Mr. Miyazawa when his term as Prime Minister was to end in October 1993.

Prof. Gregory Clark, who teaches comparative culture at Sophia University in Tokyo, describes Japan as a "sophisticated tribal society" in which people tend to make up rules as they go along rather than rely on a consistent moral code. "The tribal ethic has precedence. But it can't cope with all situations. So you have scandals," says Prof. Clark. "The problem [for the Japanese] is deciding what is a scandal." And more often than not, he says, the Japanese will wait for someone else to decide for them.

Prof. Clark stresses that the most important principle in Japanese business is not to rock the boat. "You've got to look after the people around you and keep them happy," he explains. KPMG Peat Marwick's Mr. Whitson believes this principle makes Japanese accountants amenable to cooking the figures. They would be inclined to obey a boss who asked them to falsify accounts because their first loyalty is to the company, not the code of ethics.

In an article in the October 1991 edition of Japan's Usbio magazine, Osaka University Prof. Iwao Nakatana contrasted what he called "Japan's network capitalism" with the willingness of Western people to accept a certain level of inefficiency for the sake of preserving democracy. "Whereas Japan is as society based overwhelmingly on insider relationships, the U.S. does its utmost to suppress such tendencies and create a system where all kinds of trading are entrusted to an anonymous market and [where] everyone has an equal chance," he wrote.

Japanese emphasis on personal relationships and the nation's willingness to look after its friends have given Japanese companies a major advantage over U.S. and other Western competitors in countries where bribery is a normal part of business. Prof. Wakasugi explains that Japan's history has also created a tendency to seek favors from people and companies who possess strong, centralized power. "The weaker give bribes to the stronger," he says. "It is a basic structure common to all Asian people. And [because] people think politics is a very dirty business… bribery is natural."

Already there are warning signs that some Japanese companies may be as unconcerned about ethics in the U.S. as they are at home. There have been complaints, for example, that the top jobs in many Japanese companies' Americans operations are reserved for Japanese to the exclusion of equally talented Americans, especially women. It's also alleged that some Japanese companies in the U.S. exclude Blacks and that he firms hold back high-tech supplies from U.S. customers while supplying them to Japanese companies going after the same markets as the Americans.

"They don't know the local environment so well sometimes, so they get caught doing business as usual," says KPMG Peat Marwick's Mr. Whitson. But, he adds, their damage control is extremely good, and they soon learn from their mistakes. "If morality is important to do business in the United States, then I think they would go along with it – not because it's right, but because it's good for business."

Source: Chonko (1995)

ETHICAL ISSUES ON GOOD CORPORATION

1. Indigenous People

The US-owned Freeport McMoran Copper & Gold spent US $15 million in 1997 on community programmes after much conflict with the local population in Indonesia. It faced three tribal wars in 1997, a strike the August and lawsuits from local leaders. The company had adopted a reactive strategy by building a school and a clinic without consulting the local community. Nor it had done any proper planning.

The company has set aside one per cent of its revenues (i.e., US $15 million in 1997) for community programmes targeting indigenous tribes and spending an additional similar sum on health and education. The funds were announced only in 1996 after being in operation for 25 years.

The lessons which can be learned from the experience are:

- Find local leaders.
- Agree on projects with the local government and tribal leaders on the basis of an assessment of the real needs of the local population and its wants.
- Avoid unrealistic expectations. When free-port set aside one percent of its revenues in for community programmes, these were hijacked by the local government official who wanted control over the spending. Parts of the funds were spent on costly housing projects and the rest went to seven new foundations, each for seven local tribes. Freeport intended to make available to local villages, with each village council being accountable. The company also got in trouble with the military. There were allegations of severe human rights abuses by the soldiers and this tarnished the image of Freeport. Freeport subsequently started speaking against the military.

Stakeholders Ethical Impacts of Globalization

1. **Shareholders:** Globalization provides potential for greater profitability, but also greater risks. Lack of regulation of global capital markets, lending to additional financial risks and instability.
2. **Employees:** Corporations outsource production to developing countries in order to reduce costs in global marketplace – this provides jobs but also raises the potential for exploitation of employees through poor working conditions.
3. **Consumers:** Global products provide social benefits to consumers across the globe but may also meet protest about cultural imperialism and westernization. Globalization can bring cheaper prices to customers, but vulnerable consumers in developing countries may also face the possibility of exploitation by MNCs.
4. **Suppliers and competitors:** Suppliers in developing countries face regulation from MNCs through supply chain management. Small scale indigenous competitors exposed to powerful global players.
5. **Civil society (pressure groups, NGOs, local communities):** Global business activities bring the company in direct interaction to local communities with possibility for erosion of traditional community life; globally active pressure groups emerge with aim to 'police' the corporation in countries where governments are weak and tolerant.
6. **Government and regulation:** Globalization weakens governments and increases the corporate responsibility for jobs, welfare, maintenance of ethical standards, etc., globalization also confronts governments with corporations from different cultural expectations about issues such as bribery, corruption, taxation, and philanthropy.

"Ethics should be established for the long run, being honest and straight can solve many problems."

—Li and Fund

6

Chapter

Role of Corporate Culture in Business

INTRODUCTION

Knowledge is quickly becoming the major asset and export item of global business. The greatest future and competitive advantage of the corporates will evolve from the ability to create, develop, and leverage distinctive knowledge from diverse cultures within the global context. It is universally accepted that culture exerts a phenomenal amount of influence on learning and most social interactions. Culture is often cited as the most significant hindrance to establishing universal standards on a global basis. The common organism that exists within all human beings is the brain. Research has shown that humans can, when necessary, solve the most complex problems. In this context the corporate culture is also developed consisting of many human brains, experience, practices, beliefs and so on. Corporate culture has become a widely accepted term in mainstream of business. Many executives pay as much attention to culture as strategy in shaping a business plan. Some mergers are shunned because of cultural differences; other proceeds, because the cultures of the merging partners line up. Edgar Schein of M I T the author of *Organisational Culture and Leadership* who offered the bold in sight that, "there is a possibility, under emphasized in leadership research, that the only thing of real importance that leads to is to create and manage culture and that the unique talent of leaders is to work with culture". Another book John Kotten and James Steskett's *Corporate Culture and Performance* offers the companies to demonstrate with strong culture for the massive margin. Throughout human history and across national boundaries, culture articulates a distinctive way of life. According to the Forunte Magazine in 1995 on corporate reputation survey says "There is growing concern that companies cannot live by numbers alone. The one thing that set the top ranking companies in the survey apart is their robust cultures". History yields values, values create forms and shape behaviour. Heroic figures exemplify core values and beliefs. Rituals and ceremonies dramatise core values and provide delightful material for companies for company events. International corporates like Google, IBM, Toyota, TATA, Infosys, etc., are some of companies practising a strong culture in the organization.

CULTURE

Culture refers in general term to an organization value, beliefs and behaviours. In general, beliefs and values on the basis of which people interpret experiences. But there is no comprehensive, or commonly accepted, definition of culture. As it differs from person to person, family to family, business to business, society to society and nation to nation. There is no commonly or widely accepted concept of culture. Some researchers perceive cultures as systems that link people to their ecological environment. According to Stares (1968) culture consists of groups behaviour patterns in their individual ecological environment. There can be strong culture and weak culture. Both depend on leaders, persistence practices, employees training for best behaviour in the organization.

Organisational culture is an idea in the fields of organisational studies and management which describes the psychology, attitude, experiences, beliefs and values both personal and cultural of an organization. It has been defined as "the specific collection of values and norms that are shared by the people and groups in an organization and the control the way they interact with each other and with stakeholders outside the organizations (Charles WL Hill). It can also be explained for organizational values as also known as beliefs, and ideas about what kinds of goals members of an organization should pursue and ideas about the appropriate kinds as standards of behaviour organizational members should use to achieve those goals. From organisational values, develop organizational norms, guidelines or expectations that prescribe appropriate kinds of behaviour by employees in particular situation and control the behaviour of organization members towards one another.

CORPORATE CULTURE

Corporate culture is the collective behaviour of people using common corporate vision, goals, shared values, beliefs, habits, working language, systems and symbols. It is also referred to an organization's values beliefs and behaviour. According to the Marketing Information Centre, "Corporate culture is referred to as the particular strategies, style, systems, environment and shared values with the organization which contribute to its individuality."

The concept of corporate culture is understood according to business. Operate culture is the total sum of values, customs, traditions and meanings that make a company unique. Corporate culture is often referred as "the character of an organization," since it embodies the vision of the company's founders.

Corporate culture, embedded deeply in the organization in the behaviour of the people, is necessary to equalize to the image of the company. Therefore, it is difficult to determine an organization's culture from outside. Culture may be based on the theory of "Onion Skin", which is as follows:

Culture	Mechanisms	Strategy	Customers
• Assumption	• Rewards	• Product	• Suppliers
• Beliefs	• Systems	• Services	• Shareholders
• Values	• Structure	• Customers	• Competitors
• Norms	• Capabilities	• Colleagues	• Government
• Styles			• Society.

RESEARCH VIEW ON CORPORATE CULTURE AND ETHICAL VALUES

Corporate culture is a multifaceted construct. For example, in describing corporate culture, Goffman (l959-1967) focused on the *observed behavioral regularities* in people's interactions; Homans (1950) wrote of *norms* that evolve in working groups; Ouchi (1981) stressed the *philosophy* that influences organizational policy, and Van Maanen (1976) emphasized the rules for getting along in an organization. More recently, corporate culture has been defined as the assumptions, beliefs, goals, knowledge and *values* that are shared by organization's members (Deal and Kennedy 1982; Sathe 1984; Schein 1985; Schwartz and Davis 1981). Though values, according to this view, are but one dimension of corporate culture, they have been, theorized to be highly influential in directing the lie of individuals in society in general and organizations in particular (Rokeach 1968, 1973; Yankelovich 1 1981). For *society*, values help define the "core" of people what they love, hate, or are just indifferent to. They help explain why people make sacrifices and what they are willing to give up to attain goals. Values encompass a larger view of what people are, can be, and will become (Mitchell 1971). For an *organization,* 'values serve to convey a sense of identity to its members, enhance the stability of its social system, direct managers' attention to important issues, guide subsequent decisions by managers, and (most important for our research) facilitate commitment to something larger than self (Deal and Kennedy 1982; Smircich 1983).

Organizations may have many values that are distinctly marketing in character, for example, values that guide product and service quality, advertising content, selection of distribution channels, and treatment of customers. However, underpinning all of these specific values are corporate *ethical* values. These values help establish and maintain the standards that delineate the "right" things to do and the things "worth doing" (Jansen and Yon Glinow 1985). In turn, such ethical standards can influence individual's choices, and lead to actions that are desirable to organizations (Conner and Becker 1975). More specifically, when the ethical standards/values of an organization, are widely shared among its members, organizational success will be enhanced (Badovick and Beatty 1987; Brown 1976; England 1967; Keeley 1983; Koch and Fox 1978). As Peters and Waterman (1982) point out in their study of excellent companies, virtually all the superior performance firms have at the core a well-defined set of shared values, particularly ethical values.

Marketing has increasingly considered exchange to be its central concept, a trend that culminated in 1985 with the AMA's new definition of marketing. Insight into the influence of shared values on desirable organizational outcomes can be gained by examining the exchange relationship between individuals and their organizations. As in all *exchange relationships,* two sides are involved, each with something of value, freedom to agree or disagree, and the ability to communicate what is being offered. On one side are individuals, who come to organizations with certain needs and desires. Within the organization they expect to find a work environment in which they can use their abilities to satisfy many of these needs. On the other side, organizations hire individuals to accomplish the tasks necessary for the survival, growth, and prosperity of the organization. In essence, organizations satisfy individual's needs and in return, individuals work hard to accomplish organizational goals (Steers 1977). When organizations provide an environment or "culture" conducive to such exchanges (e.g., when they are dependable, broadminded, or ethical), the likelihood of receiving desirable responses from employees (e.g., high productivity and loyalty) is theorized to increase (Hrebiniak and Alutto 1972; March and Simon 1958). Though top managers must recognize that this exchange relationship is important in both the recruitment and retention (or commitment) of employees, our study focuses on the latter.

Organizational Commitment

Scholarly works on organizational commitment are numerous (see Randall 1987). Though recent reviews reveal more than 30 different forms of work commitment, they also show that each form can be relatively stable over time (Morrow 1983). Similarly, though definitions of organizational commitment abound, a common theme in most of them is that committed individuals tend to identify with the objectives and goals of their organizations and want to remain with their organizations (Buchanan 1974; Hrebiniak and Alutto 1972). Thus, organizational commitment has been described as a "psychological bond" to the organization that influences individuals to act in ways consistent with the interests of the organization (Mowday and McDade 1979; Porter, Mowday and Boulin 1974).

Commitment has been associated with many desirable organizational outcomes, including satisfaction, performance, reduced turnover, and flexibility. Most researchers acknowledge value on both theoretical and empirical grounds and most managers prefer loyal and devoted employees on practical grounds. The important issue from both research and managerial viewpoints is: How can organizations instill and maintain a high level of commitment in their members? In other words, before managers can hope to influence commitment in an informed way, the antecedents of commitment must be identified (Morris and Sherman 1981; Randall 1987).

Some research studies have shown certain personal characteristics (including age, income, and education) and certain job characteristics (including variety, autonomy, identity, and feedback) to be robust predictors of many organizational behaviours. For example, in the organization literature, age and income have been found to be related positively to commitment (Brief and Aldag 1980; Steers 1977) whereas education has been related negatively (Brief and Aldag 1980; Morris and Sherman 1981). Further, Herzberg (1966), Hackman and Lawler (1971), and Becherer, Morgan, and Richard (1982) found positive relationships between satisfaction and certain intrinsic job characteristics as measured by the Job Classification Index (JCI) (see Sims, Szilagyi, and Keller 1976). Similarly, in the marketing literature, positive relationships have been found between organizational commitment and age, income, variety, autonomy, and feedback (Hunt, Chonko, and Wood 1985). What has not been investigated *empirically* in *any* literature is the association between corporate ethical values and commitment.

CORPORATE CULTURE VS ORGANISATIONAL CULTURE

Organisational culture and corporate culture are often used interchangeably, and it is a mistake to state that they are different concepts. All corporations are also organisations, but not all organisations are corporations. Organisations include religious institutions, non-profit organisations and government agencies. There is even the Canadian Criminal Code definition of " Organised crime" as meaning "a group comprised of three or more persons which as, as one of its primary activities or purposes the commission of serious offences which likely results in financial gains'. Corporations are organizations and also legal entities.

Senior management may try to determine a "corporate culture". They may wish to impose corporate value and standards of behaviour that specifically reflect the objectives of the organizations. In addition, there will also be an extent interval culture within the workforce. Work groups within the organization have their own behavioural activities or interactions which, to an extent, affect the whole system. Roger Strrison's four-culture typology, and adopted by Charles Handy. He suggests that unlike organizational culture, Corporate culture can be imported. For example, computer technicians will have expertise, language and behaviours gained independently of the organization, but their presence can influence the culture of the organization as a whole. Whatever may be the discussion there is not much difference towards organisation culture' and 'corporate culture' as far as the business activities are concerned. All that it has as Schein (2009), Deal & Kennady (2000) Kotter (1992) and many others state, that "organizations often have very differing cultures as well as sub-cultures".

Hence, for the purpose of business ethics, both organisation culture and corporate culture are understood as same. However, it differs on the basis of environment, size and nature of the business

Again organisations have turned as the strong believer of corporate culture for the long-term results. The practice of business ethics has been adopted for the sound commercial practices. The components of the ethics have main responsibility and accountability which are practised in business by showing:

1. Responsibility for good quality of product and services, creating, friendly environment both internally and externally.

2. Responsibility for information, both to the employees and customers.
3. Equality of opportunity both to the employees and managers.
4. Equality of opportunity which distributed to all levels of personnels in the organization.
5. Working environment by incorporating work interest, belief in oneself, identifications of skill and knowledge of the individual.

CORPORATE CULTURE AND CHANGE

Culture and change go hand in hand in the present business world. The modern mantra for the best performance of the business and its result is "change". There are number of methods and recommendations which are suggested by the researchers about the change in culture. There is also a variety of phychological approaches for the best system towards learning organization and for corporate culture and evaluation. Ideas and strategies, on the other hand, seen to vary according to particular influences that affect culture.

When an individual wants to change an aspect of the culture of an organization one has to keep in consideration that this is a long-term project. Corporate culture is something that is very hard to change and employees need time to get used to the new way of organizing. For companies with a very strong and specific culture it will be even harder to change.

According to Cummings and Worley (2005) there are six guidelines for cultural change:

1. Formulation of a clear strategic commitment.
2. Displaying of top management commitment
3. Model culture change at the highest level.
4. Modification of organisation to support organization change
5. Select and socialise as the newcomers and terminate deviants.
6. Develop in ethical and legal sensitivity.

Change of culture in the organization is very important and inevitable. Culture innovation is bound to take place because it entails introducing something new and substantically different from what prevails in the existing cultures. Culture innovation is bound to be more difficult than cultural maintenance. People often resist changes, hence it is the duty of the management to convince people that are likely to gain and will outweigh the losses. Besides institutionalisation, dedication is another process that tends to occur in strongly developed organizational cultures. The organisation itself may come to be regarded as precious in itself, as a source of pride, and in some sense unique. Organisational members begin to feel a stray bond with it that transcends material returns given by the organization and they begin to identify within.

High performance corporate culture through change

(1) **Change in service:** Good service is a sustainable activity and performance in the organization and it focuses on:

- Customer focuses
- Quality focuses
- Authoritative
- Responsive to change

The four core dimensions have been adopted and successful results have been achieved by the big giants in the business world are:

- Harley Davidson
- Walmart
- Jet Blue
- Universal Fibers
- Hospitality Industry
- New Balance
- Green Mt. Coffee
- N. Western Mutual
- Whole. Foods

(2) **Change in New Age:** Change in corporate culture according to the new age is another paramount importance towards the success of the business. The corporates have changed in the core factors of the business like:

- Innovativeness
- Egalitarian
- Consensual
- Creates Change
- Long term focus
- Promotes diverse ideas

The corporates who adopted are:

- Southwest Air
- Intel
- Nucor
- Microsoft (1980)
- People Soft
- SAS Institute
- Emerson Elec
- Ebay

CORE COMPONENTS OF CORPORATE CULTURE

Corporate culture is a multidimensional activity of different activities in the organization. This may be strong or weak. Strong culture is said to exist where the staff respond to stimulus because of their alignment to organization values. In such environments, strong culture helps firms operate like well oiled machines, cruising along with outstanding execution and perhaps minor tweakery of existing procedures here and there.

Conversely, there is weak culture where there is little alignment with organizational values and control must be exercised through extensive procedures and bureaucracy.

Where culture is strong – people do things rightly because they believe it is the right thing to do. There is a risk of another phenomenon, group think "Group think" was described by Irving L. Janis as "a quick and easy way to refer to a mode of thinking that people engage when they are deeply involved in a cohesive group, when members strive for unanimity override their motivation to realistically appraise alternative in action." This is a position where people, even if they have different ideas, do not challenge organization thinking and therefore there is a reduced capacity for innovative thoughts. In fact group think is to increase in the organization towards the common goal. There are people who often turn down or are seen as a negative influence by the rest of the group, because they bring conflict. Innovative organizations need individuals who propose to challenge the status quo—be in group think or bureaucracy, and also need procedures to implement new ideas effectively.

Whether it is a strong or weak culture, the corporate should create its culture with the core components and also with "beliefs and assumption."

Beliefs and assumptions are sounded by:

(i) **Mission:** The image of the corporate is created through the mission which focuses on external environment.

Mission should be based on

- Strategic direction and intent
- Goals and objectives
- Vision

(ii) **Consistency:** Another stable activity shown in the external environment of the organization with

- Core values
- Agreement
- Co-ordination and integration

(iii) **Involvement:** This is internal focus which is flexible in nature depending up on the people in the organization. This may change status, position, mind set-ting, attitude and behaviour of the individual. Whatever may be the situation the organization should practise:

- Empowerment : Employees, managers according to their responsibilities and levels.
- Team orientation
- Capability development

(iv) Adaptability: Change in culture through innovation and getting used to it and practising the same way in is own course of time. The organization should adopt the formula of flexibility to achieve best results through:

- Creating change
- Customer focus
- Organisational learning.

The core component of the corporate culture should be based on values. Value based organizations have shown sustainability in profit maximization and continuous improvement in the long run. However, there are eight core values for strong corporate culture:

1. **Flexible Deployment:** It is to achieve for multiple skills in the workplace. Special care is to be taken towards coordination function and cross-functional multi-skilling programme.
2. **Customer focus:** The corporate culture should give prominence to the customer. There need to have qualitative and quantitative responses to survey. The co-ordinated programme inclusive of customer integration skills, customer relation management system and guideline to interact for customer–focused behaviour must be framed.
3. **Performance focus:** Role description of employees, upto-date employee role description and annual performance review must be targeted.
4. **Project based work:** Staff involvement in cross-functional project teams. And the number of skills involved in cross-functional teams. Implementation and support of works – functional project teams to deal with organization problems, challenges and need based opportunities.
5. **Human spirit and work:** Use of a quantitative and qualitative techniques in studying and surveying employee engagement in the organization. In this there need to implement on employee engagement strategy.
6. **Learning and Development:** Implementation of learning and development program emphasising job skills, personal development and enhancing problem solving capabilities. This is to spread between skill personal and problem solving personal.
7. **Open information:** This is possible only through training program and all staff must attend compulsory. In this implementation of a workplace initiative program carrying into the extent and limit of staff authority across all functions of the business.

CORPORATE CULTURE WITH THE LOGISTICS MANAGEMENT

The corporate culture based an logistics management should change its components according to the nature and size of the business and its organization function.

Logistics management should be based on the following practices:

1. **Shared basic assumption:**
    - Relationship environment
    - Nature of reality – open firm boundaries
    - Human relationship with native of human and trustworthy
    - Nature of human activity to build best relationship
    - Nature of people, who are essentially co-operative
2. **Shared Values:**
    - Trust
    - Commitment
    - Co-operative norms
    - Organisation compatibility
    - Top management support
3. **Focus form behaviour:**
    - Sharing of risk, reward and information.
    - Co-operating with other firms in implementation of supply chain management
    - Combination of efforts with other members of the supply chain.
    - Seeking out of firms that are compatible in goals and objectives.
    - Leadership and commitment to change.
4. **Supply chain partners behaviour:**
    - Seeking out of firms that are compatible in goals and objectives.
    - Co-operation with other firms in implementing supply chain management.
    - Combination of efforts with other members of the supply chain.
    - Sharing of risk, rewards and information.
    - Leadership and commitment to change.
5. **Effective supply chain management:**
    - High level of information sharing between the firms.
    - Firms sharing risks and reward.
    - Co-operation between firms.
    - Similar customer service goals and focus among firms.
    - Integration of key processes between firms.
    - Long-term relation ships
    - Inter-functional co-ordination.

CULTURE AND ETHICAL BEHAVIOUR

The origin of culture is based a on culture itself with culture's or nation's history, geography, and natural resources. For example, Italy has been a unified country only since 1861, and it was ruled for centuries by other countries. Historically, Italians have feared outsiders who may be sent by their rulers to infiltrate their cultural groups. Italians hated to pay taxes to such rulers and devised elaborate schemes for avoiding them. Today, these historical factors still play a prominent part in the ethical practices of Italians, because they tend to trust only people in their cultural in-groups and flagrantly violate the tax laws.

Geographical location also plays a major role in understanding differences in managerial ethical behaviors. Once again, Italy serves as a prime illustration as it has historically been victimized by overwhelming natural disasters: volcanoes, floods, famines, and earthquakes. As a result. Italy exudes an aura of "precariousness" (Haycraft 1985). Italians tend to accept insecurity as a fact of life. which helps to explain why they are able to enjoy life more for the moment and are willing to accept events as they happen (Gannon & Associates, 1994). Sometimes, Italian businessmen will make extravagant promises that they know how only a slight chance of ever being actualized. And this behavior is in accord with their view that all life is precarious and subject to chance. Just as a mountain is beautiful before being destroyed by an earthquake. So too an extravagant promise is acceptable if there is any chance, however slight, that it can be fulfilled.

Natural resources also influence managerial ethical behaviour. Japan for instance, is a small island nation that has few natural resources. It imported the practice of rice farming from China at about the 7th century A.D. because this type of agriculture provided at least a subsistence level of living for all Japanese. However, for each village to survive, it was necessary that all contribute and work hard at rice farming. Thus, harmony in working toward the common good became the chief value underlying the Japanese perspective; it was the first article in the country's first constitution, written by Prince Shotoku in the 7th century. Behaviors that tend to destroy this sense of harmony are frequently classified as unacceptable or unethical.

This perspective is in sharp contrast to that in the United States, where life, liberty and the pursuit of individual happiness predominates. In the United States, the abundance of natural resources and land helped to strengthen this ideological perspective. Americans in the 17th and 18th centuries had almost unlimited resources and they tended to develop practices that were wasteful and careless of resources. Even today, this wastefulness is a problem in the United States.

The next element is the national culture itself, and will focus on two overlapping aspects of it: the management practices in such areas as bribery and issuing false reports, and the basic values that lead to such clear differences in these practices. 'According to a number of investigators of national culture, the most important dimension or value across cultures may well be individualism collectivism, that is, the degree to which the individual feels that he or she is integrated into a group, even to the extent of making decisions only if they are / acceptable to the group. Research has indicated that members of collectivist cultures tend to be very cooperative with other members of their in-groups but uncooperative and hostile to members of out-groups (Brislin, 1993). Such a zero-sum or winner-loser perspective has obvious ramifications for defining acceptable managerial behaviours. For instance, a manager should always try to help members of his or her culture or in-group and act in an honest and trusting way toward them. However, this same manager may well lie to members of the out-groups and even view them as "less than human." Some Japanese managers, for instance, believe that they need to be honest only when speaking Japanese, and so they sometimes use the English language when dealing with non-Japanese managers if they want to deceive them or avoid being held to a commitment (DeMente, 1991).

Primary and secondary influences on values and behaviours constitute the third element. Parenting and socialization represent such a primary influence. For example, for the first few years of life, Japanese children are strapped to the bodies of their mothers, who encourage them to look at their faces, thus developing a relationship of dependency. These children also sleep with their parents until the age of 6 or 7, which strengthens this sense of dependency. Such parenting practices are consistent with the emphasis on harmony. By contrast, American children are strongly encouraged to explore the world about them as early in life as possible. Such patterns strengthen either a group-oriented style of ethical decision making, as in the case of Japan, or an / individualistic style, as in the case of the United States.

Education is also an important primary influence on values and behaviours. In Germany, children are separated into different types of schools at the end of fourth or sixth grade; other European countries make similar assignments at the end of eighth grade. Some of this separation is class related, because only the wealthier parents can afford to hire tutors to help their children pass the rigorous examinations required for admission to the schools that lead to a university degree and a prosperous life. Tutoring of 4-year-olds is quite common. Such educational systems reinforce the belief that there are natural and definite social class barriers in society. Although sheer ability is sometimes sufficient to overcome such barriers, in many instances individuals are born with special rights and obligations. Although it is difficult to precisely identify cause and effect, it may well be that the United States punishes more of its managers for unethical acts than all other developed countries combined, partly because of the more open educational system that exists in the United States. Some citizens, including managers, do not automatically have special rights and obligations different from those of other citizens.

Religion is a third primary influence. Many of the citizens in several developing countries believe in astrology, and some of their businessmen will not undertake a course of action until it is approved by an astrologer. Also, some of the major religions, particularly Catholicism and Confucianism, tend to have an antibusiness bias, thus making major business activity in and of itself immoral and unethical. For example, the Catholic theologian and philosopher, St. Thomas Aquinas, argued that a price should be "just," that is, just sufficient to cover the costs of labor and materials. However, his approach was antithetical to charging interest, which is a major foundation stone of modern economic life. Clearly, there are instances of companies charging a usurious rate of interest, and any American paying an interest rate of 22% on a bank credit card balance while receiving only 3% for money invested in bank certificates of deposits can easily sympathize with the concept of the just price. Still, as Max Weber has persuasively argued, it was the Protestant ethics and its emphasis on relating worldly success to divine salvation that was a major precondition for modern capitalism and its high standard of living.

There are also secondary influences on values and behaviours that are not as direct as the primary influences, and these include laws, organizational cultures, and human resource management (HRM) systems. They still, however, exert a powerful influence. Thus, Title VII of the Equal Employment Opportunity Law and its extensions have changed life dramatically in the United States for many groups, including women, African Americans, and the disabled. There are various HRM policies in the areas of recruitment, training, performance evaluation, and reward systems that exert a powerful influence on ethical practices. For example, Sears, Roebuck and Co. recently changed its policy of paying its employees in auto services on a commission basis, because some of them deliberately charged customers for services that were never rendered. In Japan, where the customer is considered king, it would be hard to imagine a similar situation occurring at a prominent company.

Also, IBM had a no-layoff policy until recently and it supposedly led to a more conservative approach to decision making and, by extension, what was acceptable or ethical behaviour. Similarly, many large Japanese organizations guarantee lifetime employment to a core set of managers and employees and, although this has led to an increase in feeling of company loyalty, it has also been accompanied by conservative decision making and the treating of some employees performing approximately the same jobs in radically different ways. An employee who has been guaranteed lifetime employment may receive twice the salary of his short-term counterpart.

Organizational cultures also represent a potent secondary influence. Thus, in Japan, the Sony Corporation has a more innovative and risk-taking organizational culture than that of many older and more established companies such as Mitsui, partly because Sony was established about 300 years later than Mitsui, when conditions were quite different. Sony needed experienced managers and so it did not follow the practice of "maturing" managers and hiring them directly from schools and universities. Rather, Sony started to hire managers away from other Japanese companies. Still, Sony and Mitsui are more similar to one another in terms of their organizational cultures than to such American companies as Xerox or RCA.

There is, however, a trend for large companies in one nation to implement changes in their organizational cultures that make them more similar to companies in other nations. Honda, for many years, followed the Japanese emphasis on harmony, which led to a slowing down of the decision-making process in the organization. Managers did not want to openly criticize the ideas of their peers and superiors, and frequently problems were not even discussed until it was too late to solve them. Recently, however, Honda has encouraged such American-style practices as openly confronting a problem at a meeting, even if some loss of face occurs, and rewarding successful managers much more than in the past. This abrupt change in the management systems has been difficult for many of the Honda managers to accept, especially because what was previously unacceptable and unethical is now considered acceptable and ethical.

Both primary and secondary influences have significant effects on the values and beliefs of individual managers. It also shows that individual values and beliefs are then related, although imperfectly, to subsequent behaviours or decisions. It should be recognized that these secondary influences can overwhelm individual behavioural propensities, as previously indicated; for example, tight management control systems decrease unethical behaviours. Thus, these secondary influences not only reflect the culture but also exert independent pressures on individuals to behave in certain ways.

There is a *modal* behaviours found in a nation, that is, points in a statistical distribution of a nation where large clusters of individuals can be found. It is impossible to identify and describe the behaviours of every individual within a nation, whereas an attempt can be made to do so.

FUNCTIONS OF CORPORATE CULTURE

As corporate culture is to be shaped by corporate vision, shared values, beliefs, assumption past experiences, learning leadership and communications. And there need to be a basis for all the activities functions of the organisations.

Corporate culture is a combination of material and spiritual body. It is under historical conditions, formed by and for businesses to follow common to all members. And the collective consciousness, ethics, values are the core of the corporate culture. The performance of corporate culture may be taken in various forms and it is understood into the functions or role in the organisations, which are discussed as under.

Guiding Function: This is the function where it is taken at the macro level. The corporate values and behaviour of the overall effect guide, indicating the direction of the development of enterprises. It guides enterprises to establish overall concept and enhance the competitiveness of enterprises. At the same time it may be taken at micro level. Here every employee, company's psychology, values and thinking, behaviour and oriented approach play a role in a timely manner to the attention of employees as well as thoughts and actions directed to the business goals.

Authority: A common enterprise to follow the spirit of enterprise, business ethics, corporate fashion, corporate values and codes of conduct and other cultural factors, must penetrate into every employee's ideas, psychological and behaviour, and thus the ideas of each employee psychological and behaviour constraints and norms play a role.

Cohesion function: The core of the corporate culture that values are a driving force, able to unite all staff of enterprise, thereby creating a huge centripetal force and cohesive force. In fact, if all the staff together to create a collective consciousness, its employees if they are recognised, it will create a bonding effect, from all levels of staff. It will gather together all kinds of subtle ways to communicate thoughts and feeling of employees integration with employees' ideas, beliefs, style, sentiments. This can be trained and inspire the staff, which may lead to form a coherent organic whole.

Integration: Corporate culture and the social and cultural interpenetration, mutual influence and mutual integration are the functions in respect of integration. On the other hand, in the common business practice in the formation of corporate culture, not only by the majority of staff to comply, with and because the corporate culture factors in the psychological impact of employees. Education, guidance and adjustment, allow business and employees, gradually adjust among themselves blending into one.

Stimulants: Corporate culture on employees can produce a tremendous impetus, can enhance the sense of honour and confidence so that the employees produce a sense of responsibility and mission. In this respect employees produce a high growth from the inner emotions and forge ahead with spirit, inspire and motivate the common goal of the enterprise.

From the above functions it can be decided that the corporate culture is only a sound mechanism, can act as a powerful source in formation of organisational effectiveness.

Achieving or effective functioning of corporate culture:

(1) **Explicit mechanism:** The functions of corporate culture must be primarily achieved through the explicit mechanisms. This carries outside of the corporate culture formed by physical and chemical culture. The culture of this reflection is reflected in corporate image, spirit and values, the more deeper physical and chemical influence will be. In order to make a good culture, it is necessary to promote enterprise culture.

(2) **Implicit mechnism:** The implicit mechanism of corporate culture is the second in which multiple levels are present. Each level has a different function of the culture, and play a role in different ways. In deep analysis of corporate culture that makes the accumulation of core value system. This has a special function, has impact on employees as an inner guide, to meet psychological needs. By shaping corporate culture employees in the organisation create a sense of responsibility and mission and create a value for conscious dedication towards their work in the organisation.

(3) **The corporate culture may be regulatory machanisms:** Quality level of corporate culture determines its size. The quality of corporate culture is adjustable and building of enterprise culture proved the quality of corporate culture which is directly related to function effectively. The most fundamental factor corporate culture is to improve the quality and level of the same which may result in excellent result. The organisation's spirit, the collective consciousness, value, visual image, reputation and so on are adjusted levels of corporate culture.

(4) **Transmission mechanism:** The corporate culture and its functions depend on the external communication. The external staff, senior managers, marketing officials and body dealing with the public should be communicative of corporate culture to the public of various communities and society in general. An effective communicative channels, welfare activities, public relative activities to the society may uphold a good corporate culture image.

Corporate culture should make total quality management in the organisation.

TQM and Corporate culture model

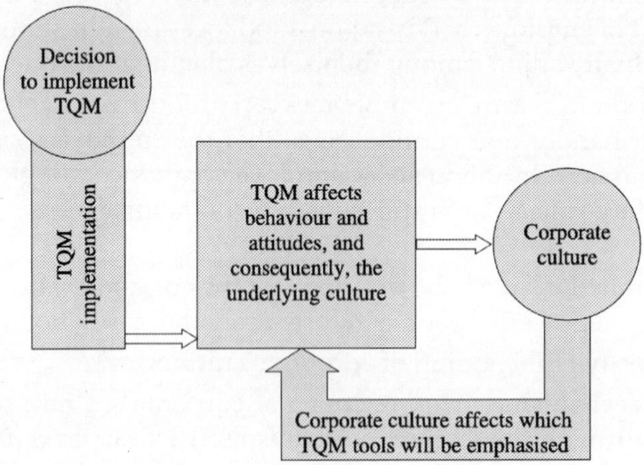

Some of the organisations adopt different functions based on the nature and size of the organisation, some of them are:

- → To set a stategy } Adoption function
- → To outsource skills }
- → To train the managers and engineers and integrate skills } Acceptance Function
- → To test to, just see and observe }
- → To disappoint or be unconvinced by the basic arguments. } Doubts (without any function)
- → To find out more resource and benefit without any extra cost. }
- → To deny or disinterest in hearing any matter which is not necessary } Unknown function
- → To make note of things which are never heard. }

RESEARCH STUDY ON CHANGE IN THE CORPORATE/ ORGANISATIONAL CULTURE

Corporate culture is a great influencing factor for effective business world. To uphold its importance and practice systematically various research studies have been taken place all over the globe. There are various contributions towards the corporate culture by

(1) Arthur F. Carmazic (2007) – 5 major types of corporate culture.
(2) Hofstede (1980) – 5 dimensions of culture.
(3) Charles Handy (1985) – Four type culture
(4) Edgar schein (2004) – Model on organisational culture
(5) Robert Cooke – Culture and organisational expectation.

Each of the above researchers study is discussed briefly.

CHANGE IN THE ORGANISATIONAL CULTURE

Types of Corporate Culture

(1) Corporate culture
- Shared value
- Team culture, cultural intelligence
- Building a team culture
- Strategies for building growth culture.

Two sources of corporate culture

(a) Adoptive culture
(b) Growth culture

(2) Innovative – adopt culture
- Innovation
- Creating culture for innovation
- Strategies for creating a culture and innovation.
- Transformation of innovation and creative culture.

(3) Winning organisation culture
- Organisational sources 360 Five Basic Elements.
- 75 models.

(4) Employee Empowerment culture
- The Tao of Employee Empowerment
- Getting rid of Bureaucracy

(5) Innovation – Friendly Organisation
- Corporate innovation system
- Entrepreneurial organisation
- Guiding principles to liberalise employee.
- Leveraging the power of diversity

(6) **Continuous Improvement Firm [CIF]**

- Kaizen – It is an integral part of corporate culture both conscious and subconscious thinking about improvement and effectively integrating Kaizen, into corporate culture.

  Eg. Toyota.

(7) **Sustainable growth strategies**

- Strategies of market leaders.

(8) **Corporate leader**

- Business architect
- Business performers

(9) **Cultural intelligence**

- Managing culture differences
- Competitive advantage: Firm vs different corporates

  Eg: US vs Japan
- Cross China vs India
- Cross – Cultural Differences

  Eg: Chinese vs Americans

  Japanese vs Indians.

(10) **Competitive Culture**

Competitive philosophy is described by Sun TZU as "The Way" or corporate culture or corporate mission. Clear philosophy makes decision making effective, strong philosophy, strong competitor.

Changing organisational culture will result in 5 major types of corporate cultures

According to Arthur. F. Carmazic, "Lessons from the Monkey King Leading change to create Gorilla sized Results ". (2007) There are 5 major types of corporate culture which are explained under:

(1) **Blame corporate culture:** This culture is where the individual will not act actively for a change to better, with the reasons of traditional practices and are not interested in the new ideas. This is based on following characteristics:

(a) Trust level is low (b) Act self interest (c) Do not take many risks (d) Little innovation (f) Pay check driven (g) Inefficient action (h) High lend of fear

This culture cultivates distrust and fear, people blame each other to avoid being reprimanded or put down, this results in no new ideas or personal initiative because people don't want to risk being wrong.

(2) **Multi-directional corporate culture:** This is another culture where it has a lot of confussion, no clarity and lack of communication. The characteristics are:

(a) Little communication (b) Exclusive (c) Lots of gossip (d) Criticise other departments (e) Little co-operation (f) No common vision.

This culture cultivates minimized cross-department communication and co-operation. Loyalty is only to specific groups (departments). Each department becomes exclusive and is often critical of other departments which in turn creates lots of gossip. Lack of cooperation and multidirection is manifested in the organization's inefficiency.

(3) **Live and let live corporate culture:** This kind of culture orgnisations will be flexible, adjustable and situational. Here the following are the characteristics:

(a) Complacency (b) Mental stagnation (c) Low creativity (d) Average cooperation (e) Moderate communication and (f) Little future vision.

This culture is complacent, it manifests mental stagnation and low creativity. People here have little future vision and have given up their passion. There is average cooperation and communication, and things do work, but they do not grow. People have developed their personal relationships and decided who to stay away from, there is not much left to learn.

(4) **Brand congruent corporate culture:** Here the company will to the reputation and brand based on the characteristics followed.

(a) Believe in product (b) Feel about the company (c) Co-operative (d) Similar goals and (e) Solving problems actively.

People in this culture believe in the product or service of the organization. They feel good about what their company is trying to achieve it. People here are passionate and seem to have similar goals in the organization. They use personal resources to actively solve problems and while they don't always accept the actions of management or other around them, they see their job as important. Everyone in this culture operates at the level of group.

(5) **Leadership enrich culture:** A leader has prime role in the organisation culture with the following characteristics:

(a) Aligned with the organisation (b) Feel good about company (c) Leadership at all levels (d) Leadership to develop in all levels.

People view the organization as an extension of themselves, they feel good about what they personally achieve through the organization and have exceptional cooperation. Individual goals are aligned with the goals of the organization and people will do what it takes to make things happen. As a group, the organization is more like a family providing personal fulfilment which often transcends ego. So people consistently bring out the best in each other. In this culture, leaders do not develop followers, but develop other leaders. Everyone in this culture operates at the level of organization.

Carmazi's model requires application of his directive communication psychology to evolve the culture. While the idea of having a leadership enriched organization is, inspirational, it would require substantial leadership resources to develop. The concept of evolving the culture assumes that "every individual in the organization wants to do a good job", and the behaviours, that result in poor performance are manifestations of psychology the group or organization has created through policies, leadership and poor communication.

Methods of corporate or organizational cultures

Many research studies have been done to describe the organisational culture all over the world. Some of them are discussed in brief below.

(1) Five dimensions of culture

Hofstede identified five dimensions of culture in his study of national influences. The five dimensions are:

Hofstede (1980) demonstrated that there are national and regional cultural groupings that affect the behaviour of organizations.

He looked for national differences between over 100,000 of IBM's employees in different parts of the world, in an attempt to find aspects of culture that might influence business behaviour.

- **Power distance:** The degree to which a society expects there should be differences in the levels of power. A high score suggests that there is an expectation that some individuals wield larger amounts of power than others. A low score reflects the view that all people should have equal rights.
- **Uncertainty avoidance:** Reflects the extent to which a society accepts uncertainty and risk.
- **Individualism vs. collectivism:** Individualism is contrasted with collectivism, and refers to the extent to which people are expected to stand up for themselves, or alternatively act predominantly as a member of the group of organization. However, recent researches have shown that high individualism may not necessarily mean low collectivism, and vice versa. Research indicates that the two concepts are actually unrelated. Some people and cultures might have both high individualism and high collectivism. For example, someone who highly values duty to his or her group does not necessarily give a low priority to personal freedom and self-sufficiency.
- **Masculinity vs. femininity:** Refers to the value placed on traditionally male or female values. Male values for example include competitiveness, assertiveness, ambition, and the accumulation of wealth and material possessions.

(2) Four classifications of Deal and Kennedy

Deal and Kennedy defined organizational culture as the way things get done around here. They measured organizations in respect of:

(i) Feedback – quick feedback means an instant response. This could be in monetary terms, but could also be seen in other ways, such as the impact of a great save in a soccer match.

(ii) Risk – represents the degree of uncertainty in the organization's activities.

Using the above parameters, they were able to suggest four types of organizational culture:

- **The Tough-Guy Macho Culture:** Here feedback is quick and the rewards are high. This often applies to fast moving financial activities such as brokerage, but could also apply to a police force, or athletes competing in team sports. This can be a very stressful culture.
- **The Work Hard/Play Hard Culture:** It is characterized by a few risks being taken, all with rapid feedback. This is typical in large organizations, which strive for high quality customer service. It is often characterized by team meetings, jargon and buzzwords.
- **The Bet your Company Culture:** It is where big stakes decisions are taken, but it may be years before the results are known. Typically, these might involve development or exploration projects, which take years to come to fruition. Such as oil prospecting or military aviation.
- **The Process Culture:** It occurs in organizations where there is little or no feedback. People become bogged down with how things are done not with what is to be achieved. This is often associated with bureaucracy. While it is easy to criticie these cultures for being overly cautious or bogged down in red tape, they do produce consistent results, which is ideal in, for example, public services.

(3) Charles Handy – Four type culture

Charles Handy (1985) popularized the 1972 work of Roger Harrison of looking at culture which some scholars have used to link organizational structure to organizational culture. He describes Harrison's four types thus:

- **Power Culture** which concentrates power among a few. Control radiates from the centre like a web. Power and influence spread out from a central figure or group. Power derived from the top person and personal relationships with that individual matters more than any formal title of position. Power cultures have few rules and little bureaucracy; swift decisions can ensue.
- **Role Culture,** people have clearly delegated authorities within a highly defined structure. Typically, these organizations form hierarchical bureaucracies. Power derives from a person's position and little scope exists for expert power, controlled by procedures, role descriptions and authority definitions. Predictable and consistent systems and procedures are highly valued.
- **Task Culture,** teams are formed to solve particular problems. Power derives from the expertise as long as the team requires expertise. These cultures often feature the multiple reporting lines of a matrix structure. It is a small team approach, who are highly skilled and specialist in their own markets of experience.
- **Person Culture** exists where all individuals believe themselves superior to the organization. Survival can become difficult for such organizations. Since the

concept of an organization suggests that a group of like-minded individuals pursue the organizational goals. Some professional partnerships can operate as person cultures, because each partner brings a particular expertise and clientele to the firm.

(4) Edgar Schein Model on organisational culture

Edgar Schein, an MIT Sloan School of Management professor, defines organizational culture as: "A pattern of shared basic assumptions that was learned by a group as it solved its problems of external adaptation and internal integration, that has worked well enough to be considered valid and, therefore, to be taught to new members as the correct way you perceive, think, and feel in relation to those problems" (Schein, 2004).

According to Schein, the culture is the most difficult organizational attribute to **change**, outlasting organizational products, services, founders and leadership and all other physical attributes of the organization. His organizational model illuminates culture from the standpoint of the observer, described by three cognitive levels of organizational culture.

At the first and most cursory level of Schein's model is organizational attributes that can be seen, felt and heard by the uninitiated observer – collectively known as **artifacts**. Included are the facilities, offices, furnishings, visible awards and recognition. The way that its members dress, how each person interacts with others and with organizational outsiders, and even company slogans, mission statements and other operational creeds.

The next level deals with the professed culture of an organization's members — the **values**. At this level, local and personal values are widely expressed within the organization. Organizational behaviour at this level usually can be studied by interviewing the organization's membership and using questionnaires to gather attitudes about organizational membership.

At the third and deepest level, the organization's tacit assumptions are found. These are the elements of culture that are unseen and not cognitively identified in everyday interactions between organizational members. Additionally, these are the elements of culture which are often taboo to discuss inside the organization. Many of these 'unspoken rules' exist without the conscious knowledge of the membership. Those with sufficient experience to understand this deepest level of organizational culture usually become acclimatized to its attributes over time, thus reinforcing the invisibility of their existence. Surveys and casual interviews with organizational members cannot draw out these attributes – rather much more in-depth means is required to first identify then understand organizational culture at this level. Notably, culture at this level is the underlying and driving element often missed by organizational behaviorists.

Using Schein's model, understanding paradoxical organizational behaviours becomes more apparent. For instance, an organization can profess highly aesthetic and moral standards at the second level of Schein's model while simultaneously displaying curiously opposing behaviour at the third and deepest level of culture. Superficially, organizational rewards can imply one organizational norm but at the deepest level imply something completely different. This insight offers an understanding of the difficulty that organizational newcomers have in assimilating organizational culture and why it takes time to become acclimatized. Cultural norms are generally not understood before would-be change agents begin their actions. Merely understanding culture at the deepest level may be insufficient to institute cultural change because the dynamics of interpersonal relationships (often under threatening conditions) are added to the dynamics of organizational culture while attempts are made to institute desired change.

Again according to Edgar Shein, there are three levels of corporate culture and they are:

(1) Surface level : At this level, culture is both enacted and reinforced through visible appearances and behaviours, such as physical layouts, dress codes, organisational structure, company policies, procedures, programmes and attitudes.

(2) Middle level: Here, culture is manifested through our beliefs and values.

(3) Deepest level: At this level, culture is manifested through assumptions – our long learned, automatic responses and established opinions.

One of the best examples of corporate culture is Toyota company.

(5) Culture and Organisational Expectations

According to Robert Cooke, in this research: "The Organisational Culture Inventory: Culture Clusters.," defines culture as the behaviours that members believe are required to fit in and meet expectations within their organisation. The organisational culture inventory measures twelve behavioural of norms that are grouped into three types of cultures:

Construction culture	*Passive/Defensive culture*	*Aggressive/Defensive culture*
In this members are encouraged to interact with people and approach tasks in ways that help them, meet their higher order of satisfaction needs.	Here the members believe they must interact with people in ways that will not threaten their own security	In which members are expected to approach tasks in forceful ways to protect their status and security.

(1) Constructive cluster

It includes cultural norms that reflect expectations for members to interact with others and approach tasks in ways that will help them to meet their higher order of satisfaction needs, for affiliations, esteem and self-actualisation.

The four cultural norm clusters are:

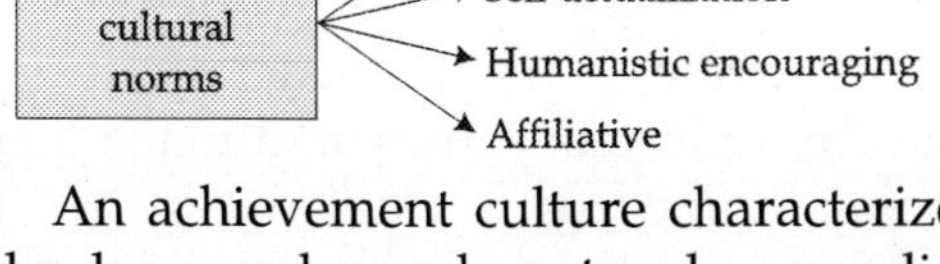

(i) **Achievement:** An achievement culture characterizes organizations that do things well and value members who set and accomplish their own goals. Members are expected to set challenging but realistic goals, establish plans to reach these goals, and pursue them with enthusiasm.

(ii) Self-actualizing: A self-actualizing culture characterizes organizations that value creativity, quality over quantity, and both task accomplishment and individual growth. Members are encouraged to gain enjoyment from their work, develop themselves, and take on new and interesting activities. (thinking in unique independent ways).

(iii) Humanistic Encouraging: A humanistic-encouraging culture characterizes organizations that are managed in a participating and person-centred way. Members are expected to be supportive, constructive, and open to influence in their dealings with one another. (Helping others to grow and develop.)

(iv) Affiliative: An affiliative culture characterizes organizations that place a high priority on constructive interpersonal relationships. Members are expected to be friendly, open, and sensitive to the satisfaction of their workgroup. (dealing with others in a friendly way).

Organisations with constructive cultures encourage members to work to their full potential, resulting in high level of motivation, satisfaction, team work, service quality and sales growth. Constructive norms are evident in environments where quality is valued over quality. Creativity is valued over conformity, cooperation is believed to lead better results than competition, and effectiveness is judged at the system level rather than the component level. These types of cultural norms are consistent with the objectives behind empowerment, total quality management, transformational leadership, continuous improvement, reengineering and learning organisation.

(2) Passive/ Defensive cluster

In this culture cluster, norms that reflect expectations for member to interact with people in ways that will not threaten their own security are in the passive/defensive cluster present.

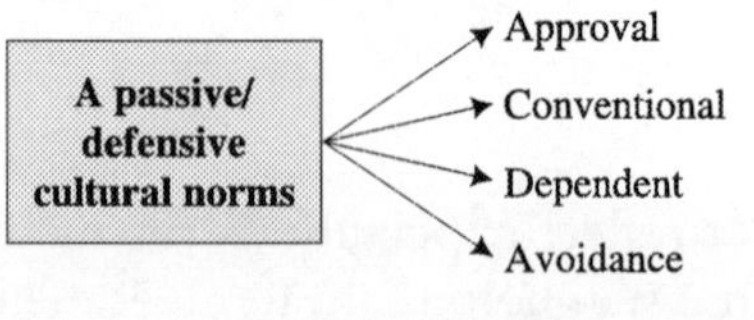

(v) Approval: An approval culture describes organizations in which conflicts are avoided and interpersonal relationships are pleasant at least superficially. Members feel that they should agree with, gain the approval of, and be liked by others. ('going along" with others).

(vi) Conventional: A conventional culture is descriptive of organizations that are conservative, traditional, and bureaucratically controlled. Members are expected to conform, follow the rules, and make a good impression (always following policies and practices).

(vii) Dependent: A dependent culture is descriptive of organizations that are hierarchically controlled and non-participative. Centralized decision making in such organizations leads members to do only. What they are told and to clear all decisions with superiors (pleasing those in positions of authority).

(viii) Avoidance: An avoidance culture characterizes organizations that fail to reward success but nevertheless punish mistakes. This negative reward system leads members to shift responsibilities to others and avoid any possibility of In being blamed for a mistake (waiting for others to act first).

In the organisations with this sort of culture, the members feel pressured to think and behave in ways that are inconsistent with the way they believe they should in order to be effective. People are expected to please others. Particularly the superiors and avoid interpersonal conflict, rules procedures, and others are more important than personal beliefs, ideas and judgement. Passive/defensive cultures experience a lot of unresolved conflict and turnover, and organisational members report lower levels of motivation and satisfaction.

(3) The Aggressive / Defensive cluster

This is third type of cluster includes cultural norms that reflect expectations for members to approach tasks in ways that protect their status and security.

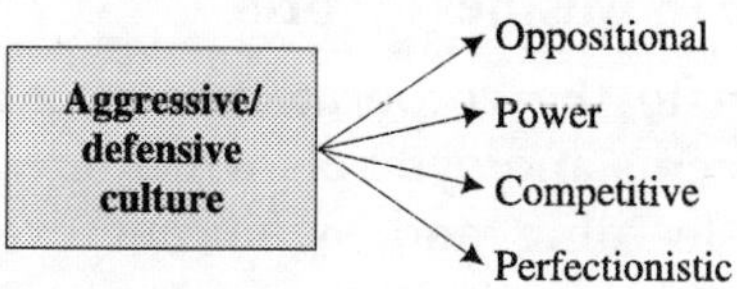

(ix) Oppositional: An oppositional culture describes organizations in which confrontation and negativism are rewarded. Members gain status and influence by being critical and thus are reinforced to oppose the ideas of others. (pointing out flaws).

(x) Power: A power culture is descriptive of non-participative organizations structured on the basis of the authority inherent in members' positions. Members believe they will be rewarded for taking charge, controlling subordinates and, at the same time, being responsive to the demands of superiors. (Building up one's power base).

(xi) Competitive: A competitive culture is one in which winning is valued and members are rewarded for outperforming one another. Members operate in a "win-lose" framework and believe they must work against (rather than win) their peers to be noticed (turning the job into a contest).

(xii) Perfectionistic: A perfectionistic culture characterizes organizations in which perfectionism, persistence, and hard work are valued. Members feel they must avoid any mistake, keep track of everything, and work long hours to attain narrowly defined objectives (doing things perfectly).

Organisations with this type of culture encourage or require members to appear competent, controlled and superior. Members who seek assistance, admit shortcomings or concede their position, are viewed as in competent or weak. These organisations emphasise finding errors, weeding out "mistakes", and encouraging members to compete against each other than competitors. The short term gains associated with these strategies are often at the expenses of long-term growth.

Elements of Entrepreneurial Culture

1. People and empowerment focussed
2. Value creation through innovation and change
3. Attention to the basics
4. Hands-on management
5. Doing the right thing
6. Freedom to grow and to fail
7. Commitment and personal responsibility
8. Emphasis on the future.

Impact of Corporate Culture in Business World

Corporate culture in addition to the corporate vision, goals, shared values, beliefs, habits, working language, systems and symbols which are interwoven with processes, technologies, and also with learning and significant events. In addition, different individuals bring to the workplace their own uniqueness, knowledge and ethnic culture. So **"corporate culture encompasses moral, social and behavioural norms of the organisation based on the values, beliefs, attitudes and priorities of its members."** Corporate culture can be transformed, but leadership to sustain anything that sweeping has to come from the top executives.

The impact of corporate culture based on adoptive culture: In this corporate culture is good only if it fits its context, i.e., business space and business strategy. In today's rapidly changing economy, "Only cultures that can help organisations anticipate and adapt to environmental change will be associated with superior performance over the long term." Research findings show, cultures that are externally oriented (e.g., risk taking, readiness to meet new challenges) tend to be more strongly associated with organisational performance.

Exhibit

A brief note on corporate culture of Toyota

The spiritual centre of Toyota city a huge company turn of 4,00,000 people outside the industrial city of Nagoya. Once in a while, Toyota employees from around the globe come to the company's Toyota city plant near Nagoya, Japan for indoctrination in the "Toyota Way."

The company's commitment to team work is exemplified on the factory floor, where workers grab parts from trolleys that move with the line, one of the time saving innovations proposed by the workers themselves. Slogans written by employees hang from the ceiling, and each production team has its own melody that rings art when a member needs to catch many events attention. Toyota's devotion to Kaizen, or continuous improvement, showing up throughout the company and is a lesson that will serve all managers.

Toyota's global competitive advantage is based on a corporate philosophy known as "Toyota Production System". Toyota's philosophy of **empowering its workers** is the centre piece of a human resources management system that fosters creativity, continuous improvement and innovation by encouraging employee participation, and that likewise engenders high levels of employee loyality.

Impact of Corporate Culture

Culture leads to energise the leaders and groom strategic planners in an appropriate communication and direction. Leaders may stand by examples. In respect of **General Electric** [GE] a popular company, the corporate values are so important, the **Jack Weich,** the former legendary CEO of the company, had them inscribed and distributed to all GE employees, at every level of the company. The sum is greater than its parts at GE both business and people diversity is utilised in most effective way. A major American enterprise with a diverse group of huge business, GE is steeped in learning culture and it makes GE a unique company.

As Jack Welch puts it, "what sets GE apart is a culture that uses diversity as a limitless source of **learning opportunities**, a storehouse of ideas whose breadth and richness is unmatched in world of business. At the heart of this culture is an understanding that an orgnisation's ability to learn, and translate that learning into action competitive business advantages There is a great impact of corporate culture, when it is seriously adopted. Some of them are discussed below.

(i) Impact on winning organisation

Corporate culture will support in formulating winning organisation. Create hot teams, inspire and empower employees, cultivate leaders and so on. It also creates an adoptive organisation. Build a growth culture. Search for synergies, leverages and diversity, etc.

(ii) Impact on setting a common goal

Corporate culture will set a common goal mobilising people around a common goal. Help them feel a part of something genuine, special and important and it will inspire real passion and loyality.

(iii) Impact on Employees

Leadership and business practices are interlinked for attaining competitive advantage. To attain competitive advantage a strong culture in the organisation is required.

Model on competitive advantage

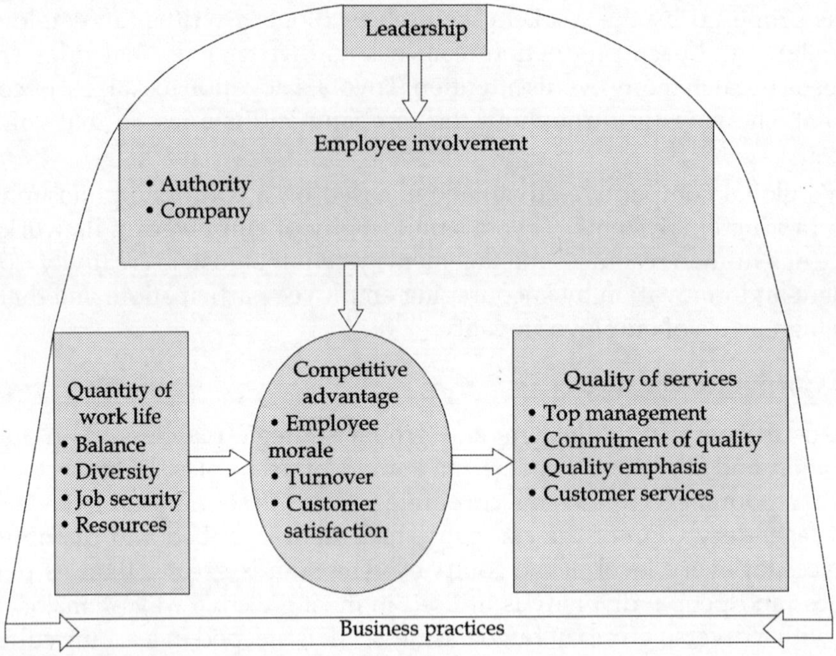

Culture is a strong and adoptive practice in the business without which it will lose its identity in the long run. If the culture starts fading away it is a sign of losing the organisation. Discouraging culture like no shared values, lack of trust, blame culture, focus on problems, no opportunities, diversity which is not celebrated, failures are not tolerated, people start losing confidence in their leaders and system are signs of bad culture. No organisation attains success in business without heart such culture.

Best practice of organisation culture through employees

Employees are main pilliars of the organisation. Their mindset and strong will towards organisation culture will attain the success in the business. There are six golden situations that employees can adopt for a strong culture which are given below:

- Do more than just get by.
- Train and be trained.
- Take advantage of every opportunity.
- Be fair to the company
- Seek solutions and not problems.
- Enjoy your work and smile.

Nature of winning culture

Winning culture is the end result of corporate culture which are mentioned below:

- Inspiring
- Value-based activity
- Strategically aligned
- Adaptive
- Collaborative
- Inclusive
- Team culture
- Diversity friendly
- Improvement oriented
- Quality focused
- Customer oriented
- Competitive.

ELEMENT OF CORPORATE CULTURE

It is of paramount importance in the organisations and adoption of culture is very essential. The culture is to be shaped by eight elements, namely

- Corporate vision
- Shared values
- Beliefs
- Assumptions
- Past experience
- Learning
- Leadership
- Communication.

Selected culture to prepare models in the organisation

- Team culture
- Inspiring culture
- Growth culture
- Adaptive culture
- Competitive culture
- Play it safe culture
- Continuous improvement culture
- Innovation culture
- Quality culture
- Coaching culture
- Questioning culture

Additional suggestions towards corporate culture

(1) There should be close relationship between individual culture and organizational culture.

(2) The organization should be very challenging to use one's talent as a problem solving technique.

(3) The traditional values and practices should be given due respect.

(4) The employees must be identified individually on the basis of their education, experience and skills.

(5) The organization should provide ample opportunities for employees empowerment.
(6) The organization's need to have encouragement for innovation and entrepreneurship.
(7) There must be family values and culture in the organization.
(8) There need to be various stress busting techniques and orientations to the employees to ease their minds.
(9) The organization should always have a helping hand and support the employees in the event of any crisis.
(10) Every individual must be treated equally with a high degree of dignity and goal achievement.

Entrepreneuriship and culture

According to Stephen Mc Guire: "An entrepreneurial organisation culture (EOC) is a system of shared values, beliefs and norms of members of an organisation, including valuing creativity and tolerance of creative people, believing that innovating and seizing market opportunities are appropriate behaviour to deal with problems of survival and prosperity, environmental uncertainty and competitors' threats and expecting organisational members to behave accordingly."

Entrepreneurial culture

The future business scenario is going to be different with newer challenges in each and every field. But like in the past, the wisdom and competence of human resources will be the reckoning force to meet the challenges of new scenario as well. Along with many new cultures, the culture of entrepreneurship will be needed to run business organizations. The human resources development will be needed in building and harnessing the culture of entrepreneurship.

It calls for reorientation of HRD process in transformational strategies for the new millennium. Assuring fit between person and organization is critical to entrepreneurial and creative success. The following steps will be needed for building entrepreneurial cultures.

(1) Encouraging and rewarding entrepreneurial behaviour
(2) Identifying and developing organization specific entrepreneurial competence
(3) Developing creative and innovative skills
(4) Assessing internal and external opportunities
(5) Imbibing motivation directed style
(6) Entrepreneurs as core competency

The presence of entrepreneurship culture can be said to be high in a public sector organization of India if value orientation and behaviour outcome among the managers meet the following criteria:

- **Achievement Directed:** Managers are highly achievement oriented and they take risk.
- **Business Directed:** Managers take initiative to grab opportunities having high business potential for their organization or department/unit.
- **Decision Directed:** Managers take decisions quickly and they involve departments concerned in decision-making process to add value to the decision.
- **Innovation Directed:** Managers pursue to see that their ideas are realized in products, proceses or services.
- **Motivation Directed:** Managers take actions to motivate others to move to new directions.
- **Opportunity Directed:** Managers constantly scan and understand the environment as a source of various opportunities.

Innovation and culture

The dictionary defines innovation as the introduction of something new or different. Innovation is implementation of creative inspiration. The National Innovation Initiative (NII) defines innovation as "the intersection of invention and insight, leading to the creation ·of· social and economic value."

Innovation is fostered by information gathered from new connections: from insights gained by journeys into other disciplines or places: from active, collegial networks and fields, open boundaries. Innovation arises from ongoing circles of exchange, where information is not just accumulated or stored, but created. Knowledge is generated anew from connections that weren't there before".—Margaret J. Wheatley

Innovation is the process of making changes to something established by introducing something new, new idea, method or device.

The term innovation may refer to both radical and incremental changes to products processes or services. The often unspoken goal of innovation is to solve a problem. Innovation is an important topic in the study of economics, business, technology, sociology, and engineering. Innovation is considered a major driver of the economy.

Corporate Culture and Computers

Information technology is an excellent example for innovation, computers and its related functions are the main source of innovation in the business culture.

The impact of culture by the effect of computers has become basic topic for discussion on corporate culture.

The large scale computerisation of white-collar work has altered the very fabric of social behaviour, rituals that used to be social are now machine dictated. Face-to-face communication is more often than not replaced by impersonal electronic exchange. This new white-collar work place culture is different from any that history has ever known.

Traditional cultures were human creations designed to bring meaning to time spent at work. Cultures consisted of thousands of rituals of workday activity, reinforced by peoples telling stories about what so and so had done and what it meant in the grand scheme of things. Routine was punctuated periodically by social gatherings–celebrations of culture values. These reassured people that adhering to cultural practices would serve them in good stead over the long haul. Actions by managers since the early 1980s, as we have noted, have undercut the prevailing belief systems of corporate life. The operative assumption for decades had been, "work hard and stick within the norms of this organisation and you will have job for life or for as long as you want one". The new corporate dictates it clearly, "Look out for yourself and don't trust the organisation to provide you with anything but a temporary job, as long as it serves its purpose to do so".

Around the world, effect of computers is strong and there are a lot of changes in the organisational culture. More than half of the workforce are computer officials in today's organisations. Much of an organisation's cultural life was conducted in informal gatherings coffeestops or in the local pubs. For most people, it worked and gave meaning to the majority of their working hours, which they spent in the workplace. For companies that cared about the social context of the work environment, all this kept the company together and led to superior performance over long time.

Computer-mediated life in the modern corporation

An employee comes to work in the morning. For many employees who do routine work, their daily agenda is dictated by the computers. The employee logs into the appropriate system or file and begins to move forward the daily transactions.

Even with top-end computer technology, a user gets tired. Inevitably, after a couple of hours, it's time for a break. The employee logs off, stretches to ease the strain in back and shoulder muscles, caused by working at a console, and runs off to the kitchen or coffee station. There is no set time for this break. Employees know the quantity of work expected and speed themselves to meet the required standard. As likely as not, there is no one else in the kitchen; cup of coffee in hand, the employee returns to his or her work station alone. The chance for a routine conversation is not a regular part of the break. Sipping coffee/tea the employee checks the company Jokeline to find out the laugh of the day. Then it is time to log back on and get back to work.

Since most modern organisations are saturated with computer technology and each and anything through information technology, the culture of the individual, environment, managers, employees and corporates are entirely changed. There is a transformation from old culture to new culture not only among business houses but also in the society as a whole.

Modern communications capabilities are superb. But how often are they used to reinforce core cultural messages rather than just to communicate the latest corporate downsizing skills associated with working in the modern computerised environment are valuable and transferable.

Computer technology is a double-edged sword. Computers can be used to enhance the skills of workers and broaden their impact on wider field of corporate endeavour. But they can also be used to trap workers in the dead end jobs. There is a lot cross-cultural changes among the corporates. There is a lot of influence of western culture all over the world. The eastern countries especially the people in urban areas are changed to the western culture. The corporates in the western countries have started giving the weightage to eastern culture and values, like replacing systems into human. Even this culture may change into technology culture.

Cross-culture

Cross-culture describes the relationship between individuals and groups of individuals to which they belong. The different countries exchanging their beliefs, knowledge, experiences, practices and values among with other countries is referred as cross-culture. Economic liberalisation and globalisation have opened the doors to the world economy. As a result the investors from different nations started exchanging their products, technology, knowledge, services and so on. This brought a great transformation in the world economy. Cultural exchanges in the business provided a lot of business opportunities and potential for economic growth. There are both individual and collective cultures. Western countries perceive individuals as separate entities, e.g., Canada, Australia. In these countries, individual culture views themselves as independent, self-contained and autonomous. Whereas some of the countries like Hongkong, Korea, individuals are inter-dependent. In these countries they define themselves as collectivist cultures, value relationships, meeting the needs of the group and support transformational leaders efforts to align sub-ordinate values and needs with those of the organisation.

Individualism culture affects reasons for complying with organisational requirements with 'more involvement' in an organisation. Whereas the collective culture enjoys the strong organisational effectiveness through moral involvement. Whereas in respect of individualistic culture, there is calculative involvement. This cross-culture differences are followed for more clarity:

Cross-culture

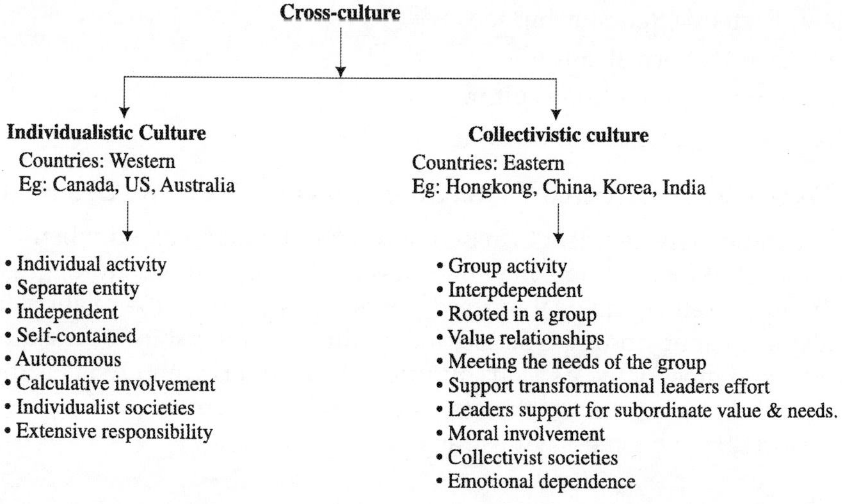

Global organisations should function based on different cultures for their growth, sustainability, continuous improvement and meet competitive advantage. The success in multicultural ventures requires improving the effectiveness of the managers managing these organisations. Managerial style is one of the important dimensions of organisational effectiveness.

In the growing global market, more and more business find themselves confronting new obstacles. Obstacles that can endanger the success of global joint venture. Problems encountered during inter-cultural business interactions lie in the misunderstanding of basic cultural guide lines present in each country. In order to conduct business across cultures, there need to put in effort to understand and work within the culture, guidelines and legal aspects of different countries. Each culture has its own unique way of handling business as well as social interactions and the visitors in particular culture must recognize the difference.

Cultural diversity can never be underestimated. People of different cultures share basic concepts but they view it from different angles and perspectives. As a result one group may behave in a manner which the other may consider irrational or even in direct contradiction of what others hold scred.

Organisations should understand the new culture and its differences, build flexibility, share information and develop collective know-how into worldwide network. Add to these, there need to be communication, negotiation, understanding each other's values of different nations which are dealt with.

The following basic requirements of cross-culture are:

(a) Language (b) Non-verbal communication (c) Space and time orientations (d) Religion and belief system (e) Pattern of thinking (f) Self-image (g) Set of values (h) Material culture (i) Aesthetics (j) Social practices (k) Nature of government and policies.

Richard. R. Gesteland in this book "Cross-cultural Business Behaviour" Expresses various patterns on cross culture as:

- Deal Focus Vs Relationship focus
- Informal Vs Formal culture.
- Rigid time Vs Fluid time culture.
- Expressive Vs Reserved culture.

(1) Deal Focus – Task Oriented Vs Relationship Focus – People Oriented

There will be conflict between deal focussed and relationship focussed when they work together. Relationship focus people may find deal focus people as pushy, aggressive and offensively blunt. In return the deal focused people may point at the relationship focus people as dilatory, vague and inscrutable, for example, relationship focussed countries are Arab world, and most of the African countries, Latin America and Asia Pacific region. Here the personal contacts, trustworthiness play the role in the business. But these people will be uncomfortable in business with strangers.

Whereas the people in countries like Northern Europe, North America, Australia and NewZealand, are relatively open in doing business with strangers. In this, market can initiate contact with the prospective buyer, without any previous relationship or connection. This type of business culture is uncommon in Japan. In Japan, the third party introduction or the customers may get contact through the trade-shows and trade missions and so on.

In deal focus the business relies on written agreements to prevent misunderstandings and solve problems. Relationship focus culture depends mainly on relationship to prevent difficulties and to solve problems and use indirect language, the body language. This makes the difficult communications easy.

(2) Informal Vs Formal culture

Differences in cross-cultural behaviours create invisible barriers to international trade. Variation and verbal and non-verbal behaviour can cause culture clashes, but a skilled interpreter can often smoothen over verbal problems. In respect of formal culture, the business people will not be comfortable with easy going counterparts who are informal. The informal people may see their formal counterparts as stuffy, distant and arrogant. In formal culture the people value status, hierarchy, power and respect. But informal culture status maintains equality. Ignorance of this distinction can cause serious problems across the bargaining table. Formal people consider the way of addressing people as an important way of showing respect to persons of high status. Informal culture is followed by Australia, USA, Canada, New Zealand, Denmark, Norway and Iceland. The formal culture is followed by most of Europe and Asia, the Mediterranean region, Arab world and Latin America.

(3) Rigid-time Vs Fluid-time culture

In rigid time culture, people worship the clock and they follow scheduled worshipping culture. Edward T. Hall used the term "mono-chronic" to describe them. Another culture known as "poly-chronic" culture. Here the people place less emphasis on strict punctuality and are not obsessed with deadlines and scheduling. In these two types of culture there is a conflict as some visitor belonging to rigid culture regard their fluid cultures people as lazy, undisciplined and rude while the later often regards the former as arrogant martinets enclaved by arbitrary deadlines. Nordic, Germanic Europe, North America and Japan have monochronic culture whereas Australia, New Zealand, Russia, most of East Central Europe, Southern Europe, Singapore, Hong Kong, Taiwan, China, South Korea and South Africa have moderating mono-chronic culture. The Arab world, most of Africa, Latin America, South and Southeast Asia have poly-chronic business culture. When mono-chronic and ploy-chronic people have to do the business deal, one needs to put a comfortable margin in scheduling and then maintain a close relationship with his counterparts. Along with verbal communication, non-verbal as well as para-verbal communication causes problems when dealing with the business across culture.

(4) Expressive Vs reserved culture

An expressive person uses different ways verbally, non-verbally or para-verbally to communicate than their more reserved counterparts. This may result in lot of differences, one can harm the best effort to market, sell, negotiate or to manage people across cultures. Countries in the Mediterranean region, Latin Europe and Latin America have a very expressive culture. USA, Canada, Australia, New Zealand, Eastern Europe, South Asia and Africa have a variably expressive culture. But East and South east Asia including India, Nordic Germanic Europe share a very reserved culture. Even the vocal volume and silence have to be adjusted when one from a very expressive culture negotiates with reticient group.

The following table shows the crosscultural behaviours between American and European resulting in main ethical issues.

American Behaviour		*European Behaviour*	
Behaviour (a)	*Believe in (b)*	*Behaviour (a)*	*Believe in (b)*
• Trust more	• Constructive	• Trust less	• Realism
• Make more friends	• Friendly, open	• Have few close friends	• Discretion in depth
• Smoothen differences	• Co-operative	• Dispute difference	• Refining trust through dialogue
• Collaborate easily	• Others will join with their common interest, caspiracies are evil	• Collaborate	• Others will block your cautiously conflicting are normal
• Be optimistic and	• Life is rich	• Be cautious express reservation	• Resource limited
• Seek opportunity	• The right time now	• Act out of purpose	• The right time will show itself
• Mis-business and pleasure	• Life is a continuum	• Separate business and private life	• Everything has its time and place
• Think, act loud Brain storm	• Ideas, the better the product for solution	• Prepare what you say	• Be accountable for your words
• Behave spontaneously	• Free, creative	• Behave logically, rationally	• Mature, responsible
• Decentralised politics	• People can solve their own problems	• Centralised policies	• Controls and limits, ensure every one is cared for
• Do it, theories later	• Be practical	• Theory before action	• Doing it right
• Create open information flow	• Enables the relationship	• Gaurded information flow in direction	• Enables the relationship

Contd...

Contd...

• Take pride in accomplishment	• One becomes some one through doing things	• Take pride in one's self and one's group	• Maintain dignity by living out one's calling
• Attack because of the result	• Getting things done is what counts	• Attack because of the process	• Correctness and style are paramount
• Base authority and hierarchy on accomplishment	• Position exist while they are practical and functional	• Accept hierarchy as based in the nature of things	• Position is based on the kind of person
• Avoid differentiating female and male roles	• Trying to be more fair and egalitarian	• Differentiate male and female roles	• Both men's and women's roles have their own prestige
• Treat children as adult	• Making choices helps them grow up	• Discipline children	• Discipline creates character
• Put freedom and initiative first	• Respecting the individual	• Put duty and obedience first	• Respecting common good
• Forgive mistakes	• Trying is what count you will get	• Avoid mistakes	• Mistakes are often irreparable
• Consume	• Being alive, moving spirit filled	• Be frugal	• Strive for quality not quantity.

Source: Dr. George Simmons (1990), "Transuntra Leadership"

CROSS-CULTURE AND ITS ISSUES IN ETHICS

Cultural diversity is not something that is going to go away tomorrow, enabling to plan the strategies on the assumption of mutual understanding. It is in itself a phenomenon with its own riches, the exploration which could yield in calculate benefits, both in terms of wider vision and more profitable policies and activity. People of different cultures share basic concepts but view them from different angles and perspectives, leading them to behave in a manner which may be considered irrational or even in direct contradiction of what is sacred. The behaviour of people of different cultures is not something willy-nilly. There exist clear trends, sequences and traditions. Reactions of Americans, Europeans and Asians alike can be forecasted, usually justified and in the majority of cases managed.

The corporate today is increasingly multi-cultural. In an environment where markets and competition are globalising. Organisations have to interact, manage, negotiate and compromise with people from different cultures. When working with people whose values and beliefs are very different from one's own can make for costly misunderstanding and even business failures. If ignored or mismanaged, cultural differences can lead to great frustration and ineffectiveness internationally for otherwise successful managers and organisations. When successful managers, however, differences in culture can lead to effective and sustainable sources of competitive advantage.

Cross-cultural challenges and issues

Culture is dominant in the world of human relations. Humans are the only species that have created culture. This teaches, "It is not just what to think, but how to think". Actually, it is this same culture that influences the development of embedded knowledge, beliefs, biases, and prejudices in the limbic brain and will influence learning and cognitive development throughout life. Cultural influences are strong and even dominant in guiding our thought preferences and influences our learning. Strong cultural beliefs distrust toward the citizens of another country, or region can be very difficult to reverse or transfer sufficiently to find a lasting compromise. There are four types of corporate culture as (i) fulfilment oriented culture (ii) project oriented culture (iii) person oriented culture (iv) role oriented culture. These are not mutually exclusive and it is very common to identify overlapping cultures with a perceptible dominant type. Most of business administration and its practices are largely driven by American culture and the same may pose certain problems. The European countries are fully acceptable to the Americans, whereas the Americans are not accepting European culture fully. Europeans see American behaviours as superficial, insincere, lack of conviction, containing hidden agenda, foolishness, aggressiveness. They also say scatter brained undisciplined, irresponsible, immature, no substance, unprincipled, small minded, poor judges of character, debasing both women and men and children are load and intrusive delingment, socially irresponsible, overreaching themselves, wastefulness and quantity over quality and so on.

On the other hand, Americans see Europeans' behaviour as, cynicism, cold, distant, argumentative, distrurstful of each other, pessimistic, out of touch, compartmentalised, cautious, guarded, lacking spontaneity, beureacratic and dictatorial tendencies, impractical. They are also secretive, variety without substance, uncommitted to results. Added to that autocratic, non-democratic, sexist, preserving art moulded tradition, blind obedience, prone to dictatorship, overcautiouns, miss opportunities, smallness, meanings obsessed with thing and not people and so on.

The other issues are cross-cultural behaviour between American and Asian business professionals. There will likely be a very distinct difference in the order in which the information or message is organised. The American is likely to first state the issues and then presents the supporting information. The Asian would likely to present the support facts and conclude with the issue statement (Scollon and Scollen 2001).

There are a lot of issues among Asian countries in respect of cultural behaviours. People's Republic of China was founded in 1949. In late 1970s the new pragmatic leadership adopted economic reform policies to accelerate economic development and took to be opening to the outside world to attract foreign investment into China in 2001. China successfully acceded to the WTO. Now China is firmly committed to economic reforms and opening to the outside world devoting efforts to establish a socialist market economy system in future. In personal relationship and interpersonal favours and cultural values have been considered of great importance as people attach meaning to working and also for understanding organisational behaviour and management.

Overall, with the rapid development in economy, and society in modern China, traditional confucianism and western values are mixed together, which result in the cross-cross vergence of cultural values as well as the complexity of meaning of working among chinese people. The family oriented work values and attention on interpersonal relationship and harmony atmosphere are increasingly becoming blended with individual achievement and personal growth. And contemporary human resource management and development based on scientific theories mixed with traditional culture values is being more and more attentive in China due to Chinese typical situation.

In respect of Germany, the people here consider work as duty and entitlement. Korea is based on modernisation whereas Lekanon is based on family support and difference to authority and United States based on rags to riches.

The organisations dealing with multiple activities of business connected to various countries around the globe should be conscious in handling the cultural values of different people or employees, situation, environment, language, working hours and working conditions. Each and every dimensional variance of the activities must be carefully analysed, and tackled to attain the organisational goals, meet vision and mission and objectives. Proper planning, training, co-ordinating and mutual study of different cultures is essential to meet the competitive advantage in the global economy. There may be cross-cultural exchanges like East meeting West and West meeting East. Flexibility, acceptance of different people with different cultures is the "Mantra for organisational ethics" and success.

OVERVIEW ON DIFFERENT CASES RELATED CULTURE

1. Changing Corporate Image: Reliance Industries

V. Balasubramaniam (Balu), India's foremost lobbyist and the unofficial 'ambassador' of Reliance Industries Limited (RIL) in Delhi was raided on 28 October 1998. Balu's alleged crime: possession of confidential government documents.

When Romesh Sharma, pointsman for Dawood Ibrahim, was arrested on 21 October 1998 in connection with the theft of a helicopter, he informed the police that the papers were with Balu. The police contacted Balu, who invited them to collect the papers. Sharma also informed the police that he was a partner in two companies—Reliance Developers and Investment Private Ltd, and Reliance Estate Private Ltd.

Balu approached Sharma to help Dhirubhai Ambani's son-in-law, Raj Salgaonkar to extricate himself from the problem. Salgaonkar was being threatened by Dawood's henchman, Abu Salem. Balu contacted Salem and resolved the matter.

RIL however denied any connections, contacts or dealings directly or indirectly, with Romesh Sharma and/or any of his associates.

It was the second time that Reliance and the underworld had been intertwined in this way. Earlier, in August 1989, RIL's general manager (PR), Kirti Ambani was arrested in Mumbai for trying to organize the supari killing of Bombay Dyeing Chairman, Nusli Wadia.

Today, the Ambanis are supposed to have transcended the manipulative image they acquired in the 1980s, and become a professionally-run, forward-looking company with a global vision. Anil and Mukesh Ambani try and project the Wharton Business School image.

2. Reputation

Reputation is both a product and a by-product of competition. It depends on a company's uniqueness—on its ability to separate itself from others. Sometimes, being unique, credible, and consistent may lead to imitation by others. Names convey tacit information. They can also have an economic value, e.g., Michael Jordan, the basketball legend became a most sought-after corporate spokesman.

Corporate identity conveys the values and principles of the employees and managers associated with a company. Reputation is the net emotional reaction of customers, investors, employees, and the general public to a company's name.

For instance, in one survey, a perceptual map was drawn for each store and of its reputation. The map used a two-dimensional image, of luxury-thriftiness and tradition-innovation which shows the store's reputation in New York. For instance, Macy's has a reputation for tradition and thriftiness, while Bloomingale has a reputation for luxury and innovation.

Fombrun (1996) considers three elements which constitute reputation: trust, credibility and responsibility.

ORGANISATIONAL CULTURE

A Practice in Wipro through his Founder

Among others, Wipro won the prestigious 'Risk Management Award,' instituted by the *Financial Times The Banker Magazine*. What is that which makes this company so successful? "An obsession for excellence," says Azim Premji, Chairman & Managing Director, Wipro Limited.

Chairman and Managing Director of Wipro, Premji is credited with transforming Wipro, his family's vegetable oil business, into one of the world's foremost software company.

Although one of the richest Indians, he flies economy class and is happiest when hiking, reading or discussing the foundation he has set up to promote primary education.

These are changing times. Yet in the middle of all the changes there is one thing that constantly determines success. Some call it leadership. But it is the single-minded pursuit of excellence.

Excellence endures and sustains. It goes beyond motivation into the realms of inspiration. Excellence can be as strong a uniting force as solid vision.

Excellence does not happen in vacuum. It needs a collective obsession as one will have experienced the benefits of excellence in one's own life. Excellence is a great starting point for any new organisation but also an unending journey. What is excellence? It is about going a little beyond what we expect from ourselves. Part of the need for excellence is imposed on us externally by our customers. Our competition keeps us on our toes, especially when it is global in nature.

But the other driver of excellence is internal. It is found that excellence is not so much a battle you fight with others, but a battle you fight with yourself, by constantly raising the bar and stretching yourself and your team. This is the best and the most satisfying and challenging part about excellence".

How does one create excellence in an organisation? Eight step plan by Azim Premji

First, we create an obsession with excellence. We must dream of it not only because it delivers better results but because we truly believe in it and find it intrinsically satisfying to us.

We must think of excellence not only with our mind but also with our heart and soul. Let us look outside, at the global standards of excellence in quality, cost and delivery and let us not rest till we surpass them.

Second, we need to build a collective self-confidence. Organisations and people who pursue excellence are self-confident. This is because excellence requires tremendous faith in one's ability to do more and in a better way. Unless, we believe we can do better, we cannot.

Third, we must understand the difference between perfection for its own sake and excellence. Time is of essence. Globalisation has made the customer only more impatient. This may seem like a paradox: should we aim for excellence or should we aim for speed?

Excellence is about doing the best we can and speed lies in doing it quickly. These two concepts are not opposed to each other; in fact, speed and timeliness are important elements of quality and excellence.

Fourth, we must realise that we cannot be the best in everything we do. We must define what we are or would like to be best at and what someone else can do better.

Excellence is no longer about being the best in India. It is about being the best in the world. We have to define what our own core competencies are and what we can outsource to other leaders. Headaches shared are headaches divided.

Fifth, we must create processes that enable excellence. Today, there are a number of global methods and processes available whether it is Six Sigma, CMM or ISO. Use them because they are based on distilled wisdom collected from the best companies in the world.

Also, we must build a strong foundation of information technology, because in this complex, dynamic world, it is imperative that we use the most modern tools to keep processes updated.

Sixth, we must create a culture of teaming. I have found that while great individuals are important, one cannot have pockets of excellence. Quality gives ample opportunities to build a culture of teaming. Cross-functional teams that are customer facing can cut through an amazing amount of bureaucracy, personal empire building and silos and deliver savings that one would not have imagined possible.

The other advantage of building teams focussed on quality is that the teaming culture eventually spreads to the rest of the organisation and teaming becomes a way of life.

Seventh, invest in excellence for the future. Future always seems to be at a distance. But it comes upon you so suddenly that it catches you by surprise, if not shock. What constitutes excellence in the future will be significantly different from what it is today.

In these days of severe market pressures, there is big temptation to sacrifice the future to look good in the present. We must certainly trim our discretionary expenses, but we must ensure that our investments in strategic areas that lead to excellence in the future are protected.

Finally, excellence requires humility. This is especially needed when we feel we have reached the peak of excellence and there is nothing further we can do. We need an open mind to look at things in a different way and allow new inputs to come in.

Otherwise, there is a real danger of becoming complacent or even downright arrogant. I would like to end my talk with a story that illustrates this very well.

A brilliant young professor went to meet a famous Zen master to have a discussion with him on Zen. He found himself in front of a modest house. He rang the doorbell and waited. A while later, he heard shuffling footsteps and the door was opened by the Zen master.

He invited the professor to sit with him on the dining table. The professor was a little disappointed with the shabby appearance of the Zen master. He started quizzing him immediately on comparative philosophies and the Zen master gave some brief answers.

When the professor began to debate with him on those answers, the Zen master stopped speaking and kept smiling at him. Finally, the professor got angry. He said, "I have come from a long distance just to understand the relevance of Zenism. But apparently you have nothing to say. I have not learnt anything from you at all."

At this point, the Zen master asked the professor to have some tea. When the professor held the cup, the Zen master started pouring tea into it. After some time, the tea started spilling and the professor shouted, "Stop! The cup can contain no more."

The Zen Master stopped and then, once again smiling, he said, "A mind, full of itself can receive nothing. How can I speak to you of Zenism until you empty your mind to learn." The professor understood and apologized to the Zen master. He parted from the Zen master as a wiser man.

ORGANIZATIONAL CULTURE AND MANAGERIAL ETHICAL BEHAVIOURS

Within national cultures, there are also variations in organizational cultures but of course there is some relationship between the two. One example of variance in organizational cultures within a country, where, the differences in the organizational cultures of Sony and Mitsui in Japan were described. Mitsui is a company that is several hundred years old but Sony was created just after World War II, and their respective situations were quite different. Mitsui is far more bound by traditional Japanese thinking than is Sony. The culture of an organization reflects the patterned way of thinking, feeling, and reacting that exists in that organization. Thus, the organizational culture might be viewed as the modal organization personality (Hofstede, Nevijen, Ohayv, & Sanders. 1992). Organizational culture helps to create a certain homogeneity of behaviour within an organization. It does this in a variety of ways, for example, by providing norms for what types of people and behaviour are appropriate for the organization.

Much of organizational culture involves codes of unethical behaviour, whether written out in a formal way or existing by informal understanding (Ott, 1989). Such culture is also manifested in a wide variety of formal company management approaches and in the extensive informal reinforcement activities that take place daily, such as the informal or formal mentoring programmes of a company. Once established, the culture of a company tends to perpetuate itself and is not easy to change. Some of this inertia is due to the fact that the culture determines who will be pre-selected and hired. how they are to be socialized, and how deviates will be removed (Sathe. 1985).

Although organizational culture will reflect national culture to some degree, there is a great deal of variation within a national culture. Even in countries with a very strong national culture, such as Japan, there can be extensive differences between companies such as Sony and Matsushita. Of course, virtually all organizational cultures within a nation will be at least somewhat congruent with national cultures; if they are, not, then certain negative consequences such as low job satisfaction among organizational members is likely to be the result (Triandis, 1994). DeGeorge (I993) has described how organizational cultures can significantly influenced the ethical behaviours of managers. He points out that sometimes there are ethical ideals in the organizational culture and at other times no such guides. Organizational cultures in which efficiency is overemphasized may detract from considerations such as ethical behaviour.

Thus, the behaviour of managers is influenced by both national culture and organizational culture. The relative importance of these two sources in influencing the behaviour of managers is not precisely known, but one estimate by Hofstede (Hofstede et al., 1992) indicates that organizational culture might account for about 30% of the variation in the individual behaviour of managers within a society. One basic difficulty that multinational companies face is that of preserving their organizational cultures across national borders (DeGeorge, 1993). Although there is generally some correspondence between a national culture and an organizational culture, in international operation this may not be the case.

There is a variety of ways to classify differences in organizational culture. A study by Hofstede et al. (1992) on 10 firms located in Holland and Denmark identified some differences in organizational culture that would appear to be especially instrumental in explaining managerial ethical behaviours. The following critical organizational cultural differences were identified in this study:

1. *A process versus a result orientation:* In the process orientation, there is a primary concern with how something is done and an expectation that if things are done according to prescription, then the results will be satisfactory. The results orientation, on the other hand, focus on the results obtained without much regard to how they were achieved.
2. *A loose control versus a tight control orientation:* Tight control firms are characterized by many formal practices and policies that act to restrict and control the behaviour of organizational members. Loose control organizations obviously allow employees considerable latitude.
3. *An employee orientation versus job orientation:* The difference is focused on the value and importance placed on people versus the work to be done. An organization with a high employee orientation emphasizes helping employees and fulfilling their needs.
4. *Achievement versus avoidant orientation:* In the achievement-oriented firms, there are very high expectations for performance and also policies and practices that facilitate them. In avoidant organizations, there tends to be a higher prevalence of safe and passive practices.
5. *Open communication versus closed communication orientation:* There is a much higher degree of information sharing in a firm emphasizing open communication between individuals; levels, and superiors and subordinates.
6. *Customer orientation versus internal orientation:* In firms with customer orientation, there would obviously be a closeness to the customer and a strong desire to meet customer needs. The firms with an internal orientation tend to be less flexible in dealing with customers and more inclined to demand strict adherence to inviolable rules.

These differences are likely to affect the choice of management practices and thus have ethical implications. One would expect, for example, that firms with a result orientation as opposed to a process orientation would have more ethical problems. It can also be hypothesized that firms with loose controls would have more ethical problems. Organizational cultures with a higher respect for people should have fewer ethical problems in personnel matters than their counterparts. Also, firms with very high people orientations may create very strong firm loyalties, which may cause their members to put the organization's interests above those that might be best for outside groups such as customers. Achievement-oriented cultures probably have more ethical problems than avoidant cultures. Open communication cultures should have fewer ethical problems than closed communication cultures, for we would expect less suppression of such problems by organizational members. Finally, we might expect that highly customer-oriented firms may actually have more ethical problems than firms with an internal orientation. This is because such firms may be motivated to meet customer demands by unethical means, as compared to firms that see company rules as inviolable.

"Whatever a gerat person does is followed by others, people go by example persons set up."

—Bhagavat Gita

7

Chapter

Perception and Practices of Marketing in Business Ethics

There are many researches, which lead to a more complete and scientific understanding of social responsibility in marketing and marketing ethics (Donald – P. Robin). Corporates should follow ethics in marketing, if not, society will suffer. Hence, it is necessary for corporates to follow ethics in marketing. The practice of integrity, honesty, dignity in the marketing activity, treating the consumer with dignity and respect by not cheating them, not forcing the customers to purchase the product, fairness in marketing activities such as product, pricing, advertisements, sales and distribution are some of the ethical practices in marketing. Deception, false promises, non-disclosure of the product defects, misleading labels, exorbitant packages, price discounting, unclear printing of pricing, advertisements on socially abused products, uncultured and immoral advertisements, misleading advertisements, high pressure persuasion on customers are some of the unethical practices in marketing. Generally, it is expected that any of the marketing activities based on laws are ethical. Ethics and law go hand in hand. But in some cases ethics is beyond law. To determine an activity to be ethical there must be legal and ethical foundation in marketing. The following are some of the laws connected to marketing activities:

A. Relating to Consumers

- The Consumer Protection Act, 1947.
- The Drugs and Cosmetic Act, 1940.
- The Essential Commodities Act, 1955.
- The Drug and Magic Remedies (Objectionable Advertisement) Act, 1954.

B. Relating to Pricing and other Marketing Practices

- Monopolies and Restrictive Trade Practices Act, 1969.
- The Bureau of India Standard Act, 1986.
- Prevention of Food and Adulteration Act, 1947.
- Weights and Measures Act, 1976.

C. Relating to the General Public

- The Environment (Protection) Act, 1986.
- The Protection of Civil Rights Act, 1955.
- The Indian Penal Code 1860.
- The Agriculture Produce (Grading and Marketing) Act, 1937.

D. Relating to Other Activities

- The Trade and Merchandise Marks Act, 1958.
- The Indian Contract Act, 1872.
- The Sale of Goods Act, 1930.
- The Specific Relief Act, 1963.

Ethics in marketing is discussed below with following headines

(i) Ethics in marketing related to laws.
(ii) Ethics in marketing related to fairness in marketing.
(iii) Ethical issues in marketing related to products.
(iv) Ethical issues in marketing related to pricing.
(v) Ethical issues in marketing related to advertisement.
(vi) Ethical issues in marketing related to sales and distribution.
(vii) Summary of relationship of different corporate sectors studied through 'F'-Test and Chi-Square test.

Reseach outcome on laws relating to different aspects of marketing

Laws relating to business activities other than marketing activities like the Trade and Merchandise Marks Act and Sale of Goods Acts are practised more by the corporates, next to this, are law towards pricing and practices.

Corporate priority of law related to customer

- Between private limited and public sector companies, the practice of law towards customer is comparatively higher but they differ in practice. The Consumer Protection Act, the Drugs and Cosmetics Act, the Drug and Magic Remedies Act were in dominant practice among corporate sectors. Most among them were pharmaceutical companies.
- The practice of law towards customers by multinational companies and public limited companies is more or less the same. Further, the public limited companies show higher performance level with regard to the Essential Commodities Act, than multinational companies.
- However, the performance of law towards customers of different corporates show the non-signification level through the 'F' value.

Corporates priority of law towards pricing and other marketing practices

- Between public sector and public limited companies the performance level is comparatively equal but they differ in some respects. The public sector shows more performance towards the Weights and Measures Act than the public limited companies, whereas with respect to the Prevention of Food and Adulteration Act, the public limited companies show more performance than public sector companies.
- Between multinational companies and private limited companies, multinational show more performance level in the Bureau of Indian Standard Act than private limited companies. Whereas with respect to the Prevention of Food and Adulteration Act and the Weights and Measures Act, private limited companies perform better than multinational companies.
- The overall performance level of different corporates on law with respect to pricing and marketing activities are the same and the difference is insignificant.

Corporates priority level of practising law towards general public

- Between public sector companies and multinational companies the practice of law towards general public can be placed at a higher level, however they differ to some extent. The public sectors perform high performance in respect of the Environment (Protection) Act, and the Indian Penal Code than the multinational companies.
- Between private limited companies and public limited companies, the private limited companies show a higher level in practice of law like, the Environment (Protection) Act and the Protection of Civil Right Act than public limited companies.
- The overall comparison between the different corporate practices of law towards general public is insignificant.

Corporates priority of law towards other activities

- There is a variation between the public sector and multinational companies with respect to the performance of law relating to other activities, namely, the Indian Contract Act, the Sale of Goods Act and so on, whereas the variation is insignification. However, they differ in practice, regarding the law relating to the Indian Contract Act, the Specific Relief Act, and the performance level is high by public sector and low with regard to multinational companies.
- Between public limited companies and private limited companies the performance levels differ with respect to law relating to the Trade and Merchandise Marks Act, on this, public limited companies show higher performance than private limited companies.
- However, all corporates show the some level of performance with respect to law on other activities like the Sales of Goods Act.

- The 'F' value reveals that the overall performance of different corporates with respect to the law mentioned above is non-significant.

Facts/Practice through interpretation on

1. Corporate response towards adequacy of law with respect to marketing activities

- As the attitudes towards law among different corporates vary there is a relation level of attitude to certain extent between private limited companies and multinational companies. The attitude on adequacy of laws relating to the consumers, prices, general public, the private limited companies are on high opinion than multinational companies, and multinational companies are not happy over the functioning and adequacy of law. This is upheld by some of the corporates through their expressions as: *"Law is an agency without teeth"* (Toyota) *"legal processes are mere formality, the customer must establish their rights without emotions, any defect in the product they should demand for the product replacement directly to the companies instead of complaining in the customer courts"* (AKAI). *"The law and regulatory bodies are not proper because a person who is not following law is the officer and the same person will question the corporate officials, regarding the practices of Laws."*
- The public limited and public sector companies are related to certain levels with respect to attitude towards law. However, they differ a lot in their attitude towards the adequacy of law with respect to laws related to the prices and the general public. Public limited companies show high attitude levels with respect to prices and general public. One of the corporates said *"we follow Minimum Wages Act and no child labour is entertained"* (Arvind Mills) and public sector companies show low attitude levels as they express their opinion as *"for every six months laws keep on changing with respect to Essential Commodities Act"* (HPC), *"practice of law is not conducive to hospitals/education, law is very loose"* (KAPL).
- The statistical result reveals that the differences in the attitude level of different corporates like public sector, public companies, private companies and multinational companies are insignificant (1.82), but in reality the attitudes differ. This will be proved by some of the statements expressed by the corporates like *"None of the laws are applicable to the Indian citizen "*(BPL). *"our company is very rigid towards law as the law is very peculiar"* (Gokuldas). *"Law in India is very expensive"*(NTC). *"The most we value determined by law every individual should do some sort of social services, there must be steps to improve the pollution"* (Bal Pharma). *"In the legal opinion, the human system cannot be explained"* (Broun and Burk). *"Law does not have teeth and not fully compromises"* (Rallis India). *"Law needs to be transparent and clearly defined and law relating to customer need is to be more specific"* (Sonal Garment). *"Laws and acts do not make us to be consolidation"* (Toyota).

2. Corporates attitude on fairness in various marketing activities

- Both the private limited companies and multinational companies show high attitude level with respect to fairness in the practice of marketing activities, however, they differ slightly with some of the factors in the practice of law, unfair behaviour, integrity, honour and customer problems and so on. The public limited companies stand on a little higher level than the multinational companies with respect to the opinion that ethics and law should go hand in hand. As one of the multinational companies said that *"law is an agency without teeth* "(Ravindra Toyota), in practice on unfair behaviour in marketing as one of the corporate points it out as *"integrity and transparency are our promise and the component of our marketing activities"* (Wipro). The public limited companies show more interest than multinational companies.
- Even though the difference in the attitude level between the public sector and the private limited companies are more or less the same, still there is a slight difference. The public sector shows a high attitude with respect to marketing responsibility for the consequences of their activities and establishment of firm procedure in determining the customer problems than private limited companies. With respect to ethical problems not to refer to the legal department and not to force customers to purchase the products, the private limited companies show higher attitude level than public sector companies.
- The statistical result to measure the different attitude on fairness in marketing by the different corporate through 'F' value shows non-significant. This is confirmed by some of the corporates expressing their opinions like *"there is transparency and uncompromising quality"* (Akai), small retailers are unethical *"there must be buyers markets"* (HMT), *"sellers market is bad, consumers and others must be given a chance"* (KAPL), *"We induce the customer to purchase and not to force them"* (Micro Lab), *"never please the customer at the cost of displeasure with other customers"* (Medreich Sterilab), *"Ethics in marketing cannot be 100% true"* (I.T.I), *"we believe a lot in customer relation"* (Coats India), *"we go by value and we don't give false promises"* (HPC), *"no lies in marketing"* (Arvind Mills), *"customer service is our motto, we conduct a training for inhaling, since we have to pay back to the customer and we must be 100% ethical"* (Astrazeneca), *"in marketing there must be ethics"* (Shahi Export), *"To follow 100% ethics in marketing is difficult because of the competitions, we never curb competitions, we try to be ethical to our customer"* (Philips India).

3. Corporates responses on opinion on ethical issues in products

- The public sector companies show high performance than multinational companies in case of product satisfaction, misleading the consumers through false promises and much of labelling giving misleading information about the product. The public sector companies show more concern over the product satisfaction, they mislead the consumers through false promises and much of the labelling gives misleading information about the product than multinational companies.

- The public limited companies show a high performance level comparatively with private limited companies with respect to product satisfaction, avoiding of product connected to public sentiments, unsafe products, product boycott. Again the private companies have strong opinions on misleading information on product labels and on packages causing environmental pollution, than the public limited companies.
- The differences on overall attitude towards ethical issues in products by the difference corporates are not significant.

4. Corporate response on fairness in pricing

- Between public limited and public sector companies show more performance level with respect to legal provisions. Both of them do agree that there must be practices of the Monopolies and Restrictive Trade Practice Act, whereas public limited companies agree to follow the Bureau of Indian Standard Act.
- Multinational companies show keen interest on following the MRTP Act than the private limited companies and private limited companies are much interested in the Bureau of Indian Standard Act than multinational companies.
- With respect to fairness in pricing the public sector and multinational companies show high opinion on pricing level, however they show slight variation as public sector shows a high opinion with respect to few competitors who will set the pricing and not following the nature, purpose and effect judgement on unit pricing and the unclear printing of pricing on the product. Multinational companies are of high opinion on price discounts as being beneficial to the business and not to the consumer.
- As one of the corporates say *"in pricing the profit should not be the motive all the time but it should be a part of the business and totally to the customer's satisfaction. Pricing is not a one time market"* (MSIL).
- Between the private limited and public limited companies, the private limited companies show high opinion on price discounting as being beneficial to the business and not to the consumers, not to reduce the prices due to the competitors and so on, more than public limited companies.
- The overall opinion on legal provision and opinion and practices on fairness in pricing and ethical issues in pricing are the same by all the corporates. They favour the issue of fairness in pricing as some of them say *"we give value for money and customers should be created with post purchase feeling"* (Philips India Ltd). *"In our company pricing is fixed on the basis of activity based costing"* (BPL), *"pricing is fixed on the basis of customer psychology"* (Bata India), *"It need not to tell everything to the customer. Sometimes the pricing can be kept hidden"* (NTC). They show a slight difference however the difference is insignificant.

5. Corporate responses towards opinion and practices on ethical issues in advertising

- Between multinational companies and public sector companies, the multinational companies show high practising level and very close to this is the public sector companies. They slightly differ from the opinion on advertising products must be based on legal provisions as legal measures have little effect in controlling the advertisement. As one of the corporate admits it as *"In India there are checks and balances, the problem in India however, is lack of education and lack of awareness"* (IBM) than the public sector companies. However, in some respects the public sector companies which have a high opinion on practising also show a high degree of controlling unfair advertisement copies (like surrogate advertisement) (UB) i.e. advertisement of not accepted products through accepted products (Kingfisher mineral water), advertisement focused on children is unfair as one of the public sector corporate expresses as, *"no single media is especially adopted to the children. Children are becoming more of Robots, they lose human feeling, too much is given towards technology, children are very much attached to the bad things"*(MSIL). Another opinion like *"the models must be morally aware otherwise they will have an undesirable impact on the younger generation"* this is supported by one corporates under the public sector by expressing *"women are not commodities, they are human beings and the good quality of the product need not be advertised at the cost of women who are exploited by the media"* (MSIL).
- Private limited companies show more concern regarding targeting children on advertisement, moral awareness of both men and women models than public limited companies. But the public limited companies show more awareness on legal provisions on advertisement and publicity than the private limited companies.
- The response on the ethical issues in advertisement with respect to opinion and practices are very encouraging as they put it as *"advertising is a powerful promotion tool and message and the medium should be objective"* (IBM) *"advertising is compressive and customers are the best advertisers"* (HPC) *"When there is permission to clubs, why restrictions on advertisement, there must be separate place for smokers and it can be called* 'smoking zone' *or place for smokers and like bar and this is followed in western countries"* (KS and DL) *"promotion planning is also done on practical basis and it is done on all technology and our product is very friendly"* (LG), *"our advertisements are value oriented, we never mislead the customers, our advertisements are very decent and family oriented"* (Philips India). There are some corporates who are not happy about some of the opinions and practices of advertisement like *"National culture will be weak if the advertisement made to change"* (Micro Lab), *"there is no control over private channel"* (BPL), *"In our country, many of the private firms are unethical"* (I.T.I), *"With respect to under- garments it has to face the outside world and it should be checked and most important is clothing is very close to the nature"* (Coats of India), *"Advertisement is nothing but touching person-*

al feeling of the customers, ethics is involved very less in advertising, we have to bother for the personal feelings" (NTC) *"In India advertisement is not maintained properly, Law is not proper and misleads the customers"* (Astra Zencea), *"Advertising like 'Coke' and other soft drinking have lot of unethical acts and they try to connect with other products"* (Asian Paints), *"there is too much of exposure on women in advertisements, there are better way of advertising the products, the whole family should view the advertisement"* (Li and Fung), whatever may be the positive or negative opinion on advertisement and its ethical issues the statistical result through 'F' value reveals the difference in opinion and practices of different corporate sectors are non-significant.

6. Corporate response towards practices of ethical and opinion on ethical issues towards sales and distribution

- Between private limited and public limited companies, the private limited companies have a higher level of opinion with regard to *"sales people are boundary spanners to the corporate and do not act independently"*, *"salesman will exert high pressure persuasion on customers"* and *"sales people work under the pressure of the corporate where the consumers are not benefited"* than the public limited companies. Whereas the public limited companies have a high opinion regarding *"relationship marketing"*, *"Sales representatives misrepresentation"* and *"the retailers charging high prices to the consumers"*, than the private limited companies.
- Between public sector and multinational companies who show less level of opinion and practices statistically, with that of private limited and public limited, the public sector companies show high opinion on *"sales people generally receives very little training"* than multinational companies. However, multinational companies are of high opinion on practicing *"relationship marketing"*, *"salesmen do not misrepresent the product"* and *"training to treat the customers equally in their organization"* than the public sector units supporting to this one of the multinational companies corporate expresses it as, *"In IT industry, where the vendors and the buyers are knowledgeable and educated, training of salesman in presenting facts and putting them with objectivity leaves no room for unethical practices"* (IBM).

CODE OF ETHICS

In India research study on ethics in general and business ethics in particular are not many. Few studies on integrated business ethics and marketing have been done. This is dealt with one of the research study on corporate social responsibility business ethics and ethics in marketing activities. The outcome of the same has been discussed below:

Good ethics and good business are synonyms from the moral, legal and practical point of view. Business ethics is science of conduct. Corporates are to be regarded as social institutions with ethical principles and rules of conduct that reflect their dignity, authority and social responsibility.

Keeping these facts in view, some of the principles are suggested to prepare code of ethics. The suggestions are based on references from relevant books, articles, journals, academicians, self (researcher),

Some of the Principles:

(i) General

- Recognise the concept of corporate responsibility in the widest sense with obligations to the community as well as customers and employees.
- Usher in a spirit of healthy competition in business without suppressing the voice of competitors.
- Develop corporate mission, long-term vision, credo, state business objectives and strategies that focus on customers, government, shareholders and society.
- Optimise the core values of good citizenship in organization.
- Adopt sound ethical business and marketing practices.

(ii) In Particular

In the area of marketing activities

Marketers must accept responsibility for the consequences of their activities and make every effort to measure their decisions, recommendations and functions in order to identify, serve and satisfy all relevant to customers, organisations and society. The marketing activities must be based on the following:

- Substitute buyers market with the sellers market (essential goods).
- Achieve market leadership by customer satisfaction through products and services of international excellence.
- Develop and adopt marketing culture like transparency, honesty, integrity, discipline, human dignity and esteem.
- Create relationship marketing for sound business and prosperity of the customers.
- Practice the various legal provisions in marketing.
- Avoid deceptions, false promises, misleading and unfair activities in the marketing sector.
- Consciously integrate and interact with the departments of the organisation so as to ensure smooth functioning of the company.
- Arrange a contact of marketers with other areas of organisation in which they have contact.
- Protect the customers right to safety, to choose, be informed and be heard of their grievances.
- Optimise "after sales services" in an attempt to build good relationships with customers.
- Stop privileging certain customers at the cost of displeasing other customers.

- Develop code of ethics in marketing and arrange for programmes on ethics for marketing managers.
- Learn ethical theories as an analytical tool for dealing with ethical problems in marketing.
- Emphasise the importance of Consumer Courts, Consumer Redressal Forums to meet the customers expectations of appropriate ethical behaviour.
- Prepare checklists that act as self *regulatory* tools in the marketing activities.
- Set up a Department of Ethics attached to legal department or human resource department of the organization.

In the area of product and product promotion

- Products and services should meet customer satisfaction and establish relationship based on integrity and trust.
- Develop and maintain total quality in product development and production.
- Develop the product to meet customers' needs in time, satisfy the customers through fair product pricing, product quality and product safety.
- Ensure a continuous improvement in product production and development.
- Ensure the corporate specifications remain fully competitive in the market in which it operates.
- Get ready for the product recall from the market if the product is harmful and unsafe to the customers.
- Avoid producing socially controversial products harmful to society and physical environment (alcohol, cigarettes and gutkha).
- Avoid false promises and misleading promises on product quality usage and services.
- Take immediate legal action in checking the spurious products in the market.
- Arrange for appropriate product packages which is optimally priced. .
- Make sure that warning labels and instructions are clearly visible on product packages.
- Avoid the products which are not environment friendly.
- Prepare a strong code of conduct and ethics for products production.
- Determine the pricing policy on the basis of legal provisions.
- Formulate an ethical way of fixing the price on the basis of cost and competitive perceived value.
- Determine the price depending upon scalability, reliability and upgradeability, brand products and material acceptance.
- Maintain fair prices and not vary on the basis of competition.
- Create customer satisfaction through fair pricing policy.
- Avoid unclear printing of prices.

- Avoid misleading prices, tags through marketing practice such as 'sale every day', 50% OFF half price sale, and clearance sale, etc.
- Avoid too much of disparity between wholesalers and retailers through fixing maximum and minimum price.

In the area of advertisement

Advertisement is a powerful tool to fulfill society's dreams, ambitions and goals. It tends to reflect the prosperity and standards of living of a country. Critics of advertising accuse advertisements of being immoral and a parasitical force which exalts false values and induces people to buy things they may not need to or cannot afford it The corporates should be responsible in advertisement by adopting the following suggestions:

- Frame principles for strong self-regulatory body to act within the purview of Advertising Council of India.
- Develop advertisements based on ethical systems at the level of external as well as personal systems. At the external level it can be based on mandatory institutional codes, guidelines, formal regulations and organisational procedures. At the personal level emphasis should be placed on human judgement and moral values.
- Promote social welfare and modify attitudes and behaviour of the receiver of the message.
- Control puffery, deception and misleading advertisements and, communicate only factual information.
- Avoid advertisements threatening national culture and existing social set-up.
- Avoid highlighting strong social values of family, culture, brotherhood with socially controversial products
- Avoid surrogate advertisement in advertising socially controversial products (e.g., mineral water, apple juice).
- Avoid targeting children in advertisements which exploit their innocence.
- Avoid advertisement copy based on excessive and irrational exposure of women which lowers the dignity of women and treat, them as objects of sex.
- To train models both men and women on moral awareness, failing which they would have an undesirable impact on the younger generations and society.
- Develop more use of selective relevant humour containing moral family values and culture in their advertisements. These factors enhance the value of advertisements and appeal to all.
- Arrange for consumer education in the Indian context.
- Avoid too much of exaggeration, aggressiveness and irrationability in advertisement copy, otherwise it will have a negative impact on younger generation (toys like pistol, guns, etc,).
- Regulate private television channels and avoid advertisements which are not morally acceptable.

- Regulate advertising industry and work in tandem with media agencies and government bodies.

In the area of sales and distribution

Studies and situations show that business in India will be dominated by retail business in manufacturing and services sectors. They serve as a vital link between the customer and the company. The following points can be considered by the corporates to prepare a code of ethics in this area:

- Develop a sound training programme to the sales managers and sales persons in order to understand consumers mind, needs as well as promote sales.
- Avoid high pressure persuasion on customers.
- Arrange for moral awareness to the retailers and other business persons as many of their activities may be unethical.
- Promote direct sales to the customer to understand his needs and serve better.
- Promote relationship marketing both in product and service.
- Train that the sales representatives do not present the product to the consumers in order to please the company and to improve sales.
- Avoid misrepresenting customers through seconds sale and clearance sale which will dupe the customers with substandard products.

Implementing tool for code of ethics in an organization (action plan)

The objective of business is not only to earn profit but also to ensure the welfare and happiness of people. As corporates are not mere business institutions they are also unique institutions vested with the responsibility of changing socio-economic structure. The corporate should act according to the environmental factors consisting of social, legal and ethical factors. It is advisable that the corporate can make use of the research study and adopt the recommendations with action plans (tools for implementation) into their practices, which will help in bridging the gap between the perception and practice.

- Follow "positive attitude oriented approach", calm and stability of mind through yoga, meditation, transitional course, mind resting programmes before formulating or altering company's programmes, policies, rules, decisions, strategies and the like.
- Appropriate training programme and awareness for Total Quality Management (TQM), through suitable techniques to develop organisational mission, vision, values, culture, commitments, devotion and promotions.

  Establish good culture of developing relationship among employees through:

  (a) Job security — avoid 'hire and fire' practices.

  (b) Flexible working hours.

  (c) Flexible organizational structure.

  (d) Awareness about corporate performance.

  (e) Awareness about business goals.

- Establish family values and work culture through:
  - (a) Employee involvement and development schemes (EIDS).
  - (b) Evaluate employee suggestions.
  - (c) Evaluate employees current skills and knowledge levels. Identify gaps between current training and ethical training.
  - (d) Provide the cross-cultural training to employees by contacting various other organisation employees to visit and orient about their organisational culture and vice versa.
  - (e) Evaluate and improve training programmes every year.
- The organisational effectiveness can be ensured through:
  - (a) Creating work ethics and culture through Total Quality Management, Time Management, Production Management and the like.
  - (b) The work culture should be based on time where the hoarding of,

"Time and devotion
lead to promotion"
and
"Think twice and ask for advice" to be displayed.

- A strong mind of corporate social responsibility through:
  - (a) Matching of mind and action *"one mind and one word"* should be the policy.
  - (b) Establish link between perception and practice through *"think good and act good"* policy.
  - (c) Frequent discussion on ethical dilemmas and decisions.
- Involving employees for community development programmes through:
  - (a) Arranging for blood donation camps in the organization.
  - (b) Health services through pictures, community service programmes like AIDS awareness programmes and slides and films on AIDS, alcohol and cigarettes.
  - (c) Arranging frequent orientation, awareness and training classes on mind resting, siddha samadhi yoga, vipassana — a meditation technique and stress management classes and develop human values.
- Encouraging customers and suppliers to participate in the community services by giving additional gifts or discounts.
- Formulate environmental committee and air pollution committee to monitor pollution levels both in the organisation and outside the organization.
- Establish tools and technique for practising ethics.
- Arranging for ethics training to CEO's, executives, employees and everyone in the organisation in the convenient timing probably before the closing of working hours for about 10-15 days. This can be arranged equally in batches without distinguishing the differences.

- Encourage moral stories, moral behaviour, Vedas, Upanishads, philosophy, Bhagavad Gita and education on Thirukural and Basaveshwara Vachannagalu in the organisation which will uphold Indian values and culture. Appropriate hoardings and signboards on the saying of the above must be displayed at both internal and external places of the organization.
- Arranging spiritual teachings, discourses twice or thrice a year.
- Ethical watch on employees and making necessary entry in the service record and profile.
- Adopt the Japanese model on 5S concept namely

  Seiri – Straighten up

  Seitan – Put things in order

  Seiso – Lean up

  Seiketsu – Personal cleanliness

  Shitsuke – Discipline

Tool for Marketing Ethics

- Customer-centric programmes and their approval through social sanctions.
- Periodical survey on marketing position, quality of product, product approval by the society / customers, product positioning in the market, retailers' unfair activities on the companies' product.
- Ensuring quality product services by maintaining and following world leaders in business.
- Issue code of marketing ethics/guidelines for fairness in marketing activities to all personnel in the marketing department, suppliers, wholesalers and retailers of the company.
- Issue 'check list' consisting of various ethical activities in marketing to mark whenever and wherever it is necessary as an analytical tool to the marketing managers.
- Competition should be met only through ethical marketing and business practices through quality products and services.
- Identify key customers and relationships.

(iii) Tools for Ethics in product

- Products with 'customer-centric' and not profit oriented.
- Product development should be based on urban, rural areas (e.g., Bata Shoes Co.), environment friendly, with continuous improvement through innovation, suitability, cost-benefit oriented, and meeting the customer needs and delight.

- Product recall—whenever product is not meeting customer safety and need to introduce new product with modification and necessary alteration.
- Product planning should be on the principle as "Human system will be a failure but not the product."
- Check, regulate and take necessary legal action immediately to cut spurious products by appointing area inspectors.

The tools for implementation are intrisinic and inclusive task for any organization. It demands a separate department for implementation. And this may be named as "Ethics Department".

Tool for establishment of ethics department

- The ethics department may be attached to human resource or communication department. It should be an independent department, headed by the trained, qualified and appropriate person who strongly believes and practises honesty, integrity, cultural values, yoga, meditation, love towards human kind, sound knowledge of organisation and who can stand as a friend, philosopher and guide.
- Periodical check/audit in quality, individual work culture, organisational culture by the department of ethics.
- A checklist or manager manual to be issued to all the executives and employees, manual should consist of ethical guidelines for the individual, organisation and different departments.
- Clean the organisation with ethical activity, eradicate unethical activities which will serve for long through practice of honesty, from top management, integrity, compassion organisational culture and commitment.

Develop *ethical stamina* to each and every individual in the organization.

The corporates can adopt any village which may be small or moderately big, impart education, right from school level and give necessary vocational training suitable to the organisation and the same students can be employed in the one's own organisation. In this way the corporate social performance will have more meaning both to the corporates and to the society. This is advantageous, as the corporates are teaching organisational culture, work culture right from the inception of school education of the child. It will build family values and strong relationship and integrity.

"After all;
What is *ethical and not ethical*
is *a matter of adjustment*
of others and one's own judgement."

Ethics Department and Organisation Culture

Establishing an ethical corporate culture is more than providing ethics training.

Ethical decision making must be integrated into the day-to-day decisions undertaken by marketing professionals. Establishing an ethical corporate culture might include the following:

1. Ensuring that a code of ethics is in place and enforced.
2. Ensuring that a whistle-blowing or ethical concerns procedure (or both) is established for internal ethical problem solving.
3. Involving marketing professionals in the identification of ethical issues to gain understanding and resolve those issues.
4. Determining the relationships in which marketing professionals are involved and making them known to all those who are involved in those relationships.
5. Integrating ethical decision making into the performance appraisal process.
6. Publicizing, in all organization communications, top management ethical priorities (Harrington, 1991, p. 28).

A culture does not appear suddenly. The development of a culture requires countless individual events, attitudes, policies, and beliefs (Hyman, Skipper, & Tansey, 1990). Every marketing decision made in the organization, no matter how trivial, becomes a part of the organizational culture. So developing a culture of ethical behaviour is a long-term process. No single action can turn a culture around. Every day, each marketing professional must endorse the culture through his or her actions. If the culture is not supported, actions that go against the ethical culture will destroy it.

Ethics Training Programmes

Ethics training and seminars have been used by some organizations to assist them in dealing with ethical problems. For example, the National Association of Purchasing Managers has an ethics committee that offers opinions on ethical questions and provides educational seminars on the subject of ethics (Cummings, 1979). Training and seminars have the objective of training marketing professionals to examine the ethical nature and implications of their decisions. Organizations must provide for the education of marketing professions in specific ethically related practices.

The two most common reasons for establishing an ethics training programme are: (a) developing employee awareness of ethics in business and (b) drawing attention to ethical issues to which the employee may be exposed, by raising awareness, organizations hope to aid decision makers in the following ways:

1. Establishing the recognition of the ethical components of business decisions.
2. Legitimizing the consideration of ethics as part of decision making.
3. Avoiding variability in decision making caused by the lack of awareness of rules and norms.
4. Avoiding ambivalence in decision making caused by an organizational reward structure in which a person experiences being pulled in psychologically opposite directions.

5. Avoiding ambivalence in decision making caused by confusion as to who is responsible for misdeeds, particularly when an employee has received an order from a superior.
6. Providing decision-making frameworks for analyzing ethical issues and helping employees to apply such frameworks (Jansen & Von Glinow, 1985).

In most companies, ethics training is a communications device used by top managers to emphasize the importance of including ethical considerations in decision making. Codes of ethics are reviewed and a case study approach is often used. But a few organizations really seek to raise the level of ethical thinking among employees (Harrington, 1991). Employees must sense that top management is sincere before any real influence is accomplished. So once again, we see the imperative that top management must establish an ethical culture supportive of the messages being conveyed in ethics training.

Training programmes have been shown to lower the extent to which employees perceive they have to engage in unethical behaviours to get ahead in their organizations. Furthermore, when ethics training programmes exist, employees tend to refuse to take unethical actions when faced with serious ethical dilemmas (Delaney & Sockell, J., 1992). So although the jury is still out, the existing evidence speaks in favour of the ability of ethics training programmes to reduce the incidence of unethical behaviour.

Despite the good news presented in the preceding discussion, organization ethics training programmes can and do fail. One reason for this is that such programmes 'can operate under the misconception that their primary focus should be to ensure the ethical behaviour of marketing professionals (Rice & Dreilinger, 1990). When this is the focus, the training programme tends to become little more than a series of "thou shalt nots." In other words, marketing professionals learn what they *should not do* in certain situations, but they do not learn what they *should do* in those same situations. Most marketing professionals have a pretty good idea of what not to do. Where they need help is in the area of what the company expects them to do in those situations. In other words, the primary reason for the failure of ethical programmes is that they do not take a proactive approach for solving ethical problems by making recommendations that will work in practice.

Many companies have implemented ethics training in the belief that it is an integral feature in the development of an ethical company culture. But few of these companies have extended their ethics training toward strategic issues in other words, toward the long run (Harrington, 1991). To have a long-term perspective, companies should seek to answer questions such as the following:

1. How can ethical considerations be incorporated into long-term planning?
2. How can we identify ethical issues in which the company may or may not be involved?
3. How do each of these ethical issues affect the company?
4. What is the likelihood of occurrence of each of these ethical issues?
5. What is an appropriate response(s) to each ethical issue?

6. How can an individual's, department's, and company's performance be monitored regarding each of these ethical issues (Harrington, 1991).

Ethics training, like all other ethics programmes, is really a part of a larger effort to instill an ethical behavioural culture in the organization. Furthermore, it is just one of the many parts of the puzzle designed to instill an ethical culture that will benefit the company in the long run. Ethics training will be *effective* only if the larger ethics oriented effort of the company (e.g., codes, top management actions, ethics advisers) are effective.

Ethics Advisers

Just as organizations use consultants for solving business problems, they can also use ethics advisers. These advisers could occupy staff positions in the organization, their major function being to oversee ethical concerns (Keichel, 1979). Individuals occupying such positions would review decisions for their ethical content in an attempt to improve the overall ethical climate of the organization.

Ethics advisers come by a variety of tides and in a variety of forms. These include ethical officers. ethical ombudsmen, ethical devil's advocates, and special audit committees (Werner, 1992). Whatever they are called, their purpose is to seek out unethical behaviours taking place in the organization. Although their specific responsibilities vary from one organization to the next, most agree that the ethics adviser must maintain a central position in the organization. That is, he or she must have access to everyone in the organization, at all levels of the organization.

Although it is imperative that ethical advisers have direct contact with top management, this contact is also the source of one of the problems associated with ethical advisers. They become "appointed" with top management. When this happens, ethics advisers can lose their effectiveness with people at lower levels of the organization. This occurs because lower-level employees feel that the ethical adviser is simply someone whom top management has assigned as a "watchdog." In actuality, the ethical adviser is charged with trying to instill behaviours that will work for the long-term good of the organization and the individuals in that organization.

Many colleges and universities have also added ethics-related courses to their curricula. Much is being said and written about the effectiveness of such courses in promoting ethical behaviour in marketing situations.

The Ethics Code of Johnson and Johnson, "Our Credo".

- We believe our first responsibility is to the doctors, nurses and patients to mothers and all others who use our products and services.
- In meeting their needs everything we do must be of high quality. We must constantly strive to reduce our costs in order to maintain reasonable prices.
- Customers' orders must be serviced promptly and accurately.
- Our supplier and distributors must have an opportunity to make a fair profit.
- We are responsible to our employees, the men and women who work with us throughout the world.

- Everyone must be considered an individual.
- We must respect their dignity and recognize their merit.
- They must have a sense of security in their jobs.
- Compensation must be fair and adequate, and working conditions clean, orderly and safe.
- Employees must feel free to make suggestions and complaints.
- There must be equal opportunity for employment, development and advancement for those qualified.
- We must provide competent management, and their actions must be just and ethical.
- We are responsible to the communities in which we live and work and to the world community as well.
- We must be good citizens, support good works and charities and bear our fair share of taxes.
- We must encourage civic improvements and, better health and education.
- We must maintain in good order the property we are privileged to use, protecting the environment and natural resources.
- Our final responsibility is to our stockholders.
- Business must make a sound profit.
- We must experiment with new ideas.
- Research must be carried on, innovative programmes developed and mistakes paid for.
- New equipment must be purchased, new facilities provided and new products launched.
- Reserves must be created, to provide for adverse times.
- When we operate according to these principles, the stockholders should realize a fair return.

Exhibit

Consolidation of opinion/practices of ethics shared directly by the corporates

This is outcome of the research study and the response of 52 corporates belonging to public sector and multinational companies. The responses are on the basis of questionnaire developed and also personal interview and interaction. The corporates response are on the basis of perception and practices towards corporate social responsibility business ethics, ethics in marketing and ethical issues in product, pricing, advertisement and sales distribution. These are counted as the qualitative data under the research study. The extract of the same has been given under direct speech.

CORPORATE OPINION AND PRACTICES TOWARDS STAKEHOLDERS

"We are tenant in this country, we must be careful with government and people". –IBM

"Customers are kings".

"Customers are kings and customer education is very important".

– Mysore Sales International Ltd.

"Demand should be for the product replacement instead of demanding to change the parts or complaining in the consumer courts". –Akai

"Our pride is to satisfy the customers, we are role models".

–Hindustan Petroleum Corporation

"Business cannot be made at the cost of customers and society". –Akai

"Nature and customer friendly products which are to be produced".

–Asian Paints

(a) Corporate opinion and practices towards shareholders and employees

"We follow the philosophy of team spirit which is driving the employee to top level and there is self motivation and self responsibility". –L.G.

"We are 100% conscious in taking care of our employee and we give training towards safety measures". –Shahi Exports

"Meeting and developing a direct contact with the employees is beneficial and Premji is meeting 5000 employees, and delivers a 3 ½ hours speech on motivation continuously, offering 40% stock option, and showing that every year we are rich on paper". –WIPRO

"There is education within the organization". – IBM

"There is transparency to the employees for over 50 years". –TTK

"Opportunity to the employees to become shareholders". – Gokuldas Exports

"Meeting employees' needs and salary, even when there was a factory fire in 1996 and assuring them of job security." –Asian Paints

"Direct recruitment from schools is encouraged, no foul language to be used among the employees." –Arvind Mills

"There must be education within the organization." –IBM

"We start the social responsibility first to our employees, we do help each and every employee at the time of crises and we will treat all our employees as equal".

–Philips India Ltd.

"Best apprenticeship training in more than 20 countries and training concentrating on future oriented professions, free and nutritious food to employees." –MICO

(b) Corporate opinion and practices towards society at large

"Ours is an environment friendly product." –Asian Paints

"We are environment friendly and our corporate office is green and our product is nature based." – LG

"We conduct health programme and donate to Sindhi charitable Hospital".

–Gokuldas Exports

"Scholarship for handicapped and scheduled caste students."

–Hindustan Petroleum Corporation

"Conduct school programs on awareness to save the Tiger." – Britannia

"Conducting educational programmes to develop creativity, a beautiful film is screened to the children in their respective schools to develop the idea of creativity". – Coats India

"Technical education like invention of education in I.T. distant education, establishment of computer centres at Bangalore, Bhopal, Delhi, Bombay and the like. The course material for hardware and software is supplied thus education is created within the organization". –IBM

"We also give the girl child education". –WIPRO

"We promote art and culture through drama and music." –MICO

"The company has developed human resources, they act as universities, set-up colonies, townships in addition to employment. Exclusive plants were set up called 'Udaya Welfare Association' *for the disabled and the destitute."*

–Hindustan Machine Tools

"We conduct periodic health camps, blood donation camps, adopted the village called, Shivanahalli, E-mobile dispensary services, nearly 10,000 saplings were planted near Devanahalli and we have around 20 crores budget on social responsibility, every year scholarship is awarded for 10 school children who are handicapped and there is scholarship for Scheduled caste students."

–Hindustan Petroleum Corporation

"We conduct health programmes, we give importance to higher education and grant educational loans". –Karnataka Soaps and Detergents Ltd.

"The WIPRO young minds programme is conducted for government school children from Karnataka and Andhra Pradesh. We give free education from 10th standard to graduation for those children whose parents income is around rupees 1000 per month and we have technology for social work, helping the orphanage meeting their basic necessities". -WIPRO

"Adoption of village in Gujarat, we have school programmes towards environment as 'Save the Tiger' and we promote art and music by conducting a festival called Britannia classical music festival for the last 25 years in Mumbai". –Britannia Ltd.

"We have effluent treatment and environmental protection". –Bata India

(c) Corporate attitude towards business ethics

"Honesty is fundamental, housekeeping boy, corporate ethics are beyond law and we are true almost". –Karnataka Antibiotics and Pharmaceuticals Ltd.

"I need not to tell lies and I need not tell everything to the customers."

–National Textile Corporation

"Customers are kings" –Mysore Sales International Ltd.

"Ethics should be established for the long run, being honest and straight can solve many problems." –Li and Fund

"We are going down as our R and D decision is not sound". –I.T.I

"It is difficult to be ethical in business, personally one may be ethical and to practice the same it is very difficult in the organization, in the business world due to the competition, many are not ethical, even if he thinks to be ethical, the organization may not allow and vice versa".–Chestline

"Even to be unethical, it is highly expensive (like tenders)".

–Indian Telephones Industries

"Ethics is not beyond profit, every small businessman wants to make profit rather than being unethical, every individual goes for basic needs like food, shelter, education, meeting marriage expenditure and he will be in that sphere, there is no question of ethics, thus the same is applicable to the corporates and everybody is making lots of money by cheating the customers". –NTC

"Public sectors are more ethical and private sectors do not bother for ethics; people buy oil from us and fill in the other cylinders and sell it, it is very difficult to prastice ethics in India, because everybody should get profit for the money invested". –Indian Oil Corporation

"Private sectors are not practicing ethics" –Hindustan Petroleum Corporation

"Ethics depend upon the product and no quick money"

–Mysore Sales International Ltd.

"There must be newly formed constitution, A Government which is thinking of only people's welfare should come to power and it must check irregularities". –(Birla 3M)

"In export business one must be ethical and we do follow that since ours is 100% export oriented organization". –Chestline.

"Ethics is our business and we are very much in right ways, no short cuts, we have open policy with nine branches". –Aravind Mills.

"Ours is one of the TATA Group of Companies and ours is 100% transparent".

–Rallies India

"We believe in being transparent and promote transparency, where we consider it as healthy sign of the business." –L.G.

"We are 100% transparent". –Philips India

"Where is the question on ethics when we are running the company for the sake of the employees survival, though we are running on loss". –Subadra Textiles

"Ethics is partially agreeable and partially disagreeable". –Shahi Exports

"Ethics is a subject but being too ethical is not practical". –TTK

"Our concept of business is family based". –Bada India

"Ethics is an agency without teeth". –Toyota

"Corporates should be focused on the survival of the fittest. Logically ethics may be true and transparent and practically it is very difficult". –Sangli Textile

"Our company is running in an ethical manner and it is integrated with 80 corporates".

–Wipro

(d) Corporate response towards adequacy of law with respect to marketing activities

"Law is an agency without teeth". –Toyota

"Legal processes are mere formality, the customers must establish their rights without emotions, any defect in the product they should demand for the product replacement directly to the companies instead of complaining in the customer courts". –AKAI

"The law and regulatory bodies are not proper because a person who is not following law is the officer and the same person will question the corporate officials, regarding the practices of Laws".

–Birla 3M

"We follow Minimum Wages Act and no child labour is entertained".

–Arvind Mills

"For every six months laws keep on changing with respect to Essential Commodities Act".

–HPC

"Practice of law is not conducive to hospitals/education, law is very loose."

'–KAPL

"None of the laws are applicable to the Indian citizen". –BPL

"Our company is very rigid towards law as the law is very peculiar".

–Gokuldas

"Law in India is very expensive". –NTC

"Every individual should do some sort of social services, there must be steps to improve the pollution". –Bal Pharma

"In the legal opinion, the human system cannot be explained".

–Broun and Burk

"Law does not have teeth and not fully compromises". –Rallis India

"Law needs to be transparent and clearly defined and law relating to customer need is to be more specific". –Sonal Garment

"Laws and acts do not make us to be consolidation". –Toyota

"To follow 100% ethics in marketing is difficult because of the competition, we never curb competition. We try to be ethical to our customers." –Philips India.

"No lies in marketing." –Arvind Mills

"Customer service is our motto, we conduct a training for inhaling since we have to pay back to the customer and we must be 100% ethical."

"In marketing there must be ethics." –Shahi Export

"There must be buyers markets." –HMT

"Sellers market is bad, consumers and others must be given a chance."

–KAPL

"We induce the customer to purchase and not force them." – Micro Lab.

(e) Corporate response on fairness in pricing

"In pricing the profit should not be the motive all the time but it should be a part of the business and totally to the customer's satisfaction. Pricing is not a one time market". –MSIL

"We give value for money and customers should be created with post-purchase feeling". –Philips India Ltd

"In our company pricing is fixed on the basis of activity based costing". –BPL

"Pricing is fixed on the basis of customer psychology". –Bata India

"It need not to tell everything to the customer. Sometimes the pricing can be kept hidden". –NTC

(f) Corporate responses towards opinion and practices on ethical issues in advertising

"In India there are checks and balances, the problem is the lack of education and lack of awareness". –IBM

"No single media is especially adopted to the children. Children are becoming more of Robots, they lose human feeling, too much is given towards technology, children are very much attached to the bad things". –MSIL

Another opinion like "the models must be morally aware, otherwise they will have an undesirable impact on the younger generation".

"Women are not commodities, they are human beings and the good quality of the product need not be advertised at the cost of women who are exploited by the media". –MSIL

"Advertising is a powerful promotion tool and message and the medium should be objective." –IBM

"Advertising is compressive and customers are the best advertisers". –HPC

"When there is permission to clubs, why restrictions on advertisement, there must be separate place for smokers and it can be called "smoking zone" or place for smokers and like bar and this is followed in western countries". –KS and DL

"There is too much of exposure on women in advertisements, there are better ways of advertising the products, the whole family should view the advertisement". –Li ang Fung.

"Promotion planning is also done on practical basis and it is done on all technology and our product is very friendly". –LG

"Our advertisements are value oriented, we never mislead the customers, our advertisements are very decent and family oriented". –Philips India

"National culture will be weak if the advertisement made to change". –Micro Lab

"There is no control over private channels". –BPL

"In our country, many of the private firms are unethical". –I.T.I.

"With respect to undergarments it has to face the outside world and it should be checked and most important is clothing is very close to the nature."

–Coats of India

"Advertisement is nothing but touching personal feelings of the customers, ethics is involved very less in advertising, we have to bother for the personal feelings". –NTC

"In India advertisement is not maintained properly, Law is not proper and misleads the customers". –Astrazencea

"Advertising like Coke and other drinking have lot of unethical acts and they try to connect with other products". –Asian Paints

(g) Sales & distribution

"We have direct marketing, we have relationship marketing even at the level of customers and consumers." –Coats India

"We give best training to our salesman to explain to the doctors since they are involved with human life". –Astrazeneca

(h) Corporate response towards practices of ethical and opinion on ethical issues towards sales and distribution

"In IT industry, where the vendors and the buyers are knowledgeable and educated, training of salesman in presenting facts and putting them with objectivity leaves no room for unethical practices." –IBM

"Sales people should be constantly trained for being upgraded, effecting marketing behavioural science, direct dealing to the rural area a speacilly designed product for rural peoples for their hard work". –Metreich Sterilab,

"We have direct marketing, we have relationship marketing even at the level of customers and consumers". Coats India,

The overall response on ethics in marketing and ethical issues in marketing activities in product, pricing, advertisement and sales and distribution are very encouraging by the different corporate, namely public sectors, public limited, private limited and multinational companies.

(i) Corporate practices on business ethics

"Our company is running in an ethical manner and it is integrated with 80 corporates (Wipro) and they have fear on expressing ethics, too much of ethics is to be avoided". –TTK

"Our concept of business is family based". –Bata India

"In export business one must be ethical and we do follow that since ours is 100% export oriented organization" –Chestline

"Ethics is our business and we are very much in right ways, no short cuts, we have open policy with nine branches". –Aravind Mills

"We believe in being transparent and promote transparency, where we consider it as healthy sign of the business". –L.G.

"We are 100% transparent". –Philips India

"None of the laws are applicable to the Indian citizen". –BPL

MODEL FOR CORPORATE ETHICAL HOUSE

To sum up, we give below a schematic model of ethics for forging corporates into good corporate citizen. This model can be used as the basis for incorporating ethical issues in the mission / vision statements of companies. The model also helps the companies to develop "ethical office". Ethical office is a culture that fosters mutual respect, trust and honest communication among co-workers, ethical office is becoming another means for achieving competitive advantage, as companies see the link between healthy profits and ethical cultures. The significance of this concept lies in the fact that it promotes effectively corporate conscience, a commitment to accountability and ongoing communication about ethical issues.

MODEL FOR CORPORATE ETHICAL HOUSE

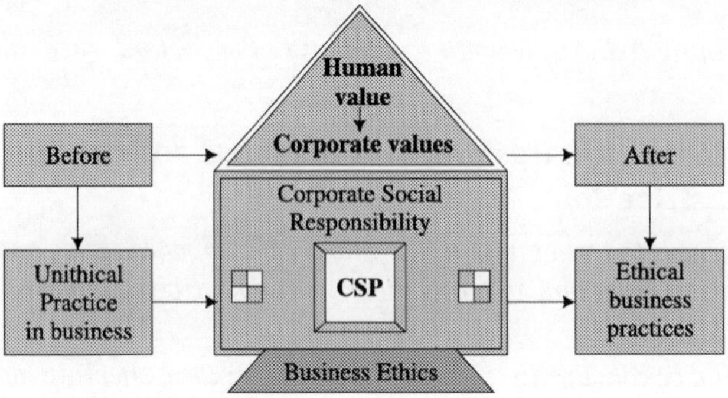

Reflecting on it fully, act as you will

–Bhagavad Gita, Chapter XVIII, Sloka 63

To transform a corporate house in to Ethical house it should have a strong foundation of business ethics with the regent wall of corporate social responsibility and concert roof of corporate values twisted with human values.

Index

A

Abdul Kareem 88
Accounting 111
Adidas 159
Advertising
  and culture 169
  and law 168
  ethical issues in 167
  social welfare and 170
Advice channels 110
Aggressive cluster 305
American Marketing Association's Code of Ethics 182
Anglo-American model 262
Applied ethics 13
Armstrong, Neil 48
Auditing 111

B

Bhagavad Gita
  value-based leadership in 90
BHEL disinvestment 191
Bhopal gas tragedy 144
Bofors guns case 46
Boundary spanners 179
Business community
  responsibility of 237
Business ethics 4, 5, 12, 327
  argument for 28
  arguments against 29
  basics of 27
  characteristics of 13
  factors influencing 15, 25
  functional areas of 8
  principles in 46
  scope of 6
  world centres for 214

C

Chambers of Commerce and Industry 246
City development 249
Classic yogas 79
Clearance sales 182
Coca-Cola 160, 176
Code of ethics 109, 334
Comeco Corporation 51
Committees 110
Computer viruses 208
Consumer protection 181
Contemporary ethical theories 68
Corporate culture 26, 282, 283, 285
  and change 286
  components of 287
  elements of 309
  ethical values and 283
  functions of 294
  logistics management in 289
  role of 281
Corporate environment 7
Corporate ethical house, model for 352
Corporate ethics 4, 5, 34
Corporate governance 258
  models of 261
  principles of 266
Corporate social responsibilities 34, 219
  features of 224, 225
Creditors' responsibility 227
Crisis management 41, 43
  responses to 43
  types of 44
Cross-culture 313, 317
Culture 62, 282
  and ethical behaviour 291
  five dimensions of 300
Customers' responsibility 227
Cyber law, global trends in 198

D

Dalda 175
Deal and Kennedy 300
Defensive cluster 304, 305

Deontological theories 20
Descriptive ethics 13
Discourse ethics 71
Discrimination 119
Domino's 230
Dow Chemicals 50
Dynamic complexity 133

E

Economic responsibility 224
Edgar Schein model 302
Egoism 17
Emotional honesty 81
Employees' responsibility 227
Environment protection 49
Ethical business performance 25
Ethical dilemmas 213
Ethical issues
  case studies on 45
Ethical responsibility 225
Ethics 5
  as a tool 30
  theories of 16
  types of 10
Ethics advisers 344
Ethics consultants 111
Ethics education and training 111
Ethics in management 108
Ethics managers 110
Ethics of principle 100
Ethics of virtue 96, 100
Ethics training programmes 342
Ethics, promotion of 235
Expressive vs reserved culture 316

F

Fair wages and salary 113
Family system 63
Feminist ethics 70
Financial management, ethical aspects of 184
Flexible working patterns 117
Fuller, H.B. 229

G

Gender issues 134
General business ethics 37
German-Japanese model 263
Gurgaon Foods 52

H

Handy, Charles 301
HR management, ethical practices in 112, 130
Human-centric model 128

I

IBM's tangle in Argentina 46
Ideals 102
IEEE code 210
India, e-commerce in 207
  cyber law in 198
Indian-South Asian model 264
Individual ethics 10
Informal vs formal culture 315
Information ethics 204
Information technology 197
  ethical issues in 199
Issues management 35

J

Job stress 125
Johnson & Johnson 160

K

Kalam, APJ 86
Kant's categorical imperative 20

L

Lakme girl 173
Legal responsibility 225

M

Managerial ethical behaviours 322
Marketing ethics 149
Marketing
  ethical foundation in 151
  moral values in 150
  social responsibility and 151
Meta ethics 13
Mission 109
Mobil 50
Moral psychology 13
Moral standards 16, 62

N

Nestle infant formula 158
New Dalda 176
Normative ethics 13

O
Organisational culture 285, 320, 322
Organizational commitment 284

P
Participatory ethics 11
Passive cluster 304
Pepsi's Burma connection 46
Personal ethics 57
    components of 59
    evaluatory changes in 65
    factors influencing 64
    false notion on 63
Personal selling 178
Pfizer 161
Philanthropic responsibility 225
Philip, Morris 160
Phillip Morris's troubles 46
Plato 97, commentary on 99
Pricing, ethical issues in 164
Principle of proportionality 23
Product
    boycott of 157
    ethical issues in 152
    global marketing of 157
    labelling of 155
    marketing of 152
    packaging of 155
Professional business ethics 12

R
Rawls' principle of maximum justice 22
Recognitional ethics 12
Relationship marketing 179
Reliance Industries 319
Reliance's corporate governance 268
Religious culture
    ethical issues in 47
Rigid-time vs fluid-time culture 315
Risk analysis and management 110
Ross's prima facie duties 21
Rural development 248

S
SAIL 230
Seconds sales 182
Self, value of 59
Sexual and racial harassment 120
Shareholders' responsibility 226
Single-tier board structure 262
Situational ethics 19
Social responsibility, Indian perspective 222
St Joseph health system 87
Stress management 127

T
Tampax Corporation 159
Tata, JRD 240
Technology ethics 193, 210
Teleogical theories 17
Toyota 306
Transactional ethics 10
Trusteeship 238

U
Utilitarianism 18

V
Value statements 109
Virtue ethics 68
Virtue of humility 68

W
Workplace misbehaviour 132, 133